Search for Human Security

The Shifting Paradigms

SEARCH FOR HUMAN SECURITY

THE SHIFTING PARADIGMS

Narottam Gaan

4831/24, Ansari Road, Darya Ganj,
New Delhi-110002
Tel. : 23260807, 41563444
Fax : 011-41563334
E-mail: info@essessreference.com
www.essessreference.com

Reference Press
4831/24, Ansari Road,
Darya Ganj,
New Delhi-110 002.

Tel.: 23260807, 41563444
Fax: 41563334
E-mail: info@essessreference.com
www.essessreference.com

© 2009 by Narottam Gaan

Rs.1295/-

While extensive effort has gone into ensuring the reliability of information appearing in this book, the publisher makes no warranty, express or implied, on the accuracy or reliability of the information, and does not assume and hereby disclaims any liability to any person for any loss or damage caused by errors or omissions in this publication.

All Rights reserved. No part of this publication may be reproduced, stored in a retrieval system, transmitted in any form or by any means, mechanical, photocopying recording or otherwise without the prior written permission of the publisher/copyright holder.

First Published - 2009

ISBN: 978-81-8405-048-6

Published By Reference Press and printed at Salasar Imaging Systems

PRINTED IN INDIA

Dedicated to

SWAMI GURUPREMANANDAJI

Our Loving Mother

Whose bosom of omnipresence I pillowed on

as a babe of eternity

to drink

the nectar of Her immortal Love, Joy and Bliss

Contents

Acknowledgment

My dream to write a book on security could not have found its reification without help and cooperation from others. My unbounded thanks and gratitude flow from the core of my heart to a galaxy of scholars to name a few like Dr. Arthur H. Westing, Dr. Thomas F Homer Dixon of Toronto University, Dr. Richard A Matthew of California University, Barry Buzan, Ole Waever, Jaap de Wilde, Johan Eriksson, Giampiero Giacomello, J. Ann Tickner and Norman Myers, Valerie M. Hudson and Andrea M. Den Boer on whose works I depend and who have played a key role in shaping my views and vision about the multidimensional aspects of human security from different perspectives. From the abyss of my heart I always convey my sense of gratification to a host of erudite scholars for the materials, articles and books they have provided me without exhibiting even a shred of evidence of their being hesitant. I will fail in my duty if I do not give my heart rendering thanks to the authorities of European University Center for Peace Studies, (EPU), Stadtschlaining, Austria and the Austrian Government for having privileged me with a much coveted scholarship to go to Austria and Hungary and to have higher studies on International Relation. This helped me a lot come in contact with a number of great scholars like Arthur H. Westing, Gunther Bachler and Johan Galtung whom I consider as yet the very prominent authorities to have provided me different perspectives to my work.

Words are inadequate to express my humble

gratitude and indebtedness to an eminent scholar of international repute Dr. Sukh Deo Muni, former professor of Jawaharlal Nehru University in School of International Studies and ambassador, Dr. S.R.Chakravarty, former Professor in South Asian Studies in the School of International Studies, Jawaharlal Nehru University, New Delhi, Prof. Mahendra Prasad Lama, former professor, South Asian Studies, School of International Studies, Jawaharlal Nehru University and Vice Chancellor Sikkim University, Prof, Annpurna Nautiyal of HNB University, Garhwal, Srinagar, my teachers Dr. Benudhar Pradhan, Director, Gandhian Institute for Peace Research and Action, and Dr. Asha Hans, former Professor in Political Science, Utkal University, Vanivihar, and S. N. Girish, I.A.S, a man of honesty, exemplary probity and humanist, and P.K. Chaudhury, dedicated the cause of poor for their inspiration, kind help and choicest good wishes kept in store for me.

The floodgates of my unbounded gratitude remain always flung upon to Prof. Dietrich Fischer, a great scholar of international eminence and Academic Director, European University Center for Peace Studies, Austria for having ungrudgingly consented to write a foreword to this book.

I am extremely grateful to my parents, my life partner Reena and my two loving beautiful flowers Tattwamasi and Yogeswar who have always spurred me inspiringly to the daunting task of trailblazing and emerging shining, and withstand difficulties in the preparation of the book. My eldest son Tattwamasi deserves all credit and exacts my love and blessings for having computerized the entire work to my utmost satisfaction. Behind all these and the sole doer, but for who it is not possible to write such a book are our all adored Guruji Paramhamsa Prajnanananda and Gurudev Paramhamsa Hariharananda. I deem it a God given privilege to sing in paeans of their Beatific Bliss and Glory in this humble work, which I consecrate at their Lotus Feet.

Preface

The moment a child falls on the ground from mother's womb his/her search for security begins apparently culminating in state. This was admitted by no less a person than Thomas Hobbes in his autobiography that his mother had given birth to twins- myself and fears. Many centuries back the individuals living within a territory had ensconced their faith in the prince/king for their security as a collective unit. The prince was the symbol of their identity in a definitive political unit spatially distanced from similar other units to the extent that they were not conquered over by other princes. With Westphalian convention recognizing the identification of the entire people with a sovereign state hammered out on the basis of a definitive territorial exclusiveness and nationality, a clear concept of security strewn around state emerged. What accorded identity to the people as a collective unit was the state, a metaphorical representation of the former. With evolution of monarchies into democratic systems, the prince was only replaced by the people as a part of political fulfillment but the same absolute, indivisible and inalienable sovereign state continued independently of who holds or represents it. State as the ultimate referent of security and identity of the people continued to define the nature and concept of security by its uncontested absolute military power.

The transference did not bring any change in the existence of an absolute state sovereignty whether the government is democratic or undemocratic. The prince got transformed into people as the sole owner of sovereign state. But it was rhetoric as there was no change in the nature of the absolutism of state. This is what entitles it to be guarantor of security as there are no other institutions to challenge its claim to assume the status of the referent of security of the people supposedly constituting the state. Since state is the sole referent of security, its existence as a sovereign state assumes importance in the classical or traditional realist paradigm of security. The continuing arms race and strive for weaponization among nations in the international system conceived in the Hobbesian state of nature can be explained by this fact of state being in 'existence in perpetuation'. As Hobbes' Leviathan admonishes any disobedience to it would back the people again into the anarchic state of nature, the people finding security and identity in the state are made to believe that any deviance from this will make them insecure and their life miserable. This ingrained belief of people in the state as the ultimate referent of security is what gives the legitimacy to the state, and constitutes the foundation of realist paradigm of security. The growing competition among nations and super power conflict during the cold war for dominance is partly to be explained on this Hobbesian epistemology.

An ontological discrepancy exists. Prince was replaced by people in democracies but the indivisible absolute state sovereignty continues in abstraction and assumes the character of mythology drawing legitimacy from people to those who claim to be acting on behalf of state. Like prince dethroned, the absolute state he/she presided over could not be replaced or conceived differently. This entrenched discrepancy continues to constitute the security/identity problematic when people, individuals or groups, women or children came to realize the yawning dissonance between security of state and their security. If the very nature of the absolute state sovereignty is understood then it is indifferent to the type of government which gets the mandate from people to rule. That means it has an existence independently of the type of government exercising power on its behalf but not independently of people constituting the state. Gradually, the security of state was conflated with security of the government in power. The political-economic ideology of the government becomes that of the state. The western more so American political system based on Hobbes and Locke's possessive individualism for providing a commodious living and inordinate life style to its dominant majority rich class found in this realist paradigm of security a convenient hypothesis to dominate other nations and nature. This resulted in the establishment of a liberal capitalist market oriented political system ultimately finding its culmination in globalization. Any kind of challenges to the political-economic metaphysics is interpreted as a threat to the sovereign state system. What was thought as settled and non-existent in homogenous societies like America and other western societies that security of state is coeval with security of people, has now come to surface in view of the deep economic crisis there. Their very belief in the neoliberal political- economic order free of any state interference, which accorded legitimacy to the government that it would solve all problems, has now turned out to be a mythological superstitious belief challenging the established view that the security of state means security of the people.

Thus, the sovereign state system, which was in 'existence in perpetuation' independently of any political colour and transferred from prince to the people for their identity as a collective unit was gradually knitted into what the western nations define it as the realist paradigm of security. All the nations of the world crafting their statecraft on the Westphalian thematic are guided by this realist paradigm of security and the concept of development built into it for ensuring a commodious and inordinate life style based on western liberal market economy. This would help the western powers led by America grow in power both in military and economic terms.

In heterogeneous societies as many countries in Asia and Africa are, the people as a collective unit was put to tatters. The people tend to seek identify in terms of categories such as class, gender, race, language, caste, religion, environment etc. The inherent ontological discrepancy comes to the fore bringing to limelight the fact that the security of state is no longer the security of the people. Many global crises such as poverty, malnutrition, spread of infectious diseases, gender inequality, food insecurity, terrorism, environmental changes and climate change afflict the people not as a 'collective unit' but as different categories demonstrating the utter inadequacy of state and its attributed military apparatus to meet these challenges. In the 1980s a spurt of intellectual activities went on to explore alternative approaches to this antiquated realist paradigm of security. Keeping in mind the multifarious crises, which the realist paradigm did not conceive then, many alternative approaches emerged to challenge the realist paradigm built into sovereign state. A marked shift from it strewn around state towards other categories or referents is perceived in these approaches. None of the theories on security built on realist paradigm has been able to answer the question put to its political-economic metaphysics by the climate change.

This book has been a laudable attempt to succinctly blend into its tapestry all different strands of approaches made so far in international politics in contrast to realist paradigm. What comes out important is the very recognition among the scholars of these alternative approaches of the fact that the individual human being is entitled to be the legitimate claimant to the status of being referent of security in place of state. This does not imply the throwing of state into the scrapheap as Marxists would prophesize. What the analysis in the present book of all these approaches, condescends is that there is urgently required an ontological revision of the very realist paradigm built around state, which is a political existence in perpetuation. When we think it not independently of the political attributes of the power that be, it becomes problematic, as Marx would say an instrument of class exploitation, or capitalists attribute to it a liberal- market oriented economic order or Hegel apotheosizing as the march of God. Thus, the attributions or staining it stems from the ideological-cultural dominance of the class that is in power within a state or a nation in the world. The ethnocentrism of western paradigm scripting not only the economic and political theme of the entire world but also staging it as a liberal market based political order, an euphemism for globalization needs reinvention to ensure security to individual human and non- human being. The synoptic essence of all the current themes on security as described in this book hovers on not security of state but on security of individual under the rubric 'human security'. Of course the critics take strong umbrage at any thing that harms the individual being christened as human security on the pleas that such an attribution will denude security of its pith and marrow and the very raison detre of state will be torpedoed. Shifting away from state to individual categories while defining security does not warrant any diminution or dilution in its primary role as an 'existence in perpetuation' to found a people as a definitive political category ending its wilderness. Human security rather gives it new responsibility and insight to redefine security not exactly as homogenizing or universalizing concept emanating from it or from similar states but in terms of differentiated and diverse categories either affected by states or non-state actors. The very belief in the realist paradigm of security as the panacea for all ills plaguing human beings fossilized into a superstitious mythology among the nations of the world needs to be critically reviewed.

This book, I hope, will be able to earn the laurels from all those who evince greater interest in having all theories on security starting from orthodox classical models to the current analysis on human security encapsulated in succinct lines.

Dr. Narottam Gaan

Foreword

This is a monumental work, a comprehensive overview of many schools of thought about security. It documents the gradual shift from the traditional idea that security is first of all a question of securing state sovereignty, by military means, to the evolving insight that the primary goal must be to meet the security needs of all human beings.

Johan Galtung summarized the traditional "security discourse" as follows: "We have a problem, our enemies who seek to harm us. Through military superiority, we can deter or defeat them, to achieve security, and through this peace." He contrasts this with the more sensible "peace discourse", which briefly argues, "We have a problem, an unresolved conflict. Through peaceful conflict transformation, we can achieve peace, and through this mutual security."

Richard Falk argued that "the greatest utopians are those who call themselves 'realists', because they falsely believe that we can survive the nuclear age with politics as usual. The true realists are those who recognize the need for change." Thus, Narottam Gaan is indeed a true realist.

This book gives ample evidence that the search for peace and human security is a positive-sum game, in which everyone can gain, different from the pursuit of military superiority, which is a negative-sum game, because a competitive arms race makes both parties worse off.

One can distinguish between military, economic, political and cultural power. They correspond to four basic human needs: survival, welfare, freedom and a meaningful life (the opposites of direct violence, misery, oppression and alienation). Misery and oppression are two aspects of what Galtung calls "structural violence," the loss of life and well-being that is not caused by weapons, but by unjust social structures with extreme wealth and waste at one end, and needless deprivation at the other end. An estimated 125,000 people die every day from hunger and preventable or curable diseases. Therefore the loss of life from structural violence far exceeds that from direct violence, i.e. wars and violent crimes. Cultural violence justifies direct and structural violence through nationalism, racism, sexism and other forms of discrimination in education, the media, literature and art.

Human security means protection against all forms of violence—direct, structural and cultural. It protects humans from the threats of aggression and violent crime, but also ensures that people's material needs for food, shelter and health are met, and their spiritual needs for education, freedom of choice a meaningful life or "identity". Ensuring human security also requires the preservation of a livable environment. As Dr. Gaan points out, weapons are useless to deal with threats such as the growing ozone hole or global warming.

Preventing climate change requires the cooperation of all nations. If even a single country releases excessive amounts of pollutants that cause global warming with possible disruptions of food production, or a thinning of the protective ozone layer leading to increased rates of cancer and genetic mutations, everyone on earth is exposed to dangers. To ensure global cooperation by all requires global treaties and measures to implement them. Many governments today are still reluctant to join global agreements, for fear of giving up some of their national sovereignty. But that fear is mistaken. No country today, for example, has sovereign control over the ozone layer. By cooperating at the world level on such issues, we do not lose any control over our destiny. On the contrary, we gain added control that we did not possess before and will never be able to achieve at the national level alone.

Common problems, which could not be solved by an individual family or village, gave rise to the first advanced civilizations about six thousand years ago. The recurrent droughts and floods in the Euphrates, Nile and Yellow River valleys could be brought under control only by constructing dams and irrigation systems through large-scale coordinated efforts. This led to the emergence of the first states in Sumer, ancient Egypt and China, to the development of written language, codification of laws, the evolution of mathematics and early technology, and a flourishing of the arts.

Today, humanity faces problems that exceed the capacity of even an entire nation to solve. Preventing such dangers now requires global cooperation. Hopefully, this necessity will provide an impetus towards the creation of some form of global order and civilization enabling us to deal with these problems before it is too late.

Prof. Dr. Dietrich Fischer,

Academic Director, Haus International,
Kirchenplatz 8, A-7461 Stadtschlaining, Austria
Tel +43-3355-20726, Fax +43-3355-2666,
Mobile +43-664-511-1889
Email fischer@epu.ac.at Website www.aspr.ac.at
PEACE CENTER BURG SCHLAINING
ASPR Austrian Study Center for Peace and Conflict Resolution
EPU European University Center for Peace Studies
1995 UNESCO PRIZE FOR PEACE EDUCATION

1
Security and Securitization: The Copenhagen School and Beyond

The word "security" has been too elusive to be defined in precise and concrete terms as was used to be by the traditionalists. With the end of cold war the relative dominance of the military-political security plummeted reflecting the widespread recognition of the sources of security being diversified away from the centre stage i.e. the state. In recent years what have catapulted into the centre stage of both policy and strategic thinking are the environmental apocalypse, poverty, economic decline and other social crisis of identity, drug and human trafficking and politics of racism, minority, human rights and feminist indignation and the issues relating to the very survival and dignity of human beings brushing aside the political-military construct of security hovered around state and its apparatus to the fringe. The growing disenchantment with the inadequacy of state to meet all these security challenges from diverse sources making a mince meat of the realist and neorealist understanding of security gave rise to the "wide" versus "narrow" debate about security. The widening of the base of security threats as outlined above and confinement to the use of force blurs the distinction between the traditional and wide concept of security and endangers the intellectual coherence of security and dilutes the meaning. If sources of security threats have been diversified, to cling to Westphalian thematic of security built around state and its military apparatus seems not in congruence with the old logic and the changing and plurality of security threats. As a response and solution to these threats it is not always the state and its military apparatus but the some collective security thinking appears logical as found required in the case of climate change. As a result of the end of the cold war a global reconceptualisation of security has emerged, that geographically widened due to globalization. With the approaching shift in earth history from the 'Holocene' to the 'Anthropocene 'new objective security dangers have been socially constructed since the 1980's. Now global problems pose fundamental threats, challenges, vulnerabilities and risks for individual human beings and humankind (Brauch 2008:1).

Security is a basic term and key concept in the social sciences that is used in intellectual traditions and schools, conceptual frameworks, and approaches. The term 'security' is associated with many different meanings that refer to frameworks and dimensions, apply to individuals, issue areas, societal conventions, and changing historical conditions and circumstances. Thus, security as an individual or societal political value has no independent meaning and is always related to a context and a specific individual or societal value system and its realization (Ibid).

Security is a societal value or symbol that is used in relation to protection, lack of risks, certainty, reliability, trust and confidence, predictability in contrast with danger, risk, disorder and fear. As a social science concept, security is ambiguous and elastic in its meaning. Arnold Wolfer pointed to two sides of the security concept: "Security, in an objective sense, measures the absence of threats to acquired values, in a subjective sense, the absence of fear that such values will be attacked."

For the constructivists, security is interred subjective referring to "what actors make of it ". Thus, security depends on a normative core that cannot simply be taken for granted. Political constructions of security have real world effects, because they guide action of policymakers, thereby exerting constitutive effects on political order. Security is the result of a speech act, according to which an issue is treated as : "an existential threat to a valued referent object " to allow" urgent and exceptional measures to deal with the threat". Thus, the "securitizing actor" points "to an existential threat "and thereby legitimizes "extraordinary measures".

'Security in an objective sense' refers to specific security dangers, i.e. to 'threats, challenges, vulnerabilities and risks' to specific security dimensions and referent objectives as well as sectors while 'security in a subjective sense' refers to security concerns that are expressed by government officials, media representatives, scientists or 'the people' in a speech act or in written statements by those who securitize 'dangers' as security 'concerns' being existential for the survival of the referent object and that require and legitimize extraordinary measures and means to face and scope with these concerns. Thus, security concepts have always been the product of orally articulated or written statements by those who use them as tools to analyse, interpret, and assess past actions or to request or legitimize present or future activities in meeting the specified security threats, challenges, vulnerabilities, and risks. The Copenhagen school did not review the sectorialization of security from the perspective of national (international, regional) and human security.

Influenced by different worldviews, rival theories and mindsets, security is a key concept of competing schools of a) war, strategic or security studies from a realist perspective, and b) peace and conflict research from an idealist or pragmatic view (Brauch 2008:5).Since 1990, interparadigm debates emerged between traditional, critical, and constructive approaches. Within the UN and NATO, different concepts coexist, a state-centred political and military concept, and an extended security concept with economic, societal, and environmental dimensions. A widening and depending of the security concept prevailed in OECD countries, while other countries adhered to a narrow military concept.

Not only the scope of 'securitization' has changed, but also the referent object from a 'national' to a human-concerned' security concept, both within the UN system, and in the academic security community. In European security discourses, an 'extended' security concept is used by governments and in scientific debates Miller distinguished a 'national' and three expanded security concepts of 'social', human and environmental security .

While since the 19th century the key 'actor' has been the state, it has not necessarily been a major 'referent object' of security which is often referred to as 'the people' or 'our people' whose survival is at stake (Brauch 2008:6).

Whether a threat, challenge, vulnerability, and risk (Brauch 2005a, 2006) becomes an 'objective security danger' or a 'subjective security concerns' also depends on the political context. While in Europe climate change has become a major security issue, in the US, during the administration of George W. Bush this problem was downgraded. Labelling climate change a security issue implies different degrees of urgency and means for coping with it.

The traditional understanding of security "as the absence of existential threats to the state emerging from another state" has been challenged both with regard to the key subject (the state) and carrier of security needs, and its exclusive focus on the "physical or political dimension of security of territorial entities" that are behind the suggestions for a horizontal and vertical widening of the security concept. The meaning of security was also interpreted as a reaction to globalization and to global environmental change.

Those arguing explicitly and lending support for widening include Ullman(1983), Waever (1987) , Matthews (1989), Brown (1989), Nye (1989), Crawford (1991), Haffendorn (1991), Tickner (1992) and Waever et al (1993). There are others who establish a link between patterns in economic and military sectors. They include Gilpin (1981), Crawford (1993, 1995), Gowa (1994), Mansfield (1994). Being a widener, Buzan has been skeptical about the prospects for coherent conceptualization of security in the economic and environmental sectors. Since the melting down of glaciers and ice sheets in the Artic region has been a reality because of global warming, the cascading consequences of climate change in terms of flood, cyclones, expansion of desertification, intensified search for food, unprecedented migration and devastating health hazards will bind states not to narrow national security but to a new and dynamic security dimension in terms of collective security in a fragile and interdependent world. Ullman (1983) and Buzan (1991) have specifically widened the definition of threat away from a purely military to a more general formulation.

The traditionalists demonstrated strong proclivity toward putting primacy on military security despite a vast array of nonmilitary security threats affecting humanity at large. They are not averse to looking at these nonmilitary security threats and conflict in the international system yet are prompt to loosen their state centrism without making an attempt to defend and stick to their conventionally understood centrality of state in security terrain when many nonstate actors are in the fray along with state to claim equal status in the military game. An excerpt from Chipman (1992: 129) buttresses this above stand:

> The structuring element of strategic analysis must be the possible use of force.... Non – military aspects of security may occupy more of the strategist's time, but the need for peoples, nations, states or alliances to procure, deploy, engage or withdraw military forces must remain a primary purpose of the strategic analyst's inquiries.

Chipman marks certainly a shift from the state centrism and includes peoples and others in the strategic thinking and user of forces in the international system. On the other hand, Stephen Walt maintains a strongest stand on the traditionalist position by asserting that moving away from state centrism and widening the agenda outside the military domain runs the risk of expanding "Security Studies" excessively; by this logic, issues such as pollution, disease, child abuse, or economic recessions could all be viewed as threats to "security". Defining the field in this way would destroy its intellectual coherence and make it more difficult to devise solutions to any of these important problems (Walt 1991: 212-213).

The wider agenda extends the call for state mobilization to a broad range of issues. Walt allows economics and security into his schema but only as they relate to military issues rather than as economic security per se. Deudney is opposed to calling it environmental security as it will be counterproductive. The traditionalists are of the view that there is no point in calling it environmental security if solutions to the global environmental crisis are found in the instrumentality of state military apparatus. What they miss is that the global environmental crisis does not always seek solutions in the military apparatus of the state, which appears inadequate and redundant. How a state can stop the ozone hole by missiles or sea level rise by its nuclear weapons? New devices other than retreat into the instrumentality of state are needed to find out solutions.

The debate about levels of analysis has assumed significance in security studies in international relations. The five most frequently used levels of analysis are international systems, international subsystems like OAU, NATO, SAARC, ASEAN etc, units, subunits and finally at the bottom individuals. On the question of selecting a referent as the main security unit, the traditionalists put a primacy on state. This level of analysis has been closely associated with *neorealism* as it professes state centrism holding subunits as within states and sub systems and systems as made up of states. This has been criticized for reinforcing state centrism and inside-outside assumptions typical of international relations (Walker, 1993, Onuf, 1995). Since the sources of security threats have been diversified away from the state and a myriad of units other than states have equal claim to the status of state as the level of analysis, there is no point in privileging state as the main security referent object.

Sectorization of international relation has been very common as with the widening of the security agenda diversifying away from the state. To study international relation in terms of sectors—political, societal, economic, military, environmental has become the dominant tendency with new issues coming up to challenge the state centrism in security thinking. Buzan (1991:19-20) delineates sectors in security analysis as follows:

> Generally speaking, the military security concerns the two level interplay of the armed offensive and defensive capabilities of states, and states' perceptions of each other's intentions. Political security concerns the organizational stability of states, systems of government and ideologies that give them legitimacy. Economic security concerns access to the resources, finance and markets necessary to sustain acceptable levels of welfare and state power. Societal security concerns the sustainability, within acceptable conditions for evolution, of traditional patterns of language, culture and religious and national identity and custom. Environmental security concerns the maintenance of the local and planetary biosphere as the essential support system on which all other human enterprises depend.

Among all these sectors state is the central referent object in traditionalists' concept of security. If multi sectoral approach to security has been the fait accompli, referent objects other than state are bound to creep into the mainstream of security study. Each sector tries to look at the whole through the lens of its own reality. What the analyst does at best is to disaggregate the complex whole into divergent simplified threads and reassemble and weave these into a grand tapestry highlighting the interplay among all these.

With the end of cold war and demise of bipolarity interest in regions as a focus for security was seen as it was envisaged that the world would witness a more pluralistic and regionalized society. With the Soviet empire crumbled to smithereens the ideological accent explaining the super power rivalry and looking at the regional conflicts through their own lens lost its leverage. The super powers tended to avoid wider political and military engagements leaving the regions to resolve their conflicts without being entwined into super power fray. Further, the diffusion of industrial, military and political capability among a wide range of states shifted the focus of security centring on super powers to the regional levels and has increased the importance of territorially defined subsystems in geographical clustering in the security analysis. Hans Mouritzen (1995, 1997) has given the general explanation of regional state system. According to him the units (states) are fixed rather than mobile. In contemporary international relations theory, it is the considered view that the main political units are fixed not mobile. This enables each unit to face a relatively stable regional environment consisting of the major units in its geographical proximity; each unit will be characterized by a specific location in the system's structure (Mouritzen, 1980: 172,180).

CLASSICAL SECURITY COMPLEX THEORY

This theory was first designed by Barry Buzan in his book Peoples, States and Fear in 1983 (pp.105-115) and applied to South Asia and the Middle East (Buzan, 1983) and later applied to Southeast Asia (Buzan 1988). Vayrynen (1988), Wriggins (1992) and Ayoob (1995) have applied the versions of this theory to several region cases. Buzan and Waever (1992) and Waever and colleagues (1993) have applied it to study the post-cold war transformation in Europe.

According to Buzan, "classical security complex theory posits the existence of regional subsystems as objects of security analysis and offers an analytical framework for dealing with those systems" (Buzan, Waever, Wilde, 1998:11). In chime with traditional approach, this theory has put primacy on the state as the key unit focusing on military and political sectors. While highlighting the relative autonomy of regional security relations, this theory tries to set those relations within the context of the unit (state) and system levels. The emergence of neorealism in the late 1970s (Waltz, 1979) hinging exclusively on the power structure at the system level exacerbated the tendency of power theorists to underrate the significance of the regional level in international security affairs. The purpose of this classical theory is to obviate this tendency.

All of the states in the system are woven in a global web of security interdependence. The normal pattern of a globally set of security interdependence in a geographically diverse, anarchic international system as a whole far from being uniform has been one of regionally based clusters, which is defined as security complexes. Because potential military threats always stem more easily from neighbours over short distances than over long distances. Thus insecurity is always associated with proximity and the states fear the threats from the neighbours more intensely than from the distant states. For this reason, security interdependence is more intensely felt among states inside such complexes than among states outside the complexes. In the words of Buzan:

"A security complex is defined as a set of states whose major security perceptions and concerns are so interlinked that their national security problems cannot reasonably be analyzed or resolved apart from one another" (Buzan, Waever, Wilde, 1998:12) The interactions among the actors within the complex and their security perceptions constitute the formative dynamics and structure of the complex. The dynamics of security interdependence among states can be seen in a spectrum of whether there is enmity or comity among them. At the negative end lies conflict syndrome in which interdependence stems from fear, rivalry and mutual perception of threats (Senghaas,1988; Vayrynen 1984). In the middle lie security regimes in which states still treat each other as potential threats but have made reassurance arrangements to reduce the security dilemma among them (Jervis, 1982). At the positive end of the spectrum lies a pluralistic security community in which states no longer expect or prepare to resort to force in their relations with each other (Deutsch et al 1957: 1-4). Buzan cited two conditions to explain why a security complex may not be present:

> First, in some areas local states have so few capabilities that their power projects little, if at all, beyond their own boundaries. These states have domestically directed security perspectives, and there is insufficient security interaction among them to generate a local complex. The second condition occurs when the direct presence of outside powers in a region is strong enough to suppress the normal operation of security dynamics among the local states. This condition is called overlay, which normally involves extensive stationing of armed forces in the area overlain by the intervening great powers and is quite distinct from the normal process of intervention by great powers into the affairs of local security complexes Buzan, Waever, Wilde, 1998:12).

Looking at the pattern of interactions among them and seeing them as subsystems within their own structures provide the crucible to identify and assess the changes in the pattern of regional security. Essential structure composed of three components is the yardstick to assess significant change in a classical security complex. These are: (1) the arrangement of the units and the differentiation among them, (2) the patterns of amity and enmity, and (3) the distribution of power among the principal units. Major shifts in these components mark the need to redefine the complex security system. According to Buzan et al, four broad structural options are available for assessing the impact of change on a security complex:

"**Maintenance of the status quo** means the essential structure of the local complex- its distribution of power and pattern- remains fundamentally intact. The outcome does not mean no change has taken place. Rather, it means the changes that have occurred have tended, in the aggregate, either to support or not seriously to undermine the structure.

Internal transformation of a local complex occurs when its essential structure changes within the context of its existing outer boundary. Such change can come about as a result of regional political integration, decisive shifts in the distribution of power, or major alternations in the pattern of amity and enmity.

External transformation occurs when the essential structure of a complex is altered by either the expansion or contraction of its existing outer boundary. Minor adjustments to the boundary may not significantly affect the essential structure. The addition or deletion of major states, however, is certain to have a substantial impact on both the distribution of power and the pattern of amity and enmity.

Overlay means one or more external powers moves directly into the regional complex with the effect of suppressing the indigenous security dynamic.This situation is distinct from the normal process of intervention by great powers into the affairs of regional security complexes" (Buzan Waever, Wilde, 1998:13-14).

Security complexes are theoretical constructs the

analyst imposes on reality. They are not insulated from the established pattern of global politics rather they reflect its working pattern. The members of the security complexes are distinguished from other neighbouring states in that they have a distinct territorial exclusiveness and geographical cluster. Divagating from the extremes of national and global security, the classical security complex theory adverts on the region, where these two extremes interplay and where most of the action takes place. This theory also links the studies of internal conditions in states, relations among states of the region, relations among regions and global powers. In the words of Barry Buzan et al:

> The theory offers descriptive concepts for both static and dynamic analysis and provides benchmarks for locating significant change within the structure of international security relations. Once the structure of any given complex has been identified, it can be used to narrow possible options for change. The theory is prescriptive to the extent that it identifies appropriate (and inappropriate) realms for action and organization and suggests a range of states of being (conflict formation, security regime, security community) that can serve as frameworks for thinking about policy objectives (1998:15).

TRAVERSING BEYOND CLASSICAL SECURITY COMPLEX THEORY

Classical security complex theory was a political military construct and states were its referent objects. Security regions had the following characteristics:

1. They were composed of two or more states.
2. These states constituted a geographically coherent grouping
3. Security interdependence marked the relationship

among the states either positively or negatively but which must be stronger among them than between them and outside states.

4. The pattern of being interdependent had to be deep and durable.

Security regions were a type of international political sub systems, relatively autonomous and miniature versions of larger international political systems. Because the units of analysis were states, security regions tended to be a fairly large scale phenomenon. At present the concept of security moves beyond the classical security complex theory and is open to a wider range of sectors. In the analysis many questions crop up to challenge the confinement of classical security complex theory to state and its politico- military denomination. What will be the extent of regional pattern when one no longer sticks to the state and privileges its dominant political- military sector? Will the security dynamics in the non-traditional sectors generate significant regional formations? Will their security logics place their main focus on higher or lower levels? Even if regions are found in several or all sectors, will they line up- for example, are the regions in the environmental sectors at all like those in the political sector?

According to Buzan et al, there are two possible ways of opening security complex theory to sectors other than the military- political and to actors other than states:

1. Homogeneous complexes. This approach sticks to the classical assumption that security complexes are concentrated within specific sectors and are therefore composed of specific forms of interactions among similar types of units.

2. Heterogeneous complexes. This approach rejects the assumption that security complexes are confined to specific sectors. It is based on the fact that the regional logic can integrate different types of actors interacting across two or more sectors.

Homogeneous or sector specific security complexes, which are basically state dominated models and classical political- military constructs require the construction of separate frames for each sector being insulated from other sectors in security dynamics. A formidable challenge of how to weave the sector wise separate frames into a holistic tapestry remains central to this complex. Heterogeneous security complexes have the merit of linking the across sectors, thus enabling the analyst to spin the entire picture in a single canvass with a record of the inevitable spillovers between sectors.

When security is studied sector wise the question of where security is located and what are the trends, becomes important. Two types of considerations affect very much the answer chosen to these questions. First is the facilitating condition for securitization or the cause and effect nature of the issues around which securitization is strewn. Second is the very process of securitization. Facilitating conditions are sometimes clearly located on a level and sometimes not. Issues are clearly global when they have global causes and effects-for example, the issue of global warming and sea level rise. They are local when the causes and effects are local – for example the pollution of river caused by upper riparian affects the lower riparian. Rising sea level is different. It is a global phenomenon in terms of its effects but the cause is local; caused for example by the inordinate consumption and exorbitant life style of the rich North countries. It is possible to mix levels and have local causes and global effects or global causes and local effects such as holes in the ozone layer. This situation, however, is all about the level of the issue, not necessarily of its securitization. In classical security complex theory the concern hovers on which actors are actually linked by their mutual security concerns. So far as the facilitating conditions are concerned, the criterion for answering the level question is ultimately political: what constellation of actors forms on the issue. The nature of issues- causes and effects- can often be an indicator of the likely level. In the process of securitization, the key issue is for whom security becomes a consideration in relation to whom.

SECURITY: A CONCEPTUAL ANALYSIS

When state is the main referent object, any kind of threat from similar outside states to it is considered a threat to its survival or existence. If the state is held synonymous with its people, territory and society, then the threat is designated as threat to the entire people and state is legitimized to use force as it conduces adequate to meet the challenge to its existence as a political entity. In the words of Barry Buzan et al:

> The invocation of security has been the key to legitimizing the use of force, but more generally it has opened the way for the state to mobilize, or to take special powers, to handle existential threats (Buzan et al 1998:21).

Traditionally, by saying "security", a state representative declares an emergency condition, thus claiming a right to use whatever means are necessary to block a threatening development (Waever1988, 1995b). When the threat to state is not considered as threat to its people or the very nature of threats other than from outside states requiring not its military capability to meet the challenge or the utter helplessness of its weapons before the threats, the referent object is no longer the state, it is people in a wider agenda to come within the ambit of existential threat. Here the existential threat to people is the threat to state and its institutions.

In the military sector, the referent object is usually

the state. Traditional security studies tend to see all military affairs as instances of security. Where there is military coup against the existing government and its policy, it is suggestive of the fact that there has been threat to the survival of military forces, which has elevated these forces to referent object status.

In the political sector, existential threats are traditionally defined in terms of constituting principle-sovereignty but sometimes also ideology of the state. Sovereignty can be existentially threatened by anything that challenges recognition, legitimacy or governing authority.

In the economic sector the referent objects and existential threats are not easily identifiable. Firms are existentially threatened by bankruptcy or by changes in the laws that declare them illegal. National economies have greater claim to the status of referent object when they are bankrupted and fail utterly to provide the basic needs to the population. Here the survival of the population is the bench mark, any kind of threat to it can be considered as security referent object.

In the social sector the analyst looks at the systems in terms of patterns of identity and the desire to maintain cultural independence. Here the referent object is large scale collective identities that can function independent of the state such as nations and religion. Collective identities evolve in response to internal and external developments but if these tend to threat their identity, they are considered as security referent objects. That migration or rival identities can be considered an existential threat depends on whether the holders of collective identity have relatively a closed or open mind to accept them into their mainstream

In the environmental sector the referent object is very

vast ranging from the individual species to plants, habitats, maintenance of climate, biosphere and existence of human beings. Here the securitization of one is not at the expense of the other. This is concerned about the relationship between the human species and the rest of the biosphere and, remains crucial to whether that relationship can be sustained without risking a collapse of the achieved level of civilization, total destruction of planet's biological domain or both.

SECURITIZATION

Securitization is the shift of security referent object into the centre stage of a state's military apparatus in response to the sources of security threats to its normal functioning and existence in an extraordinary way. It ranges from being non- politicized in a spectrum through being politicized to being securitized. It takes the form of presenting something as existential threat to referent object. This is not securitization itself but a securitizing move; the issue is securitized only if and when the audience accepts it as such. In the words of Buzan et al:

> In security discourse, an issue is dramatized and presented as an issue of supreme priority; thus by labeling it as security, an agent claims a need for and a right to treat it by extraordinary means. For the analyst to grasp this act, the task is not to assess some objective threats that "really" endanger some object to be defended or secured; rather, it is to understand the processes of constructing a shared understanding of what is to be considered and collectively responded to as a threat. The process of securitization is what in language theory is called a speech act (Buzan et al, 1998:26).

What is important to note that the security speech act is not defined by just uttering the word "security". It must be presented as an existential threat requiring emergency or special measures and that presentation must be accepted by a sizable audience. Acceptance by the audience means an act of renewing and reinforcing the legitimacy they have already given to the political regime to recourse to extraordinary measures. The sources of security being diversified away from the traditionally understood military construct of the state, the act of securitization is an inter-subjective establishment of an existential threat with large scale political effects providing the set to ensure a negotiation between the authorized agency of the state and the audience. Because of its inter-subjective characteristics, the security studies are being applied to a variety of sectors. Sectors are "views of the international system through a lens that highlights one particular aspect of the relationship and interaction among all of its constituent units" (Buzan, Jones, and Little, 1993:31). The purpose is to differentiate types of interactions among these sectors and identify units and values characteristic of and rooted in particular sectors. The nature of survival and threat will differ across different sectors and types of unit.

SUBJECTIVE, OBJECTIVE, AND INTER-SUBJECTIVE SECURITY

The main thrust of the above analysis is that securitization, like politicization, has to be understood as an essentially intersubjective process. The orthodox view of security holds that security can be understood both objectively and subjectively. Even if one wanted to take a more objectivist approach, it is unclear how this could be done except in cases in which the threat is unambiguous and immediate. No security theory has yet provided an objective measure of security.

Securitization is a political act, which has consequences in the sense that it causes the actors to act in a different mode than he or she would have otherwise. This is exactly symptomatic of the classical realist nuance that good statesmanship is one which understands the thresholds at which other actors will feel threatened and therefore more generally understands how the world looks to those actors, even if one disagrees (Carr 1993; Kissinger 1957; Waever 1995d). But this seemingly objectivity becomes complicated because of the fact that different nations and states have different threshold to define security.

In some cases, however, the judgment about reasonableness of a securitization assumes importance, because this influences how other actors in the system will respond to a security claim. What is a legitimate securitization within a given political community may appear paranoid to those outside it. Conversely, outsiders may perceive that a political community undersecuritizes a "real" threat and thus endangers itself or free rides. The way the securitization processes of one actor fit with the perceptions of others about what constitutes a "real" threat plays a great role in shaping the interplay of securities within the international system. "Both within and between actors the extent of shared intersubjective understandings of security is one key to understanding behavior" (Buzan et al, 1998: 31). It will be a futile exercise to define what constitutes a 'real security' outside of the world of politics. Such rationalistic universalism is of little significance in political analysis. A deep understanding of the processes and dynamics of securitization will enable one to know who can "do" security on what issue and under what conditions, and possibly to manoeuvre the interaction among actors and thereby curb security dilemmas.

The distinction between subjective and objective is

useful to know how to avoid a view of security that is given objectively, and emphasize that security is determined by actors and in this respect is subjective. The label subjective, however, is not fully adequate. Individuals cannot decide alone whether an issue is a security issue. Securitization is intersubjective and socially constructed. It is a social quality, a part of a discursive, socially constituted intersubjective realm to hold that referent object having general legitimacy should survive to which actors can make reference and point to something as a threat and get others to follow or tolerate actions not otherwise legitimate. For individuals or groups to speak security does not guarantee success (cf. Derrida, 1977a; Waever 1995b). Successful securitization is not decided by the securitizer but by the audience of the security speech act. The audience is to accept that something is an existential threat to a shared value. Thus, security (as with all politics) ultimately rests neither with the objects nor with the subjects but among the subjects (cf. Arendt 1958, 1959; Waever 1990; Huysmans 1996).

SOCIAL POWER AND FACILITATING CONDITIONS

All the actors are not equal and their relationship is not symmetrical. Securitization in order to be successful is dependent very much on the position or power an actor enjoys in comparison to others. Security is thus very much a structured field in which some actors are placed in position of power by virtue of being generally accepted voices of security by having the power to define security (Bigo 1994, 1996). This power, however, is never absolute. No actor can guarantee that it has the ability to make people accept its own version of 'what security is' and its claim for necessary security action (see Wavear 1995b). To articulate alternative interpretations of security is neither forbidden to anybody. The field is structured or biased but no one conclusively has the rein over the power of securitization. Therefore, according to Buzan et al (1998: 32), "one cannot make the actors of securitization the fixed point of analysis – the practice of securitization is the centre of analysis. In concrete analysis, however, it is important to be specific about who is more or less privileged in articulating security. To study securitization is to study the power politics of a concept."

To stipulate objective standards of securityness and apply those in political field is highly impossible because they are about the future, about alternative future – always hypothetical and contrary to facts. A security argument always involves two predictions: What will happen if one does not take "security action and what will happen if one does. "A security theory that could tell politicians and citizens what actually constitute security problems and what do not would demand that such predictions should be possible to make on a scientific basis, which means society would have to be a closed mechanical, and deterministic system"(Buzan et al: 32). This is not the only condition. Apart from being a matter of degree (how threatening), securityness is also a question of quality. It may so happen that an actor may choose to handle a major challenge in other ways and thus not securitize it. In politics it is not possible to decide by investigating the threat scientifically. Thus, the use of a specific conceptualization is always a choice.

The impossibility of an objective measure for security does not denude the study of securitization of its significance, and make the study of features of the threat itself irrelevant because the security quality is supplied by the politics. On the contrary, these features rank high among the "facilitating conditions" of security speech act. Facilitating conditions are the conditions under which the speech act works, in contrast to cases in which the act misfires or is abused (Austin 1975 [1962]). Conditions for a successful speech act fall into two categories: (1) the internal, linguistic- grammatical – to follow the rules of the act (or, as Austin argues, accepted conventional procedures must exist, and the act has to be executed according to these procedures), and (2) the external, contextual and social – to hold position from which the act can be made. "The particular persons and circumstances in a given case must be appropriate for the invocation of the particular procedure invoked" [Austin 1975(1962):34]). Among the internal conditions of a speech act, the most important is to follow the security form, the grammar of security, and construct a plot that includes existential threat, point of no return, and a possible way out- the general grammar of security as such plus the particular dialectics of different sectors, such as talk identity in the societal sector, recognition and sovereignty in the political sector, sustainability in the environmental sector, and so on (Waever, 1996b).

The external aspect of speech act has two main conditions. One is the social capital of the enunciator, the securitizing actor, who must be in a position of authority, although this should not be defined as official authority. "The other external condition has to do with threat. It is more likely that one can conjure a security threat if certain objects can be referred to that are generally held to be threatening- be they tanks, hostile sentiments, or polluted waters. In themselves, these objects never make for necessary securitization, but they are definitely facilitating conditions" (Buzan et al, 1998: 33).

ACTOR AND ANALYST IN SECURITIZATION STUDIES

Approaching security from a speech act perspective raises questions about the relationship between actors and analysts in defining and understanding the security agenda. Although analysts unavoidably play a role in construction and deconstruction of security issues, it is not their primary task to determine whether some threat represents a real security problem. The debate is going on about the securityness of America in Iraq war.

To Buzan et al an objective security assessment is beyond their means of analysis. The main point is that actors and their audiences securitize certain issues as a specific form of political act. Actors who securitize do not necessarily say "security" nor does their use of the term *security* necessarily always constitute a security act. The point is whether the actors take the form of 'politics of existential threats' with the argument that an issue takes priority over everything else and therefore allows for a breaking of the rules. It is the political actors not the analysts who give the designation of what constitutes a security issue. Analysts on the other hand interpret the justness of political actors' actions and to see to what extent their actions fulfill the security criteria.

It is further, before the analyst judges whether the actor is effective in mobilizing support around this security reference, the attempted securitizers are judged first by other social actors and citizens. The degree of their following is then interpreted and measured by the analysts. Finally, to assess the significance of an instance of securitization, analysts study its effects on other units. The actor commands at only one very crucial step: the performance of a political act in a security mode. The actors play a crucial role in deciding whether an issue constitutes an existential threat. This defining security role of actors does not bind the analysts to their self assessment. When the issue of 'what are the effects of these security acts' and ' who influences the decisions comes up, the actors do no longer enjoy that defining role. "Thus, a concept such as security complex is defined not by whether actors label themselves a complex but by analysts' interpretation of who is actually interconnected in terms of security interaction" (Buzan et al 1998: 34).

This does not suggest that the analysts are in fully agreement with this securitizing act. Their main purpose is to find out whether a certain issue is worth securitizing. One cannot simply contest a securitizing attempt by saying 'this is not worth securitizing' or 'you are not threatened'. " But it is possible to ask with some force whether it is a good idea to make this issue a security issue- to transfer it to the agenda of panic politics- or whether it is better handled within normal politics" (Buzan et al, 1998: 34). As witnessed in the discussion about environmental security, even environmentalists have had strong second thoughts about the effects of putting the environmental agenda in security terms. "The securitization approach serves to underline the responsibility of talking security, the responsibility of actors as well as of analysts who choose to frame an issue as a security issue"(Ibid).

An emerging school of 'critical security studies' (CSS) wants to challenge conventional security studies by applying postpositivist perspectives, such as critical theory and poststructuralism (Krause and Williams 1996, 1997). They like Buzan deal with social construction of security. But they differed from Buzan and others in that they intend to change the society as known from constructivists and poststructuralists because things are socially constructed.

Buzan and others are of the view that what is socially constructed is often sedimented as structure and becomes stable in practice. On the basis of that it continues one can have understanding of the social construction of security not only to criticize this but also to understand the dynamics of security and thereby manoeuvre them. This leads them to put emphasis on collectivities and on understanding thresholds that trigger securitization in order to avoid them. With this securitization perspective

Buzan and others remain abstained from attempts to speak about what real security would be for people, what are actual security problems larger than posited by the elites. To be able to talk about these issues requires different ontological choices with an emancipatory ideal than what are followed by Buzan and others. Buzan and others are of the view that their approach and the approaches made by critical security studies (CSS) and constructivists are complementary to each other excepting that the latter can do what the former remains abstained from and the former can do what the latter is unable to do. Buzan prefers to sit on the fence keeping a distance from the scene in order to understand the mechanisms of securitization and the latter are intent on getting involved in the process in order to change it. Other differences exist between these approaches. While much of critical security studies, structuralists and constructivists put emphasis on individual as the true reference for security culminating in human security, Buzan's rest on collectivities. The analysts in the former studies prefer to put aside the existing security construction disclosed as arbitrary and look to other issues that are more security problems. On the other hand, Buzan and others prefer to focus on existing modus operandi and assume that future management of security rests on handling of these actors. In this sense the latter is closer to traditional security studies and the former is akin to go at the current power wielders hammer and tongs. Buzan and his colleagues claim to be constructivists at some point in holding security to be a political construction and not what the analysts hold as true security is. That means they give more importance to understanding of securitization than judging its justness. On the other hand, the critical theorists are bent on changing the system as it is a social construction.

THE UNITS OF SECURITY ANALYSIS: ACTORS AND REFERENT OBJECTS

The speech –act approach to security requires a distinction among three types of units involved in security analysis.

1. **Referent objects :** things that are seen to be existentially threatened and that have a legitimate claim to survival.
2. **Securitizing actors :** actors who securitize issues by declaring something- a reference object- existentially threatened.
3. **Functional actors :** actors who affect the dynamics of a sector. Without being the referent object or the actor who significantly influences decisions in the field of security. A polluting company for example, can be a central actor in the environmental sector- it is not a referent object and is not trying to securitize environmental issues (quite the contrary).

In traditional paradigm state has been the referent object for security and, in a more hidden way, the nation. For a state, survival is about sovereignty, and for a nation it is about identity (Waever et al. 1993. chapter 2). In the securitizing process as described above the securitizing actors can attempt to construct anything as a referent object other than the state. Size or scale seems to be one crucial variable in determining what constitutes a successful referent object of security. Individuals or small groups may not be able to establish a wider security legitimacy in their own right. Human security can cover the smaller groups or individuals who claim freedom from want and freedom from fear. At the system end of the scale the nuclear apocalypse during cold war could be able to constitute all of humankind as a security referent in much the same way as the fears of climate change or environmental catastrophe constitutes at present.

It has been found in practice that the middle scale of collectivities such as states, nations, and civilizations as anticipated by Huntington have been most amenable to securitization as durable referent objects. In the process they have been able to reinforce their identities as rivalries to other limited collectivities and construct their interactions in a 'we' versus 'they' feeling. The construction of 'we' versus 'them' is the facilitating condition for successful securitization. In this respect the middle level collectivities get an advantage over the system level.

Thus, the primacy of the middle level collectivities has led the traditional state centric security analysts to attack the approach made by Buzan and his colleagues. From traditional perspective, security by definition, centres on the state, and the state is and should be about security. With exclusive emphasis on military and political security a hard-line liberal might say the state has no legitimate functions other than security. When security is defined beyond the state centric logic securitizations become problematic such as environmental security and human security. Similarly, when the state expands beyond security, problems such as the conflation of economic security with protectionism do appear.

Buzan and his colleagues (1998: 37) while rejecting the narrow state centric move "have constructed a wider conceptual net within which the state-centric position is a possible but not a predetermined outcome". In their analysis state still retains its primacy as the most important security referent even though security is not equally available to all other states and social movements. "Security is an area of competing actors, but it is a biased one in which the state is still generally privileged as the actor historically endowed with security tasks and most adequately structured for the purpose".

Being a middle-level, limited collectivity is insufficient for achieving status as a referent object. This is probably best illustrated in the case of economic security, where one would think firms are the natural limited collectivity units. But by their very nature, firms rarely have a strong claim to a right to survival. If the survival of a firm is threatened, the firm will not be able to legitimize action beyond the normal, legal rules of the game.

The environment is becoming an interesting case, because groups are using a securitizing logic that exactly follows the format prescribed in the previous section. The environment has to survive, therefore, this issue should take priority over all others, because if the environment is degraded to the point of no return all other issues will lose their meaning. Sustainability might be the environmentalists' equivalent of the state's sovereignty and the nation's identity. It is the essential constitutive principle that has to be protected. If environmental degradation with its disastrous consequences could be considered as the threat to humankind, it has all the arguments of being the security referent object.

"Humankind as a whole achieved some status as a referent object in relation to nuclear weapons and could do so again- perhaps more successfully- in relation to environmental disasters, such as new ice ages or collisions between the earth and one or more of the many large rocks that occupy near- earth space"(Buzan et al 1998 : 38). A small group of individuals having no freedom from want and fear can claim the status of being the security referent within the rubric of human security. The level of human civilization could also become the referent object in relation to environmental threats. In the economic sector, system-level referents may be more effective vehicles for security discourse than limited collectivities, such as the firm and the state. Already, systems of rules or sets of principles, such as "the liberal world economy" and "free trade", have some status as referent objects in the economic sector (Ibid).

The individual is again a factor in security debate. As urged by Ken Booth (1991, 1994, 1995), much of security analysis have ignored taking into account the effects of various issues on actual human beings. The thrust of his argument is on securitizing concrete individuals in their competition with aggregate categories. Emma Rothschild (1995) has argued that historically a major part of liberal thought is built on a philosophical tradition to consider the individual as the referent of security. In the 1980s projects like the Brandt and Palme Commissions focused on individual as the fulcrum of security referent object. Thus, security being gravitated toward the individual Rothschild argues convincingly that regardless of whether it is intellectually coherent or ethically ideal, securitization of the individual is a real political practice of our times (Buzan et al 1998:39).

Traditionally, the middle level has been the most fruitful generation of referent objects, but lately more has been heard about system and micro level possibilities (Rothschild, 1995).Referent objects must establish security legitimacy in terms of a claim to survival. This means security analysis is interested mainly in successful instances of securitization- the cases in which other people follow the securitizing lead, creating a social, intersubjective constitution of a referent object on a mass scale. Bureaucracies, political regimes and firms can seldom be classed as security referent as they lack the legitimacy of being a claimant to survival. In practice, security is not totally subjective. There are socially defined limits to what can and cannot be securitized although those limits can be changed. " This means security analysis is interested mainly in successful instances of securitization-the cases in which other people follow the securitizing lead, creating a social, intersubjective constitution of a referent object on a mass scale" (Buzan et al, 1998: 39). Unsuccessful or partially successful attempts at securitization are interesting primarily for the insights they offer into the stability of social attitudes toward security legitimacy, the process by which those attitudes are maintained or changed, and the possible future direction of security politics.

Is securitization necessary to treat threat as threat? According to Buzan et al, without it one is not able to show that this is a threat. "The securitization perspective, which basically removes the objective ground from the dominant discourse, opens the possibility of problematizing both actual securitization and the absence of securitization, but it cannot do so by proving that something "is" a security problem- at least not without shifting from the role of analyst to securitizing actor"(1998: 40).

SECURITIZING ACTOR

A securitizing actor is someone, or a group, who performs the security speech act. Political leaders, bureaucracies, governments, lobbyists and pressure groups are included in this group. These actors cannot be considered as referent objects of security because in their security speech act they do not refer to the need to defend their own survival. Their argument is generally based on the need to defend the security of the state, nation, civilization, or some other larger communities, principle, or system.

The notion of an "actor" is in itself problematic because any collectivity can be disaggregated into subunits and on down to individuals. One can say that it is not really the state but some particular departments or in the last instances individuals who act. "But to disaggregate everything into individuals is not very helpful, because much of social life is understandable only when collectivities are seen as more than the sum of their 'members' and are treated as social realities"(Buzan et al, 1998: 40). Identifying actors is thus more complicated than identifying referent objects. The former involves a level of analysis problem. The same event can be attributed to different levels for instance individuals, bureaucracies, state etc. It is individuals who are really actors or perform the speech act in the sense that the collectivities whether state, government are authoritatively represented by the individuals. When it is said a nation for instance, America says this, it means the nation, the collectivity is represented by some individuals who act ultimately on behalf of the state. Focusing on the organizational logic of the speech act is probably the best way to identify who or what is the securitizing actor.

The difference between actor and referent object in any specific case will also usually mean there is a separate category of "audience", those the securitizing act attempts to convince to accept exceptional procedures because of the specific security nature of some issue. One danger of the phrases securitization and speech act is that too much focus can be placed on the acting side, thus privileging the powerful while marginalizing those who are audience and judge of the act (Huysmans, 1996). When securitizing actors such as state, nation are reified it means forcing the audience to accept the securitizing logic and support the securitizing act.

The distinction between securitizing actor and referent object is less of a problem in the context of the state. There are explicit rules regarding who can speak on behalf of the state. It is the government which is authorized to act on behalf of the state. The government in this case is the state in practice. No such formal rules of representation are found in case of nations or the environment. "Consequently, the problem of legitimacy is larger in these cases than in the case of the state. When someone acts in the name of a nation, certain discursive rules are imposed on the actor, because he or she has to speak in terms of identity, in terms that follow the logic of 'nation', and these terms shape the discourse and action in a way that differs from that appropriate to other referent objects" (Buzan et al, 1998: 41). The rules for what one can do in the name of a nation are less rigid than those for a state. Therefore, it will be easier to talk of the state acting than of the nation doing so. It feels more correct to make the distinction between who actually does the acting and what those actors are referring to as that which should survive and then see how successful they are in asserting a claim to speak for that higher entity.

But the distinctions between securitizing actors and referent objects are contextual rather than intrinsic to specific units. In many cases, the securitizing actors will be different from the referent object, but in others- most notably the state-the referent object will in a sense speak for itself through its authorized representatives. In all cases, however, the analyst is obliged to question the success or failure of the securitizing speech act. Even governments can fail at securitization, as happened to Britain over the Suez, the United States in Vietnam, and the European Communist regimes domestically in the late 1980s.

REGIONS AND OTHER CONSTELLATIONS OF SECURITIZATION

Is a security complex defined by actors or referent objects ?The security complex is actually a constellation of security concerns, the different instances of securitization as such form the nodes among which the lines can be drawn and the complex mapped. Security actors speak and act in the name of referent objects, and they generally see threats as emanating from other referent objects. There is thus a real sense in which India and Pakistan, Turkey and the Kurds or Chile and ITT interact.

Since referent objects are the socially constituted units, they are often actors for each other, even if some analytical theories point to other links in the chains as the actors. For instance, states are to some extent real as states and they act as states even if the literal acting is done by statesman, because states ascribe intentions and responsibility to each other as states (Manning 1962).

In classical security complex theory (CSCT), the definition was outlined in terms of primary security concerns. In the current framework, it must be instances of securitization that connect and form the complex. In discussions of the concept of security, some participants claim an actor-based threat is a precondition for something to be a security problem (Deudney 1990).

What interests Buzan is the attribution of security problems to specific sources rather than the actual origins of what appear as security problems. According to attribution theory, the degree of choice is overemphasized. The other side is actorized and considered a wilful chooser rather than a chain in a series of events. In most cases, the fact that the other is a strategic actor with several choices is an amplifying factor in any threat perception and therefore assists in pushing an issue across the security threshold. Because the other is an actor, not just a wheel in a machine, it has the potential of outwitting us, of having intentions, or of bending or suppressing our will to replace it with its own (Clausewitz 1983; Waever1995b). It seems that the focus is on securitizing actors rather than referent objects. What constitutes the threat for one is not necessarily the referent object for the other. This procedure was much easier in classical security complex theory where security was conducted for and by India, which was also the (perceived) threat to Pakistan and vice versa. What is drawn from attribution theory is the reason to believe that most threats are linked to actors and what is sometimes analyzed as referent objects will often be constructed by other actors as actors.

THE MILITARY SECTOR

In the military sector, the modern state defined by the idea of sovereignty is the most important player. The agenda of military security is thus focused largely around states, although other referent objects and securitizing actors are also in play.

Military security matters arise primarily out of the internal and external processes by which human communities establish and maintain machineries of government. The process of government is of course, about much more than the use of force. The terms and conditions of political legitimacy, and the extent to which those terms are accepted both between rulers and ruled and among different sets of rulers, are at least as important as military considerations. In practice, the military security agenda revolves largely around the ability of governments to maintain themselves against internal and external military threats it can also involve the use of military power to defend states or governments against nonmilitary threats to their existence, such as migrants or rival ideologies.

The maintenance of civil order and peace, as well as administration and law and territorial integrity are the principal domestic functions of the government. But territory is not always securitized, and on occasion governments freely negotiate substantial reorganizations, as in the recent splitting up of Czechoslovakia and the former Soviet Union. When the perceived threat is internal, military security is primarily about the ability of the ruling elite to maintain civil peace, territorial integrity, and more controversially, the machinery of government in the face of challenges from its citizens (Ayoob 1995).

It is noteworthy that the most extreme modern form of the state, the European or Westphalian state, has consolidated itself by a progressive disarming of the citizenry and a movement toward an ideal in which the state is the only legitimate wielder of force in society and effectively commands far greater instruments of force, both domestically and externally, than those illegitimate (mostly criminal) armed elements that remain.

REFERENT OBJECTS AND SECURITY ACTORS

Referent objects

Much of traditional theory and practice in international relations is built around the idea that the state is the only legitimate referent object for military security. In the state-centric, Westphalian conception of international society that grew up in Europe and was transplanted to the rest of the world, the state was conceived to be, and in some places came close to being the sole repository of both the right and the capability to use force (Buzan et al 1998: 52).

In the contemporary international system, some pre-state referent objects are still active. The remnants of tribal barbarians still exist in parts of Central Asia and Africa. Some hint of how these tribes worked as referent objects for military security can be gleaned from contemporary civil wars in Afghanistan and Somalia. Kings and Princes, empires and cities have largely disappeared or have ceased to play role as referent objects in the military sector, although royal families such as those in Kuwait and Saudi Arabia still preserve some autonomy as referent objects. Private armies also remain relevant, as was seen during the 1930s when the Chinese state had partially disintegrated, resulting in largely autonomous warlords ruling large swaths of territory. The Western fears of Islam, the rise of "Hindu nationalism", and theories about the "clash of civilization" (Huntington 1993, 1996) can contest state's claim to exclusively as the referent object for military security and it is not beyond challenge from both larger and smaller entities. The securitization itself has society as large as its referent object and state agents or politicians as major actors.

A final issue at the sub-state level is not massive at present. But if feminists can construct an image of collective violence being conducted by one group-men-against another- women-and, for instance, conceptualize rape as a security problem for all women because of the existence of men, new collectivities begin to emerge as referent objects on the violence agenda.

More abstractly, principles such as the balance of power, international society, non-proliferation of some types of weapons (nuclear, biological, chemical or blinding) and international law (nonaggression) can also be invoked as referent objects of military security. Again, there may be a direct link to state security, but the call for action is made in terms of some general principle, such as human rights, collective security, or international stability. Nuclear nonproliferation is particularly interesting here given that some states explicitly hinge their own security on possession of these weapons while at the same time arguing that the acquisition of these weapons by other states constitutes a security threat to the international system.

Securitizing Actors

One cannot assume, however, that the state is always coherent. In democracies, many voices, including pressure groups and defense intellectuals, public opinion will engage in the discourse of securitization-sometimes effectively, as in the case of U.S. opposition to the Vietnam War or Iraq war.

Functional Actors

The military sector is rich in actors that influence the dynamics of the sector without being either referent objects or securitizing actors. Many of these actors are either the agencies of force, ranging from assassins and mercenary companies through defense bureaucracies to armies, or providers of the instruments of force, most notably the arms industry. Subunits within the state are of interest in military security either because of an ability to shape the military or foreign policy of the state or because they have the capability to take autonomous action. Within a modern state, many subunits have the ability to influence the making of military and foreign policy. This is the familiar world of bureaucratic politics (Allison, 1971). Governments may have survival interests of their own usually wanting to keep themselves in power that can be distinguished from the national interest generally defined in terms of threats to the sovereignty or survival of the state. Since the government is the authorized securitizing actor for the state, separating the two can be difficult. Also prominent are the armed services, whose individual cultures exert strong pressures on military strategy and procurement. The preferences of navies for large surface ships and of air forces for manned aircraft, regardless of cost-effectiveness, are well known examples.

THE LOGIC OF THREATS AND VULNERABILITIES

Securitization is essentially an intersubjective process. The senses of threat, vulnerability, and (in) security are socially constructed rather than objectively present or absent. Nevertheless, it is easier to achieve securitization under some conditions than under others. Heavily armed neighbours with a history of aggression are more easily constructed as threats that are lightly armed, pacific ones. Different societies will respond to the same "objective" security situation in different ways. Short of tanks coming across the border, there are very few objective threats. But other things being equal, historical and material facilitating conditions affect the processes of securitization and desecuritization in a fairly systematic way. Once military securitization has occurred, issues such as balance and technology development take on a more autonomous role.

Other things being equal, in this sector the logic of threats and vulnerabilities between any two units in an international system is a function of the interplay between their respective military capabilities and their degree of amity and enmity, which are the outcomes of the (de) securitization process. In making these calculations, both the absolute capabilities of opponents and their capabilities relative to one's own must be taken into account. The absolute capabilities of potential attackers determine the nature and extent of military threats.

The dialectic of relative military capabilities between established rivals can be elaborated almost endlessly according to variations in strength, technology, and strategy (Buzan 1987: Buzan and Herring, 1998). The dialectic spins into the larger matter of balance of power versus bandwagoning and whether military security is best sought by internal balancing (increasing one's own strength to reduce vulnerability) external balancing (finding allies who share one's perception of threat), or bandwagoning (appeasement of, or subordination to, the main source of threat).

Geography shapes the perception and operation of military threats and vulnerabilities in two ways: through distance and terrain. Distance works on the traditional principle that military threats are more difficult to mount and easier to defend against when they have to travel over longer distances than over shorter ones. Most states have the capability to make threats of attack or invasion against their immediate neighbours and into their regions. In modern times, only a handful of states have developed the capability to operate military worldwide. As modern military capability has diffused throughout the international system, mounting a global military posture has become increasingly more difficult than it was in the days when the Spanish conquistador Pizarro was able to overthrow the Inca Empire with 164 men, 62 horses, and two cannons. Arguably, only the United States now falls into the world military power class.

The effect of distance is what underlies the regional premise of security complex theory. Although world –class powers can engage and defeat significant opponents at great distances Britain's takeover of India during the eighteenth century, the U.S. role in World wars I and II and the Gulf War, Iraq and Afghanistan war are few examples to show the military capability of great powers to target opponents at a longer distances. The general rule of military relations is that states are worried more about their neighbours than about distant powers. With nontraditional military relations, the distance rule applies more unevenly. It remains largely true for local criminal and inner-city scenarios and failed-state anarchies, but terrorists and mafias may deliver threats with little concern for distance and speculations about cyber war points toward modes of conflict in which distance may not matter much (Der Derian 1992).

Terrain works similarly to distance in that it tends to amplify or reduce vulnerability to military threats. Countries such as Poland and the Ukraine occupy largely flat terrain that poses few obstacles to military movement. By contrast,

Japan and Britain have benefitted from the logistical obstacle to invasions by neighbours created by open water. It is hard to imagine that Taiwan would exist as a separate state, were it not for the protection offered by the Taiwan Strait. Switzerland has benefitted from its mountain barriers, Russia from its distances and climate. Isreal and Kuwait, by contrast, have no strategic depth and few physical barriers to invasion.

History affects military threats largely in terms of the impact of past experience on present perception. The existence of historical enmity and repeated war will tend to amplify present perception of threat. After World War I France feared Germany even when the latter was disarmed. Poland has long historical suspicions of Germany and Russia, Korea and China of Japan, Vietnam of China, Greece and Armenia of Turkey and Iraq and Iran of each other. Such memories can be very long and deep (Vietnam and China, Iraq and Iran- especially if viewed as Arabs versus Persians). Or they can be fairly recent (France and Germany). Some seem almost ineradicable (Greece and Turkey). Whereas others have either faded from military significance or been replaced by more recent events (Britain and France, Denmark and Sweden). As was seen during the Cold War, history is not a necessary condition for strong feelings of military threat. Neither the United States nor the Soviet Union/Russia had any serious history of enmity before they plunged into the Cold War, but the existence of a bitter history and memories of previous wars facilitate the process of securitization. As Japan and Germany have learned, such memories can obstruct the process of desecuritization even when well established present political and military realities seem to pose no objective grounds for threat perception.

Political factors affect military threats in two ways: through the degree of recognition that exists between the actors and through harmonies and disharmonies in their political ideologies. In the case of the Cold War, historical enmities were largely absent, but the United States and the Soviet Union were locked into a zero-sum ideological conflict that served just as well to stimulate the process of securitization.

Ideological divisions can operate in international systems when the political units continue to recognize each other as legal equals. But one does not have to look far back in history(or perhaps far ahead into the future) to find it accepted as normal that both states and peoples should regard each other in hierarchical terms, as superior and subordinate. In historical terms, the decades since the end of World War II represent a sharp break with historical practice. Decolonization made it necessary, at least for a time, to accept all states as legal equals and all peoples as equally human. The establishment of human rights means the human side of this equation will probably endure, but there are real questions as to whether a number of post-colonial states will be able to govern themselves well enough to sustain their status as equal members of international society. Some- such as Haiti, Somalia, Liberia, Bangladesh, and Cambodia-might already be slipping into a kind of mandate status, not as colonies but as dependants on the international community.

Differences in status make a difference to military threats. When one political unit does not recognize another as of equal status or, even worse, does not recognize its political status at all, a variety of significant restraints on the resort to force are removed. The process of securitization is correspondingly facilitated, because behaviour by the other- which one would have to live with if it were a recognized state- can more easily be castigated as an unacceptable threat to, say one's supplies of necessary goods or the security of one's citizens abroad. Relations between Europe and much of Asia had this unequal quality during the nineteenth century, a story told excellently by Gerrit Gong (1984).

Elements of this "standard of civilization" approach recently reappeared in Europe when some post- Cold War successor states were confronted with conditions regarding democracy, human rights, and economic law before being accorded recognition. When political unit is not recognized by others, its sociopolitical institutions are not considered politically empty and available for occupation. "Political and social recognition do not begin to guarantee freedom from military threat, but their absence makes military threats much more open to securitization" (Buzan, 1996).

REGIONALIZING DYNAMICS?

The end of the cold war witnessed a marked shift from preoccupation with global level security to regional and local level security concerns. According to Buzan and others three types of development can undermine the natural dominance of the regional level in military security in favour of the global level.

i) "The first occurs if military threats cease to matter in international relations, in which case all of the military sector would fade into the background and emphasis would shift relatively to the other sectors,

ii) The second occurs if military technology becomes so advanced and cost-effective that distance and geography cease to matter in the transmission of military threats, in which case the distinctive logic of regional security complexes would disappear.

iii) The third occurs if the concentration of power in the international system becomes so great that the regional level either ceases to exist/ (because all states are globally operating great powers or integrated regions) or ceases to matter (because the great powers overlay regional security complexes)" (Buzan etal , 1998: 62).

A substantial part of the international system, including most of its major centres of power, now lives in a pluralistic security community in which the members neither expect nor prepare to use force in their relations with each other. Opinion varies as to whether this is evidence for the "democracy and peace or the interdependence and peace hypothesis or simply a result of historical war weariness and nuclear deterrence. Whichever is right , it has become undeniably more difficult and perhaps impossible to securitize military relations among these states. A few great powers can deliver huge amounts of military power any where on the planet within a short period of time, and the combination of nuclear weapons and long –range missiles means distance and geography matter less in relations between the great powers. The proliferation of technologies of mass destruction (nuclear, chemical, and biological) and the means to deliver them (missiles) might indicate a more general move toward global capability , but if so that move is very slow and very partial . Most existing and potential nuclear weapons states (Britain, France, China, South Korea, Japan, Taiwan, India, Pakistan, Israel, Iran, and Iraq) have means of delivery confined largely to their own regions, thus reinforcing the regional military security dynamic. For the bulk of states such weapons play no role in present status of future plans. For them, the reality remains that conventional forces are very much constrained by distance and that the regional logic of military security relations remains dominant.

In terms of the concentration of power, the direction of events seems to be firmly away from any globalizing trend and toward the diffusion of power and regionalization of interaction. The era of European imperialism and the Cold War both represent versions of power concentration that were able to override the regional logic. Most of the major centres of power are now rather inward looking concerned with their own problems, and disinclined to use military power abroad either for expansion or for more than minor peacemaking efforts in local conflicts. They will use substantial force when their interests are threatened, as in the war against Iraq, but in general the major powers are not driven to use force abroad either by rivalry with each other or by internal pressures. They have become resistant to the appeal of military securitization.

It might be argued that the United States retains a unipolar military technological superiority and level of expenditure so overwhelming as to sustain a centralizing trend. But U.S aversion to casualties and entanglements marginalizes its impact on the other factors pushing towards regionalization. As Somalia demonstrated, most states and even some non states now have the capability to resist effectively any attempt to military occupation.

The introversion of the great powers is complemented by the diffusion of power to the regional states, few of which are constrained about securitizing their relations with their neighbours. This development should extend the process begun by decolonization of increasing the importance of regional security dynamics relative to that of the great powers. The recent American intervention in Iraq and its making the latter a messy on a falsified pretext of Iraq under the hanged Saddam Hussain having weapons of mass destruction shows an outside super power military intervention is not a desired solution to the regional crisis.

The Cold War fostered a habit of superpower intervention in Third World military conflicts, both domestic and regional. Local powers appealed to the superpowers for support by trying to locate their own security concerns within the context of superpower rivalry. In turn, the United States and the Soviet Union defined their security in global terms. The Cold War facilitated the process of military securitization all around.

It would be difficult to prove that the Cold War actually generated many conflicts in the Third World except in a few instances. But the cold war logic and attempt to enlist the regional powers and weave local conflicts into their global strategy aggravated the regional conflicts. Given the absence of ideological or strategic motivation after the end of cold war, the major powers are unlikely to be easily moved to intervene directly in Third World conflicts, as they were in Vietnam and Afghanistan (Buzan et al, 1998:65). But in the absence of any military might projected to restrict American unipolarity, America could easily intervene in Afghanistan and Iraq especially after 9/11 incident as a part of its global strategy to decimate terrorism

THE ENVIRONMENTAL SECTOR

The Environmental Security Agenda

Some analysts describe environmental security as "ultimate security (Myers 1993a), others as a pollution of security proper (Deudney 1990). Most others oscillate somewhere in between. Some scholars filter environmental security through a political and military lens (Homer-Dixon 1991), others perceive it as a social welfare issue (as reflected, e.g. in Article 130R of the Treaty of the European Union). In the study of international relations, more ever, the environment seems to be a welcome garden for case studies in regime theory (Haas, Keohane, and Levy 1993). But attempts to securitize environmental values have a short history compared to what can be seen with regard to the other four sectors

Ultimately, according to Buzan and his colleagues "the scientific agenda underpins securitizing moves, whereas the political agenda is about three areas: (1) State and public awareness of issues on the scientific agenda (how much of the scientific agenda is recognized by policymakers, their electorates and their intermediaries- the press. (2) the acceptance of political responsibility for dealing with these issues and (3) the political management questions that arise: problems of international cooperation and institutionalization- in particular regime formation, the effectiveness of unilateral national initiatives, distribution of costs and benefits, free-rider dilemmas, problems of enforcement, and so forth" (Buzan eta al , 1998: 72).

The environmental sector is made complicated by its great variety of issues. This is the widest formulation of the environmental agenda and therefore includes issues the present study deals with primarily in other sectors.

- Disruption of ecosystems includes climate change; loss of biodiversity; deforestation, desertification, and other forms of erosion; depletion of the ozone layer; and various forms of pollution.
- Energy problems include the depletion of natural resource, such as fuel wood; various forms of pollutions, including management disasters (related in particular to nuclear energy, oil transportation, and chemical industries); and scarcities and uneven distribution .
- Population problems include: population growth and consumption beyond the earth's carrying capacity; epidemics and poor health conditions in general; declining literacy rates; and politically and socially uncontrollable migrations, including unmanageable urbanization.
- Food problems include poverty, famines, over-

consumption, and diseases related to these extremes: loss of fertile soils and water resources: epidemics and poor health conditions in general: and scarcities and uneven distribution.

- Civil strife includes war related environmental damage in the one hand and violence related to environmental degradation on the other.

SECURITY ACTORS AND REFERENT OBJECTS

The environment as such, or some strategic part of the environment, is the referent object of environment security. The environmental security debate has taken over from the anti nuclear weapon lobby this concern about the loss of civilization. At stake is the maintenance of achieved levels of civilization, including a development perspective free of environmental disasters. In short, environmental security "concerns the maintenance of the local and the planetary biosphere as the essential support systems on which all other human enterprises depend" (Buzan 1991:19-20).

It is in relation to this ultimate referent object (human enterprise) that a paradox arises similar to that inherent in the classic security dilemma in an anarchic system. The only way to secure societies from environmental threats is to change them.

A high degree of controversy surrounds environmental issues. In addition to securitizing actors are actors who oppose securitizing moves by either contesting or ignoring the attempt to prioritize a threat. Of course, this might also be said for the military sector, where peace movements sometimes try either to debunk state moves toward securitization (by denying the validity of the threat) or to turn the state against itself (by pointing to the securitization itself as the threat-e.g. in generating arms races or raising the risk of war). But in the environmental sector, the security status of issues has only recently been asserted and lacking any depth of social sedimentation, is much more vulnerable to such countermoves. Porter and Brown (1991) have captured this concept using the idea of lead actors, veto actors, and veto coalitions. (Their exact term is veto states, but they also apply that term to firms and other functional actors.). These categories embody both political and security moves, but they do give useful insight into the security actors in this sector.

Lead actors have a strong commitment to effective international action on an environmental issue in specific cases. These actors may be states. Australia, for example took the lead in regime formation for Antarctica. Sweden and Norway pushed international action on trans-boundary air pollution, especially acid rain. Related to the scientific agenda, however, the lead actor is not a state but a global, environmental epistemic community (Haas 1992) that investigates the urgency of a wide range of environmental subjects, constructs an agenda, and communicates that agenda to the press and political elites. It is worthwhile to consider this loose "community" as independent political force in this sector, because its members have proved able to exert major political influence. For the political agenda, the distinctive lead actors are activist and lobbying nongovernmental organizations (NGOs) of which Greenpeace and the World Wildlife Fund are among the most outstanding examples, securitizing the environment is their trade.

Porter and Brown (1991: 36-37) distinguish several strategies for lead actors, in particular the states among them. They might raise awareness of an issue by financing research and informing public opinion in target states (i.e. mobilizing the scientific agenda). For this purpose, they can make use of the environmental epistemic community to support their position abroad. These actors may take unilateral action (lead by example), or they may use diplomacy to put the issue on the agenda of international organizations or to isolate veto actors. "In most cases, however these initiatives cannot be called securitizing moves, they constitute politicization. This is characteristic of the entire practice of environmental regime formation in the international system" (Buzan eta al, 1998: 77).

When victims lack the resources to lead (as is true for most developing countries), they are likely to be support actors. Leading actors, and support actors even more so, are not by definition located at the danger spots. Especially when the issue is global (such as ozone depletion) economic (as with the demand side of the tropical forest issue), or moral (such as whaling) these actors can be found anywhere- although this generally means in countries that can afford to put energy into remote problems and in which people are free to do so. Because of the issue-specific nature of these positions, they have (so far) not cumulated in overall power constellations. Nor have environmental values (yet) become a conscious ordering device for society as a whole in the way military, economic, and identity interests have done.

As with the military sector, the environmental one is rich in functional actors. One large category is economic actors (transnational corporations [TNCs] state firms agricultural, chemical, and nuclear industries, fishing, mining, and the like) whose activity is directly linked to the quality of the environment. These are functional actors whose behavior affects ecosystems but who generally do not intend to politicize let alone securitize this activity. Their common denominator is that they are large scale economic actors, generally motivated by profit making. They exploit ecosystems to build or maintain the human habitat. Much of the environmental debate is concerned with how these actors operate. What are the acceptable types and limits of exploitation? Can one find sustainable forms living from nature's interest (and if possible increasing that interest) rather than spending its capital? This places these actors in the spotlight of environmental security debates, often in a negative sense.

THE LOGIC OF THREATS AND VULNERABILITIES

According to Buzan and his colleagues, three relationships of threat define the possible universe of environmental security.

1. Threats to human civilization from the natural environment that are not caused by human activity. Earthquake and volcanic events count (although even here there are debates about human agency) but the most incontrovertible examples are fears of large meteorite strikes and concerns about a natural swing back into a cycle of extensive glaciation.

2. Threats from human activity to the natural systems or structures of the planet when the changes made do seem to pose existential threats to (parts of) civilization. Obvious examples here are, at the global level, greenhouse gas emission and the effects of CFCs and other industrial emissions on the ozone layer. At the regional and local levels, this relates to environmental exploitation (by extraction, dumping, or accidental destruction) beyond the carrying capacity of smaller ecosystems, which upsets the economic base and social fabric of the states involved.

3. Threats from human activity to the natural systems or structures of the planet when the changes made do not seem to pose existential threats to civilization. An example of this might be the depletion of various mineral resources, which may be inconvenient but which can almost certainly be handled by advances in technology (i.e. the shift from Copper to Silicon in

the electronics industry and potentially a shift from metal to ceramics in some engineering applications).

The last of these relationships registers little in the discourse of environmental security, with the notable exception of concerns over the extinction of various animals (especially birds and large mammals). The first does register but only at the margins. It could grow if the scientific agenda provides more compelling reasons to worry about it or if those securitizing actors that have an interest in it (e.g. the space defense lobby) become more influential.

The second relationship is the main reason to talk about environmental security: It represents a circular relationship of threat between civilization and the environment in which the process of civilization involves a manipulation of the rest of nature that in several respects has achieved self defeating proportions. From a global perspective, this circular relationship is mainly the result of two developments, the explosive growth of both the world population and economic activity in the second half of the twentieth century. During the last 2,000 years, world population increased from an estimated hundred million to about 6 billion. In the 10,000 years before that, world population grew from a mere 4 million to a hundred million (Pointing 1991: 90, 92, 241: Porter and Brown 1991: 4). Between 1960 and 1990 the estimated gross world product almost quadrupled from about $6 trillion to almost $20 trillion (Porter and Brown 1991:5). Ideas for integrating environmental concerns into economic accounting are fairly new (Van Dieren 1987) but are being pushed by the rise in pollution statistics in the late twentieth century.

Crucial for understanding environmental security is the idea that it is within human power to turn the tide. The problem is one of humankind's struggle not with nature but with the dynamics of its own cultures- a civilizational issue that expresses itself mainly in economic and demographic dimensions and that potentially affects the degrees of order in the international system and its subsystems.

The basic logic of environmental security is that in a global perspective, humankind is living beyond the carrying capacity of the earth. In local and regional circumstances this condition is often even more manifest. The exact meaning of the concept carrying capacity is disputed, but for the present context it can be defined as the total patterns of consumption the earth's natural systems can support without undergoing degradation (cf Ehrlich 1994). These patterns of consumption involve several variables, such as total population, production modes, and gross per capita consumption levels. In short, carrying capacity depends on numbers, technology and lifestyle.

The security debate addresses the reliability of such predictions (Meadow's work for example, is widely contested). The prevention of breaking points and measures to reduce vulnerabilities in case prevention fails. The ultimate question is whether there are civilized ways out of the problems created by civilization. How will people adapt to the new constraints of their environment? So far, two debates about threats and vulnerabilities have arisen in response. Both are substantially affected by a lack of knowledge of the actual levels and probabilities of threat and of what measures might reasonably be taken.

The first debate is about the economic –liberal case that questions whether we should do anything. The economist (1-7 April 1995) argues for discounting the future to avoid huge, perhaps unnecessary economically disruptive expenditure in the present. The argument here is to let the future (with its presumably greater resources and more knowledge) take care of itself. Critics call this unlimited faith in the skills of future generations to deal with problems created here and now "the myth of the techno-fix" (Smith, Okoye, de Wilde, and Deshkingkar 1994).

It should be noted that a major difference in these debates involves whether one discusses causes or effects. The essence of the environmental lobby is to deal with causes- attempts to change society by coordinated effort before nature changes it through disaster. Although this policy involves many securitizing moves, it primarily results in politicization only. In terms of politicizing causes, much is happening, but most of the threats are too distant to lead to securitization. Environmental issues often point to an unspecified, relatively remote future and therefore involve no panic politics. It is assumed that it hardly matters whether we act now or next year: therefore, "urgency" becomes reappropriated as a part of "normal politics". This, of course, is exactly what radical environmentalists question. They argue that taking action is literally an urgent matter, and their rhetoric is definitely one of securitization, it will soon be too late, we have to act even when we must take unpleasant steps that would normally be totally outside the acceptable spectrum, because the nature of threat demands this.

In other words, the environmental sector provides a lens that enables us to highlight root causes of existential threats that become manifest on other sectors. This finding is similar to that for the economic sector, This may sometimes point to misperception or scapegoat functions (e.g. blaming Jews for the economic depression in the 1930s) and some times to the overspill from one sector to another: For examples, failing to distribute scarce water jeopardizes basic human need and will stimulate " my family first" policies- that is, extremism, If we define environmental security in terms of sustaining ecosystems that are necessary for the preservation of achieved levels of civilization, it follows that when and where this security fails, the conflicts will be over threats to these levels of civilization- that is, threats to non-environmental existential values. The environment, modified by human interference, sets the conditions for socio-political economic life. When these conditions are poor, life is poor.

REGIONALIZING DYNAMICS?

The contemporary environmental agenda was originally conceived as global. Its emergence is not the result of the globalization of local developments but, on the contrary, of the discovery of global consequences of seemingly harmless individual or local practices. This contrasts with the development of other security agenda which evolved out of the gradual globalization of problems that originally had a local character-military security, for example, in which it took centuries for warfare to develop on a global scale. Hence, the rhetoric of the political agenda makes us believe we are dealing with an essentially globalized sector. The bulk of the literature is arguing that, to use the words of Andrew Hurrell and Benedict Kingsbury (1992:2).

> Humanity is now faced by a range of environmental problems that are global in the strong sense that they affect everyone and can only be effectively managed on the basis of cooperation between all, or at least a very high percentage, of the states of the world, controlling climate change and the emission of greenhouse gases, the protection of ozone layer, safeguarding biodiversity, protecting special regions such as Antarctica or the Amazon, the management of the sea-bed, and the protection of the high seas are among the principal examples.

This sounds good, but it is not entirely true. The concern here is global, but most pollution related problems require first and foremost joint action by the highly industrialized states only, in principle, the protection of Antarctica, except for the hole in the ozone layer, could be left to the seven states that have legal rights there. The Amazon region (and thus, to a large extent, biodiversity) would be protected best by leaving it alone a decision that rests essentially with the Brazilian government and a few business enterprise. The global dimension is present but not as overwhelmingly as is often suggested.

Threats and vulnerabilities in the environmental sector are issue specific and seldom universal. Moreover, causes and effects may be located at different levels and in different regions. Global events seldom have the total character of a potential nuclear winter. Most global events, including climate change and massive migrations, can be compared to events such as the two world wars and the Great Depression.

A useful starting point for tracing security complexes in the environmental sector is disaster scenarios. What if the hole in the ozone layer widens, sea levels rise, massive migrations occur, or another Chernobyl type accident occurs? Who is immediately affected? How permanent is the damage? What are the regional political consequences, and are there global consequences? In other words, what is the highest level on which the effects will occur?

The next question is, at what level are the causes located? What and who are causing the hole in the Ozone layer, the sea level rise, and the like? These locations can sometimes be linked in coherent regions. For example, acid rain in the Nordic countries originates in Britain and Central Europe. Sometimes the complexes of causes and effects are less coherent. The hole in the Ozone layer (effect) can be located regionally whereas the causes are cumulative and dispersed worldwide.

The third sequence of questions is decisive; because it is here that a political constellation of mutual security concerns is formed. Who feels threatened? Who must those parties cooperate with if action is to be effective? Effects and causes are significant conditions in disposing who will become involved with whom and how, but they do not fully determine outcomes. Securitization always involves political choice, thus, actors might choose to ignore major causes for political or pragmatic reasons and therefore may form a security constellation that is different from what one would expect based on one's knowledge of effects and causes.

According to Buzan and his colleagues, the following sequence of questions should be answered for a concrete assessment of security dynamics in the environmental sector:

1. (a) What does the disaster scenario look like? How does it manifest itself in time and space? This involves mainly the scientific agenda and provides structural (physical) characteristics of the issue area. (b) Is the disaster scenario (expected to be) politicized? In other words, at what point are we talking about environmental security in this issue area? This involves the political agenda.

2. (a) Who are the veto and other functional actors in this issue area? In other words, who is causing the problems? This provides structural characteristics. (b) Who are the actual or potential lead and support actors? This provides political characteristics of the issue area. The resulting actor typology provides s strong indication of the localizing, regionalizing, and globalizing dynamics of the political agenda. If actors become interconnected in a political constellation over these security issues, they represent a security complex.

3. How independent an issue are we dealing with? (a) Is there structural issue linkage? For example, in poverty – related forms of desertification, the issue of erosion is linked to those of population growth and domestic and North– South economic asymmetries. This again mainly involves the scientific agenda. (b) Is there political issue linkage? Structurally unrelated issues may become interlinked by veto and lead actors, as, for example, when biodiversity in rain forests is linked to debt negotiations. This type of linkage will show from the political agenda (Buzan et al, 1998:89).

In sum, it can be reiterated that securitizing moves at the global level have resulted in considerable politicization, but successful securitization has been limited. Successful securitization has occurred mainly at the local level, where the actual disasters take place and thresholds of sustainability are passed .But even so, it is not necessarily the environment that is securitized: Environmental conflict often travels under the guise of political turmoil or ethnic strife.

Another difficulty in analyzing environmental security in terms of regions is that causes and effects of environmental issues frequently involve different regions and different actors- the actors who cause environmental damage are distinct from those who suffer from it. There may be one set of actors in one region whose security interdependence is high if one wants to deal with the causes of a specific ecoproblem (e.g., agricultural policies in semiarid regions), whereas another set of actors in another region may be involved in cause of failure caused by the spillover of negative developments (e.g., environmental refugees fleeing hunger after crop failure). This leads to larger and more complex patterns of security linkage.

NGO activities combined with wide media coverage turn these local problems into global issues. This global village image of the environmental sector is a strong non regional feature. Yet, many of the manifest existential threats involved are expressing themselves locally, which means people usually do not have to wait for a global – level solution to tackle these local problems.

In sum, securitizing moves are attempted at almost all levels but mostly at the global level. Most successful securitization, however, is local. Some subsystemic formations do emerge, regional as well as nonterritorial.

THE ECONOMIC SECURITY AGENDA

The idea of economic security is located squarely in the unresolved and highly political debates about international political economy concerning the nature of the relationship between the political structure of anarchy and the economic structure of the market (Buzan 1991:230). Mercantilists and neomercantilists put politics first, seeing the state as both embodying the social and political purposes for which wealth is generated and providing the security necessary for the operation of firms and markets.

Liberals put economics first, arguing that the economy should be at the root of the social fabric and that the market should be left to operate as freely as possible without interference by the state. The state is necessary to provide law and politico – military security and to support the social fabric in areas in which the market fails to do so.

Socialists falling between the two argue that economics is at the root of the entire social fabric and to the extent that states can escape this logic, their task is to reach the social and political goals of justice and equity based on economics. The security focus of socialists is toward the economically weak and against the strong.

The crushing victory of the West in the Cold War marginalized the socialist element of the ideological debate and weakened, but by no means eliminated, the economic nationalist element. In rhetorical terms, the victory pushed much of the ideological debate (probably temporarily) into the background, leaving an economic security discourse shaped largely by liberal concerns and by the effect of an international political economy attempting to operate under liberal rules. Moreover, the type of liberalism now in fashion is particularly pure. It has much less attachment to the national economy than did its nineteenth – century predecessor, and it has pushed aside much of the "embedded liberalism" (Ruggie 1982) enshrined in the post – 1945 Bretton Woods system. In its more virulent forms, this liberalism seeks to recreate Karl Polanyi's (1957[1944]) nightmare of the total subordination of social values to market values. Much of forebodings of Polyani then came true today as the American market economy slows down miserably. In practice, much economic nationalism remains, finding its political space in the ambiguity that exists within the liberal position over how large the role of the state should be and the extent to which the market should be allowed to override national and individual security. Trade continues to evoke fierce opposition between liberal and protectionist forces, but production and even more so, finances have developed an increasingly unrestricted global transnational character. The liberal ideal is ultimately to dissolve national economies, with their exclusive currencies and restrictions on factor movement, into a global economy with relatively few restraints on the movement of goods, capital, services, and (more hesitantly) people. The problems are how to maintain economic and political stability and how to handle the widening gap between the very rich and very poor that unrestricted markets tend to generate while simultaneously removing many powers and functions from states. This explains the concern within the field of international political economy(IPE) about how to maintain order and stability in a liberal international political economy, with the focus first on hegemons(Kindleberger, 1973, 1981; Gilpin 1987) and then on regimes and institutions(Keohane 1980, 1984).

These developments mean the discourse on economic security is now shaped by the dominance of the liberal agenda and by the consequences of attempts to implement that agenda in the areas of trade, production and finance. The particular characteristics of the liberal ascendance mean the contemporary discourse on economic security centres on concerns about instability and inequality. Concern about instability raises questions about the relative economic decline of the United States as a hegemon and about the domestic and international management problems arising from the increasing integration and liberalization of the world economy. Concern about inequality raises questions domestically about the role of the state and internationally about the disadvantaged economic position of most Third World states.

Alongside U.S. decline was the growing integration and liberalization of the global economy, first in trade and beginning in the 1970s, also in finance. This condition had two effects. First, it meant national economies became progressively more exposed to competition from other producers in a global market and to ever more powerful transitional corporations and financial markets. The effects of the global economy in promoting unemployment and deindustrialization came to be seen as a threat to both welfare and sovereignty by those who were not doing well within it. Some also saw the global economy as a threat to the state itself or at least to much of the traditional conception of what the state was supposed to do (Cerny 1995). Second, this condition meant all national economies that had become adapted to an open global trading and financial systems were dependent upon its continued stability and smooth functioning. All of these economies were therefore threatened by the possibility of systemic crises that might disrupt the worldwide flows of goods and capital.

The particular plight of Third World countries arose from the dependent economic position as suppliers of primary goods many had inherited from their colonial period. These countries found themselves locked into disadvantage terms of trade that some argued prevented their economic and socio-political development. Viewed from another perspective, these countries found themselves politically independent but heavily penetrated by outside market and political interests and burdened with societies and leaderships whose traditions, skills, resources, and internal divisions often provided poor foundations for the development of a modern political economy (Galtung 1971).

One peculiar characteristic of economic security under liberalism is that it is about the creation of stable conditions in which actors can compete mercilessly.

Related to hegemonic power or positions in general, states are faced with an economic security dilemma. Relative economic growth plays a major role in determining the power of states in the system (Kennedy 1989, Gilpin 1987). In contrast to military power, however, relative wealth is not normally of a zero-sum character, for example, the rise of Japan has not made the rest of the OECD poorer. If the Japanese economy were to collapse tomorrow, the resultant loss of capital and markets would drag the rest of the OECD economies down with it. In other words, economic interdependence is much less black or white when it comes to enmity and amity that military interdependence, consequently, economic security is a much more blurred concept than military security. It is often difficult to separate attempts to securitize economic issues from the more general political contest between liberal and nationalist approach to economic policy. During the Cold war, the superpower rivalry muted protectionist voices because of the overriding common military and political security concern all of the capitalist powers and shared against the Soviet Union, As long as the Soviet threat existed, the capitalist states worried more about it than about the commercial rivalry among themselves. But after 1989 with the ideological confrontation consigned to history, the common interest that had kept the capitalist economies together despite their rivalry was significantly weakened.

SECURITY ACTORS AND REFERENT OBJECTS

The economic sector is rich in referent objects, ranging from individuals through classes and states to the abstracts and complex system of the global market itself.

Only two sorts of securitizing logic can usually attempt to elevate firms to the status of referent objects. The first is local and concerns the immediate effect on individuals and towns when a firm goes under. Individual, trade unions, city governments, and the local political representatives of the national governments and the local political representative of the national government may all attempt to save the company by casting its demise in security terms. The second type of securitizing logic is national and involves the government's attitude toward the place of a firm in the state's industrial base. For example- if the government is committed to a higher degree of self-reliance for military mobilization. The Marxist logic of class "war" could be read as elevating classes to the status of referent object, with the class depending upon whose side one is on. Although politically effective for several generations this rhetoric failed to attract a wide following in international security terms. If the explicit attempt to securitize the working class failed, a case might be made that much liberal rhetoric about economic efficiency and stability masks an implicit attempt to securitize the interests of a transnational capitalist class. Such an argument would appeal to most types of economic nationalists but would be rejected by liberals on the grounds that market efficiency serves the wider community, not just the elite. Classes cannot be ruled out as potential referent objects of economic security, but so far the attempt to securitize class has had only patchy and short- lived success. It is worth noting that non monetary economic especially subsistence farmings have the family or even the extended family as their unit. Although entire regions (especially Sub-Saharan Africa) are based on this principle, there is no politicization or securitization of these economic activities except for some community based development literature.

At the unit level, states far outshine firms and classes as the principal referent objects of economic security, even for liberals. When security arguments are used to legitimize, for instance, a violation of General Agreement of Tariffs and Trade (GATT) rules, the basis is a security logic related to state interests rather than a firm.

THE LOGIC OF THREAT AND VULNERABILITIES

How do threats and vulnerabilities in the economic sector measure up to the securitization criteria? What constitutes an existential economic threat depends upon the referent objects. For individuals, economic security can be understood most clearly in terms of basic human needs. Individuals live or die (or in the case of malnutrition in children, have their development as human beings compromised) according to the provision of the basic necessities for sustaining human life: adequate food, water, clothing, shelter and education. But beyond these basics, it is not clear that the individual can legitimately be securitized in the economic sector.

Unlike firms, states do have the qualities necessary for securitization. States are thus peculiarly immune to some existential threats that bear on other actors in the economic sector. The bankruptcy of a state may threaten its political security (by having the International Monetary Fund [IMF] and the World Bank infringe upon its sovereignty) or its military security (by raising threats of forceful debt collection. As in the gunboat diplomacy of the colonial era- which is no longer acceptable, but it rarely affects a state's economic security.

Beyond this basic level however it is difficult to see how economic security can be legitimately invoked by liberals. Whereas economic nationalists have no problem invoking economic security in state terms liberals are (or should be) constrained from doing so by their commitment to efficiency and thus to openness and competition.

What is merely economic or political within the economic sector may have security implications in other sectors. Can society, with its wider set of values, survive the impact of international marketization? Will breakdowns in the international economy lead to war? Does the spread of mass consumption market economics threaten to overwhelm the planetary ecosystems? The logical difficulties within liberalism caused by the acceptance of economic insecurity as the price of efficiency work against attempts to securitize issues in the economic sector. They do not prevent such attempts, although it is easier for economic nationalists than for liberals to make those attempts. It is difficult for liberals to speak of economic security without becoming intellectually incoherent.

One interesting feature of the economic sector is that system – level structures (the market, the trading system, and the financial system) and the institutions associated with them are routinely invoked as objects of security. This contrasts with the discourse in the political sector, where, although various regimes and institutions and even international society itself can become referent objects, the anarchic structure as such is almost never invoked in this way (even though the obsession with sovereignty implies support for an anarchic structure) .When economic systems – whether abstract markets or concrete IGOs – are constructed as referent objects of security, the questions of what constitutes an existential threat can be answered only in terms of the principles by which such systems are organized. The LIEO (Liberal International Economic Order) is existentially challenged by anything that threatens to unravel commitments to remove border constraints on the international movement of goods, services, and finance. More subtly, it is also threatened by the development of monopolies, which undercut the rationales of competition and efficiency that underpin the system. The LIEO thus live in permanent tension with impulses toward both protectionism and monopoly. To the extent that these other impulses gain ground, The LIEO is diminished and eventually extinguished. The same logic applies to IGOs. In the economic sector something like the EU can be existentially threatened by whatever might unglue the rules and agreements that constitute its single market.

The increasing internationalization of the world economy and the fear of another 1920s-style collapse have led to the increasing institutionalization of system-level security guarantors in the LIEO. The IMF and the World Bank provide support for states that get into economic trouble and the GATT-WTO contributes to resilience against crises by providing rules and settling disputes. Central banks operate more and more independent of national governments and their representatives meet regularly to discuss and coordinate policy in forums such as the Bank for International Settlements and the International Organization of Securities Commissions (Underhill 1995). The major OECD banks are also connected by hot lines to enable immediate communication and coordination in case of crises. Such measures suggest a serious and sustained response to threats against economic security at the system level. One astute observer even compared the personnel involved in these arrangements to the "mafia of nuclear strategists" who once inhabited the military security world (Healey 1989: 413).

The securitization of systemic crises runs up against the arguments made earlier that within the economic sector, existential threats constitute a fairly narrow range of conditions. But given the particular nature and vulnerability of the LIEO as a referent object for economic security, the system level would seem to be the strongest legitimate candidate for securitization in this sector (as well as having impacts in other sectors). Although some other aspects of the economic sector can be securitized, they are relatively few and reflect extreme cases. Because of the basic nature of a liberal economy, much of what might be seen as economic security issues are in fact either normal or politicized economic relations. One feature of security in this sector is that although genuine economic security issues are relatively rare, normal and politicized economic activity frequently spills over into other sectors, with security consequences. Another feature is that although frequent attempts at securitization are made, covering many types of referent objects, few attract wide support. These discourses of securitization are part of the ideological disputes about policy for the political economy. When pure liberalism is in the ascendant, few economic security claims will be able to surmount the hurdle that insecurity is the price to be paid for participating in the global market economy. Under this logic, losers are part of the game, and their attempts to securitize their plight are dismissed as attempts to change the rules of the game.

REGIONALIZING DYNAMICS?

One of the problems in answering this question is the intrinsic difficulty of applying security logic to competitive economic relations. Another as shown earlier, is that whereas the strictly economic logic of security is rather narrow economic dynamics have many security effects in other sectors. These linkages are what underpin IPE as a cross- sectoral enterprise. Keeping the economic security agenda distinct from other sectors is not easy or generally a good idea.

GLOBALIZING TRENDS

The emergence and intensification of a global market economy is one the major developments of our time. And the security question arising is about the stability of this complex network of competitive and collaborative relations. There has long been a debate about the coming destabilization of the liberal international economic order consequent upon the decline (or, in some versions, corruption) of the United States as a hegemonic leader (Hirsch and Doyle, 1977;Keohane 1980, 1984 : Strange, 1984, Gilpin 1987, Kindleberger 1981). With the end of Cold War, this debate has taken on an ironic Leninist twist with the possibility that the removal of their shared fear of communism and Soviet Power will cause the main centres of capitalist power to fall into a gathering crisis of competition among themselves. The fashionable talk about competition for market shares (Strange 1994) cuts just close enough to Lenin's ideas of imperialism and to the struggle to redivide a saturated global market to generate a deep sense of unease. It also tends to undermine the main hope of political economy institutionalists, already understood as a fragile option, that shared understanding and ideologies plus a collection of international regimes and institutions (the group of seven (G7) the World Bank, the WTO the IMF) might be able to sustain the liberal international economic order on the basis of collective hegemony (Keohane 1984). Resurgence of Leninism in a new form turned to be a nightmare. The entire world is now under the grip of liberal market economy in the name of globalization controlled by the rich industrialized North countries.

This globalizing of economic efficiency is good for consumers, but it places tremendous pressures of adaptation on states and societies, which have continually to reconfigure the way in which they earn a living. As liberal economists seem too easily to forget, to be a consumer one has to produce something to trade or sell. In older developed areas such as Europe, intensified trade competition confronts states and societies with major questions about social and political values. The third world countries are plagued by the contradictions between the demands of the majority poor and the demands of the globalization

REGIONAL DYNAMICS

The economic logic of regionalism can thus be seen mainly as response to top-down threats from the dominant framework of globalization, although, as with the EU, significant bottom-up logics also support it. As long as economic regionalism remains liberal in its outlook, the two developments are compatible. Unlike the situation in the 1930s most contemporary regional blocs have fairly liberal internal trading structures and in many ways are open to world markets. Their purposes are to reduce the pressures of an open global economy without sacrificing all economies of scale and to try to reduce the overstretched management demands of an open global economy by moving many of those demands to a more intimate regional scale. And they are fallback bastions in case the global liberal economy succumbs to the effects of weak management, financial turbulence, or intensifying trade competition. Part of this function is about genuine economic logic of competition within a global market.

Although they do not point toward preparation for war, as was true in the 1930s, the contemporary economic blocs do have security roles in other sectors. They are for example, politico-cultural defense mechanisms against the powerful homogenizing effects of open markets. Liberals like to think of the global market as, ideally, a place of uniform rules and universal logics of behavior. But one aspect of economic regionalism may be culturally based. As Eric Helleiner (1994b) points out, the three main economic grouping all have distinctive characters. Europe is heavily institutionalized and is driven by social democratic values. North America is lightly institutionalized and reflects liberal values. East Asia relies mostly on transnational links and reflects national development values.

LOCALIZING DYNAMICS

Given the overwhelming force of globalization and the regionalizing responses to it, little room is left for serious security dynamics at the local level. Even the state, which has not long ago would have factored very strongly at this level, has largely surrendered to the imperatives of liberalization and globalization with domestic debates now dominated by system – level arguments. In terms of security logic, the situations where individuals have succumbed to famine, deep financial crisis, collapses in the provision of basic human needs, can clearly be constructed as security issues when they threaten the provisions of basic human needs or the survival of the state. There may increasingly be political room for actors at local levels as the state becomes weakened by the deregulating global economic order.

In conclusion it can be garnered that attempts to securitize economic issues are essentially a part of the political – ideological policy debate within IPE. In this context, the language of securitization is a way of taking economic nationalist positions in economic policy debates without having to abandon superficial commitments to the liberal consensus. Perhaps the main exception to this condition is seen in the system-level referent objects- the institutions and organizations of the LIEO. Within that context, regionalism also takes on some security qualities.

Although little of a strictly economic security agenda exists within liberalism, economic activity fairly easily triggers survival issues in all of the other sectors-sometimes on the basis of economic failure (e.g. famine, negative development) and sometimes on the basis of economic successes (cultural homogenization, loss of autonomy in military production, pollution, the gutting of state functions) . According to Buzan and his colleagues if one reconsiders the list of issues said to constitute the current agenda of economic security this overspill effect is rather clear (Buzan et al:, 1998: 116).

1. The ability of states to maintain an independent capability for mobilization is affected by the globalization of production, which gives states the choice of having lower-quality, more expensive domestically produced weapons or higher-quality, cheaper ones that are wholly or in part produced abroad. In the LIEO, security of supply is underpinned not by indigenous control of production but by the existence of surplus production capacity and a buyer's market.

2. Much of the same logic applies to concerns about security of supply. The possibility of economic dependencies within the global market (particularly oil) being exploited for political ends is offset by the existence of surplus capacity in nearly all commodities as well as a buyer's market.
3. Fears that the global market will generate more losers than winners and will heighten inequalities are not survival issues unless they undermine the provision of basic human needs. They are instead the political consequences of an economic system that requires winners and losers.
4. Fears of trade in drugs and weapons of mass destruction are socio-political and military security issues rather than economic ones, and fears of pollution are environmental security issues rather than economic ones.
5. Only fears that the international economy will fall into crisis are clearly economic security issues.

To say that economic security is difficult and blurry may be true, but this description is not very helpful. At most, it sends a warning and invites care in the use and reception of securitization attempts in this sector. But given the desire of liberals to separate the economic sector from politics, the fact that most of the security consequences of economic liberalism turn up in other sectors is of more than passing interest.

THE SOCIETAL SECTOR

Societal security is closely related to, but nonetheless distinct from political security, which is about the organizational stability of states, systems of government, and the ideologies that give governments and states their legitimacy. For international security analysis, the key to society is those ideas and practices that identify individuals as members of a social group. The organizing concept in the societal sector is identity. Societal insecurity exists when communities of whatever kind define a development or potentially as a threat to their survival as community. According to Buzan et al, "two misunderstandings about the term societal should be avoided. First, societal security is not the same as social security. Social security is about individuals and is largely economic. Societal security is about collectives and their identity. Second, a problem with societal is that the related term security is often used to designate the wider, more vague state population, which may refer to a group that does not always carry an identity' (Buzan et al, 1998: 120).

The most common issues that have been viewed as threats to societal security are mentioned below in the words of Buzan et al (1998: 121):

1. Migration : X people are being overrun or diluted by influxes of Y people; the X community will not be what is used to be, because others will make up the populations: X identity is being changed by a shift in the composition of the population (e.g. Chinese migration into Tibet, Russian migration into Estonia).

2. Horizontal competition : although it is still X people living here, they will change their ways because of the overriding cultural and linguistic influence from neighbouring culture Y (e.g. Quebecois fears of anglophone Canada and more generally, Canadian fears of Americanization).

3. Vertical competition : people will stop seeing themselves as X, because there is either an integrating project (e.g. Yugoslavia, the EU) or a secessionist "regionalist" project (e.g. Quebec, Catalonia, Kurdistan) that pulls them toward either wider or narrower identities. Whereas one of these projects is centripetal and the other centrifugal, they are both instances of vertical competition in the sense that the struggle is over how wide the circles should be drawn or rather- since there are always numerous concentric circles of identity- to which to give the main emphasis.

A possible fourth issue could be depopulations, whether by plague, war, famine, natural catastrophe, or policies of extermination. Depopulation threatens identity by threatening carriers, but it is not specifically a part of the societal sector's logic of identity. Although analytically distinct, in practice these three types of threats to identity can easily be combined. They can also be placed on a spectrum running from intentional, programmatic, and political at one end to unintended and structural at the other. Migration, for example, is an old human story. People may make individual decisions to move for reasons varying from economic opportunity to environmental pressure to religious freedom. But they may also move as part of a political programme to homogenize the population of the state, as in the Sinification of Tibet and the Russification of Central Asia and the Baltic states. Horizontal competition may simply reflect the unintended effects of interplay between large, dynamic cultures on the one hand and small, anachronistic ones on the other, but it can also become intentional, as in the remaking of occupied enemies. (e.g. the Americanization of Japan and Germany) and in the cultural aspects of contemporary trade policy, vertical competition is more likely to be found at the intentional end of the spectrum.

Society can react to such threats in two ways: through activities carried out by the community itself or by trying to move the issue to the political (and potentially the military) sector by having the threat placed on the state agenda. The choice of whether to see societal threats as a task for society itself, as one for an existing state, or as an argument for gaining or regaining statehood can have a decisive impact on regional dynamics.

SECURITY ACTORS AND REFERENT OBJECTS

The referent objects in the societal sector are whatever larger groups carry the loyalties and devotion of subjects in a form and a degree that can create a socially powerful argument that this "we" threatened. Historically such referent objects have been rather narrow. In the present world system, the most important referent objects in the societal sector are tribes, clans, nations, civilizations, religions, and races.

THE LOGIC OF THREATS AND VULNERABILITIES

Different societies have different vulnerabilities depending upon how their identity is constructed. If one's identity is based on separateness, on being remote and alone, even a very small admixture of foreigners will be seen as problematic (e.g. Finland). Nations that control a state but only with a small numeric margin. (e.g. Latvia) or only through repression of a majority (e.g. Serbs in Kosovo) will be vulnerable to an influx or superior fertility rate of the competing population (e.g. Russians, Albanians). If national identity is tied to specific cultural habits, a homogenizing "global" culture such as the U.S. Western Coca-cola (or, more recently McDonalds) imperialism, will be threatening (e.g. Bhutan, Iran, Saudi Arabia). If language is central to national identity, the contemporary global victory of English combined with an increasing interpenetration of societies will be problematic (e.g. France). If a nation is built on the integration of a number of ethnic groups with mobilizable histories of distinct national lives, a general spread of nationalism and ideas of self –determination can be fatal (e.g. the Soviet Union, Yugoslavia, Czechoslovakia, the United Kingdom, India, Nigeria, South Africa). If a nation is built on a melting pot ideology of different groups blending into one new group, the existing national identity will be vulnerable to a reassertion of racial and cultural distinctiveness and incommensurability (e.g. multiculturalism in the United States). If the nation is tied closely to the state, it will be more vulnerable to a process of political integration (e.g. Denmark, France) that will be the case if the nation has a tradition of operating independent of the state and of having multiple political layers simultaneously (e.g. Germany).

it can be concluded that the main forces in the societal sector that push toward globalization are probably (1) the cycle of poverty in the South, migration, poverty-related diseases transmitted through migration, and migration-related organized or unorganized crime and (2) the clash of civilizations, especially the dialectics of Westernization – a trend toward cultural homogenization and reactions against it. At least for the short to medium term, the second factor- the international political economy of culture is probably the more important, some claim the first factor will show its singular importance in the long run.

THE POLITICAL SECTOR

As defined by Barry Buzan (1991:118ff)

> Political threats are aimed at the organizational stability of the state. Their purpose may range from pressuring the government on a particular policy. Through overthrowing the government, to fomenting secessionism, and disrupting the political fabric of the state so as to weaken it prior to military attack. The idea of the state, particularly its national identity and organizing ideology, and the institutions which express it are the normal target of political threats. Since the state is an essentially political entity. Political threats may be as much feared as

military ones. This is particularly so if the target is a weak state.

Typically, political threats are about giving or denying recognition, support, or legitimacy (which explains why it is possible to have purely political threats, that is, threats that do not use military, economic, or other means from other sectors- words matter in relation to recognition and related political demands.). But what is politics? A short definition that covers most of what people have tried to incorporate into the concept is Buzan's in which politics is "the shaping of human behaviour for the purpose of governing large groups of people"(Buzan, Jones, and little 1993:35).

Political security as distinct from politics in general is about threats to the legitimacy or recognition either of political units or of the essential patterns (structures, processes or institutions) among them. In the classical tradition that contains Machiavelli as well as Arendt, politics is a continuous struggle to establish the quasi-permanence of an ordered public realm within a sea of change. Then, the critical variables are obviously the recognition of such an arrangement from within and without that lends it legitimacy and thereby to be about it. As argued by English school theorists (Manning, Wight, Bull and others) as well as contemporary constructivists (Wendt 1992, 1994) the identity of an international unit is not something it has for and with itself, it is very much a question of generally established categories of international subjectivity, of statehood and other forms of international being, to which the individual unit has to relate.

Political threats are thus made to (1) the internal legitimacy of the political unit, which relates primarily to ideologies and other constitutive ideas and issues defining the states, and (2) the external recognition of the state, its external legitimacy. Threats from outside are not necessarily directed at sovereignty but can very well aim at its ideological legitimacy- that is, its domestic pillar. It is possible for legitimacy to be contested from outside. In the India-Pakistan case and also during the Cold War, legitimacy was questioned externally (in the mutual exclusiveness of political forms) without this aiming to be a questioning of recognition.

Only the modern, territorial, sovereign state has a clear, standardized form of recognition that constitutes an entire international system of equal and "like" units. But all units that interact need to achieve some kind of recognition in a general sociological sense. They need to be accepted as parties to be dealt with in their own right – if possible as equals, if necessary as vassals, but definitely not through their component parts (which mean the external power has ignored and undercut the existence of the unit). Even in relationships of inequality, one wants to be recognized as vassals or as lord, if one wants to be recognized as lord or equal and achieves recognition only as vassal, this is a serious security threat, a threat to the political identity assumed by oneself. In the modern state system issues of political recognition are normally "either/ or" matters. Basically, states do or do not recognize each other as equals.

SECURITY ACTORS AND REFERENT OBJECTS

The predominant form of political organization in the contemporary international system is the territorial state, which is obviously the main referent object of the political sector. Other state like or state-paralleling political organizations (i.e. other unit level referent objects) that can sometimes serve as referent objects at the unit level are (1) emerging quasi- superstates such as the EU, (2) some of the self-organized, stateless societal groups dealt with in the societal chapter- tribes, minorities, and clans- which have strong political institutions although not of the formal type international society recognizes (only those that take on very strong political institutions although not of the formal type international society recognizes (only those that take chapter, otherwise they are dealt with as societal" and (3) transnational movements that are able to mobilize supreme allegiance from adherents. Some world religions occasionally qualify here (the Catholic Church in earlier times. Muslims at times following such appeals but lacking one generally recognized authority) and more clearly but less significantly, some smaller sects clearly operate this way. Ideological movements also take this transitional form. But this phenomenon is often blurred by the fact that a movement strong enough to operate with power in international relations has a base in one or more states in which it is in power (e.g. communism in the Soviet Union). Gradually, the state – centered raison d'etre of this homeland of the revolution comes to override the transitional logic of the movement as such (Herz 1950, Wight 1978, Der Derian 1987, chapter 7; Armstrong 1993).

The securitizing actors who can make appeals about the survival of these referent objects are – in contrast to some of the other sectors- relatively well defined. In case of a state, the government will usually be the securitizing actor. A government will often be tempted to use security arguments when its concern is actually that the government itself is threatened. This can be the case in relation to external threats as well as internal threats. Internal threats are typical of weak states (Buzan 1991:99-103). In a strong state especially a liberal – democratic one, there is a much stronger assumption that the government acts only as the legitimate agent of the nation- state and that its claims are subject to public scrutiny and are open to questioning. Also in the strong state, it is generally assumed that "national security can be viewed primarily in terms of protecting the components of the state from outside threat and interference" (Buzan 1991-100) to which should probably be added " and allegedly exceptional cases of domestic activities deemed unacceptable and threatening by a great majority of the populace (e.g. terrorism) ."When the state accepted a self limitation in the form of rule of law, this was compensated by a clearer specification of the exceptional cases in which because of security the government was to immune (Gordon 1991:33).

A final question to be dealt with in relation to referent objects and actors is that of systemic referent objects. Appeals can clearly be made about the survival of "our unit". But security structured arguments can also be made in relation to institutions, structures, or processes in the international system. At present, the main candidates are the institutions and organizations of international governance, which are generally valued (mostly by state and international business elites) as a precondition for continued political stability.

Somewhat in contrast to the more American, more utilitarian and rational choice-inspired school of institutionalism, however, the international society literature also shows how these institutions carry some element of commitment. They are interwoven with classical themes of international law, ethics and world politics and discussions of common morality and common law, thus, they carry a legitimacy not only of utility in relation to some state calculus of interests but also as manifestations of obligations beyond the nation-state or to principles held to be morally binding (Nardin and Mapel 1992; Butterfield 1965: Wight 1978: Hurrel 1993). From this dual source of collective state stability and direct commitment, various norms, principles and institutions in the international political realm gain a stability and salience that make them possible referent objects for security action.

As a next step in defining systemic referent objects, the issue has to be a threat of dramatic nature, portrayable as threatening the breakdown or ruin of some principle or some other irreparable effect whereby one can then legitimate extreme steps. A clear case is that of the basic principles of international society, as seen when the United States and the United Nations liberated Kuwait and attacked Iraq over Iraq's violation of an international principle- the sovereignty and territorial integrity of a recognized sovereign state.

In thinking about systemic referent objects in the political sector, one must keep the distinction between securitization and politicization carefully in mind. Such referent objects must have a certain stability, be seen as pillars of the general international order, and be able to break down in some drastic (not purely gradual or incremental) sense. The UN occupies a distinctive position as a systemic referent object for political stability because of its central role as the repository of the basic principles of international society and international law. At present besides UN charter, some other seems to be seen as basic, efficient, and consensual enough to legitimate action in their defense, including sovereign equality, human rights, balance of power, self determination, racial equality, human rights, environmental issues and non-proliferation of weapons of mass destruction. This does not mean these principles are always and uniformly defended not that each appeal to them will be effective but only that these are the principles at the international level to which one can make reference in a security way and have a chance of legitimating extraordinary action or of mobilizing strong international collective action (Mayall 1996: Roberts 1995-1996; Wheeler 1996).

The securitizing actors operating in relation to the systemic referent objects are first of all the states, because most of the these principles are principles of international society – the society of states- and are often legal or semi legal in international law.

THE LOGIC OF THREATS AND VULNERABILITIES

Existential threats to a state are those that ultimately involve sovereignty, because sovereignty is what defines the state as a state. Threats to state survival are therefore threats to sovereignty. Even minor violations of sovereignty are threats, because sovereignty is a principle that claims the ultimate right of self government; thus it becomes endangered if it becomes partial in any sense. Anything that can be portrayed as a violation of sovereignty can be presented as a security problem.

The specific speech act approach thus points toward a rather focused agenda and a typical sequence of securitization and counter securitization. At first this will sound strange. Because it differs from what are normally seen as political threats as a result of the difference between an objectivist and speech-act approach. In objectivist (e.g. People, States and Fear Buzan 1991) terminology, one would say the state is based on the following pillars, and one of these is undermined by this action, and it is therefore a political security problem. With the speech act approach, the focus is on the security argument, and it will be with reference to sovereignty for the securitizing state.

The distinction between strong and weak states is important here, because it highlights different degrees of vulnerability to political threat. A strong state will typically be fairly invulnerable in the political sector. It will not be ethnically divided and thus not open to secessionist action. Its government will be neither divorced from the general opinions of its citizens nor dependent upon suppressing views and information and therefore will be fairly invulnerable to external actors supporting oppositional voices.

Such states may nonetheless feel politically threatened. During the Cold War, the United States perceived a political (as well as a military) threat from the Soviet Union in terms of the question of the legitimacy and efficiency of U.S. democratic capitalism raised by the existence and performance of the Communist rival. Strong states can also experience political security threats from integration projects that threaten their sovereignty (and their recognition and status). This is clearly illustrated by the political discourse within some of the EU member states (Waever et al/ 1993, chapter 4).This is a strange kind of threat, because it is substantially self imposed. States enter a process – for economic reasons or because of regional security concerns (Buzan et a. 1990) and this process has the potential to cut away at their sovereignty. Depending upon what kind of weakness the state exhibits, it will be worried about different vulnerabilities and will therefore securitize differently.

Since the end of the Cold War, international society has been marked by a relatively high degree of homogeneity organized as concentric circles around dominant Western Centre (Bull and Watson 1983, Buzan 1993). In addition to demanding a market economy and democracy, this hegemonic set of rules prescribes self-opening if one wants to become an insider- increased interpenetration of sovereignty. The trend is toward interpreting sovereignty less as an attribute of individual countries within international society and more as operational within a collective relationship among insiders (international society) and between insiders and outsiders. One can become an insider, in which case one opens oneself (which means one defines more things as legitimate interaction and fewer as illegitimate intervention).

Political threats to international referent objects- international law, international order, and international society- are not cast in terms of sovereignty. These objects represent established orders. They can thus be threatened by non-acceptance and challenge.

REGIONALIZING DYNAMICS?

In terms of international security, the political sector by definition is not strong on localizing trends, and the decisive issue will be the balance between unit- to- unit dynamics and actions with reference to system level referent objects. The following different types of state situations as analyzed by Buzan et al 1998:155) are worth mentioning for understanding regionalizing and non-regionalizing dynamics and their geographical location:

1. Intentional threats to (weak) states on the basis of their state-nation split

Because state and nation do not line up it is possible for some other actor- within the state or neighbouring it- to raise secessionist or irredentist claims. There are numerous possible examples to prove this. : Hungary against Romania, Russia against the Ukraine, Somalia, against its neighbours, Kurds, threatening Iraq and Turkey. This kind of threat is found in almost all regions of the world (Prescott 1987). It is endemic to Eastern Europe, and Belgium and perhaps the UK are examples in Western Europe. In the Middle East, this type of threat is relevant in relation to Palestinians, Kurds, Arabs in Iran, and Shites in Iraq and the Gulf states. In Africa, many states are weak in this regard, but this situation mainly creates domestic security problems of a societal nature. In Asia, the major cases of this type are Tibet-China and Kashmir, the Tamils in Sri Lanka, various groups in India, self-claiming nations within China, and the opposite way around (with a nation covering more than one state) in the Korean situation. There are few examples in North America, by far the most conspicuous being Quebecois secessionism.

2. Intentional threats to (weak) states on political-ideological grounds

Here, the ideology on which the regime operates is not widely accepted. Threats can be levelled against the state on this basis, and the regime claims these are security problems. Examples are North and South Korea and United States against Cuba. The position of the Arab states toward Israel was such case , but even this situation is changing, This surprising situation probably testifies to the continued strength of the principle of sovereignty and nonintervention to question a regime as such is problematic, One either has a direct conflict with the country or tries to have it branded by international society as breaching more basic rules (e.g. non- apartheid, genocide), or must abstain form major moves against the legitimacy of the regime and the state.

3. Inadvertent, unit-based threats to state-nation vulnerable states

Unintentional threats should be sorted into two groups. Accidental, one-time threats are not very interesting to Buzan and his colleagues. Unavoidable, interlocking, inadvertent threats, however, happen when two or more states are locked into a security conflict because of incompatible organizing principles, here, the distinction between nation-state and political- ideological vulnerabilities can be studied to see if it produces systematic variation.

Inadvertent threats based on a state-nation split could be illustrated by the case of Estonia and Russia, in which the Estonian definition of Estonia is perceived as a threat to the Russians in Estonia (and thereby in Russian politics too), simultaneously, a Russia defined in a certain way is by definition a threat to Estonia. A Croatia defined on a territorial basis (the borders of the old part state of Yugoslavia) and a Serbia defined on an ethnic basis (the nation of Serbs) are difficult to reconcile as well (Wiberg 1993). Such security dilemmas can be handled only through processes that involve critical self-reflection by the involved parties on their own identity and concept of stateness. The political struggles within each society over how to articulate state and nation are at the heart of this type of security predicament.

4. Unintentional threats to states on political – ideological grounds

This type of threat constellation can be illustrated by the Cold War. The clearest example , however , remains that of the India – Pakistan conflict, which hinges on competing ideas of the state – different basic political legitimizing principles that are not only mutually exclusive but are also unavoidably threatening to each other . Pakistan is based on religious exclusivity whereas India is a continentwide, inclusive state able to accommodate ethnic and religious differences – thus also including Muslims. Conflicts of this type are not common. They are serious and often long standing when they do appear but are not the typical form of political security conflict.

5. Security of and against supranational , regional integration

This category is not intended to distinguish between regional and global, but there is a difference between principles and organization. Principles are relevant mainly at the global but also at the regional level. Supranational political organization is relevant mainly at the regional level. Supranational political organization is relevant mainly at the regional level and it is primarily in the EU that such organization becomes threatening to state sovereignty.

6. Systemic, Principled threats against states that are vulnerable because of a state-nation split.

A historic instance of this type of threat is the Austrian (and Austrian – Hungarian) case vis-à-vis the nationalist movement in the nineteenth century, for a time, this case seemed to be mainly of historical relevance. Again, however, we are experiencing a general wave of national self-determination of "every nation is state" thinking a new spring of nations- and all multinational and otherwise non-nation-corresponding states have good reason to be worried.

7. Structural (systemic) threats to (weak) states on political –ideological grounds

Here, a state's political system is challenged but this time not by another state but by a general development in international society on principles that are incompatible with those of the state. The classical example, now resolved, was that of antiapartheid and South Africa. The most important contemporary cases in which security actions are taken against this type of threat are in East Asia and Middle East- "Asian" values and national sovereignty defended against an allegedly Western universalism (China, Singapore, and Malaysia), and Islamic values similarly posited as threatened not only by Western culture but also by what is seen as a Western attempt to organize the international system on its principles.

These seven are the different kinds of threats to states, the main unit of this sector.

8. Threats to transnational movements that command supreme loyalty from their members

No large movements of this type are very effective today. Communist movement was a reality until the end of 1980s.

9. Threats to international society, order, and law

The most obvious example is Iraq's invasion of Kuwait. In recent years US has been seen making securitization of NPT while it makes move against North Korea and most recently against Iran. America could decimate Saddam, the ruler of Iraq on the falsified pretext of the latter having conclusion in possession of weapons of mass destruction.

In essence, the new framework for security agenda covers a wider range of sectors than the traditional military and political. Expansion of the security agenda to include economic, environmental, and societal has challenged the established frame of mind about security revolving around state and its military apparatus, and adverts to a range of new dynamics. Accustomed to defining security almost exclusively in terms of one sector, the traditional security studies avoided ever having to be opened to new sectors and new insights. Buzan and his colleagues initiated the project with the aim of how to combine the regional focus of classical security complex theory (CSCT) with the wider agenda of security studies. CSCT followed the mode of thinking of the traditional security studies (TSS) - state centric and organized around military-political security concerns. "Within the military-political nexus, CSCT gave reasons to expect regional formations, explained how these formations were structured and how they mediated intervention by outside powers, and offered ways of specifying and to a point, predicting outcomes"(Buzan et al, 1998:197). Buzan and his colleagues have not rejected its subject matter, though they have rejected the method of TSS.

Buzan and his colleagues have focused on socially constructed rather than objective security. This has been strongly built into CSCT. The idea of intersubjective constructions of securitization and desecuritization processes fits comfortably into the idea of security interdependence, which lies at the heart of CSCT. It plays the role given to amity-enmity as key structuring variable and the consequent spectrum of conflict formation, security regime, and security community. With the wider agenda, it is possible to envisage regional security interdependence arising less from interactions between units than from collective responses to shared fates arising from outside systemic pressures. When security interdependence comes top down rather than bottom up, it seems highly likely that the resultant security complex will be found at the amity end of the spectrum rather than at the enmity end. In all sectors the logic of regionalization can be the result of bottom up processes that find their upper limit at the subsystem level. But regionalization can also result from top down processes when the subsystem is triggered by global structures, interaction capacities, and processes. As explained above, security complexes are ultimately defined by the interaction among their units; thus the top- down – bottom up question is only about the causes behind that process. The security complex as such is the pattern of security interaction. This means that already in CSCT the constructivist element was that a security complex is what states actually do. According to Buzan and his colleagues (1998:200), "The novelty is that in CSCT it was also assumed that the causality behind the formation of the security complex was bottom up, that the interaction of mutual security concerns within the region had produced the complex". They have now opened up the possibility that causation can be top down. It is sometimes necessary to start from the system level to explain the formation of the complex. The complex itself is defined by the actions and relations in the region. If it was not and if it was defined solely by global level considerations and actions, it would not be a regional security complex. Keeping all these arguments in mind Buzan and his colleagues (1998:200-201) redefined security complexes:

> Security interdependence is markedly more intense among the units inside such complexes than with units outside them. Security complexes are about the relative intensities of security relations that lead to distinctive regional patterns shaped by both the distribution of power and relations of amity and enmity. A security complex is defined as a set of units whose major processes of securitization, desecuritization, or both are so interlinked that their security problems cannot reasonably be analyzed or resolved apart from one another. The formative dynamics and structure of a security complex are normally generated by the units within it- by their security perceptions of, and interactions with, each other. But they may also arise from collective securitizations of outside pressures arising from the operation of complex metasystems, such as the planetary environment or the global economy.

The question is how the particular regional formation remains relevant when the actors are synthesizing security across a range of sectors. Buzan and his colleagues have tried to resolve security complex theory with the arguments about security constellations in the light of the redefined definition. Security constellations is a much wider concept than security complexes, reflecting as it does the totality of possible security interrelationships at all levels. The concept is not to be understood in relation to security complexes but in relation to the entire framework of which they are a part. It does not mean that territorially coherent regions should involve more than one subset of security constellations as in CSCT. Compared with the CSCT framework, security constellations will almost certainly generate much fuller set nonregional subglobal patterns. The politico-military focus of CSCT allowed little room for nonregional subglobal patterns. Because politico-military relations are strongly mediated by distance, adjacency is a main element that determines interaction capacity. Thus, as with CSCT, the regional level still plays a distinctive role in security constellations. Buzan and his colleagues have put up three reasons for explaining the regional level will remain an important focus of security analysis within the new framework(1998: 202-203):

1. As long as political life is structured primarily by states, territoriality will continue to be important and will be predisposed toward regional formations. States, in other words, will tend to construct political responses in their own territorial image.
2. On current evidence, regional security dynamics remain strong in many parts of the world in the sectors in which security relations are strongly mediated by distance.
3. Some environmental and economic issues are structured so as to reinforce existing regional security complexes.

THE CONSTRUCTIVE APPROACH

At stake here is where to locate oneself analytically in a spectrum that ranges from constructivist to objectivist. On this issue, Buzan and his colleagues have compared their securitization approach to two other approaches, traditional security studies (TSS) and critical security studies (CSS). This approach is complex because the axis has to be used twice- once regarding "security" (how socially constituted is the security nature of issues) and also in regard to social relations in general. Especially in the comparison between CSS and Buzan's position, one is more constructivist on one axis and the other is more constructivist on the other axis, therefore, this must be differentiated to grasp the differences.

Traditional security studies (TSS) is usually objective regarding security. It sees states as the given, eternal form of units; it views interests as something objective; and it has rules about the behaviour of states that take on something close to natural science status, such as balance of power and arms race theory.

In contrast, critical security studies (CSS) views the system very much in constructivist terms. If states dominate the arena that is the feat of power politics representing other dimensions of reality that could potentially replace the states if an emancipatory praxis could- with the help of critical theory- empower other subjectivities than those that dominate at present. The social world does not exhibit any iron laws, all regularities can be broken and it is the task of critical theory to show this and expose the logic for this. As Buzan and his colleagues point out on the issue of security CSS is often less constructivist than one would expect. As a part of its argument against established discourses on security CSS will often try to mobilize other security problems- environmental problems, poverty, unemployment- as more important and more threatening, thereby relativizing conventional wisdom. In their views CSS often ends up reproducing the traditional and objectivist concept of security (1998: 204).

Buzan and his colleagues view securitization approach is radically constructivist regarding, which ultimately is a specific form of social praxis. Security issues are made security issues by acts of securitization. They have not peeped behind to decide whether it is really a threat, which would reduce the entire securitization approach to a theory of perception and misperception. In their words, " security is a quality actors inject into issues by securitizing them, which means to stage them on the political arena in the specific way" as mentioned above " and then to have them accepted by a sufficient audience to sanction extraordinary defensive moves"(!998:204).

Defining security as a self-referential praxis must constitute radical constructivism- on the security axis. In regard to general social relations, Buzan and his colleagues are less constructivist than most authors of CSS. " When one has adopted a basically constructivist position that assumes social relations are not laws of nature but the contingent product of human action and always potentially open for reconstruction and then base one's analysis on the possibility that it could change in part by one exposing the processes that made it what it is" (Ibid: 204).

Since security has been studied in the name of identities (societal security) it has been objectifying identities (McSweeney 1996). They have taken identities as socially constituted but not radically more so than other social structures. "Identities as other social constructions can petrify and become relatively constant elements to be reckoned with. At specific points, this ' inert constructivism 'enables modes of analysis very close to objectivist- for example, Waltzian neorealism, as long as one remembers that in the final instance the ontology is not Waltz's naturalism and atomism but some form of constructivism, or even, in line with classical realism, rhetorical foundations"(Dessler 1989; Buzan, Jones, and Little 1993, part 3).

The advantages and disadvantages of Buzan's radical constructivism regarding security have been controversial. The main disadvantage is their inability to counter securitizations with an argument that this is not really a security problem or that the environment is a bigger security problem. Since the meaning of security is to lift it to a different kind of politics, they cannot contest this in terms of truth; only pragmatically or ethically can they ask, what are the likely effects of securitizing this issue? Will doing so be a helpful way of handling this issue, and what are the side effects of doing it in a security mode? They can expose the unnecessary nature of the securitization but not its falsity.

A second kind of advantage and disadvantage of the debate relates to the kinds of analytical questions that can or cannot be dealt with. The major new opening is probably an ability to historicize security, to study transformations in the units of security affairs. Traditional security studies define the units (states) and the instruments (military) that by definition make any security phenomena elsewhere invisible. Much of critical security studies has an individualist, reductionist ontology and therefore also translates everything into a homogenous currency-individual security. Securitization studies can analyze how and when new referent objects attain the status of something in the name of which one can successfully undertake security and can study the degree to which the new sectors actually exhibit politics in the form of security. It becomes possible to draw a map of security in between the closed, predefined world of traditionalists, the very-thing-is security of the wideners, and the everything- could-be-different of CSS. To the traditionalist, this map will seem transient because it is not founded on material factors but only on sedimented patterns of security practice; to the critical theorist, it will be reactionary in reproducing the world as it is and not as it could be.

CONTRAST WITH THE TRADITIONAL APPROACH

The most obvious difference between Buzan's and traditional approach is in the choice of a wide (multisectoral) versus the narrow (monosectoral) agenda. Wideners must keep an open mind about the balance among the sectors, the cross linkages between them and the types of threat, actor, and referent object that might be dominant in any given historical time. By contrast, traditional security studies give permanent priority to one sector (the military and one actor (state) plus any links or crossovers from other sectors that relate directly to the use of force. Both approaches are incompatible in their methodology. Buzan's definition of security is based on the social construction of threats and referent objects whereas traditionalists take an objectivist view of these factors. The danger is that the traditionalists' objectification of threats and referent objects will push them onto the role of securitizing actors.

Both share a methodological collectivism that leads them to draw a boundary between international security and a wider political theory of security. Buzan's, critical security studies and traditional security studies have rejected reductionism as an unsound approach to international security. Further, for both approaches, security is an empowering word- setting political priorities and justifying the use of force, the intensification of executive powers, the claim to rights of secrecy, and other extreme measures.

With the end of the Cold War, the extension of the market economy into nearly all of the formerly Communist world, and the intensification of global finance, investment, and production, the case for a wider security agenda has become stronger. The demise of the Cold War has, at least for the time being, greatly reduced military rivalries among the great powers. Security concerns are more about the consequences of how the open international system operates – a set of issues that affects the strong actors as much as it does the weaker ones. This development is most obvious in the case of the international economy (Rosenau 1990; Ruggie 1993; Cerny 1995; Strange 1994). The rise of economic security is not just a throwback to classical mercantilism. It is a reaction against the various dangers of global liberalization – the risk of becoming a loser; the general hazard of system instability, especially financial; and the dark side of trade in the form of criminal activities in drugs, weapons, and other banned products (e.g., CFCs). The rise is also about the crossover effects of the global economy and stability, and military self – reliance. In the post cold war world, therefore it can be argued that a wider security agenda is a necessary response to the global success of the liberal project.

In the words of Buzan and his colleagues "although the multisectoralism of the approach enables a proliferation of securitization, its constructivism delivers the means for questioning and politicizing each specific instance. This contrasts with the approach of TSS, which puts a firm sectoral limit on what constitutes security but which has objectified, depoliticized, and indeed naturalized it as the only allowable understanding of security. On this test as well, the new framework can hold its own against the traditional one" (1998: 212).

BEYOND COPENHAGEN SCHOOL : A CRITIQUE

A more comprehensive theory of securitization involves understanding of security in two ways. The first understanding concentrates on the speech act event and is grounded in the concept of performativity. This understanding would correspond with an 'internalist', more poststructural/postmodern reading of securitization. An internalist understanding of security is stronger in Waever's early works but has become much weaker in the joint works with Buzan. In the words of Stritzel, "the second understanding theorizes the process of securitization based on the central idea of embeddedness. This understanding would correspond with an 'externalist' more constructive reading of securitization" (Stritzel, 2007: 359).

SECURITIZATION: AN ARTICULATION ADDING INTERNALIST FOCUS

The basic foundation of the Copenhagen School approach to security drawing on speech act philosophy rests on the assumption that the articulation of security is a crucial form of security action. It is this articulation that has the potential, the structure, the social practices that follow. That means something is articulated as posing a threat to a valued referent object considered so existential that it is legitimate to move the issue beyond the realm of normal politics authorizing the actor to deal with the issue by exceptional methods the latter considers appropriate. As Waever put it, "by uttering 'security' a state-representative moves a particular development into a specific area , and thereby claims a special right to use whatever means are necessary to block it"(Waever, 1995:55). This conceptualization of security by Waever drawing on realist rhetoric claims to exceptionality of methods and situation distinguished from normal fields of activity is based on a fundamental transformation with all the consequences that will follow.

This fundamental transformation is drawn on John L. Austin's concept of 'performative utterances' (Austin, 1962). Basing on this Waever argues that the very utterances of 'security' is more than just saying or describing something but the performing of an action. According to Austin, performative utterances do not just describe but have the potential to create (new) reality, for the Copenhagen School the modus of exceptionality, of dealing with an issue in a new way. For the Copenhagen School, the main effect of uttering security is its potential to let an audience tolerate violation of rules that would otherwise have been obeyed (Waever, 2003:11). Drawing insights from Derrida and Butler Waever stresses the always political and indeterminate nature of the speech act event whose meaning and performative force is not related to its context. This is in consonance with Derrida's famous claim that "there is nothing outside the text" and that meaning can never be fixed. Judith Butler has extended such a poststructural/postmodern position to develop the idea of speech acts having productive power (Butler, 1996, 1997). According to her concept of performativity, speech acts have the power to constitute new meaning and create new patterns of significance in social relations. Thus, according to Butler, it is the speech act itself which has the power to create authority and bring about change rather than any pre-existing context that would empower actors and/or speech acts in the first place. Agreeing with Butler and Derrida and in accordance with Schmitt and Arendt Waever stresses that a speech act has an indeterminate force of its own that is not related to features of an existing context.

TOWARDS A MORE COMPREHENSIVE FRAMEWORK: ADDING EXTERNALISM

The Copenhagen School's framework of security is characterized mainly by three elements: (1) speech act, (2) the securitizing actor and (3) the audience. According to Stritzel, the Copenhagen School has "not yet conceptualized the exact relationship between the actor and the audience very clearly" (Stritzel, 2007: 362). What does this school make it clear is that securitization is an intersubjective act of a securitizing actor acting towards a significant audience. In the words of Stritzel:

> Thus, rather than reducing threat assessments to a single actor, most often 'the state', the Copenhagen school splits the actor into two elements: the securitizing actor performing a securitizing move by uttering a security speech act, and the relevant audience accepting or refusing this move. With that a certain threat is no longer simply assessed but its interpretation and representation is 'negotiated' between an actor and the relevant audience (Ibid: 363).

Waever has rejected the traditional sender- receiver view of communication as found in realist security thinking but believes in a speaker- audience model. The question crops up: Is the speaker- audience model the most appropriate model for non-democratic regimes? What happens if there arise several audiences? And when exactly an audience is persuaded? The concepts of speech act, actors and audience are important to the Copenhagen School. Its "approach is much too silent about the exact mechanism of their trilogy and too unspecific about the substance of their terms. In particular, the Copenhagen School should say more about the relative status of the idea of a security utterance or speech act event as opposed to the idea of an intersubjectivity of actor and audience or the process of securitization"(Ibid).

How does the power of audience relate to the decisionism of the speech act event? And how can the idea of the performative force of a security articulation stressed in security? This tension exists in the Copenhagen School. To quote Buzan and his colleagues:

The process of securitization is what in language theory is called a speech act...it is the utterance itself that is the act. By saying the words, something is done (Buzan et al., 1998: 26).

This demonstrates clearly that "Waever and Buzan continuously fluctuate between the terms process and speech act/utterance as if both were synonymous. The act is at the same time defined as an intersubjective process of constructing a threat and as just an utterance itself" (Stritzel, 2007: 364).

TENSION AREAS IN THE COPENHAGEN SCHOOL APPROACH

The Copenhagen School in its articulation of securitization theory is plagued by its insufficient consideration of the situatedness of speech acts and a too static conceptualization of the speech act event in general. Stritzel outlines the tension areas in the Copenhagen School. In his words: "The first tension concerns a certain degree of implicit objectivism as opposed to a more reflectivist and relativist overall approach" (Ibid: 366). This is no where more evident than in their concept of facilitating conditions. It is more perplexing to a reflectivist scholar to read the third condition: "features of the alleged threats that either facilitate or impede securitization" (Buzan et al, 1998:33). This gives the impression "as if the Copenhagen School would attribute a causal role for a given external materiality outside its being mediated through language" (Stritzel, 2007: 366). Furthering his point Stritzel admits that "a certain tension in the argument of the Copenhagen School remains: the more poststructural one reads the Copenhagen School, the more problematic is their concept of facilitating conditions, and conversely, the more emphasis is put on the facilitating conditions, the more difficult it is to read the Copenhagen School as a poststructural position"(Ibid).

The second tension revolves on static elements of the theory as opposed to a more dynamic and contingent overall approach. It is the separation of referent object and actor and the introduction of neatly separated ' sectors' which many reflectivist scholars argue that securitizations usually escape a static' actor-referent object-sector heuristic(McSweeney,1996,1998,1999). The strong realist emphasis on exceptionality in this conceptualization has been criticized by many. Taking the realist understanding of security as an intellectual starting point, Waever perpetuates the realist vocabulary of exceptionality which many scholars consider to be empirically inadequate. Many current security practices deal with threats below the level of exceptionality (Abrahamsen, 2005; Coker, 2002). "The realist vocabulary tends to create a rather strict polarization-security dichotomy which prohibits making securitization theory more widely applicable to 'real-world' securitizations" (Stritzel, 2007: 367).

The third tension concerns the refusal of the Copenhagen School to conceptualize securitizing speech acts and securitizing actors as embedded in broader social and linguistic structures. "It is their embeddedness in social relations of meaning and power that constitutes both actors and speech acts. This neglect of 'externalism' in the concept of securitization is even more puzzling" (Stritzel, 2007: 367). Very much aware of the virtues of externalism, Waever sided with an internalist position in the conceptualization of securitization. In his joint work with Buzan he tried to move some steps towards externalism with the negative side effect that severe tensions have been created that make it difficult to move towards a coherent conceptualization of securitization.

Elements of actor –centrism of the Copenhagen School are mainly embedded in the idea of the act of utterance bringing about change in conjunction with an emphasis on decisions by the securitizing actor, often the political leader. As Michael William (2003) points out this opens the theory for a rather strong decisionist interpretation which shares central understanding with Carl Schmitt. Their claim that the success of a speech act also depends on the authority of the speaker introduces a more Bourdieuian and intersubjective audience, which presupposes a more reflected (structurationist) conceptualization of embeddedness (Stritzel, 2007: 373).

Critical approaches to security studies developed through two series of encounters between what have been construed as schools of thought (Waever, 2004a). The first encounters took place between scholars associated with the Aberystwyth and Copenhagen schools. Both schools have strong roots in political theory, as well as in IR debates and their repositioning in relation to peace research and strategic studies. The third group of academics, referred to as the Paris school, has its roots not in IR but in political theory and the sociology of migration and policing in Europe. The second series of encounters were between this third group of people and people associated with the Copenhagen and Aberystwyth schools of thoughts.

In the critical security studies literature, what is generally referred to as 'Critical Security studies' (CSS) is associated with scholars such as Keith Krause, Michael Williams, Ken Booth and Richard Wyn Jones. Owing much to the vision of critical theory in IR developed initially by Robert Cox, but the post-positivist movement in IR theory, CSS sought to make explicit the largely statist and military-oriented assumptions of traditional security studies as a means of opening the field to greater theoretical security and debate, as well as allowing it to address a broader range of issues (Krause & Williams, 1996, 1997). A further development of this critical project (sometimes called 'capital C' critical security studies) is what has come to be known as the 'Aberystwyth School'. According to Wyn Jones and Booth, the fulcrum of security studies lies on the emancipation of individuals. Booth and Wyn Jones's

Frankfurt School- oriented critical approach suggests that realism's military-focused, state centered and zero-sum understanding of security should be replaced by a collaborative project that would have human emancipation as its central concern (Booth, 2005a, Sheehan, 2005, Wyn Jones, 1999, 2001).

Whereas developments in Aberystwyth and Copenhagen took place largely within IR and through exchanges with the existing experts in the fields of international security, strategic studies and peace research, the works of the researchers associated with the Paris School had varied disciplinary locations, including political sociology, criminology, law and IR, and interacted with experts in areas broadly covered by internal security. The many changes between the members of the different approaches succinctly described above have not led to a deepening of conceptual trenches, but to the realization that there is enough common ground between the researches to facilitate constructive debate and to develop new conceptual tools and empirical research from the initial works" (Critical Approaches to Security in Europe: A Networked Manifesto, Security Dialogue 2006:37:450).

THE POLITICS OF SECURITY

Ever since Bill McSweeney (1996) first coined the term 'Copenhagen School' to refer to their work, the theoretical contributions of Buzan, Weaver and others have conceptual ideas: securitization, sectors/referent objects and (regional) security complexes (Buzan,1991,2004; Buzan,Waever&de Wilde,1998; Buzan & Waever,2003; Weaver, 1989a, 1995, 2000, 2003).The reflections of the Copenhagen school are the result of a rare theoretical merger between something like an 'English School constructivist realist' coming from a strategic studies background (Buzan) and a self-proclaimed 'post-structural realist' strongly influenced by the works of Derrida and Kissinger (Weaver).

The idea of securitization describes processes in which the socially and politically successful "speech act" of labelling an issue a "security issue" removes it from the realm of normal day-to-day politics, casting it as an "existential threat " calling for and justifying extreme measures' (Williams, 1998:435).These processes can have different referent objects, depending on whether they belong to an economic, environmental, political, military or societal sphere (what Buzan and Weaver call 'sectors'). The idea of sectors allows the authors to be more systematic with respect to their general claim that, in principle, anything can become securitized, Yet, only if a claim to treat something with exceptional measures is accepted by a relevant audience does a 'securitizing move' (the mere claim) turn into a (successful) securitization (exceptional measures are actually enabled). With regard to the societal security sector, Buzan and Waever argue that the referent object is often identity. Looking at real-world security rhetorics, they claim, one will observe that an issue like migration has often been treated as an issue of security through reference to a threat to national or transnational identity (see, for example, Huysmans, 2000). More precisely, migration is often the case of an overlap in the security rhetoric of economic ('jobs') and societal ('national identity') (Buzan, Weaver & de Wilde, 1998; Sheehan, 2005). Moreover, since identity-related securitizations often appeal to the emotions of their audiences, certain layers of the security rhetoric may also be more tacit, invoking myths of stability and unity that can only be understood fully from within a community.

It was the combination of securitization with the societal sector and the referent object of identity that led to a major controversy towards the end of the 1990s. McSweeney initiated the debate by arguing that Buzan and

Weaver treat identity as a fixed entity .This would be theoretically inadequate, because identity would always be fluid and contingent, stemming from the discursive constructions of an only imagined community. What McSweeney had in mind was thinking of identity issues as processes of identification. Therefore, he stressed always the political and decision- based nature of identity issues. With that, McSweeney opened the securitization-identity nexus to a perspective that makes it possible at examine how a securitization impacts on processes of identification. Rather than treating identity as a referent object-as for example, in the case of Northern Ireland- a securitization can lead people to identify with things because of a particular securitization. In contrast, the Copenhagen Schools treats identity issues as more stable and sedimented (Buzan & Waever, 1997; 243) by focusing on how a fluid identity is frozen by a securitizing move.

While the McSweeney debate was concerned with the micro dynamics of securitization and identity, the fully fledged regional-security-complex theory of Regions and Powers (Buzan and Waever, 2003) has introduced a broad macro perspective on world politics based on the idea of securitization. Here, the securitization of identity is just one dimension among many others that can constitute the pattern of amity and enmity in a region. The precise pattern depends on the real world securitization of actors. Thus, threats and conflicts can be perceived as mainly being military-political, environmental, societal and /or economic. In terms of regional pattern of amity and enmity, Buzan and Waever allow regions to range from conflict formation(South Asia) to the dense institutional and normative net of a security community(Europe), thereby empirically operationalizing Wendt's claim against Kenneth Waltz that 'cultures of anarchy' may range from Hobbesian to Kantian, depending on 'what actors make of it'(Wendt,1992,1999).

In other words, the concept of security complexes is broader, incorporating not only security communities but also the more realist picture of 'conflict formations' present in many regions of the world. In their own terminology, a 'security community' is a situation in which there are no securitizations among the main actors of a region, a rare case of 'asecurity' in world politics (Waever, 1998; Buzan and Waever, 2003: 343-376).

UNMAKING SECURITY: DESCURITIZATION AND EMANCIPATION

The securitization of identity has brought home the realization that discourses (and practices) have political effects .These effects range between the 'tactical attractions' of securitization as attention-grabbing and the structuring of communities on the model of 'political realism'(Huysmans,1998c, Williams,2003).

As securitization is defined in opposition to normal politics, as a politics of exception or 'abnormal politicization', unmaking it implies a retrieval of the conditions of normal politics. Desecuritization would therefore bring issues back to the 'normal haggling of politics' (Buzan, Waever and de Wilde, 1998:29). Although it has been suggested that the normal politics implied by the framework of securitization is that of liberal democracy (Aradau, 2004; Behnke, 1999; Huysmans, 2004b), normal politics remains undefined in the Copenhagen School framework.

Desecuritization can be seen as an attempt at retrieving the normality of politics. Huysmans (1998c:576) has defined desecuritization as 'unmak[ing] politics which identifies the community on the basis of the expectations of hostility'. Through being located 'within the realm of political argument and discursive legitimation, security practices are thus susceptible to criticism and transformation' (Williams, 2003:512). If desecuritization is anchored in the core of security analysis, tension between discursive construction and the meaning of exceptional politics remains to be explored.

Emancipation, in a formulation that has become defining for the Aberystwyth School, is a normative engagement with normal politics. Booth has argued that emancipation should take precedence over concerns with power and order as emancipation, not power or order, produces true security. Emancipation, theoretically, is security. The normativity of the Aberystwyth School is defined as security, given that security is a 'powerful political concept that energizes opinion and moves material power' that can be mobilized to emancipatory ends. This understanding of security has steered that critical project towards the 'realities of security' that have been made invisible by 'the traditional mindset of those who have dominated or disciplined International Relations' (Booth, 2004:8). Security-power- normality is replaced by security-emancipation-normality, with emancipation disentangling security from power and achieving a fuller and more inclusive realization of security.

The normative separation of security from power and order is problematic, as it accounts neither for the transformation of normality nor for the political effects of security. Other critical scholars who felt akin to the emancipation oriented understanding of the theory and practice of security(Wyn Jones,2005:215) have become aware of the need to reformulate the concept of emancipations in relation to normality and not simply normatively. In a Foucault-inspired approach, normality is the result of the exclusions and forms of disciplinary and biopolitical regulation of populations (Dillon, 1995; Elbe, 2005). Security is therefore not simply exceptional, but has constitutive effects on the normal. Normality is simultaneously a field of struggle, where technologies for constituting subjects and ordering the social come up against the intransigence of political agency and the resistance of political subjects.

The Paris School has also redefined normality as constituted by professionals through technologies for ordering and managing social problems. The struggle would therefore shift from political agency to the institutional level of the professionals involved in the definition of threats and the technologies to govern them. Unmaking security would entail the disruption of the 'regime of truth' created by the professionals of security.

For the Paris School, two convergent factors explain in reshaping of the concept of (in) security. Desecuritization, via reassuring discourses or different techniques of protection (e.g. video cameras), does not always reduce insecurity or increase confidence in the political. Security is not the opposite of insecurity. How security is defined conditions what is considered as insecurity. Policing insecurity is then a mode of governmentality, drawing the lines of fear and unease at both the individual and the collective level (Bigo, 2005; Huysmans, 2006).

This conception of security points towards a different understanding of securitization as meaning the capacity to control border, to manage threats, to define endangered identities and to delineate the spheres of orders. It distracts attention in three ways. First, instead of analyzing security as an essential concept, contested as it were, the Paris School proposes treating security as a 'technique of government" (Foucault, 1994). Second, rather than investigating intentions behind the use of power, this approach concentrates on the effects of power games. Third, instead of focusing on 'speech acts' the Paris School emphasizes practices, audiences and contexts that enable and constrain the production of specific forms of governmenality(Balzacq,2005; Bigo,2000; Bonditti, 2004, 2005: 131-154). Consequently, this approach argues that, today, the field of security is determined not only by the sovereign power to kill but also by the discursive ability to produce an image of the enemy with which the audience identifies. Drawing on Bourdieu, the Paris School has managed to circumscribe the problem raised by the Copenhagen school, whereby the emergence of speech acts was underspecified and their effects too broad, in comparison with other practices of power. Moreover, by focusing on practices at the expense of principles that hold together political communities, the Paris School does not leave room for the possibilities of reappropriating terms.

WIDENING THE FIELD: DEBATES

The question of the 'widening of the field of security' has given rise to fierce debates. The implicit argument of many of the 'wideners' is that by securitizing new issues such as peace and development, one encourages politicians to deal with them in a positive way. The widening of the security agenda, when justified by a concern to free people from fear and threat, might run into what is called 'security trap'. Talking about 'security trap' refers both to the non-intentional dimension of the consequences of widening and to the fact that these consequences might conflict with the underlying intention.

As many critical scholars have warned, when transforming a societal issue into a security issue, one risks having the issue securitized for oneself by more established security professionals (Bigo, 1996; Waever, 1995). In other words, even when widening the security agenda with the explicit intention of 'demilitarizing' international security, the signifier 'security' might on the contrary subordinate these issues to governmental security agencies, thus foreclosing the range of political options available to deal with the issues . Even if securitization is a political process, it might legitimate practices that depoliticize the approach to the securitized issues (Critical approaches to Security, Security Dialogue, 2006: 461).

Bigo has shown that the securitization of social issues raised the issue of protection by insecuritizing the audience the security discourses are addressing. This insecuritization will translate into a social demand for the intervention of coercive state agencies through reassurance discourses and protection techniques. In other words, the processes of securitization and of insecuritization are inseparable .This leads him to speak of the process of (in) securitization. This means that one is confronted with a security dilemma: the more one tries to securitize social phenomena in order to ensure 'security', the more one creates (intentionally or non-intentionally) a feeling insecurity. When analyzing the securitization of a phenomenon, how can one avoid playing into the hands of the 'deep structures' of the security discourse and thus participating in its discursive securitization? This question of the 'normative dilemma of security studies' is the third aspect of the security trap. Highlighting the non-intentional and adverse effects of analyzing the widening of security, it remains the most difficult to handle (Huysmans, 1998a).

PEACE AND SECURITY

According to Waever (2004b), 'peace' and 'security' are closely related concepts. During the cold war their connotations have differed fundamentally. While security has been the main focus of western nations, peace has been confined to political and academic realm. In the 1980s the relationship between the two became less hostile and the two found a common ground in the concept of security. Peace and security have become the two sides of the same coin. As early as the 1960s peace researchers began to expand violence to include structural violence. It was understood as everything that prevents people from realizing their potential. Johan Galtung (1969:183) called this absence of structural violence 'positive peace'. It does not reflect on its ontological foundations, epistemological premises, or the origins and implications of its concepts.

SECURITY AND DEVELOPMENT

The merging of security and development is most clearly represented by the concept of human security, introduced by the United Nations Development programme's (1994) Human Development Report. A plethora of other disciplines for example, new wars (Kaldor, 2001), 'greed and grievance' (Berdal& Malone, 2000), and 'failed state' models of conflict and social unrest have emerged to come under the rubric of Human Security Discourses. The political implications of the merging of security and development are profound. In these discourses, non-western war, or social unrest or conflict, has been emptied of political, social and historical content –both external, in terms of international context within which conflict occurs, and internal. Conflict is understood as a private, predatory activity, fostered by elites pursuing degenerate, criminal projects.

THE PRIVATIZATION OF SECURITY

The trend of privatizing security, as reflected in the growing role of private security companies (PSCs) and private military companies (PMCs), offers a promising research agenda for critical approaches to security. This trend is indirectly linked to the contemporary widening of the security agenda, and has been fuelled by the incapacity of public security agencies to reassure and to protect in the face of a broadening of the 'environment of threats'.

The issue of privatization is important for critical

security studies, as it allows highlighting the fact that the contemporary field of security is transversal not only to the inside/outside distinction, but also to the public/private distinction (Bigo, 2003; Olsson, 2003; Abrahamsen & Williams, 2006). The aim, here, is to understand what happens when discourses of (in) security, historically considered as enactments of state sovereignty, are said to refer to the presumably marketized, and democratized, (Thompson, 1994) realm of private security operators. Anna Leander (2005, 2006) has analyzed the political risks entailed by the commodification of violence by showing that the supply side (PMCs) and the demand side (security demand) are inseparable: 'supply creates its own demand' through the discursive process of securitization. By highlighting the structural power the privatizing trend gives to private companies, she implicitly confirms the second aspect of the security trap: the maximal security option might validate itself a posteriori by fostering a feeling of insecurity.

SECURITY AND EXCEPTIONALISM

The question of exceptionalism has recently become a site of intense political contestation over the legitimacy or illegitimacy of recent transformations in security practices, especially in the context of the 'war on terror'. On the one hand, policy makers and their supporters have frequently argued that the rules of the game have changed, that this is a new kind of war, and that exceptional times require exceptional measures. The category of the exceptional has been invoked to justify and mobilize an array of violent and illiberal practices, including detention without trial, derogation from human rights law, complicity in torture, 'extraordinary rendition', the curtailment of civil liberties and the securitization of migration.

A key point of departure is Schmitt's ([1922] 1985:5)

declaration that 'sovereign is he who decides in the exceptions'. This sharply expresses the exceptional prerogatives claimed by political authorities (however conceived) in the name of security. For the Schmitt of Political Theology, 'the exception is a situation of radical danger and contingency for which no prior law, procedure or anticipated response is adequate. For Schmitt, 'exceptionalism' is not simply an adjunct to 'normal' politics, but a more authentic expression of political authority that has the capacity to constitute new political and legal orders. The Schmittan strategy is to argue that the necessity of unlimited, unconstrained, exceptional sovereign power is brought about by the exceptional situation itself. The slipperiness of this move is exposed when it becomes clear that Schmitt's sovereign must also declare that the exception exists in the first place. Although exceptionalism legitimated on the grounds of 'objective necessity' can be performatively successful, its claimed positivistic basis resets on a hollow circular logic. Exceptionalism is from the outset fiendishly entangled in an authoritarian, decisionist politics that declares exceptional conditions (such as a state of emergency) in order to give legitimate authority to contentious policies and practices.

In contrast, Bigo (2002) argues that by focusing on elite discourses of danger and emergency, securitization theory reinforces a conception of the security field that is driven by the views and discursive strategies of elites. By focusing instead on the security professionals who manage 'unease' within society on a daily basis, exceptional security practices can be understood in the context of ongoing processes of technocratic, bureaucratic and market-driven routinization and normalization .

Williams argues that because claims about exceptions occur in the discursive field, they are open to 'a process of argument, the provision of reasons, presentation of evidence, and commitment to convincing others of the validity of one's position'. They therefore remain open to the emancipatory possibility of a communicative ethics that may 'avoid the excesses of decisionist account of securitization'.

SECURITY, RISK AND RISK MANAGEMENT

The concept of risk has recently entered into the realm of security studies. Under a rationalist tradition, the concept of risk has evolved as a basis for decision making under conditions of uncertainty (Daston, 1995; Hacking, 1990, Bernstein, 1998). Risk analysis works as an instrument in decision making by evaluating future actions in terms of risk. As Luhmann (1993:130 has argued, risk is conceptualized as "a controlled extension of rational action". Risk analysis is an estimation of future threats- an estimation that builds on the premise that risks can be classified, quantified and to some extent predicted and that rational behaviour can help to manage or may be even eliminate risk (Adams, 1995; Bernstein, 1998; Power, 2004).

The modern tradition of risk however is being contested by Beck's theory of risk society. According to Beck, late modernity is characterized by society's inability to insure itself against risks that, on the one hand, exceed the calculable and, on the other, have catastrophic effects that cannot be comprehended. Thus, according to him, the 9/11 terrorist events escaped rational predictions and have demonstrated the limits of modern insurance technology (Beck, 2002, 2003). Within IR, this has given birth to a research agenda on' reflexive security' that focuses on the management of the new and constructed risks that transcend national borders (Rasmussen, 2002, 2004).

An alternative approach addresses risk as an instrument of governance rather than an organizing principle of life. Drawing on the work of Michel Foucault, risk is recognized as a means for ordering reality- as " a way of representing events in a certain form so they might be made governable in particular ways, with particular technologies and for particular goals"(Dean,1999: 177).

Practices of security can be understood as combinations of these two strategies. Risk is therefore, a technology for the provision of security that transcends borders (Baker, 2000; Dillon, 2005; Peterson, 2006). Premised on these perspectives, a challenge for critical security studies is to engender a debate between risk- based and threat- based interpretations of (in) security that will widen the traditional critical security agenda concerned with the mutual constitution of threats and identity (Hansen, 2006; Campbell, 1998; Krause, 1998). "Addressing security as risk management opens up the logic of security and moves from the concern over identity, territory, exclusion, neutralization and elimination of others, placing the analysis on a more explicit temporal dimensions"(Critical Security Approaches, Security Dialogue, 2006: 469). Risk management locates security in a direct relation to time, owing to its reckoning of futures.

A second emergent challenge is that of exceptionalism, which is often present in routinized politics of unease (e.g. Agamben, 1998, 2005; Van Munster, 2004). As the discussion of security and exceptionalism has already indicated, the critical problem of 'the exception' is that of radical contingency. As pointed out repeatedly in Foucauldian approaches to criminology, insurance and welfare, risk management works to 'tame' contingency and order both temporal and special relations.

FROM BEING RELEVANT TO BECOMING RELEVANT

The Aberystwyth School has especially tried to show how the concept of state security does not necessarily encompass security for the people. The Copenhagen School, on the other hand, has shown how invoking the concept of security is a discursive process that erases all rules of normal politics. This alternative insight puts a special kind of responsibility on people doing security, since invoking the word starts a process beyond democratic politics.

The members of the Copenhagen school consider the military core of security studies as something to be avoided. Their estrangement from the military sector resulted in ultimately losing contact with the core element of the security concern "namely large-scale conflict, that is conflict brought to the point of mass violence, subjection, or submission"(Knudsen, Olav F.2001:357-358). Nobody can refute the fact that the concept of securitization continues to remain one of the distinctive contributions of the Copenhagen school. Having carved out middle- of the- road approach this school with its analytically sound standpoints has been able to get its concept of securitization widely accepted with great success.

The period between 1960s to 1980s witnessed frequent skirmishes between peace research and strategic studies intermediated with a mélange of political scientists of whom some were concerned with conceptualization, others theory developers and many others were busy doing empirical works. This fragmentation and fractious feuds among scholars came to an end with the demise of cold war. What added an integrative force to all these motley groups cut in a frenzy of intellectual fighting was Barry Buzan's monumental book People, States and Fear. By broadening the concept of security Ole Waever enriched the tradition in peace research. The roots of the new security thinking do not lie solely with the Copenhagen school who lent it an intellectual voice. Social democratic movements in North European region and the British Isles;

and Bjorn Moller and others who worked on related ideas, such as non-offensive defense are equally entitled to earning credits for this new security thinking.

The concept of securitization was in part a move along the path of wideners replacing the focus on violence and the business of the military with a focus on a broader agenda. What is unique in this is to draw the attention away from a mere widening of the security concept to a highlighting of the way in which issues do or do not catapult into the political agenda. Securitization marks the significance of agenda setting thus requiring the insights of political science on this. As such the items on the agenda setting assume importance not because they have inherent intrinsic values but because the effective political leadership wants them to be assumed important and form the agenda. For long security has always been privileged to remain on the top and above the agenda. The Copenhagen school deserves praises for having brought a new and broader notion of security into the agenda and arena of debate. The concept of securitization demystifies the traditional privileged position security has occupied in the agenda set by politicians, decision makers and the military establishment by holding that security is not set by nature but is embodied in their network of power and influence. "Hence, 'securitization' gave a name to the process, hitherto vaguely perceived, of raising security issues above politics and making them something one would never question" (Knudsen, 2001:359). Further, he stated that there have been already changes in the security politics before the Copenhagen school launches its concept in the post-cold war period. In his view it "is more appropriate to the security politics of the cold war years than to the post-cold war period" (Ibid).

In the Copenhagen school, threats are seen as emanating mainly from the actors' own fears, or from what happens when the fears of individuals turn into paranoid political action. In Knudsen's view, this emphasis on the subjective is a misleading conception of threat, in that it discounts an independent existence for whatever is perceived as a threat. During the cold war, threats- in the sense of plausible possibilities of danger – referred to 'real' phenomena now. The objects referred to are often not the same, but that is a different matter. "Threats have to be dealt with both in terms of perceptions and in terms of the phenomena which are perceived to be threatening" (2001: 360).

The deliberate disregard of objective factors even more explicitly demonstrated in Buzan and Weaver's joint article of the same year reduces the phenomenon of threat to a matter of pure domestic politics. It seems that the security dilemma, as a central notion in security studies, then loses its foundation. Knudsen in a riposte stated that "Weaver himself has no compunction about referring to the security dilemma in a recent article" (Ibid).

What is most discernible is the fact that the discounting of the objective aspect of threats drifts security studies to insignificant concerns. According to Knudsen, "Waever first began his argument in favor of an alternative security conception, because a convincing sense of urgency has been the chief culprit behind the abuse of 'security' and the consequent 'politics in panic', as he aptly calls it. Now, here- in the case of urgency – another baby is thrown out with the Waeverian bathwater" (2001: 360). Too much emphasis is put on the subjective side. This implies that the researches are asked to shy away themselves from the world of politics as it is and to draw their attention one-sidedly towards the politics of 'what could be'. "This aspect of Waever's approach is clearly not accidental; it is intended to be that way" (Ibid).

The problem here is that this serves to underestimate

the significance of problems that exit out there- not just in the heads of politicians and decision makers but as challenges to their experience and problem-solving efforts. The implication of the agenda-setting approach is that perceptions and images are arbitrary, a stance which in itself may be ill-advised because it detracts from the significance of issues like crisis management, which purportedly demands top priority.

Words of Knudsen : In the scintillating

> 'Securitization' is an ambiguous concept because in Copenhagen usage it refers to two things at once. On the one hand, it refers to the act (or process) of removing an issue from and raising it above politics, taking it out of the limelight. On the other hand, it points to the act (or process) of taking an issue out of obscurity or neglect and placing it on the political agenda. Hence, the same term refers at the same time to more or less inverse types of phenomena. At times, this leads to further confusion because the securitization concept assumes we know where the issue 'comes from', whereas when an issue is not on the agenda because it is a holy cow in politics (2001:361).

PARANOIA OF THE STATE

While rummaging through the debates of the 1990's one gets immediately the impression that the study of states is a 'no-no'. This is a major ingredient in the work of the Copenhagen School.

The 'referent object' is a key notion in the Copenhagen School's conceptual apparatus –that 'thing' whose security is at stake. Buzan et al. pedagogically point out the need to break away from the traditional fixation upon the state as the referent object of security. However, Knudsen gets the impression that Buzan and his colleagues keep referring to the state nevertheless. Studies of the state have not disappeared even among researches who style themselves as critical or who some-how subscribe to a 'new security studies' agenda. The upshot is that their views on the role of the state are inconsistent (2001:362).

On the one hand, the Copenhagen authors warn against 'state-centrism' and build a complicated reasoning on identity as a replacement for the state; on the other hand, they continue to reason quite conventionally about states. Hence, their position on the state is at best misleading, at worst confused. The postmodernists seem to have won out the point because there is continuing paranoia about the state in studies of international politics (Ibid). To be politically correct these days, one must disavow state centrism. But paradoxically state continues to be there as in the works of Wendt, Buzan, Walt. Holsti's work on the relationship between state and war is significant (Holsti, 1996). One must not be impervious to what these wars about. If external wars are intended to forestall the penetration of outside forces into its territorial integrity and state apparatus the internal wars attest not to the disappearance of state but its continuing importance.

To the extent that one does focus on states, there is, on the other hand, a different danger, which is to reify the state, to believe that it actually 'is' an actor with humanoid qualities. The injunction against this is, of course, another old and familiar one to generations of IR students. Again, too often the warning is mistaken as an argument against studying states as units, or 'states-as actors'. It is good practice, however, to refrain from talking about states as if they were humans. The worst sinners in this regard tend to be neorealists and their interlocutors. Their line of thinking potentially undermines a significant theme of research, already alluded to above: the transformation that occurs as actions performed by small groups or individual decision makers become perceived as actions performed by the state with which they are associated-that is, the state they are taken to represent. The phenomenon of representation in itself is at the heart of what we study in IR: the representation of the collective unit inward as well as outward.

Representation is also where the state offers politicians a possibility to abuse their role in security affairs. It is the utilization of the state machinery in the processing of threats which the Copenhagen School wants to change. How that can be done by dropping the state from the research agenda? A final danger in focusing on the state of building the illusion that states have impenetrable walls, that they have an inside and an outside, and that nothing ever passes through. Wolfers's billiard balls have contributed to this misconception (Knudsen, 2001:364).

Hence, the state must continue to be a central object of our work in IR, not least in security studies. Conceived as a penetrated state – specifically because it performs essential security functions that are rarely performed by other types of organizations, it has the following characteristics according to Knudsen (2001:363):

- The major collective unit processing notions of threat;
- The mantle that cloaks the exercise of elite power;
- The organizational expression that gives shape to communal 'identity and 'culture';
- The chief agglomeration of competence to deal with issue areas crossing jurisdictional boundaries;
- The manager of territory/ geographical space - including functioning as a 'receptacle' for income ;
- The legitimizer of authorized action and possession.

The state is also the instrument of democracy on a

large scale in its most well-functioning forms. Surveying democracy's state of heath is a crucial responsibility for social scientists. Finally when it comes to performing collective tasks on a large scale, the state is the most potentially effective organizing instrument across an almost limitless range of objectives. Security is among them.

In short, the state is too central to the large-scale business of human life to be ignored or put aside, whether for ideological or idealistic reasons. Still, we need to recognize the historical dimension in this. It is not necessarily the state's present form which makes it an important object of study; rather, it is its primary function of being the largest universal –purpose collective-action unit around. Such units require study in all civilizations and at all times in human history, regardless of their name or specific functions. The Westphalian preoccupation of IR is therefore somewhat overdrawn. There is no need to apologize for focusing on states or state-like units.

With environmental change new conceptualization of security has emerged as HUGE (Human, Gender and environmental Security) and HESP (Human and Environmental Security and Peace).

HUMAN, GENDER AND ENVIRONMENTAL SECURITY (HUGE)

The deplorable conditions of physical, environmental, human societal and gender security of a large part of humanity have inspired researchers (Oswald 2001,2006,2008 88; Moller 2001,2003:278-279)to ask security for whom(the nation state, society, human beings or humankind or the environment); for what (eternal or earthly peace, social, justice, humane livelihood, sustainable development, gender equity): from whom(state and sub-state actors, terrorists, migrants, alien cultures, multilateral organization, globalization, elites, nature, humankind, patriarchy, totalitarian integrity, national unity and identity, survival and quality of life, sustainability, equity, identity, social representations and solidarity). In synthesis, HUGE integrates social, environmental, human, cultural, political and identity concerns, aiming at solidarity, resilience, participatory democracy, peace-building and equity in a world that is facing many new security dangers and concerns due to the gradual transition from the Holocene to the Anthropocene.

HUMAN AND ENVIRONMENTAL SECURITY AND PEACE (HESP)

Policy Goals

- Policy Goals on the Societal and individual levels: Environmental Security studies should contribute to strategies for reducing the impact of environmental stress, decreasing the vulnerability and strengthening the coping capacities and resilience.
- Policy Goals on the communal, sub-national, national and international levels: strategies for coping with outcomes of environmental stress should be developed by improving disaster preparedness and response and by integrating disaster reduction into development planning and resilience-building. The resolution, prevention and avoidance of resulting violence should become a major policy goal.

HESP combines a normative orientation at the dual policy goals of sustainable development and sustainable peace with a 'people-centred' human security perspective from the individual to the global level to develop strategies for adaptation and mitigation and to reduce the likelihood and impact of vulnerability to these outcomes by strengthening resilience. Both concepts and policy goals of sustainable development and sustainable peace are as the highly contested as the security concept.

The process of rethinking or 'reconceptualization of security concepts' and 'redefinition of security interests' that was triggered by the global turn of 1989-1991 and slightly modified by the events of 11 September 2001 and the subsequent US-led 'war on terror 'has become a truly global process.

TRENDS IN THE RECONCEPTUALIZATION OF SECURITY

- Widening, deepening, and sectorialization of security concepts;
- Shift of referent object from the state to human beings or humankind(human security);
- Perception of new security dangers (threats, challenges, vulnerabilities, and risks) and securitization of new security concerns due to an articulations by national and international organizations, scientific epistemic communities ,and an attentive public with a progressing decentralization and diversity of information control through the internet;
- Search for new non-military strategies to face and cope with these newly perceived security dangers and concerns and new environmental dangers, hazards, and disasters that pose no classical security dilemma(Herz 1950,1959,1962) for states but a 'survival dilemma' (Brauch 2004) for people.

2

Neorealist and Neoliberal View of Security

Recent years have witnessed significant changes and development in the field of international relations with the concept of security remaining at the center of the discipline. The concept of security is explained by several approaches, especially constructivism, critical geopolitics, post modernism and historical sociology. Although these approaches have strongly criticized the idea of "state security" held by realists, neo- realists and neo – liberals they have not been able to dilute the centrality of security. It is little wonder therefore, that the mainstream IR theoretical paradigms like realism (and neo – realism) and neo – liberalism would contribute to the burgeoning literature on security. Security issues are nearly always dealt with as empirical issues, with a bearing on policy making. Whether the focus is on critical issues like nuclear security, international terrorism or weapons of mass destruction, or on relatively soft issues like environmental degradation, problems of refugees, migration and internal displacement, the treatment is invariably empirical without any attempt to place case studies in the broader context of theoretical or conceptual debates.

THE NEOREALIST / NEOLIBERAL ACCOUNTS OF SECURITY

Kenneth Waltz's Theory of International Politics (1979) set the tone for some of the most controversial methodological and theoretical debates in IR in the 1980's and 1990s. Much of the neorealist-neoliberal debates can be seen as a reaction to this book and a response to those reactions. The arguments, which Waltz began, underscored the importance of third-image explanations. First image explanations locate causes of international outcomes say the cause of war, "in the nature and behaviour of men. Wars result from selfishness, from misdirected aggressive impulses, from stupidity" (Waltz Kenneth, 1959: 16). Second-image explanations locate causes in the internal structure like capitalism; similarly, international peace results from a particular form of government like democracy (Ibid: 80-164). Alluding to Rousseau' stag hunt and the then prevailing game theory, Waltz stated that the first and second-image explanations were insufficient. In a situation of strategic interdependence such as that of great powers an actor's optimal strategy depends on the other actor's strategic considerations. In order to understand what the actors will do one has to take into account the constraints that define the strategic setting in which the actors interact in addition to looking at the attributes of the actors. The third image locates causes "within the state system" (Ibid: 12). An illustration from microeconomic theory explains the potential importance of third image. The price is higher and the output is lower in a monopolized market than in a competitive one. But first and second image accounts, which Waltz collectively calls reductive explanations in Theory of International Politics, do not explain these differences. In both markets, the attributes of the actors, which are firms in this case, are identical: every firm tries to maximize its profits and consequently produces the level of output at which marginal cost equals marginal revenue. What accounts for the variation in price and output between these markets is not variation in the attributes of the units but variation in the environment or market structures in which they act. This is the essence of the third image. The first and second image explanations are basically reductive. Fixing constraints and varying units' attributes comprise the essential conceptual experiment underlying reductive explanations. The third image is mainly systemic explanations. Fixing the units' attributes and varying the constraints facing the units comprise the fundamental conceptual experiment underlying systemic explanations. After highlighting the importance of third image or systemic explanations, Waltz sets the second objective in Theory of International Politics. He sees structure as a "set of constraining conditions" (Waltz: 73). A second goal for Waltz is to specify a restricted set of constraints that provide a way of conceiving of a political system and then to demonstrate the power of this formulation by showing that it tells "us a small number of big and important things" (Waltz, 1986 : 73). Waltz defines a political structure in terms of ordering principle of the system, the functional differentiation of units and the distribution of the units' capabilities. His objective is to explain why the anarchic international system tends to reproduce itself. He believes that international system has precisely defined these three dimensional structure:

1. Ordering Principle of the System

The ordering principle of the system is anarchical not hierarchical. The absence of a central authority leads to a self help system where the quest for survival requires the states to seek security through the accretion of military power. The ordering principle of the system forces the states to perform exactly the same primary function regardless of their capacity to do so.

2. The functional differentiation of units

In this anarchic system each state is a separate, autonomous and formally equal, and to realize its interests it must count only on its own resources and no one else can be counted on to do so. Then, all the important functions must be performed by each and every state.

3. The distribution of the capabilities of the units of the international system

States cannot be differentiated by its functions but they differ vastly in their capabilities. This distribution of capabilities, which is unequal and shifting, defines the relative power of the states and predicts variation in states' balance of power behaviour. This means that one international system can be distinguished from another by the distribution of capabilities between states. "Structure, properly defined is transposable" (Waltz, in Keohane, 1986 : 330).

According to Waltz, balance and bandwagon are the two choices before the states in an anarchic system. The states always prefer balance to bandwagon. The power of others is always a threat not a lure. The weak states have no other alternative than always to form alliances with leading powers.

DIFFERENCES BETWEEN MORGENTHAU'S AND WALTZ'S ANALYSIS

Classical realism is primarily based on a pessimistic portrayal of human nature. Self interested, competitive, concerned with self preservation and lust for power behaviour are found embedded in human nature. Since self preservation is the sole motive in aggrandizing power, Morgenthau argues that each state must act selfishly. Deriving its ontological foundation from Hobbes, Morgenthau argues that such behaviour leads ultimately to conflict. "What the one wants for himself, the other already possesses or wants, too. Struggle and competition ensue.... Man cannot (therefore) hope to be good, but must be content with not being too evil" (Morgenthau, 1946). In short, classical realism assumes that competition and conflict between states are inevitable, and the roots of the struggle for power emanate from the human nature.

Neorealism or structural realism pursues a different approach to explain the nature of conflict between actors in international relations. The roots of interstate conflict are found embedded in the absence of a central authority that can enforce rules and agreements, and not in the nature of human beings as in the case of classical realism. The absence of a central authority results in an insecure, self help situation in which the actors are impelled to act competitively, regardless of their individual nature or personal preferences. This situation is called anarchy not in the sense of chaos but in the sense of absence of world government, which can enforce rules in international relations. Thus, anarchy originates in an insecure international system bereft of any central government not in human nature and states must act to eliminate or reduce this insecurity through a policy of balancing against others' power capabilities, and bandwagoning a coalition that supports an aggressive state, in hopes of turning its aggression elsewhere.

In the classical realism desire for power is considered as an end in itself because the behaviour of the states leads to power oriented strategies. In neorealism the need for such strategies arises to compete for security.

On the question about the effect of polarity on war and peace both classical and neorealism differ. The key to understand this difference lies in the impact of uncertainty on the decision to go to war. The increase in the number of main actors in the international system increases uncertainty. When the number decreases, uncertainty decreases. For classical realists strategies are rooted in the human desire of power as an end in itself, then certainty leads to war because certainty simplifies the aggressors' calculations for war, and uncertainty leads to peace because action is deterred by the threat of third party intervention. In the classical realist theory bipolarity gives more certainty and leads to war and multipolarity leads to peace as it is characterized by uncertainty. On the other hand, in the neoclassical realist analysis insecurity is originated in the anarchic condition of international system, which impinges on states to accumulate more power as a systemic requirement to give more security to themselves. As the number of main actors increases, the system is more anarchic and therefore more insecure. The states are thus compelled to resort to drastic actions to reduce insecurity. In other words uncertainty gives more opportunities to aggressor to act and certainty leads to peace. In the neorealist analysis bipolarity leads to peace as it gives more certainty than multipolarity.

According to neorealism an increase in one state's security decreases the security of others. The term "security dilemma" describes the condition in which states, unsure of others' intentions, arm for the sake of security, setting in motion a vicious circle of response and counter response. Security dilemmas result from situations in the view of neo-realism and not from states' desire as in the case of classical realism.

"By concentrating on the nature of the system-level structure, Waltz avoided the need to make assumptions about human nature, morality, power and interest. Neorealists were thus able to see power in a different way. For the classical realists power was both a means and an end, and rational state behaviour was simply accumulating the most power. Neorealists found that a better guide was provided by assuming that the ultimate state interest was in security, and while gathering power often ensured that, in some cases it merely provoked an arms race. Yet while power was no longer the prime motivator, its distribution was the major factor determining the nature of the structure" (Martin Dunn).

NEOREALISM AND POST CLASSICAL REALISM

Recent years have witnessed a split of realism into two competing branches- Waltz's neorealism and post classical realism. Both are state centric; both view international politics as inherently competitive; both emphasize material factors, rather than nonmaterial factors, such as ideas and institutions; and both assume states are egoistic actors that pursue self help. Notwithstanding these similarities, differences between the two veer round the issue of whether states are conditioned by the mere possibility of conflict or states make decisions on the probability of aggression. According to neo realism the possibility of conflict decides the actions of states, which are seen as always adopting a worst case perspective. On the other hand, post classical realism rejecting the notion of worst case reasoning holds that states are understood as making decisions based on assessment of probabilities regarding security threats (See Wendt, 1992: 404 and Keohane, 1993: 282-83).

The first disagreement concerns the discount rate. It is argued that neo realism's emphasis on the possibility of conflict is emblematic of the view that actors heavily discount the future favouring short-term military preparedness over longer term objectives when they conflict. To the contrary postclassical realism does not consider the long term objectives as always subordinate to short term security requirements often requiring states to make intertemporal trade offs (Stephen G. Brooks, 1997).

The second disagreement concerns state preferences. All realists are of the view that military security is state's prime responsibility and it is founded on a state's material substructure. But disagreement brews when these priorities conflict. In the case of conflict between material capacity and military preparedness, neorealism gives primacy to the latter. In postclassical realism's analysis "the rational policy makers may trade off a degree of military preparedness if the potential net gains in economic capacity are substantial relative to the probability of security losses" (Ibid).

POSSIBILITY VERSUS PROBABILITY

Neorealism views the international system as always running high security pressures. As Mearsheimer contends, neorealists view the international system as a " brutal arena where states look for opportunities to take advantage of each other...International relations is not a constant state of war, but is a state of relentless security competition" (Mearsheimer, 1994-95: 10). In a similar vein Waltz argues that "threats or seeming threats to... security abound. Preoccupation with identifying dangers and counteracting them become a way of life. Relations remain tense; the actors are usually suspicious and often hostile" (Waltz 1989:43). Portrayal of the system as "one of high risk" does not mean "in the sense that war constantly occurs but in the sense that, with each state deciding for itself whether or not to use force, war may at any time break out" (Waltz, 1979:111, 102). Waltz argues that "in the absence of a supreme authority, there is then constant possibility that conflicts will be settled by force" (Waltz, 1959: 188). What is important is not that the conflict is always possible in anarchy but rather the relative chances that it will occur. Within neorealism, a rational state never lets down its guard: states adopt a worst-case perspective and always aim to balance the military capabilities of potential aggressors (Keohane and Martin, 1995:43; Wendt, 1992:404). For neorealists, states are conditioned by the mere possibility- and not the probability – of conflict.

According to Stephen G Brooks (1997), "neorealists regard states as adopting such a worst case perspective for three principal reasons. First, neorealists point to the potential costs of war as causing actors to focus on the mere possibility of conflict". As Mearsheimer maintains, "political competition among states is a much more dangerous business than economic intercourse; it can lead to war, and war often means mass killing on the battle field and even mass murder of civilians. In extreme cases, war can even lead to the total destruction of the state" (Mearsheimer, 1994-95: 12).

Second, neorealists argue that states will ultimately focus on other state's underlying potential for aggression- as measured by material capabilities- because " intentions are impossible to divine with 100 percent certainty", and the possibility always exist that " a state's intentions can be benign one day and malign the next" (Ibid:14). In the neorealist framework, rational states adopt a worst- case focus because this is the only way to ensure against being caught off guard.

Third, neorealists maintain that rational states will focus on the possibility of conflict because defensive precautions are considered the only true assurance against aggression. In the neorealist's view wars can be prevented by direct choice to pursue appropriate defensive preparations; "only the vigilance of defensive coalitions stands in the way of an Orwellian nightmare of huge clashing despotisms, or even a single world empire" (Liberman; 1993: 125).

Neorealists' accent on worst case and possibilistic perspective does not mean that war is highly likely. Waltz clearly states that "world politics, although not reliably peaceful, falls short of unrelieved chaos" (Waltz, 1979:114). They simply argue that the above three factors compel the rational actors to adopt a worst case and possibilistic strategy. These three factors provide the justification for neorealists' focus on worst-case and possibilistic perspective. The neorealists simply argue that given the three reasons, the rational states will react in this manner. The question remains whether rational states act on these assumptions in situations open to criticism.

"Ironically, although neorealists are leading critics of classical realist explanations of international behaviour predicated on particular conceptions of human nature, the internal coherence of the neorealist framework itself depends fundamentally on the psychological assumption that actors are characteristically highly fearful" (Stephen G Brooks,1997). Morgenthau is of the view that an aggressive animal like craving in man to dominate one's fellows results in a rapacious quest for power (Morgenthau, 1946: 192-94). Morgenthau's view of human nature thus emphasizes aggression, whereas the neorealist conception emphasizes wariness and anxiety. "These two conceptions of human nature may not be so distinct from one another: if actors are understood to be aggressive, it makes sense to assume they will also be characteristically highly fearful. In this respect, neorealists may adopt a worst case/ possibilistic perspective precisely because they implicitly accept Morgenthau's argument that actors are inherently aggressive" (Stephen G Brooks, 1997). Rightly derived from his analysis it implies that actors will seek to take advantage of weaker states whenever they have the chance, and hence military preparedness is the only true assurance against being exploited. This view is consonant with the neorealism's view that "conflict is common among states because... [of] powerful incentives for aggression"

(Mearsheimer, 1990:12) and where defensive vigilance is the only guarantee against aggression (Waltz, 1959: 188). Neorealism portrays a different view of human nature than Morgenthau. But the net result is that both view the world in very similar highly pessimistic terms. In sum, it can be said that neorealism does not move beyond the human nature arguments of classical realism; neorealists simply swap one aspect of human nature (aggression) for another (fear) (Fischer 1992: 465).

SHORT TERM VERSUS LONG TERM

Given the international system as a relentless competition for security in which states adopt a worst-case/possibilistic perspective, the neorealism assumes about a discount rate and a rational state will always seek first to maximize its short-term military security from potential rivals, even if this has negative long term repercussions for other state priorities. Neorealists never say that long term state goals are unimportant. But they view such concerns as subordinate to short term military security requirements when the two conflict. The very view that the neorealism heavily discounts the future is not shaped by "the anarchic nature of the international system per se, but rather reflects the theory's assumption that states are shaped by the mere possibility of conflict and hence seek to be prepared for all contingencies regarding the short-term use of force by potential rivals" (Brooks, 1997).

MILITARY VERSUS ECONOMIC CAPACITY

Surviving in anarchy requires both a potent military deterrent and a dynamic productive base. Waltz contends that states will be concerned, above all else, with securing their survival (Waltz, 1979: 91). The question remains about how the rational state balances the military security component of a survival strategy in relation to the economic capacity element. Will a rational state always maximize its military security, even if doing so sometimes significantly constrains its economic capacity? Alternatively, will a state sometimes attempt to enhance its economic capacity? Alternatively, will a state sometimes attempt to enhance its economic capacity, even if it thereby reduces defensive vigilance and potentially exposes economic capacity, even if it thereby reduces defensive vigilance and potentially exposes a state's vital interests to some military danger? Waltz's argument that states pursue survival thus contains an underlying tension between military security and economic capacity; however, Waltz skirts this trade-off by describing "moves to increase economic capacity, to increase military strength" as both being elements of an internal balancing strategy. (Ibid., 118).

Of course, economic capacity and military preparedness are not always incompatible. Yet, heightened military preparedness often leaves less resources available for economic priorities, especially over the long term. This is not to say a fixed inverse relationship exists between the two objectives, where increasing attention to military security always necessarily causes a corresponding decrease in economic capacity. (For a good summary as to why an ironclad trade-off does not exit between military security and economic capacity under all circumstances, see Friedberg 1989).Moreover, as John Lewis Gaddis, Paul Kennedy, and William Wohlforth emphasize decision makers very often perceive that they face such a trade-off and hence design policy based on the assumption that they cannot fully satisfy both objectives (See Gaddis 1982,58,133-35;Kennedy 1983; and Wohlforth 1994-95).

How do neorealists envision states making this trade off? Neorealism's worst case/possibilistic perspective and high discount rate reflects the view that rational states will seek first to ensure military security before advancing other objectives, such as economic capacity. This is not to claim, as Richard Rosecrance does, that neorealists maintain "economics need not be included in a valid conspectus of international politics" (Rosecrance 1981, 693; see Rosecrance 1982, 682). Neorealists certainly do not view economic capacity as unimportant. However, neorealists consider it irrational for a state to focus on enhancement of economic capacity to the extent that the likelihood of being subjected to military defeat by potential rivals increases to any degree. As Mearsheimer maintains,"states operate in both an international political environment and an international economic environment, and the former dominates the later in cases where the two come into conflict. The reason is straightforward:the international political system anarchic" (Mearsheimer 1992: 222 (emphasis added)).

This neorealists view that security priorities trump economic capacity whenever the two conflict implicitly presumes favor short-term military security over long-term military security. Why? Economic capacity ultimately provides the foundation for future military security; as a result, engaging in intertemporal trade-offs between short-term military security and long-term economic capacity is also a choice between military security in the short term versus the long term. This implicit neorealist argument that protection from short term potential trumps long-term military security is consistent with the theory's underlying view that actors heavily discount the future. Given that long term economic capacity and long term military security overlap, the most precise articulation of neorealism's conception of state preferences is consequently that short-term military security requirements supersede both short-term and long-term economic capacity. Waltz recognizes states have other important objectives besides military security, and he does not argue that states will devote all, or even anywhere near all, of their resources just to ensure this objective. (Waltz 1979,92).The neorealist perspective allows states to pursue economic capacity to a significant degree but not to the extent that doing so leaves a state potentially vulnerable to military exploitation by a possible military rival. Waltz carefully argues that just as firms are free to pursue other objectives to the detriment of profit maximization, states similarly have latitude to pursue other goals to the detriment of their chances for continued existence (Waltz 1979,92). Just as firms that ignore market forces will be punished, Waltz similarly argues that "a unit of the system can behave as it pleases," but "the international arena is a competitive one in which the less skillful must expect to pay the price of their ineptitude" (Waltz 1986, 331). Neorealists recognize states may decide to pursue economic capacity at the expense of military preparedness vis-à-vis potential rivals, but such decisions are seen as having been caused by a lack of proper understanding of the fundamental competitive tenets that govern international politics.

This analysis makes it easier to understand why neorealists resist broadening the concept of security beyond military factors to include an economic element, as David Baldwin suggests (Baldwin 1995).Neorealism's worst-case focus and conception of the discount rate culminates in a particular understanding of state preferences –where short-term military security concerns always trump those of economic capacity whenever the two conflict which then leads neorealism's proponents to focus on the military aspect of security while downplaying the economic element. Broadening the concept of security to include economic factors simply cannot be accomplished within the neorealist framework, since it would require dismantling the underlying assumptions that provide neorealism with its internal coherence. Not surprisingly, therefore, neorealists prefer to respectively define the concept of security in military terms. Taking this line of argument to its logical conclusion makes it easier to understand why Waltz ultimately concludes that it is possible, indeed productive, to ignore the economic domain when theorizing about international behavior (Waltz 1979: 79-80).

THE POSTCLASSICAL REALIST CONCEPTION OF STATE BEHAVIOUR

Does realism admit any other understanding of state behaviour that can be contrasted to the Waltzian neorealist conception? Robert Gilpin argues that all realists share an assumption regarding "the essentially conflictual nature of international affairs" (Gilpin 1984: 290).Gilpin's argument is accurate but underspecified; the crucial question is the extent to which international affairs are conflictual. Does the level and form of conflict vary over time? If so, to what degree and according to which factors?

A variety of current realist writers provides very different answers from those advanced by Waltzian neorealists. Although some of these realist scholars have attempted to merge their analyses into the Waltzian framework, their analyses do not follow from neorealism's worst-case/ possibilistic assumption. Instead, they can best be understood as reflecting a competing branch of realism – what is termed here "postclassical realism" – which views actors as being conditioned by the probability of conflict.

COMMONALITY BETWEEN NEOREALISM AND CLASSICAL REALISM

Before delineating how postclassical realism differs

from Waltz's neorealist theory, it is necessary to show how the postclassical realist conception of state behaviour outlined below simultaneously stands in contrast to classical realism. According to Stephen G Brooks, the term "postclassical realism" was chosen to designate a branch of realism that does not share four important characteristics that are held in common by classical realism and Waltz's neorealist theory. Specifically, neorealism and classical realism share the following characteristics: (1) they have a highly static conception of international relation; (2) they rely on particular aspects of human nature –aggression for classical realists, fear for neorealists - to generate hypotheses; (3) they assume that states tend to rely primarily on the use or threat of military force to secure their objectives; and (4) they concentrate on the balance of military capabilities, with neorealists excluding and classical realists generally downplaying other international-level influences on state behaviour. Postclassical realism does not subscribe to these four characteristics (Brooks, 1997).

POSSIBILITY VERSUS PROBABILITY

Consistent with their worst –case/ possibilistic perspective, Waltzian neorealists place the emphasis on a single endogenous factor as affecting the likelihood of conflict: the balance of military capabilities (Mearsheimer 1990, 21; Haggard 1991, 421; and Wendt 1995, 78-79). Aggression is seen as less likely when states balance the capabilities of potential aggressors. Do any other variables besides the distribution of military capabilities cause the likelihood of conflict to vary systematically? This question has been addressed extensively by nonrealist theories. Liberals argue that the probability of conflict depends on whether or not states are democratic (Russett 1993, 1995), and on institutional linkages between international actors

(Keohane and Martin 1995). Constructivistis argue that the likelihood of conflict depends on the nature of shared understandings regarding norms and identities between actors (Wendt 1992, 1995).

That realists often disagree with liberals and constructivists should not obscure the fact that an expanding literature exists in which a variety of realist scholars –all of whom, as will be seen, are best understood as falling outside Waltzian neorealism - have sought to answer the very same question that guides nonrealist analyses: which factors besides the distribution of military capabilities systematically cause the probability of conflict to vary? These realist scholars point to three material factors other than the distribution of capabilities that affect the probability of conflict: technology, geography, and international economic pressure. First, the importance of technology is identified by realists such as Robert Jervis, Barry Buzan, Charles Glaser, and Stephen Van Evera. Technology innovation affects a range of factors that have a beating on conflict, such as the offense-defense balance and offense-defense differentiation (Jervis 1978; Quster 1977; and Glaser 1994-95), (2) "interaction capacity," that is, the volume, speed, range, and reliability of communication (Buzan 1993,72-80); (3) reconnaissance capabilities (Gaddis 1987, 232) ; and (Waltz 1979) ; and (4) the case of extracting economic resources from conquered territory, which depends substantially on whether productive capacity is based on knowledge-intensive/ technological industries or more traditional "smokestack"/ natural resource industries (Van Evera 1990-91,14-16;and Kaysen 1990,49,53). Second, realists, including Stephen Walt and Stephen Krasner, identify the importance of geography, which affects both the utility of employing military force (Walt 1987,23-24;Jervis 1978, 183-86,194-96;and Bueno de Mesquita 1981,40-44) and access to raw material (Krasner 1978; and Jervis 1978,179).Third, realists such as Gilpin and Wohlforth underscore the significance of international economic pressure, which lead to fluctuations in the economic opportunity cost of an assertive foreign policy stance (Gilpin 1977;Wohlforth1994-95;and Kennedy 1987) and affect whether or not states can most cost-effectively influence other states through informal economic, as opposed to formal military means (Gilpin 1981,especially 132-33,138-40;Huntington 1993;Lake 1996 ;and Pollins 1994).

None of the aforementioned material factors involves ideas or institutions, which are the focus of nonrealist theories such as liberalism and constructivism (Wendt and Friedheim 1995: 691-92). These material factors make conquest more- or- less cost effective- and therefore more-or-less likely-irrespective of institutional characteristics or shared understanding about norms and identities. This is not to suggest that these material factors provide a comprehensive understanding of the cause of conflict, nor that they are of equal importance. Rather, what it underscores is the fact that realist scholars identify a range of material factors other than the distribution of military capabilities that influence the probability of conflict.

Until now, there has been confusion whether the preceding realist arguments can be incorporated into the Waltzian neorealist framework. Some of these realist writers portray themselves as amending and revising, rather than critiquing the Waltzian neorealist approach (Glaser 1994-95;Buzan 1993;and Walt 1987). As emphasized, neorealism's conception of state behavior is based on the assumption that states are conditioned by the mere possibility of conflict. The preceding analyses simply do not follow from neorealism's worst –case /possibilistic assumption ; the underlying argument advanced by these realist scholars –that the probability of conflict varies systematically according to factor other than the distribution of capabilities –instead serves to undermine this neorealist assumption. With their implicit emphasis on probabilities, these analyses are incompatible with the Waltzian framework: incorporating any of these factors into neorealism would gut the theory's worst-case / possibilistic assumption, thereby destroying neorealism's internal coherence. This helps to explain why Waltz is so resistant to include any additional international –level variables beyond the distribution of capabilities into his theory. In the end, each of the preceding argument can be more productively incorporated into a competing realist framework –postclassical realism-that is based on the underlying assumption that actors make decisions based on the probability of conflict.

Before outlining postclassical realism's remaining two assumptions about state behavior, it should be noted that the possibility/ probability distinction outlined here subsumes an emerging debate within realism between what Jack Snyder terms "aggressive" and "defensive" realists (Snyder 1991,11-12). Snyder argues that aggressive realists, who are sometimes also referred to as "offensive" realists, believe offensive military action often contributes to security, whereas defensive realists reach the opposite conclusion (Ibid. ,12). In turn, Benjamin Frankel maintains that aggressive realists" posit that security in the international system is scare," whereas defensive realist contend security is more plentiful and are "more optimistic about the likelihood of avoiding war" (Frankel 1996: xv-xvi).

In practice, an implicit worst-case assumption regarding the expected future behavior of rising powers leads aggressive realists like Mearsheimer to assert that states" seek opportunities to weaken potential adversaries" as a means of enhancing security, and hence to regard security as being scare in the system

(Mearsheimer 1990 :12). Within a worst –case framework, states focus on the balance of capabilities and are conditioned by the fear that a rising power might become aggressive at some point. In this view, states are inclined to undertake offensive military action to remove or cripple rising powers in order to forestall the possibility of coercive behavior once potential competitors become predominant.

In contrast, adopting a probabilistic view leads to a different conclusion: given that preventive war is risky and costly, acting preemptively contribute to security only when a significant probability exists that the rising power will aggressively use military force when it becomes predominant in the future–which, for defensive realists such as Jervis, Glaser, and Walt, depends not just on the balance of capabilities, but also on technology, geography, and international economic pressures. Ultimately, defensive realists have a much more conditional view than aggressive realists as to whether offensive military action enhances security –and hence see security as often being plentiful – exactly because of their implicit focus on the probability of conflict.

That the aggressive / defensive debate ultimately reflects a deeper divergence within realism regarding assumption does not in any way diminish its significance. Understanding that the aggressive /defensive debate is rooted in the possibility /probability distinction is vital, however, because it helps explain why this intra –realist dispute is in fact occurring and more importantly it underscores the need to delineate the assumption according to which realists diverge. Tracing empirical disputes such as the aggressive/defensive realist debate back to underlying differences regarding assumption is imperative to promoting cumulation within realist theory; focusing on assumptions makes it possible to interconnect a whole series of empirical disputes within realism and promote aggregation across a broad range of cases.

SHORT TEAM VERSUS LONG TERM

When security pressures are immediate and high, a rational actor will significantly discount the future in order to protect it from elimination by stronger forces. " The focus of postclassical realism on the probability- and not on the possibility- of conflict results in a conception of the international system as often having lower security pressures than neorealists assume" (Brooks, 1997). In the postclassical realist paradigm the states discount the future to a lesser degree than is assumed by Waltzian neorealists. That does not mean that the postclassical realism subordinates the long term state objectives to short term military security arrangements. Rather, the states are seen as making regularly intertemporal trade offs.

Gilpin's realist analysis makes an excellent contrast to Waltzian neorealism regarding intertemporal trade-offs. In his analysis, the actors do not make worst-case assumptions but are instead conditioned by the probability of conflict. Adding to this he further stated that the actors will often make trade offs between short term and long term objectives.

In comparison to Gilpin's more dynamic realist framework, Waltzian neorealism has been criticized on the ground that it is a very static theory (Ruggie, 1983; and Nye 1988: 245). It should not be seen as an omission on the part of Waltz and his followers. The static nature of neorealism reflects its worst- case/possibilistic focus. As a result, neorealism always holds that the rational actor will always focus on short term objectives.

POWER VERSUS SECURITY: POSTCLASSICAL REALISM AND WALTZIAN NEOREALISM

The prevailing tendency among scholars has been

to understand Gilpin's analysis of state preferences as reflecting Waltzian neorealism not as providing a different and competitive understanding. Gilpin argues that all realists are united in assuming "the primacy in all political life of power and security in human motivation" (Gilpin 1984: 290). While setting a clear objective before actors, Gilpin's analysis is complicated and ambiguous "by the fact that the pursuit of power and security do not always perfectly overlap" (Brooks, 1997). Gilpin defines power as resources: the combined "military, economic, and technological capabilities of states" (Gilpin, 1981:13). Power within it contains two different elements- military preparedness and economic capability, which sometimes will be incompatible. When it is said that states are seen as pursuing power, it leads to a different view about state behaviour than when they are said as maximizing security. Maximizing security implies that military security arrangements will trump those of economic capacity whenever these two are in conflict as neorealists argue. To say that states pursue power is suggestive of the fact that states will make trade offs between economic capacity and military preparedness, given that power is ultimately a function of both economic and military might. Thus, it is unclear whether Gilpin views states as ultimately pursuing power or security (Grieco, 1997).

On the other hand, Waltz has been very clear on this issue while arguing "the ultimate concern of states is not for power but for security" (Waltz, 1989:40). In his view the pursuit of security and power do not always coincide. He has been very explicit to say that a rational state will seek power only if security objective has first been ensured. Contradicting Waltz, Mearsheimer asserts that states ultimately "aim to maximize their relative power" (Mearsheimer, 1994-95:12). Notwithstanding this, his ultimate conclusion has been to show the military basis of power and to assert that states aim "to acquire more military power at the expense of potential rivals" (Ibid:13). Apart from military capability, economic capacity has been another component of power. In his analysis Mearsheimer ends up concluding that states above all seek to maximize their security but in doing so will sometimes increase their power. "In circumstances where the pursuit of power and security do, in fact, conflict, Mearsheimer would undoubtedly end up agreeing with Waltz's view that states first seek to ensure their military security before they pursue power" (Brooks, 1997). In contrast, the neorealists view that states ultimately seek security not power.

HIERARCHY OF OBJECTIVES

What adds confusion to Gilpin's analysis is whether he views states as having a hierarchy of objectives when he views that although states have a wide variety of objectives, all of the "more noble goals" of society "will be lost unless one makes provision for one's security in the power struggle among groups" (Gilpin, 1984: 290-291). What is inherent in this analysis is the fact that security requirements trump the pursuit of other state objectives. Hence his analysis is compatible with the Waltzian neorealist conception of state preferences (Grieco, 1990:39). At the other end Gilpin maintains that states do not have a hierarchy of objectives; instead he argues that theories that "assume that one can speak of a hierarchy of objectives" actually "misrepresent the behaviour and decision making processes of states" (Gilpin; 1981:19). In the end, he asserts that "it is the mix and trade offs of objectives rather than their ordering that is critical to an understanding of foreign policy" (Ibid:22). While arguing that military security is the vital priority of a state, he does not view rational states as privileging short term military preparedness over economic capacity in the manner that neorealists argue. "Gilpin can be best understood as arguing that states do have a hierarchy of objectives, yet it is a much more flexible hierarchy than neorealists envision" (Stephen G Brooks, 1997). It can be said that postclassical realism views power as the ultimate objective of states unlike neorealists who view security as the ultimate goal.

The postclassical realist view that states pursue power is compatible with Gilpin's contention that it is the tradeoffs not ordering of objectives that is important. As Stephen G Brooks remarks: "In marked contrast to neorealism, postclassical realism argues that a rational decision maker may decide to trade off military preparedness to some degree when the potential net gains in terms of enhanced economic capacity are substantial relative to the probability of security losses. States will be especially likely to make such trade offs when their economic resources are highly constrained". He cites Gilpin and Kennedy's argument to show "that a declining power may rationally decide to retrench from some of its external positions, enhancing long term economic capacity at the cost of somewhat reducing short term protection vis-a-vis potential military adversaries" (Gipin,1981:194-97; Kennedy, 1987 and Wohlforth, 1994-95).

CONCEPT OF POWER: DIFFERENT PERSPECTIVES

'The idea that state seeks power provided the foundation of the classical realism of Morgenthau, Reinhold Niebuhr and others. Is the post classical realist view of power different from classical understanding of power as the dominant goal of international actors? In practice, a crucial difference exists between the two approaches concerning their view of power. Specifically, although both theories regard the international system as a competition for power, they disagree as to the form and intensity that the pursuit of power will take.

Classical realism views decision makers as constantly

striving to dominate other : policymakers are characterized as being guided by a rapacious lust for power Within classical realism, therefore, power is regarded as an end in itself: for Morgenthau, one's "lust for power would be satisfied only if the last man became the object of his domination" (Morgenthau 1946, 193). As a result, states are viewed as always actively seeking any possible means to advance their power over other nations, taking military advantage of weaker states whenever they have the chance (Zakaria 1992: 194; and Schweller 1994:104-105).

Postclassical realism advocates a very different perspective: state decision makers do not maximize power because of an insatiable desire to dominate others; rather states pursue power because doing so allows for maximum flexibility in achieving the nation's instrumental interest. In other words, postclassical realism holds that decision makers pursue power because it is the mechanism by which to achieve the state's overriding objectives (Gilpin 1996: 6; and Gilpin 1975: 23). States are seen as seeking to enhance their share of economic resources, and hence their power, because it provides the foundation for military capacity and furthermore because economic resources can themselves be used to influence other international actors. Because power is viewed as a mechanism, and not an end in itself, states are expected to pursue power subject to cost-benefit calculation. In this respect, Gilpin argues that "there have been many cases throughout history in which states have forgone apparent opportunities to increase their power because they judged the cost to be too high" (Gilpin1981: 51).

The postclassical realist assertion that states pursue power does not mean that states are seen as necessarily engaging in conquest in order to capture economic resources controlled by other states is a method to increase power, but it is not the only method. States can also enhance their relative share of economic resources, and hence their power, through nonmilitary means, such as: (1) by actively seeking changes in international trade patterns (Krasner 1976; Lake 1984;Huntington 1993;and Gowa 1994) (2) by creating more efficient institution to reduce transaction costs and better ensure property rights (North 1990;Alt and Shepsle 1990;and Kang 1995,563-66); (3) by using economic leverage to secure supplies of inexpensive raw materials and other supplies from weaker states (Hirschman 1980;and Krasner 1978) and (Waltz 1979 and (4) by reducing nonproductive expenditure to free up resources for economic advancement (Kennedy 1987;and Gilpin 1981). The post-classical realist conception of international behavior asserts that in situations when the first strategy, conquest, is the most cost-effective means to increase power, states will be prone to use military force in order to enhance their power. In contrast, in situation when one or a combination of the earlier mentioned nonmilitary strategies provides the most cost-effective means to increase power, international competition will still be endemic, but states will not be prone to use military force to further their power; rather, as is the case today among the major industrialized powers, states will rely on nonmilitary means to enhance their power. "In comparison to neorealism, therefore, postclassical realism advances a much more conditional view of whether incentives for military aggression exist in the system; this conditional assessment undergirds the postclassical realist view that states will not make worst-case assumptions but will, instead, be conditioned by the probability of conflict (Brooks,1997).

In summary, postclassical realism regards states as ultimately seeking to increase their share of economic resources and, hence, their power. This focus on power resembles classical realism, but postclassical realism has a very different understanding of how and why states pursue power in the international system.

WALTZ'S DEFINITION OF STRUCTURE: A CRITIQUE

As mentioned above, Waltz defined a political structure by its ordering principle, the distribution of capabilities, and the functional differentiation or non-differentiation of the units. According to this definition, the nuclear revolution in military technology is a unit-level change and not a structural change (Waltz, 1986 : 327). Joseph Nye finds it " particularly odd to see nuclear technology described as a unit characteristic" (Nye, 1988 : 243). He and Keohane argue that such factors as "the intensity of international interdependence or the degree of institutionalization of international rules do not vary from one state to another on the basis of their internal characteristics... and are therefore not unit-level factors" (Nye and Keohane, Autumn 1987: 725-53). They conclude that "making the unit' level the dumping ground for all unexplained variance is an impediment to the development of theory" (Ibid) .The purpose of not including military technology in his definition of structure "was to give a purely positional picture of a system so the notion of structure would be transposable from one substantive context to another" (Robert Powell, 1994:325).

Inclusion of military technology in the definition of structure would make the system less transposable. Looking at the cost of greater transposability, Robert Powell is of the view that "Waltz's theory cannot account for variation in outcomes like the probability of war that may be due to the nuclear revolution" (Ibid). The question crops up while military technology was not included in his notion of structure given his goal of transposability, why the distribution of capabilities across states "be included in the definition and not other characteristics of states that could be cast in distributional terms?" (Waltz, 1986 : 329). Waltz is of the view that state "behaviour varies more with differences of power than with differences in ideology, in internal structure of property relations, or in governmental form" (Ibid). Others are of the view that the definition of structure based on the distribution of capabilities rather than distribution of something else seems to have greater explanatory power (Buzan, Jones and Little, 1993: 54-56). The criticisms of Waltz's spare definition of structure does not any way diminish the gravity of the consequences of nuclear revolution and the latter does not depend on whether the title one attaches to "structural" or "unit level" to this change.

NEOREALISM AND NEOLIBERAL DEBATE

Neorealism greatly discounts the role of international institutions in shaping the international politics and holds that the prospects for cooperation in anarchy are nebulous. Neoliberalism questions the logical coherence of the neorealist argument finding out a mistake in the logic. Further, it argues that the explanatory power of neorealism is weak when compared to neoliberalism. Surveying the neorealist research programme Keohane in his contribution to neorealism and its critics questions the predictive power of neorealism and advances " a modified structural research programme", which would " pay much more attention to the roles of institutions and rules than does structural realism. Indeed, a structural interpretation of the emergence of international rules and procedures, and of obedience to them by states, is one of the rewards that could be expected from this modified structural research program" (Keohane, Theory of World Politics 1986 : 194).

Advocating an institutional approach more clearly seen in his work, After Hegemony (Keohane, 1984), Keohane challenges neorealism. He puts the question "Under what conditions can independent countries cooperate in the world political economy (Ibid: 9)? Is cooperation among states is possible in the absence of a hegemon? Keohane begins his analysis "with realist insights about the role of power....[Keohane's] central arguments draw more on the institutionalist tradition, arguing that cooperation can under some conditions develop on the basis of complementary interests and that institutions, broadly defined, affect the patterns of cooperation that emerge" (Ibid: 9). In short institutions play a significant role in promoting international cooperation in ways that neorealism has failed to appreciate.

Keohane challenged both the logical coherence and the explanatory power of neorealism. Attacking the logic, Keohane writes, "I propose to show, on the basis of their own assumptions that the characteristic pessimism of realism does not follow. I seek to demonstrate that realist assumptions about world politics are consistent with the formation of institutionalized arrangements, containing rules and principles, which promote cooperation " (Ibid, p.67). In sum, Keohane intends to start with the same set of core assumption that neorealism does and then shows that cooperation is compatible with these assumptions.

Keohane attempts this demonstration in the context of the repeated prisoners' dilemma. There are two steps to the demonstration. The first is to argue that the repeated prisoners' dilemma is a reasonable model for the international system envisioned in neorealism, that is, this model is compatible with realism's central assumption about the international system. Although he does not develop this point at length, Keohane claims," Not all situations in world politics or international political economy take the form of prisoner's dilemma, but many do" (Ibid., p. 68). As further support for the claim that the repeated prisoners' dilemma is generally seen to be compatible with realism's basic assumption, he might also have referred to Jervis's belief that this game is an appropriate model for studying the security dilemma (Jervis, January 1978 : 167-214 and 170 in particular). The second step in Keohane's argument is to appeal to the folk theorem, which shows that the mutually cooperative outcome can occur in equilibrium in an infinitely repeated prisoners' dilemma, if the actors do not discount the future too much (Fudenberg and Maskin, 1986 : 533-54). These two steps taken together imply that cooperation is compatible with realism.

Writing in 1983, Keohane believed his neoliberal institutional approach would prove to have greater explanatory power than neorealism. But, a definitive test of his institutional approach was not yet possible because the world was "only just entering the posthegemonic era." (Keohane, 1984a: 218). It was too soon to test the explanatory power of an argument that predicted that international institutions and cooperation would persist despite the absence of a hegemon. Instead of a test, Keohane offered a "plausibility probe" of his institutional approach in the cases of international trade, finance, and petroleum (Robert Keohane in Baldwin, 1993 : 269-301, and particularly p. 292; and Keohane, After Hegemony).

According to Robert Powell, "one can envision two general types of response to Keohane's neoliberal challenge to neorealism. The first addresses Keohane's challenge to the logic of neorealism's analysis of the problem of international cooperation. This response would show that Keohane had really not based his argument on the same set of core assumptions that neorealism does. If this were the case, then Keohane's argument that neorealism's conclusions about the prospects of international cooperation do not follow from its assumptions would be invalid. If, more specifically, the repeated prisoners' dilemma is incompatible with neorealism's core assumptions about the international system, then showing that cooperation in this game is possible would say nothing about what follows from neorealism's assumptions" (Robert Powell,1994: 328).

The second type of response is more empirical. It would say that neorealism never claimed that international cooperation was logically incompatible with neorealism's assumptions. So, showing that cooperation is possible given these assumptions does not contradict neorealism. The real question is how much international cooperation exists and whether neorealism or neoliberalism does a better job of accounting for the observed pattern of international cooperation. This response would then go on to compare the relative explanatory power of these two approaches.

Joseph Grieco developed both types of response to the institutionalist challenge. He argued that Keohane had not started with the same assumption neorealism does. In using the repeated prisoners' dilemma, Keohane implicitly had assumed that states try to maximize their absolute gains. According to Grieco, however, neorealism requires a state's utility function to reflect a concern for relative gains (Grieco," Anarchy and the Limits of cooperation," p. 129). Gowa made the same criticism of Axelord's use of the repeated prisoners' dilemma (Axelord, 1984) when he used this game to model international politics. (See Joanne Gowa," 1986 : 167-86 and particularly : 172-79). Consequently, Keohane does not "show, on the basis of their [realists'] own assumptions, that the characteristic pessimism of realism does not follow," as he claimed (Keohane, 1984a, p. 67). In cooperation Among Nations, Grieco tried to assess the relative explanatory power of neorealism and institutionalism. He considers the case of negotiations over nontariff barriers during the Tokyo Round of the General Agreement on Tariffs and Trade, a case that he believes poses a hard test for realism, and concludes that realism explains this case better than does institutionalism. The latest round of the debate between realism and liberalism was now fully engaged (See Nye, 1984).

On three issues- the meaning and implications of anarchy, the problem of absolute and relative gains and the tension between cooperation and distribution- the debate between neorealists and neoliberals rests.

THE MEANING AND IMPLICATIONS OF ANARCHY

Waltz's central assumption is typically Hobbesian. He wrote: "The state among states, it is often said, conducts its affairs in the brooding shadow of violence. Because some states may at time use force, all states must be prepared to do so- or live at the mercy of their militarily more vigorous neighbours. Among states, the state of nature is a state of war (Waltz, 1979:102). Nevertheless, Waltz thinks that chaos, destruction and death are closely associated with hierarchy (government) than is the case with anarchy. Thus, he argues that the criterion of use of force or the constant fear of its use is not sufficient to explain the domestic / international divide. This has more to do with the different modes of organization in the use of force employed by the government within its territorial limits and states outside in the context of anarchy (Ibid:103).

According to Grieco, neoliberalism entails five propositions out of which the last three are worth quoting. "Third, international anarchy is the principal force shaping the motives and actions of states. Fourth, states in anarchy are preoccupied with power and security, and predisposed towards conflict and competition, and often fail to cooperate even in the face of common interests. Finally, international institutions affect the prospects for cooperation only marginally" (Grieco, 1988 : 118-19). Keohane used the prisoners' dilemma to show that anarchy did not imply a lack of cooperation. In Grieco's analysis Keohane's model was misspecified because he neglected states'concern for relative gains. Duncan Snidel then tried to show that anarchy does not imply a lack of cooperation even if states are concerned with relative gains (Grieco, Powell and Snidal, 1993: 729-43).

There are two formulations of anarchy. The first is that anarchy means the "lack of a common government" that can enforce agreements among the states or more generally among the units (Robert Axelrod and Robert Keohane, 1988: 226). Robert Art and Jervis together explain that "international politics takes place in an arena that has no central governing body. No agency exists above individual states with authority and power to make laws and settle disputes. States can make commitments and treaties, but no sovereign power ensures compliance and punishes deviations. Thus, the absence of a supreme power is what is meant by the anarchic environment of international politics" (Robert Art and Robert Jervis:1).

This above formulation is silent about the means the units have at their disposal to further their interests. It says only about the lack of a central authority that can prevent them from resorting to means they have. "One advantage of defining anarchy without reference to the means available to the units is that it makes the concept of anarchy readily transposable different substantive domains.... Waltz weighed this advantage heavily in constructing his formulation of structure, so it is hardly surprising that he would adopt this first definition of anarchy" (Robert Powell, 1994: 331).

The second notion of anarchy refers to the means available to the units. In "Coordination and Collaboration," Arthur Stein begins by observing that many international relations scholars use anarchy to describe "the classic characterization of international politics as relations between sovereign entities dedicated to their own self-preservation, ultimately able to depend only on themselves, and prepared to use force" (Stein, "Coordination and Collaboration,"in Baldwin 1993 : 30). In effect, this second formulation adds another dimension to the lack of a central authority: namely, that one of the means available to the units is the use of force.

According to Robert Powell, "the addition of this second dimension has two consequences. First, it makes the transposability of the concept of anarchy more problematic. What, for example, is the analogue to using force for a firm facing a high risk of bankruptcy? If there is no analogue, then a group of firms facing a high risk of bankruptcy would not form an anarchic system according to this definition. If we want to argue that there is an analogue, what are criteria for establishing that one of the means open to a firm is analogue to a state's ability to resort to force? Of course, a definition of anarchy that reduces its transposability may have compensating advantages. Whether these potential advantages outweigh the disadvantage of a less transposable definition will be discussed below.

Second, adding another dimension raises important questions for international relations theory. Do the pattern of behavior generally associated with anarchic system, such as the tendencies for balances of power to form and-at least for neorealists-the limited prospects for international cooperation result from the lack of a central authority? Or, are these patterns more heavily influenced by implicit and unarticulated assumption about, say, the nature of military force that are subsumed in the second definition of anarchy?" (Powell, 1994:331).

Two arguments suggest that the emphasis on anarchy has been misplaced if anarchy means the lack of a central authority. These arguments suggest that conclusions often claimed to follow from the absence of a central authority do not. These conclusions require other supporting assumptions. The first argument is really an empirical observation. Keohane notes in his assessment of the debate between neorealism and neoliberalism that the modern state system, conventionally dated from 1648, has always been anarchic in the sense that it lacked a common government (Keohane, 1993). "Thus, anarchy, while perhaps a necessary condition, is certainly not sufficient to explain any of the variation in international politics during the modern era. In particular, anarchy cannot account for whatever variation in the level of international cooperation and institutionalization there has been" (Ibid).

The second argument is more theoretical and begins with a recent attempt to formalize the classic guns-versus-butter problem (Robert Powell, 1993 : 115-32). To summarize the model, there are two states. In each period a state must decide how much of its output to consume, how much to allocate to its military sector, and whether or not to attack the other state. Each state's utility is the discounted sum of its consumption in each period. As long as neither state attacks, the game continues. If a state attacks at some time, the game effectively ends in one of two ways. Either one state or the other will prevail by conquering the other. The odds that a state will prevail are simply the ratio of its military allocation to the other state's military allocation. The fact that a state's probability of victory depends on its military allocation creates a trade-off between current and expected future consumption. The more a state consumes today, the smaller its military allocation, and the higher the probability of defeat. Because defeat means a loss of future consumption, consuming more today reduces expected future consumption. The formal analysis of the game determines each state's equilibrium level of consumption and military spending that balances this trade-off.

The guns-versus-butter model shows that our emphasis on anarchy is misplaced. Neorealism expects balance-of-power politics to prevail whenever the system is anarchic and the units want to survive (Waltz, 1979 : 121). The guns-versus-butter model indicates that this expectation is too broad. Whether or not the states balance in the model depends on an assumption about military technology. Generalizing beyond this model, whether units balance or not depends as much on other features defining the strategic situation in which they interact as it does on the presence of anarchy.

To see that balancing depends on underlying assumptions about military technology, note that the guns-versus-butter game presumes a conventional military technology in which the probability of victory or defeat depends on the relative sizes of the opposing military forces. Given this stylized assumption about military technology, the states balance against each other in the way we would expect the units to do in an anarchic system (Ibid: 168). Now suppose that the states' strategic setting is different. Formalizing and stylizing the nuclear revolution in military technology, assume that there is, to use Bernard Brodie's term, an absolute weapon (Brodie, 1959). The probability of victory no longer depends on the relative size of the states' military forces. Rather, once both states have attained secure second-strike forces, war is certain to take a toll far higher than any potential gain. If we solve the model based on this assumption about military technology, the states will spend enough to acquire second-strike forces. But they will not spend more even if the other state does. There is no balancing here even through the system remains anarchic and the units still seek to survive. Buzan, Jones and Little reach the same conclusion in The Logic of Anarchy. They and Morrow offer the expansion of the Roman Empire as an important example of the failure of balances to form (See James Morrow, October 1988 : 75-97). The first notion of anarchy, albeit very transposable, does not imply balancing.

If defined as the absence of a central authority, anarchy encompasses systems in which states do and do not balance. Conversely, if anarchy is defined by addition of the notion of the potential use of force to the lack of a central authority, the transposability of the concept seems to be greatly limited, even if units generally will balance in such a system. The disadvantages of this limited concept of anarchy are quite high. "Even if neorealism's expectations about anarchic systems in which the use of force is a serious potential concern are correct, the arguments underlying these expectations cannot be transposed to systems in which the use of force among units is not at issue. Neorealist expectations about these systems may of course still prove to be correct, but they lack theoretical foundations" (Robert Powell, 1994: 333).

From this central assumption, Waltz developed several key propositions regarding anarchy. Thus, he seeks to define the formal organization of a sphere which would decide the possibility of co-operation, interdependence or integration among units. Within formally organized realms, units are forced to specialize, since the resultant interdependence does not threaten their survival. In a sphere where there is no central, authoritative regulator, benefits of increased specialization become relative. Specialization therefore enhances rather than decreases competition. The different units become closely interdependent, in direct proportion to the degree of specialization achieved by them. Within an anarchic structure units co-act while within a hierarchical realm they interact. In an anarchic set up, units are self-help entities. The idea of interdependence has a different meaning within nations than what it is among nations (Kenneth Waltz, 1979: 104). The structure of anarchy thus limits co-operation in two ways. First- it creates the possibility of unequal distribution of co-operative gains. Second, it obstructs cooperation by accentuating some form of dependence on others through co-operative endeavours and exchange of goods and services (Ibid:106).

For Waltz, the meaning of anarchy is not only the absence of government but also the presence of chaos and disorder. Although it can be argued that the international system is very often orderly and peaceful, permitting a whole range of institutions seems to modify the behaviour of the units. Waltz believes that such views confuse structure with process. Further although, they could be accurate in describing the given reality, they detract from the explanatory power of the theory particularly as their exponents were unable to supply any third principle to describe societies that were neither anarchic nor hierarchical. Waltz's conclusion is emphatic, "Hierarchic elements within international structures limit and restrain the exercise of sovereignty but only in ways strongly conditioned by the anarchy of the larger system. The anarchy of that order strongly affects the likelihood of cooperation, the extent of arms arguments, and the jurisdiction of international organization" (Ibid: 115-116).

Waltz's treatment of the concept of balance of power also reflects his structural or systematic perspective. For him, balance of power is not a preferred option. In an anarchical milieu devoid a central regulator, survival becomes the primary objective of states and balance of power provides the mechanism through which they secure their survival. In Waltz's words – "If security is something the state wants, then this desire, together with the conditions in which all states exist imposes certain requirements on a foreign policy that pretends to be rational. The requirements are imposed by an automatic sanction. Departure from the rational model imperils the survival of the state" (Ibid: Kenneth Waltz, 1990: 198). Unlike the classical realists, however, Waltz did not base the theory of balance on the psychological predisposition of statesmen and realist politicians. He preferred to use the game theory to justify the theory of balance. He, however, admitted that general games might provide two different solutions. Participants may either prefer maximization, where all the players will cooperate to achieve the largest possible gain. Alternatively, players may be more interested in dividing the gains amongst themselves than increasing the undifferentiated gain itself. In this case, instead of cooperating with each other to maximize individual benefits, players are more interested to increase their own share or preserve their initial advantage. This tendency is referred to as a zero sum or a constant sum game which reflects more accurately the empirical domain of international politics. Thus, the goal of sheer survival makes balance of power inevitable. In Waltz's formulation:

> If some states seek an advantage over others, they combine; if other states want to counteract this advantage, they in turn combine. If the advantage sought is measured in terms of power to destroy or damage another state, then the threatened state refrains from the effort to increase its strength only at the risk of its survival. Pursuing a balance of power policy is still a matter of choice, but the alternatives are those of probable suicide on the one hand and active playing of the power politics game on the other (Ibid:110).

To summarize, Waltz conceives the international system as self help system and treats states as defensive actors in as much as their primary, though not exclusive intention is self preservation. Thus, while states are not necessarily self aggrandizing, they are compulsively self help units, looking for their own security amidst an anarchical milieu where the probability of threats to their survival is always real. Thus, states are primarily concerned about their own security and forced to view other states as potential threats. This makes balance of power the only theory of international politics, which explains fully the systemic or structural logic of anarchical order. Having ruled out the possibility of any third kind of system- other than the hierarchical and the anarchic- Waltz could confidently talk of the self-perpetuation of the international system, as states can only logically be self help units within an anarchical system devoid of an authoritative or commanding sovereign regulator. Balance of power is essentially a balance of capabilities and states have to continuously judge the capabilities of other states to maintain the balance. Balance, again, is defined by the number of poles in the balance which refer to the number of states who can seriously threaten the existence of others.

Waltz, contrary to many other neo-realists, thought that the bipolar balance was the ideal mechanism for the international system since it was easier to manage with a lesser number of interested and capable players involved. What is the value of neorealism, then, as a theory of security, if it cannot explain major foreign policy outcomes in different parts of the world? In his defence, he has provided two fold texts for his theory of security. First – he emphatically pointed out that no theory can ever claim to explain "everything" and neorealism was no exception. Second – the validity of neo-realism did not depend on empirical cases; its validity rested on the internal consistency of propositions constituting the theory and its utility depended on its capacity to generate a sophisticated research programme on security at the systems level. For Waltz, it was sufficient to establish that, contrary to the claims of the interdependency, functionalist and pluralist scholars, there was no fundamental change in the logic of the system, and the fact that such an alternation was not possible without the contemporary international system changing from anarchical into a hierarchical one. At a normative level; neorealism did not rule out the possibility of an eventual transformation of the anarchical self help system into a world government based on collective security, no more than its predecessor, classical realism had conceded the logical or theoretical possibility and normative desirability to substitute a balance of power system based on threats and counter threats for a new world order or a stateless society with perfect co-operation at all levels. However, the primary endeavour of the neo-realist intervention was to precisely deny the possibility of any alteration in the anarchical system, a denial which was not based on the amorality inherent wickedness of a handful of crafty statesmen, a neo-classical realism but on the structural attributes of the system and the logic of survival of the units.

In the post cold war period of international politics the neorealists argue that the states will start competing and balancing over economic issues after the end of the cold war much as they competed and balanced over security issues during the cold war. Samuel Huntington resting on neorealist analysis predicated of the continued importance of US primacy (S. Huntington 1993: 68-83). He and others are of the view that the prospects of "military conflict between major states is unlikely" (Ibid: 93). As the analysis of two definitions of anarchy shows, "neither definition of anarchy provides adequate theoretical support for the neorealist analysis of international politics if the use of force is not a relevant concern" (Robert Powell 1994: 334). The first definition of anarchy can be transposed readily to a system in which the use of force is not at issue. This does not support the neorealist claims that anarchy implies balance of power politics. The second definition of anarchy implying balancing when force is at issue cannot be transposed to a domain in which force is assumed not at issue. Huntington puts emphasis on the importance of international primacy believing that the politics of international economics is more like a system with conventional military technology. In contrast, Jervis questions the importance of international primacy believing that the politics of international economics is more like a system with an absolute weapon (Jervis, 1993 : 57-59). In the words of Robert Powell (1994: 334) "In either case, the neorealist- neoliberal debate's emphasis on the lack of a central authority is misplaced". As Charles Lipson describes, "The idea of anarchy is, in a sense, the Rosetta stone of international relations... But what was once a blinding insight-profound and evocative- has ossified and become blinding in other sense of the word- limiting and obscuring" (Lipson, 1984 : 80).

THE NEOREALISTS AND NEOLIBERALS ON ABSOLUTE AND RELATIVE GAINS

The second major issue remaining at the crux of the debate between neorealism and neoliberalism is the problem of absolute and relative gains. Neorealism assumes that states are solely concerned with relative gains. In the words of Waltz " states that feel insecure must ask how the gain will be divided. They are compelled to ask not 'Will both of us gain?' but 'Who will gain more?'" (Waltz, 1979 :105). In contrast, Keohane in After Hegemony advancing his institutional challenge assumes that states are trying to maximize their absolute gains, that is, the states' preferences " are based on their assessment of their own welfare, not that of others" (Keohane, 1984a : 66). He then analyzes the problem of cooperation in terms of repeated prisoners' dilemma.

Criticizing Keohane's advocacy of absolute gains, Grieco asserts that " realism expects a state's utility function to incorporate two distinct terms. It needs to include the state's individual pay off... reflecting the realist view that states are motivated by absolute gains. Yet it must also include a term integrating both the states' individual pay off... and the partner's payoff... in such a way that gaps favouring the state add to its utility while, more importantly, gaps favouring the partner detract from it" (Grieco, 1988 : 129). It may be said that the debate about absolute gains and relative gains is the debate about states' utility functions.

On the other hand, carrying forward the debate Robert Powell advocates the need to distinguish between two possibilities. "The first is that a state's concern or, more precisely, the degree of its concern for relative gains is the product of the strategic environment in which the state finds itself. If so, then the degree of concern is likely to vary as the environment, say the intensity of the security dilemma, varies. In this case, the strategic setting facing the state induces a concern for relative gains. The second possibility is that a state's degree of concern does not vary and is the same regardless of its environment" (Powell,1994: 335).

Both neorealism and neoliberalism agree on this fact that this concern is induced. Grieco believes that a state's sensitivity to relative gains "will be a function of, and will vary in response to, at least six factors" (Grieco, 1988 : 610). These include the fungibility of power across issues, the length of the shadow of the future, and whether the relative gains or losses occur over military or economic matters (Ibid: 610-11). In a similar vein neoliberalism admits that the degree of concern varies. Similarly, Keohane in his appraisal of the neorealist- neoliberal debate emphasizes that the concern for relative gains is conditional.

In the opinion of Powell two implications follow from the above conclusion that the degree of a state's concern for relative gains is conditional and varies from situation to situation. "The first is that the debate about what to assume about a state's preferences or utility function is largely irrelevant and reflects a basic misunderstanding of the role of models". The concern for relative gains can be induced in two ways. The constraints that lead to this concern can be explicitly represented. While assuming that the states are concerned with maximizing absolute gains, they are as such induced to be concerned with relative gains by the strategic environment or setting in which they are attempting to do so. "The second way to induce a concern for relative gains is to represent this concern in the state's utility function. When done in this way, the model is in effect a reduced form for some more complicated and unspecified models in which the strategic constraints would induce this concern" (Powell, 1994: 336).

The question arises about which approach to modelling a state's concern is better? In Power's opinion this cannot be answered a priori. The models are simply tools. It is like asking "whether a hammer or saw is better. The answer depends on whether the task at hand is driving nails or cutting wood". In his words "the debates about what to assume about preferences cannot be resolved without reference to an overall evaluation of the entire model and the substantive problem being modelled. By focusing solely on what to assume about preferences and not evaluating this assumption in the overall context of the entire model, the neorealist-neoliberal debate about states' preferences seems largely irrelevant. It reflects a basic misunderstanding of the role of models" (Ibid: 336-37).

The second implication is that the degree of a state's concern for relative gains is a function of, and depends on strategic environment. "A concern for relative gains is an effect and not a cause... Cooperation and concern for relative gains may co-vary, but one does not cause the other. The causes for both are the underlying features of the states' strategic environment that jointly induce a concern for relative gains and thereby make cooperation difficult" (Ibid:337).

Lipson tries to relate differences in strategic environments inherent in military and economic issues to differences in state's discount factors and through the differences in those discount factors, to the likelihood of international cooperation in military and economic affairs (Lipson, 1993: 408-20). In approval of this need Jervis is eloquent: "The conditions under which states seek to maximize their relative as opposed to their absolute gains need more exploration" (Jervis, Realism, 1988). The arguments for explaining the concern for relative gains might seem to be based on the notion of anarchy that there is lack of a central authority, which leads to balancing and a concern for relative gains. "This answer, however, fails at least for two reasons. Anarchy has been a constant feature of the modern international system. It cannot therefore account for variation in the degree of a state's concern for absolute gains...anarchy does not imply balancing" (Powell, 1994: 337).

As stated earlier, the neo-realists do not rule out the prospects of co-operation altogether. Similarly, the neo-liberals, who have been much more optimistic and enthusiastic about the possibility of co-operation and peace within the international system, do not deny the assumptions of anarchy and the international system being primarily a self-help system. The neorealist neoliberal controversy revolves around issues of co-operation and conflict between or among states, the extent and range of co-operation, the impact of institutions on state motivation and behaviour, the nature and consequences of anarchy, priority of state goals, intentions and capabilities, and the vital issue of absolute and relative gains. The neorealists and neoliberals are divided on the nature and consequences of international anarchy, even while agreeing on the anarchical nature of international system.

The liberals however, are divided on the prospects of international cooperation in security or military matters. While analysts like Arthur Stein believe that much depends on the issue on which co-operation is sought, others such as Charles Lipson, admit the limits of meaningful inter-state co-operation or the prospects of liberal institutionalism in security issues (Charles Lipson, 1984).

Lipson argues that political and economic relationships are far more institutionalized than military and security affairs and therefore should be accepted as frames of references when we talk about inter state co-operation. However, staunch liberals like Robert Axelord and Robert Keohane dismiss Lipson's suggestive case for dichotomous frames and focus on issues such as mutuality of interests, the shadow of the future, and the number of players involved in a co-operative game etc (Keohane and Axelord in Baldwin, 1993).

Keohane and Axelrod argue that any standard payoff structure is a combination of both conflictual and cooperative payoffs, so that a game might become more or less conflictual with time.

The shadow of the future is an interesting formulation developed by liberals, particularly Axelrod. Put simply, it means that the actor's perception about the future prospects of a peaceful interaction process promotes co-operation modelled on regular Prisoners' Dilemma games. The shadow is made up of four analytic components such as long term horizons, regularity of states, reliability of information about the action of others and a quick feedback (Keohane and Axelrod, Ibid. 1993: 91-92). These components explain the differences regarding the extent of co-operation achieved in security and economic issues. The reason is that while retaliation is virtually automatic on economic matters – particularly in highly institutionalized domains the same cannot be guaranteed in security affairs. Such a prospect of limited co-operation between national actors in security affairs undoubtedly pushes the liberals towards the realist case. Keohane and Axelord, nevertheless, maintain that the shadow of the future does not depend on the "objective attributes" of the above situation. Further, they argue that institutions could play a significant role in modifying standard state behaviour. Institutions thus become significant in determining the extent of the shadow of the future, since they "embody and affect actor's expectations" (Ibid: 94). The number of players engaged in a Prisoner's Dilemma game and the structure of their mutual relations also determine the prospect of co-operation. Axelord's hypothesis regarding "effective reciprocity" is based on three conditions: the players' ability to precisely identify defectors; focussed retaliation against such defectors; and sufficient long run incentives for all to punish any defector (Ibid: 94-95).

Axelord and Keohane find a convenient via media in the idea of regimes which provide standards against which actions can be measured, supply information about actor's compliance", build and maintain "reputation" and undertake responsibility for decentralized agreement of rules" (Ibid: 97). Emphasizing the merits of institutions, they maintain: "Institutions alter the pay off structures facing actors, they may lengthen the shadow of the future and they may enable N-person games to be broken down into games with smaller number of actors" (Ibid:98).

The most significant aspects of the argument of liberal scholars is that co-operation and defection do not mutually cancel each other. In a wide variety of co-operative sum games, involving multiple actors, solutions are either co-operative or conflictual, depending on several factors. Axelord and Kenneth Oye, among others, have worked on the concept of iterated or repeated games as a strategy to increase co-operation among rational, self interested actors (Oye Kenneth A. 1985: 1-24; Axelrod Robert 1984).

The realists have strongly responded to the liberal view point, which in the absence of a better alternative, can be described as liberal institutionalism. For instance, Grieco criticizes the liberals for having grossly underestimated the significance of survival instinct or self preservation as the basic motivation for state behaviour, which he thinks, is a natural consequence of anarchy (Grieco 1993:126). For Grieco, the issue is not whether states seek co-operation because co-operation is good and therefore, desirable states are individualistic, but their mode of calculation resembles more of Hobbesian pessimism than Lockean optimism. Thus, states may seek cooperation, but they would definitely prefer relative gains over absolute gains in any pattern of interaction with similar units (states). He reiterates the conventional realist wisdom- "there is no overarching authority to prevent others from using violence or the threat of violence, to destroy or enslave them" (Ibid). Further, states do not aspire to achieve highest possible individual gain or pay off. Instead, as Grieco argues, "the fundamental goal of states in any relationship is to prevent others from achieving advances in their relative capabilities (Ibid:127). Grieco also maintains that while the liberals have adopted the anarchy problematique, they have failed to comprehend the implications of an anarchical order namely, the constant possibility of inter state –violence. His arguments how ever, are mainly structural. He argues that states would be concerned about relative gains not because of the problems of mistrust, cheating and free riding, but due to their structural setting in an anarchical environment.

Robert Jervis has shown how the gap between pristine realism and neoliberalism is being narrowed by the defensive realists. Neoliberals believe that modifications in the preference structure of actors are sufficient to produce mutual benefit and advance the case for building co-operation through institutions. Institutionalized co-operation continues even when "the initial propitious conditions have disappeared" (Jervis R. 1999: 51). Aggressive realists on the contrary emphasize the intractability of the security dilemma and argue that "the institutionalization or standardization of information through regime building cannot lead to conflict changes in preferences over strategies" (Ibid). The persisting security dilemma and the unchanging nature of beliefs held by states regarding their adversaries operate in a vicious cycle while enhancing the risks of war may lower the possibilities of violent conflict, the changes in the preference structures or beliefs can seldom produce co- operation, as such changes rarely take place, given the security dilemma of states. Defensive realists negotiate between liberals and their more aggressive counter parts by subtracting their differences. They advance case-specific hypothesis. Thus while they come close to aggressive realist and of the continuum, when it comes to the behaviour of states vis-à-vis aggressive adversaries, they move closer to neo-liberals in more benign or peaceful situations.

All realists nevertheless agree on several points. However, it can be agreed that there is little difference in the positions held by the realists and the neoliberals, despite their disagreement on the issue of relative versus absolute gains.

What mainly negates the distinction between the neorealists and neoliberals is their general acceptance of the anarchy paradigm. Although the neorealists and neoliberals draw different implications from such an anarchical setting, there is no fundamental disagreement between the two groups about the anarchical nature of the international system. First, the assumption of anarchy rules out any dissimilar conceptualization of the international system particularly of a federative or universal kind. Second, both sides divide the agenda of international relations into security and other dimensions, and agree on their fundamentally different underpinnings. The only difference between them relates to the extent to which co-operative mechanisms can be stretched across sectors. The realists, by and large believe in the centrality of the security dilemma and the natural preponderance of relative gain considerations as sufficient causes limiting the potential for co-operation based on calculation of absolute gains. The liberals counter this view and agree that co-operation is possible even between adversarial actors, provided such actors are rational enough to understand the overall benefits of any Pareto – optimal solutions worked out through mutual interactions. Neither do realists deny the fact of institutionalization, nor do liberals dismiss the primary of security. Realists hold that norms, beliefs and institutions do not alter the primary motivation of states in an anarchical system in the absence of a centralized security-enforcement mechanism. The liberals endorse the primacy of self preservation, but draw attention to extensive co-operation despite the predominant security concerns of states. They do not emphasize the constitutive character of anarchy, but co-operation among states despite the absence of a central regulatory agency. A reading of neorealist text makes it evident that basically they are not against co-operation; neorealists have no problem with co-operation as long as this does not translate into disproportionate security assets which upset the existing balance of capabilities amongst the actors. While the neo-realist case for co-operation is severely restrictive, the neo-liberals take a much more optimistic position on this score.

Third, both neorealists and neoliberals endorse the idea of balance of power. The neorealist view of the balance of power follows logically from the structural, realist perspective. No major neoliberal analyst has advanced a strong theoretical case against balance of power, although they have at times questioned its efficacy, empirical validity and inevitability. In a sense, the neoliberals are simply "unconcerned" about balance of power mechanisms and their security ramifications. Their concern for politico-economic issues make them more focused on the prospects of institutionalized or regime induced cooperation in various sectors which are conditioned by security consideration of states.

COORDINATION AND DISTRIBUTION

The third issue between neorealism and neoliberalism rests on the problems of coordination and distribution. The main thrust of the neoliberal approach is that "institutions, broadly defined, affect the patterns of cooperation that emerge" (Keohane, 1984a : 9). While analyzing the importance of institutions, Keohane emphasizes market failures and explains that institutions can help independent actors overcome these failures by providing information and reducing transaction costs (Ibid:246). Institutions may make it possible to realize joint gains and move out toward the Pareto frontier. But there are many ways to realize these gains, with some ways giving a larger share to one state and other ways giving a larger share to another state. "There are", as Stephen Krasner observes " many points along the Pareto frontier" (Krasner, Global Communications and National Power in Baldwin, 1993 : 235). These multiple ways of achieving the joint gains from cooperation can create conflicts over how those gains will be distributed. Reflecting on the debate, Keohane believes that he underemphasized "distributive issues and complexities they create for international cooperation" in After Hegemony (Keohane, 1993 : 446-47). As quoted from Robert Powell about Keohane's views about distributive problems:

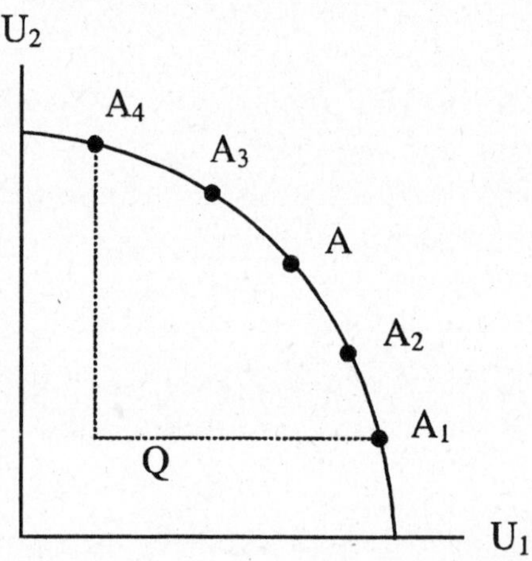

Fig. 1. Distributional conflicts: U_1 = the utility of state 1 (S_1); U_2 = the utility of state 2 (S_2); Q = status quo; A_1 through A_4 = possible agreements along the Pareto frontier

The distributive problem arises because there are many ways to divide the cooperative gains. Figure1 illustrates this problem when two states, S_1 and S_2, are trying to cooperate. S_1's utility is measured along the vertical axis. Q is the status quo. A_1 through A_2 are possible agreements that lie along the Pareto frontier. Both A_2 and A_3 lie on the Pareto frontier and are Pareto-superior to Q; i.e., both S_1 and S_2 prefer A_2 to Q and A_3 to Q. A_2 and A_3 are different ways of realizing the joint gains from cooperation. But, S_1 prefers A_2 to A_3 because A_2 yields a higher utility. Similarly, S_2 prefers A_3. Thus, there is a distributive conflict over A_2 and A_3. More generally, S_1 prefers agreements closer to A_1 and S_2 prefers agreements closer to A_4 (Powell Robert, 1994: 339).

Krasner also used these distributional issues to challenge the neoliberal approach. The main thrust of his argument is that "the nature of institutional arrangements is better explained by the distribution of national power capabilities than by efforts to solve problems of market failure" (Krasner, Global Communications and National Power: 235). In the words of Powell : " If cooperation can take many different forms and these alternative forms have distributional consequences, then the arrangements themselves can become the object of negotiation. Indeed, given the absence of a supranational authority, the states cannot bind themselves to any particular initial institutional arrangement and corresponding allocation of cooperative benefits. The institutional structure is always subject to renegotiation if a state believes it worthwhile" (Powell, 1994: 340).

The perpetual possibility of renegotiation can be both static and dynamic. In the static way the institutions might be a means of overcoming market failures or, more generally, of realizing joint gains from cooperation. While emphasizing monitoring and reducing uncertainty Keohane tries to explain how institutions can serve as a means to achieving the joint gains from cooperation. Focusing on another aspect of the explanation of institutional structure Krasner argues that the actual institutional arrangements that will emerge from the set of potential institutional arrangements that fulfill the functions will tend to reflect the desires of the more powerful actors. Thus, Powell views "Krasner's and Keohane's analyses of the static issue complement each other" (Ibid: 340).

From the dynamic perspective, suppose two "states want to move out to the Pareto frontier", they will "create an institution that reduces transaction costs and uncertainty. In this way the institution is a means to the end cf realizing the joint gains of cooperation. But there are also distributional conflicts, so both the states also use their political power to shape the institutional arrangements in order to obtain a larger share of the joint gains" (Ibid).

There is every possibility that the existing institutional arrangements and distribution of benefits may show a disparity with the underlying distribution of power. Robert Gilpin sees this as the cause of hegemonic war. The international order created by the hegemon to skew the associated distribution of benefits to its favour may not continue for long and over time gives way to another hegemonic war because of uneven economic growth and distribution of benefits no longer reflect the distribution of power (Gilpin Robert, 1981). Similarly, Krasner's metaphor of tectonic plates reflects a disparity between distribution of benefits and power. "When regimes are first created, they generally reflect the underlying distribution of power. But the pressure to change the regime builds over time as the distribution of power changes. In the tectonic plate metaphor, this pressure does not lead to a smooth adjustment. Rather, the pressure grows until it is suddenly relieved in an earthquake in which the regime alters in a way that realigns it with the distribution of power" (Powell: 342).

In the neorealist- neoliberal debate, as Keohane points out, market failures, transaction costs, uncertainty, information, and institutions play an important role in promoting cooperation. He also argues that international institutional history matters. In his words Powell expresses the views of Keohane: "Once institutions or regimes are established, actors behave in ways that whether deliberately or not, make it costly to change the regime or build a new one. Thus, even if the original distribution of power underlying the regime shifts, the now more powerful states will not change the regime unless the distribution of power has shifted to such an extent that the benefits of a new regime, which would reflect the new distribution of power, outweigh the cost of changing the existing regime. The cost of changing or constructing new regimes thus gives existing regimes some resilience to shifts in the balance of power" (Ibid: 342). "The high costs of regime – building help existing regimes persist" (Keohane, 1984a : 103).

SOME THEORETICAL EXTENSIONS OF STRUCTURAL REALISM

Structural realism has remained the most dominant paradigm of security studies within despite several limitations. In recent times, there has been a renaissance of sorts within the field of security studies (Lipschutz Ronnie D. 1995; Brown M.E. et al 1995) with attempts to broaden the neorealist idea at two levels. At one level – several scholars have sought to broaden the neorealist security agenda to include a wider range of potential threats, such as environmental issues, human rights and population displacement. At another level, attempts have been made to simultaneously deepen the agenda of security by addressing the issue at several levels from human or individual security to security at the international or global level with regional and societal security occupying possible intermediate positions. Once again traditional neorealists, such as Mearsheimer and Gray, have strongly countered these tendencies. They agree that such extension dilute the core values of the neorealist paradigm, making it theoretically incoherent and practically irrelevant.

Balance of power remains the key concept of neo-realists. Waltz explains, balance of power by two factors, the structure and anarchy and unlike Hans. J. Morganthau claims it as a law. Thus, for Waltz, balance of power is not the result of successful diplomacy rather it arises out of the logic of the structure of the international system itself. Subsequently, Waltz's formulations on the subject have come in for closer examination and detailed research. Some of the recent neorealists scholars have found fault with some of these formulations and have come out with alternative explanations.

The states, in an anarchical system, balance each other and do not bandwagon. Waltz argues that bandwagoning refers to allying with the strongest power. Balance of power theory believes that such an alliance will be dangerous for the survival of the weaker states and therefore, they should instead oppose or try to balance against the hegemon.

It is instructive to note, however, that whereas Waltzian structural balance of power theory defines balance. Simply in terms of capabilities, Waltz seeks to define these concepts by threat. Walt argues that capabilities alone cannot explain balance behaviour of states. He maintains: "By focusing solely on the distribution of capabilities, structural balance of power theory ignores the other factors that statesmen will consider when making alliance... As a result, the theory cannot explain why balance often fails to form" (Walt Stephen M. 1988: 277). Walt therefore modifies a crucial assumption of the structural theory. In his words "states seek allies to balance threats and that power is merely one element in their calculations – albeit an important one" (Ibid). Accordingly, "an imbalance of threat occurs when the most threatening state or coalition is significantly more dangerous than the second most threatening state or coalition." (Ibid: 280). The degree of threat depends upon aggregate power, geographic distance, proximity, offensive capability and the aggressive intent of a threatening state or coalition. In addition to the theoretical reformulations of Walt significant contributions to balance of power from within the neo-realism paradigm have come from Stephen Walt, Michael, Mastanduno and Randal Schweller, Barry Posen, and Stephen Van Evera among many others.

Mastanduno's contribution lies in further refining the balance of threat theory which, he like Walt finds more appropriate than the conventional Waltzian balance of power (Mastanduno Michael 1991:73-113). He refines neo-realist structuralism by clearly separating state behaviour in security and economic realms. While states balance against threat in the affairs of security, the economic behaviour of states in the post cold war era seems to suggest a balance of power rather than threat. There is no indication in Mastanduno's works of any awareness of the possible implications of his efforts at silencing what is definitely a conspicuous theoretical contradiction of neo-realism. This is captured best in the manner in which he handles the empirical evidence in support of his theoretical disjunction regarding state behaviour in security and economic affairs respectively. His perception for balance of threat theory is as follows – " Balance of threat theory predicts that the United States will use its economic relationships and power as instruments of state craft to reinforce its security strategy toward other major power" (Ibid 1997: 73). Again his prediction for balance of power theory is: "U.S. economic strategy thus far has reflected, consistent with balance of power theory, a greater concern for the pursuit of relative economic advantage than for using economic relations to support the preferred national security strategies of reassuring and engaging potential challenges" (Ibid:82-83). His emphasis on this distinction makes the prediction for balance of threat theory consistent with the assumptions of structural realism.

Randall Scheweller has further complicated the debate by refusing the dominant perspective held by Waltz and Stephen Walt, namely that states prefer balancing to bandwagoning (Schweller Randall 1992: 235-69). In fashioning an "alternative theory of alliances" based on balance of interests", Scheweller finds Waltz wanting on his insistence on balancing because of an unwarranted bias / preference for status quo power. He further claims that his theory is more realist as it is more in line with classical realism's preference for power than the Waltzian strive for security (Vasquez John A. 1998: 261). He redefines bandwagoning to mean siding with the stronger power for an opportunistic gain. It should be noted here that Schweller drops the connection of bandwagoning behaviour with either preponderance of power or threat by an adversarial power.

Christensen and Snyder have built on the manifest weakness in the theoretical accounts of polarity as originally developed by Kenneth Waltz (Christensen Thomas J. 1997: 65-97). Waltz's theory about state alliance strategies in multipolarity predicts the possibility of both "chain ganging and buck passing" behaviour. To use Christensen and Snyder's own terms:

"This is a problem because for a particular state in particular circumstances, any foreign policy and its opposite can sometimes be deducted from Waltz's theory.... On the one hand, they may chain themselves unconditionally to reckless allies whose survival is seen to be indispensable to the maintenance of the balance.... On the other hand, they may pass the buck, counting on third parties to bear the costs of stopping a rising hegemon (Christensen and Jack Snyder 1990:138).

Christensen and Snyder have sought to resolve this problem inherent in Waltz's structural perspective at the level of foreign policy behaviour of individual states by adding a variable from Robert Jervis' theory of the security dilemma: the military decision maker's perception regarding the relative advantage or disadvantage of offence or defence. This apparently explains the different kinds of foreign policy errors that led to the two world wars. Thus, (mis) perceived offensive advantage led to unconditional alliances and chain ganging while an equally erroneous perception of defensive advantage created the tendency to "free ride on the balancing efforts of others" (Ibid:167).

Van Evera and Barry Posen have attempted to accommodate the concept of nationalism within the neo-realist paradigm, perhaps to rescue the latter from the onslaught of social constructivism and historical sociology which inter alia, targeted the asociological basis of the paradigm's central building block- the idea of the state (Posen Barry 1984). They have developed a theory of nationalism as a fait accompli through the canons of methodological individualism that contains no explanation whatsoever of the why and how of nationalism.

Van Evera formulates a series of hypotheses about nationalism and then seeks to test their validity (Van Evera, 1986: 80-117; 1994: 5-39). In these he treats nationalism as an empirical fact and defines it as a political movement which is based on the loyalty of the members to their own national or ethnic group striving for an independent homeland. The groups which make nationalism are primarily linguistic entities having "dormant or manifest aspirations for statehood." In a sense, Van Evera's perspective is typically Gellnerian bereft of the latter's functional sociology or modernization underpinnings. Thus, Van Evera ultimately reduces nationalism to capability, engendering the aspiration for statehood (Ibid 1994: 16).

Barry Posen on the other hand, traces the growth of nationalism to the development of large armies and the critical imperative of states to maintain such armies for sheer survival. Nationalism therefore, becomes a function of the international system and its systemic pressures: a response to the existence of other states with nationalistic ideas and institutions making the new states capable of establishing or mobilizing large armies.

Posen is not surprised at the coincidence of nationalism and warfare; nationalism is "... purveyed by states for the express purpose of improving their military capability (Posen: 81). Nationalism is conceived as a medium of mobilization which elites use to generate military capabilities consistent with emotionally surcharged contexts. Nationalism thus facilitates the creation of large armies, backed by an entire social structure, which could then be mobilized rapidly in times of war.

Like Van. Evera Posen treats nationalism as a given, a sociological fait accompli, without tracing its origin in ideational terms. Van Evera fails to account for why a certain "capability" would give rise to nationalism and not to some things else. Posen is silent about how nationalism came into being (Krause Keith 1996: 240). For even though one can accept the view that nationalism spreads as a chain reaction or strategy of survival, the origin of the phenomenon remains uninvestigated. Their inability to address identity questions or ideological factors as possible explanations of the genesis and evolution of nation and nationalism results in a theory which fails to explain the origin and causes of nationalism as a social or political phenomenon. Their inability to provide a comprehensive sociological account of the "nation state", more than anything else, exposes neorealism to the critiques from other perspectives, particularly social constructivism and postmodernism.

As seen from the above analysis, Waltz's neorealism contains several shortcomings. Walt finds the balance of power theory to be inadequate, and develops a new balance of threat concept which he does not think challenges the basis of neorealist paradigm. He feels that there is a qualitative difference between balance of power and balance of threat. Walt's inclusion of the perception of enemy's intent as a key variable of the threat calculus introduces a degree of subjectivity, which is not consistent with Waltzian structuralism. While Waltz has developed a structural theory of international relations quite distinct from foreign policy theories worked out at the unit level of analysis, Walt's case studies are more about unit level foreign policy behaviour.

Mastanduno's analysis confuses more than it clarifies. He agrees that post-cold war unipolarity could undermine theoretical claims of neorealism and prefers the balance of threat perspective over balance of power. Yet he does not think that these developments in any way challenge neorealism's claim to complete theoretical dominance, particularly in the sphere of security studies. His views regarding the concept of balance of power stand in sharp contrast to some of the fundamental attributes of realism, both classical and structural. Schweller feels that states prefer bandwagoning to balancing; but it is hard to see how this can be reconciled with the theoretical structure of neorealism.

The attempts by Christensen and Snyder to construct a foreign policy level theory developed on the basis of Waltzian neorealism do not reflect the structural logic of the original formulation. Moreover, by bringing Jervis and Waltz together, they have once again introduced certain variables which are hardly compatible with the logical requirements of the original formulation. To take an illustration, both Christensen and Snyder do not make an attempt to explain how a key psychological factor like the decision-maker's perception of defensive or offensive capabilities fit into the neorealist paradigm. In methodological terms, Van Evera and Barry Posen's uncritical acceptance of neorealism makes their analysis of nationalism and war inadequate.

CONCLUSION

Neorealists view the international system as a relentless competition for security; in contrast, postclassical realism is agnostic about security competition in the international system: within postclassical realism, the strength of security pressures fluctuates according to a host of material factors besides the distribution of capabilities, namely technology, geography, and international economic pressures. Within realism the possibility/probability distinction exists. First, neorealism views states as discounting the future to a greater degree than is assumed within postclassical realism. Second, realism is divided regarding state preferences: neorealism emphasizes military security as the overriding priority, whereas postclassical realism maintains that states ultimately pursue power- a concept that contains an inherent tension between military security and economic capacity.

The neorealist versus neoliberal debate has in no way helped scholars to comprehend limitations of the realist orthodoxy. In a way, the neorealists have done better than the neoliberal because within the sphere of security at least, the neoliberals have very little differences with their rivals. While neorealists argue the case of an anarchic international system, which security comes by way of efficient balancing strategies built on sound military capabilities and indeterminate alliances, the neoliberals present a slightly more optimistic, but nevertheless anarchic world where co-operative economic strategies complement conventional balances to provide a better, more reliable less risky and more efficient security. That a compromise between the two is after all not very difficult is evident from the development of a perspective such as contingent realism. Most neorealists would agree that liberal institutions, democratic structures and norms and liberal economics are vital to comprehensive peace. Neoliberals would likewise complain much against competitive balancing strategies, prioritizing national interest over genuine collective commitments or the need for faithful allies in the uncertain world of global politics.

The real threat to the neorealist dominance in security studies comes from the broadening of the agenda of security in recent times, both in terms of issues and methodology. The new threat therefore is two fold. On the one hand, one witnesses increasing threats to human existence, at all levels of collective living that can hardly be explained by the narrow perspective of neorealism. We can refer to the threats of the environment to the rise of fundamentalism, ethnicity and a new politics of identity and so on. The other threat to neorealism comes from new methodological breakthrough in the social sciences which are percolating the study of IR. In concrete terms, the greatest challenge to the epistemic monopoly of neorealism stems from social constructivism and post-positivist writings on security.

3
Poststructuralist View of Security

Poststructuralism advocates a position different from both the traditional realist and idealist perspectives in international relations. It throws insights on the construction of the national-international dichotomy, the relationship between national identity and security politics, the discursive character of the concept of security and the late modern transformation of security. It is mostly concerned with whether and/or how to expand the concept of security. Supporting and reinforcing the stand taken by Ole Waever, it advocates that security is a discursive practice and that the concept of security cannot be solely confined to the military domain. What remains cynical to its central argument is that it is not to establish an objective relationship between the concept and the possible domain of security but to study whether and how an issue is securitized.

The second half of the 1980s, witnessed the advent of post structuralism in international relations and ushered in the post modern challenge strengthened with the writing of James Der Derian (1987), Michael Shapiro (1988), Richard Ashley (1987) and R.B.J.Walker (1987).

The shafts of poststructuralist challenges are pointed

towards the theoretical and philosophical scaffolding of international relations as well as the traditional perspectives peeling off the transformative trajectory from a modern to a post modern or post sovereign world. Strict adherence of both realism and liberalism in their classical as well as in their current scientific formulation to the inexorable principle of rationality gluing to the idea that "behavior that can be adjudged objectively to the optimally adapted to situations" (Herbert Simon quoted in Keohane, 1989:160) constitutes or should constitute the basis for the calculation of interests, remains a fundamental problem, as viewed by post structuralists.

In their alacrity to meet the epistemological and methodological standards of natural science the neo-realism and neoliberalism shared this rationalist ontology, ensconcing emblematic faith in science's ability to narrow the gaps in the belief by providing common standards to test beliefs, and therefore disciplining our minds, protecting as to some extent from bias. (Keohane, 1991, 46, Waltz, 1997, 1-17)

The very egoistic thematic of the modernists' ability to put the moves and unmoves in the world to rationally understood and scientifically analyzable and explicable laws and theorization is replaced in poststructuralism by disbelief in unproblematic notions of modernity, enlightenment, truth, science and reason. As enunciated by Jim George, postmodernism reformulates basic questions of modernist understanding in emphasizing not the sovereign subject (e.g., author/independent state) or the object (e.g., independent word/text) but instead the historical, cultural and linguistic practices in which subjects and objects (and theory and practice, facts and value) are constructed (George, 1994: 192).

The espoused claims of various international relation schools to science, reason and truth are not mere a statement of the world as it is, but as a set of theoretical and political demarcation of what constitutes reality and knowledge. This led poststructuralists to adopt a different view of the discipline than one held by neorealists and neoliberals. In Walker's words "theories of international relations are more interesting as aspects of contemporary world politics that need to be explained than as explanations of contemporary world politics" (Walker, 1993:6).

In contrast to rationalist perspective hinged on empiricist and positivist epistemologies and methodologies, poststructuralism espouses the anti-methods of deconstruction, geneology, and inter- texuality.

Deconstruction demonstrates how dichotomies are fundamental to construction of meaning by first, identifying the hierarchical relationship between the two concepts of the dichotomy, secondly, reversing the hierarchy, and thirdly, by this procedure undo the pairing. (Gregory, 1989 xv-xviii)

A geneology is a listing of the present based on three methodological principles :

First, it does not look for a continuous history, but for discontinuity and forgotten meanings.

Second, it does not look for an origin, indeed it is assured that one cannot be found.

Third, it does not focus on the object of geneology itself but on the condition, discourses and interpretations surrounding it (Huysmans, 1997, 340-2)

POSTSTRUCTURALISTS' VIEW OF SECURITY AND CONSTRUCTION OF THE INTERNATIONAL

To realists the world is cleft into two separate domains- the national and the international. The world on the outside of the state is considered as threats and the states in the end are concerned with their own self. The international order can never be a realm of order equivalent to that found in the national community.

Through the application of deconstruction techniques, Richard Ashley has shown how realism has understood the world as division between natural and international through a double move. First the community is understood in its meaning as traditionally held in domestic politics. It is seen as a timeless, universal entity characterized by rationality, reason progress and order. Second the community does not know any limits until the realist statesman appears to establish the border between inside and the outside. He knows and his mission is to show that the national community cannot be extended into the international realm, which is radically different from the national ridden by anarchy, rather than order, repetition rather than progress and raw power rather than reason (Ashley, 1987:416-17). The realists view is based on the fact that the outside states are always threats to national security and accordingly, the states prepare to fight these threats and debunks the idealist illusion that the national community can be extended into the international and the border between outside and inside is non-existing or at best can be dissolved. Thus, the national and international aspects of realism are different and mutually exclusive and independent zones standing in opposition to each other. International sphere of realism is not a conceptualization of universalization of nation state in its extended form, but a description of a condition of state of war existing among the states. It is not a stated objective or goal of nation state as the idealists conceive in terms of global community.

The realists tended to conceive that the modern state system is not a particular historical form of social and political organization created in a specific condition and has moved through a process of reforms and changes or needs to be supplanted in the evolution towards a higher or ideal form of organization. Rather, what is initially developed as a western concept came to dominate as a western straitjacket and an eternal reality beyond time and space. To questions of political identify and existence, which cropped up in the Westphalian convention, the investiture of sovereign on the state system came as a potent solution. If divided the world not into mutually dependent islands to be weaved into an archipelago of universality, rather into clear cut inside and outside with the latter being always a threat to the former. All claims by other than the state to the status of political comity were forever sealed and defined as threats to national security to be met by political and theoretical resistance. (Walker, 1990.6). Crowned with sovereignty, the state security assumed primacy and monopolized on what security can be, who it can be for. All other claimants to securitization of the issue without state being the referent object were considered rather threats to the conventional understanding of security.

Hinged on Ashley and Walker's deconstructions of the national international dichotomy of International Relation, other poststructuralists have dealt more explicitly with the connection between security and the construction of national identity. Instead of subscribing to the traditionalist view of security being confined to the defence of a state or an alliance of states, these post structuralists conceive security as one of the most important practices through which states construct their identity. In "security matters the enemy is specified in a series of security discourses, tied to the functioning of the state security and defence agencies". (Dalby, 1990:7). In Bradley Kleins formulation:

*...modern military practice can be understood as recurrent and always incomplete attempts to constitute

and create what from a traditional perspective looks like a self-evident project- the state. In this manner, strategic violence is less a function of the state than an instance of its own assertion. (Klein, 1994:7)

In traditional understanding of security, national identity is held synonymous, with state sovereignty and considered settled forever. The post structuralists on the other hand denied this as a settled fact and the recreation of identity has to be "secured by the effective and continual ideological demarcation of those who are "false" to the defining ideas". (Campbell, 1992:105). As David Campbell opines:

> Indeed, in a world in which state identity is secured through discourses of danger, some low tactics are employed to serve these high ideals. These tactics are not inherent to the logic of identity, which only requires the definition of difference. But securing an ordered self and an ordered world-particularly when the field upon which this process operates is as extensive as a state –involves defining elements that stand in the way of order as forms of 'otherness' (Campbell, 1992: 55)

No doubt, he agrees that security is necessary for the state but not in the way the traditionalists tend to think that a state is to be protected from outside or external threats. Making the traditional understanding of security upside down, Campbell argues that the identity of state is based on threats and it needs a sense of insecurity. Threats and insecurity are not just potentially undermining state, and something which could be eliminated, they constitute the state. By that the state is able to know who it is and what is in the face of the threatening order. The very traditionalist understanding of state as ahistorical and uniform entity unamenable to any change is replaced by deconstruction of its different historical forms of representation (Hansen, 1997 : 376).

SECURITY AS BOTH DISCURSIVE, POLITICAL AND SPEECH ACT

To the traditionalists state stands a representation of an objectively threatening reality. On the contrary, the poststructuralists look upon security as both a discursive practice and political practice which are closely connected and integral. The interconnection between the two is brought out by Waever:

> In this usage security is not of interest as a sign that refers to something more real; the utterance itself is the act. By saying it, something is done (as in betting, giving a promise, naming a ship). By uttering "security", a state-representative moves a particular development into a specific area, and thereby claims a special right to use whatever means are necessary to block it. (Waever, 1995a: 55)

The invocation of the word 'security' implies the catapultation of state into a special position to act extraordinarily by extraordinary means. In the traditional parlance the very word 'security' is synonymous with state and the latter's existence is symbiotically inherent in the security. It is the promptness and abruptness of state military action that outbids any outside military threat to existence. According to traditionalists, it is the threat of military force that constitutes and defines 'security'. It is a final act of military response to the security threats. But the post structuralists aimed at construction of a threat. That means security and insecurity are of in binary opposition, rather security can "only be thought by incorporating the trace of insecurity in the very articulation of security itself". (Dillion, 1995:162). In the words of Waever:

> "Security" signifies a situation marked by the presence of a security problem and some measure taken in response. Insecurity is a situation with a security problem and no response. Both conditions share the security problematique. When there is no security problem, we do not conceptualize our situation in terms of security. Instead, security is simply an irrelevant concern... Consequently, transcending a security problem by politicizing it cannot happen through thematization in terms of security, only away from such terms. (Waever, 1995a:56)

In the traditional perspective security firstly reinforces or consolidates identity and distances away the otherness, which appears to threaten or threaten the identity built around the rubric 'state'. In other words, it creates logic of us–them for politicization of security. Secondly, it also implies the defence of those who have a stake in the existence and perpetuation of state and finally, it defends the status quo and meaning the protection of these who are the representational elements of state and easily identify their security with the security of the state. Increasing security stands at one extreme of the spectrum and at the other end stands increasing insecurity or vulnerability.

On the contrary, the poststructuralists aim at desecuritizing the issues and shifting them from the realm of security into the realm of politics opening up the options about politicizing what is seen as given institutions and practices. The left out and the little cared for marginalized groups and lone voices are pitch-forked into the center stage. In the scintillating words of Lene Hansen:

"Securitization, on the contrary, moves an issue out of the realm of politics into the realm of security, which has the positive effect of heightening the awareness of an issue, but also a negative one, in as much it becomes more difficult for non-governmental or non-elite groups to influence the formulation of issue" (Lene Hansen. 1997 : 377).

DER DERIAN'S GENEALOGY OF SECURITY

He drove back to the very root of what the word "security" has had the meanings and discovers the connotations it had prior to the present one (Der Derian 1995:27-8).

Paying attention to political theory, he identifies four realist forms of security : Hobbes' epistemic realism, Marx's social realism, Nietzsche's interpretative realism and Baudrillard's hyperrealism. He subscribes to Nietzsche's interpretative realism for a philosophical conceptualization of security as Nietzsche sees the desire for security as the desire to be protected from the unknown, for obliterating the differences. To him the desire for security is the predominant desire in the security and what renders life worth living is ambiguity, uncertainty and paradox which the modern sovereign state envisages to remove in their quest for security.

Established on philosophical stand of Nietzsche and insight of Baundrillard, Der Derian's concept of security accepted simulation as crucial for an understanding of security. Simulation is the generation of real by models without origin or reality: a hyperreal (Baudrillard, 1983:2). It does not refer to anything real but is a part of self – referring system, which is perceived by more real than reality. Der Derian presented the Gulf war in January 1991 as the clearest case so far of the transition towards virtual security. The Gulf war composed of a "technologically generated, televisually linked, and strategically gamed form of violence that dominated the formulation as well as the representation of US policy in the Gulf" (Der Derian, 1992 :175), the use cf computer-simulation prior to the US – led liberation of Kuwait, and the extent and form of the media coverage located in 'real time', showing things 'as they happened', to a global audience, which would watch a powerful combination of the latest technology, the lowest quality image, the highest representation of reality" (Der Derian 1992:180)

Another crucial feature of Derian is his inter textuality analysis of the variety of the material : -quotes by post modern philosophers; interpretations of public statements by former president Reagan, top military staff, and government officials; and a vast number of references to popular culture, rock music, movies and novels.

Michael Shapiro in his works has also demonstrated the potential of inter textual techniques and the relevance of popular culture for the study of security, which proves how the media and popular culture have come to render impossible an undisputed hegemony by the strategic discourse of government officials, academics, journalists, and defence intellectuals" (Shapiro, 1990), citing the cases of Miami Vice story an American Contra connection before the scandal was revealed, LA Law featuring an Iranian woman suing the American government officials for the loss of her family in the drowning of Iranian Air bus or the trial of young soldier who refused to fire at civilian houses during the American intervention in Panama.

Emphasis on space and geo-politics has been traditionally the main focus of international relations. But wars on virtual security and popular culture prove that space and geo-politics are becoming less important than flows, acceleration and pace –what Der Derian calls "chronopolitics" and Luke "streams in flow" (Der Derian, 1992,Luke, 1991).

If time is becoming more important than space, it will crumble the very foundation of the modern state system of the last 400 years. If the principle and practices of state sovereignty are no longer to be the principle of political organization, will security so closely linked to state assume a new meaning? What the security will mean in that state? Addressing the question implies questioning the entire package of political concepts which are articulated within the current understanding of security as a practice of the sovereign state (Dalby, 1992 : 106).

POSTSTRUCTURAL VIEWS OF SECURITY

Poststructuralists envisage a different view of security. They did not confine the concept of security to the military domain and viewed security can be constructed as emanating from diversified sources. The think of the matter is that whether an issue is securitized and successfully put into the language of security or not. Security is not constituted prior to but in language as a discursive practice. This discursive definition of security implies that an "unlimited explanation of the concept of security is avoided" (Waever, 1995a; Buzan,1997 : 13-15)

According to Walt, the three issues play an important role in the security studies establishment's vision of and aversion to post structuralism:

First, the "lack of real worldism" seems to imply that post structuralism has confined itself to the linguistic realm, whereas security studies deal with material side of security. Post structuralism refuses, however, simply to accept the dichotomy between material and linguistic issues.

Secondly, poststructuralism thinks it impossible to distinguish between real and false or perceived threats and that real threats therefore will be (mis) treated in the same way as perceived ones. Realists subscribed to Arnold Wolfer's version of security in both objective and subjective sense. In the objective sense, security is absence of threats to acquired values. In a subjective sense, security is absence of fear that such values will be attacked (Wolfers, 1962 :151)

On the other hand, the poststructuralists condescend to the view that security threats as constructed throw discursive practices do not imply that threats should be seen as false.

In the conventional understanding of security, since security threat is external and objective, there is an outside standard against which threats are to be measured.

Since standard of measurement of security threat is purely objective and depends on the state threatened or threatening others, such standards can never be known or discovered. According to poststructuralists not every body gets to define what constitutes threats and security still remains a prerogative of the state. In the words of Lene Hansen, "whether something is characterized as a real threat should therefore be seen as part of a political and material struggle rather than as corresponding to an immanent quality of the situation" (Hansen Lene, 1997:383). It is a question of what constitutes a theory.

Thirdly, to realists security is almost technocratic management of international security based on a mechanical interpretation of the balance of power. Post structuralists on the other hand disagrees that a scientific theory is the goal in and of itself.

In the words of Klein :

> To make the claim for a particular theoretical framework on the basis of these new facts that have appeared for observation/ measurement would be to rely upon an outmoded and indefensible methodological empiricism as the desideratum for testing

> theory. It would mean that on some observable scale, theoretical frameworks have the function of conforming themselves to an independent, empirically ascertainable external reality, whose flow and contour exist outside of the framewords we bring to bear. (Klein,1994:134).

It is not just a debate over the importance of linguistics and ideas on the one side and material forces on the other, but a clash between different ontological and epistemological position. In the rationalist, realist view, any theory conceived in the lines of anti foundationalist as post-structuralism, is bound to mean a movement into the world of uncertainty, relativity and political paralysis (Williams, 1997 : 6)

In the words of Lene Hansen :

"Poststructuralists argue that discarding a rationalist ontology and adopting an anti-foundation epistemology brings us – paradoxically and contrary to what Walt holds – closer to multi faceted analysis of the world. This may very well lead to situations where making political decisions about security becomes more difficult, but a less mechanical and more open handling of politics is exactly what post structuralism advocates" (Lene Hansen, 1997 : 384).

POST STRUCTURALISM AND ALTERNATIVE SECURITY

Both poststructuralists and peace researchers have questioned the realist vision of how security should be defined and understood and the privileged role and primary referent object assigned to the state. According to Waever, both 'traditional alternatively' and realist thinking view security as a condition given prior to language, and both hold that security is a desirable condition or good, that the more national / global / individual security one has the better (Waever, 1995a :46).

The poststructuralists questioned both of these premises. To them, security is a discursive practice through which a condition of insecurity is identified, threats are pointed out, and the object of security (usually the state) is constructed. Further, the poststructrulists argue that a securitized situation is not necessarily to be strived for. The above premises of the traditional approaches rest on an objective view of security and making security correspond to real security (Buzan and Waever, 1997 :246).

The protagonists of traditional security have often advocated a shift in the meaning of security from being confined to the state to being about people's security, global security and a change in the identification of security with military forces towards an approach integrating cultural, environmental, gender, social and economic issues. Galtung advocates to locate the concept of security in a theory of basic human needs. As Peter Lawler argued, basic human needs approach " requires for its defense a prior standard of human excellence upon which an ethics of needs satisfaction can be grounded" (Lawler, 1995 :140 and 136-44).

On the other hand post structuralist tend to work within or the margins of, not out side of, the discourse of national security. As pointed out by Lene Hansen, one may find in poststructuralist "smaller remnants of the 'traditional alternative' security thinking critized by Waever and Der Derian. While arguing for a change in the conceptualization of security to a positive post cold war formulation, Dalby put forth the case of the poor, women and the children to be included within the ambit of security who have so far remained outside the apparatus of the state (Dalby, 1992 : 116). Even R.B.J. Walker held that the security of state is not synonymous with the security of the people, and is identified with the interests of elites and governments. The primary object of security is people not states, nor elites, nor the affluent, nor the stronger (Walker, 1988a :124-8).

The poststructuralists on the other hand hold that shift of focus of security on state to the people, though is a fundamental theme of traditional alternativism, is not a sufficient conclusion. The amount of political identity invested in a state has not been given due importance. The state is not just an institution clearly separated from the people, but a political practice and principle of political organization that needs to be taken into consideration. In the words of Lene Hansen: "identifying the hierarchical relationship between 'people' and 'state' embedded in the concept of 'national security' constitutes a first step in a deconstructive procedure, reversing this hierarchy by privileging 'the people' rather than the 'state' forms a second step, but traditional alternativism ... does not go far enough in attempting to undo the state-people dichotomy itself and this does not complete the third deconstructive step" (Hansen Lene:387).

Poststructuralism strongly opposes the idea of treating the people as separate descriptive political category away from and independently of the state. In Walker's analysis the world security is closely connected to his deconstruction of the principle of state sovereignty. Social movements are doubly excluded : first they are excluded from the sphere of international though situated inside, second : they are perceived by social and excluded from the sphere of political. In his view this implies that these social movements and world politics require some kind of mediating agent. First the serial has to find expression within the explicitly political practices of the state and then the state has to mediate with other states (Walker, 1994: 670).

POSTSTRUCTURALISM, NEOREALISM AND SOCIETAL SECURITY

The state centeredness of security as advocated by neo-realism has been castigated with introduction of new non state referent object of security into the conceptualization of security. To say that referent objects are historically contingent implies that the state is not the sole referent object of security. But other referent objects of security appear besides the state deserving due status and attention along with that given to the state. The concept of societal security is a glare illustration of Waever's attempt at reconciling a reconstructed neorealism with poststructuralizm.

Societal security concerns the ability of a society to persist in its essential character under changing conditions and possible or actual threats. More specifically, it is about the sustainability, within acceptable conditions for evolution, of traditional patterns of language, culture, association, and religious and national identity and custom. The definition makes it difficult to give any objective definition of when there is a threat to societal security. We can best understand it by studying the processes whereby a group comes to perceive its identity as threatened, when it starts to act in a security mode on this basis, and what behavior this triggers. Societal security is about situations when societies perceive a threat in identity terms (Waever, 1993 :23).

Buzan and Waever ask "can one not think of identities as definitely being constructed by people and groups through numerous processes and practices, and that when an identity is thus constructed, and becomes socially sedimented, it becomes a possible referent for security?" (Buzan and Waever, 1997:243).

While constructivists and postructuralists focus on

the pre-sedimentation of identities, the neorealism and neoliberalism are concerned with consequences of sedimentation on the other. The poststructuralist do not confine themselves to a pre-sedimentation phase, on the contrary they demonstrate how sedimentation and institutionalization are ongoing project and processes (Williams, 1997 a). In other words there is no simple dichotomy between being and becoming, between a constructivist stage and a consequential stage.

In the conclusion it can be said that a study of a genealogy of security as started by Der Derian would provide one with the knowledge of how the practice of security has been constituted historically, what characterized it before being catapulted into the center stage of territorial state.

Another key concept of poststructuralism has been that of 'the other'. Many insightful analyses have been made by poststructuralists to show how identities become constructed through the practices of 'the other' (Neumann, 1996). Identity in principle can be constructed through relation of differences, state identity requires otherness, discourses of danger and insecurity (Campbell, 1992:12). In the words of Lene Hansen, "there might be a tendency within poststructuralism to conclude too quickly that the only possible relationship between state and others is the latter one, and that all foreign and security policies therefore have to be built on a conquest of the other" (Lene Hansen, 1997 : 390).

4

Environmental Security: A New Dimension of Human Security

The late 1970s witnessed a spurt of activity resulting in a myriad of calls to redefine security in non military terms that include rising poverty, rapid population growth, spread of infectious diseases, and environmental degradation. The realist understanding and definition of security was state centric connected with state secrecy, nuclear and military power. The realist framework of national security as a function of the successful pursuit of interstate power competition through military means continued right through the cold war. According to Dalby, "cold war versions of security have usually been understood in spatial terms as moves of exclusion and protection is a spatial exercise in distancing and boundary making" (Dalby S.1990 : 171-88). This means in geopolitical parlance, the spatial limitation of Soviet political control. During the last half century, security has been primarily a matter of concern for states and their military alliances. The legitimacy of the governments is generally understood in terms of provision of internal security for the inhabitants residing within its territorial jurisdiction. Where stability of the regime has been held synonymous with national security serious inroads into the realm of human rights, and internal repressions have been rationalized in the name of national security. Where political instability has been identified as threat, national security is understood as containing and limiting political change and legitimizing the status quo. The intensification of cold war climaxed in the proliferation of nuclear weapons and in the Reagan administration's Strategic Defence Initiative and Star wars merely exposed the paradox of security where the enhancement of nuclear power does not mean the enhancement of security to the people. The problems plaguing the entire humanity in terms of grinding poverty, burgeoning population growth, spread of diseases, scarcity of resources and environmental degradation could not be comprehended within the realist framework based on state centric military capability. Thus, the dominant realist paradigm to understand the current realities seems to be inadequate. It has "become an anachronism that has lost much of its explanatory and prescriptive power" (Holsti O.R.1991: 94).

ENVIRONMENTAL SECURITY

The state-centric and military perspective of security has lost both practical relevance and intellectual credibility in the context of a number of historic forces and events in the contemporary age. These include the end of cold war, global integration of national economies, erosion of national identifies and cultures, the shift in priority from military rivalry to economic competition, and the diminishing role of state as the dominant actor in international politics. On the other hand, there have emerged diverse new issues-ranging from poverty to refugee crises, information privacy to cyber- terrorism, environmental problems to natural disasters – which require non-state and non military policies and strategies. These newly emerging security concerns have been characterized as non-traditional, and are now considered a major component of what is christened as comprehensive security. Among these emergent problems replacing the threat of East-West ideological divide, military aggression and struggle for global preponderance is the global environmental crisis. It looms large in terms of global warming, sea level rise, acid rain, greenhouse effect, diminishing capacity of the agricultural system, depletion of earth's finite resources, punching holes in the ozone layer, and biodiversity loss. Simply put, the global agenda has expanded since the demise of cold war as has the need for urgent attention to these problems for solution. It is thus seen that "welfare not warfare, will shape the rules and global threats like ozone holes and pollution will dictate the agenda."(Joffe J, 1992:35). It is within this context that the environmental question has gained worldwide significance as a security issue. In fact, environmental security stands out as perhaps the most widely debated issue especially due to its all pervasive nature, cross national scope and inter-generational implications (Haque M. Shamsul, 2002:24).

While many of the past, present and future causes of conflict and war may seem to have little or no direct connection with the environment or with resources, a strong argument can be made for linking certain resource and environmental problems with the prospects for political frictions and tensions, or even war and peace. At the centre of ongoing debate is the assertion that resource scarcity and certain forms of environmental degradation are important factors contributing to political instability or violent conflict at local, regional and interstate levels. There is a growing perception that local, regional and global environmental deficiencies or resource scarcities will increasingly produce conditions that may lead to conflict

(Gleick Peter H, 1998: 105-106).

This conceptual shift towards environmental security in the context of collapse of Soviet Union and diminution of security threats associated with cold war, pitchforked into the mainstream security debates urging the policymakers to cast about for a new security focus. Despite contentious debates within the field of environmental security, a wide variety of recent comments by senior diplomats and policy makers are symptomatic of the recognition that issues related to environmental security have ascended to the highest levels.

In 1987, the General Secretary of the Soviet Union, Mikhail Gorbachev stated:

> [The World] is not secure in the direct meaning of the word when currents of poison flow along river channels, when poison rains pour down from the sky, when an atmosphere polluted with industrial and transport waste chokes cities and whole regions, when the development of atomic engineering is justified by unacceptable risks...The relationship between man and the environment has become menacing. Problems of ecological security affect all the rich and the poor (Gorbachev M, 1987:3257).

In November 1989, British Prime Minister Margaret Thatcher gave a speech to the United Nations General Assembly-saying:

> While the conventional political dangers – the threat of global annihilation, the fact of regional war- appear to be receding, we have all recently become aware of another insidious danger. It is as menacing in its way as these more accustomed perils with which international diplomacy has concerned itself for centuries. It

> is the prospect of irretrievable damage to the atmosphere, to the oceans, to earth itself (Gleick, 1998:106).

In April 1997, as United States Secretary of State, Ms Albright went on to say:

> Not so long ago, many believed that the pursuit of clean air, clean water, and healthy forests was a worthy goal, but not part of our national security. Today environmental issues are part of the mainstream of American foreign Policy (US Department of State, 1997).

It was in this backdrop of future non-military threats that a number of studies and research institutions undertook works to determine if and how environmental factors were related to the intra and inter state conflicts or violence that appeared to be surfacing around the globe (Gurr Ted, 1993). These studies varied in their approach, their terminology, and their specific findings and consistent in their explanations suggested that environmental stress, operating through a set of intervening variables, could contribute to violent conflicts, and thus constituted a threat to national and international security. Furthering this argument that the mounting environmental problems and the associated issues need an attention with which the conventional outlook of national security appears to be incongruent, Jeremy Rifkin points out: "The environmental threats facing the planet are not simply the result of scientific miscalculation. Nor are they merely the consequences of ill conceived management decisions. Ironically it is the notion of security upon which our entire modern world view is based that has led us to the verge of ecocide... In less than a century the practice of geopolitics thus pushed the world to the brink of both nuclear Armageddon and environmental catastrophe forcing us to reconsider the basic assumptions of security that animate the modern world view" (Rifkin J, 1991:2).

Similarly, Lodgaard feels that "the concept of environmental security challenges established frames of mind and political conflicts. It conveys a message that environmental problems have a legitimate claim for status as military problems have" (1990: 18).

Another proponent of environmental security in the same vein opines:

> ...national security is not just about fighting forces and weaponry. It relates to watersheds, croplands, forests, genetic resources, climatic and other factors that rarely figure in the minds of military experts and political leaders, but increasingly deserve in their collectivity to rank along side military approaches as crucial to a nation's security (Myers Norman, 1986:251).

The growing significance of environmental security is quite evident in major international forums. Some well known examples include the UN Conference on Human Environment (1972), Ottawa Conference on Conservation and Development (1986), United Nations Conference on Environment and Development (1992), World Summit for Social Development (1995) and UN Symposium on the Global Environment in the 21st Century (1997). These conferences and symposia eventually resulted in various international conventions and protocols for environmental protection or security, such as the Vienna Convection for the protection of the Ozone Layer, the Convention on Biological Diversity, the Framework Convention on Climate Change, the convention to combat desertification, and the Kyoto protocol (Haque M. Shamsul, 1992: 199-222). Harking back to as far as 1987, for example, The World Commission on Environmental Development (Brundtland Report) entitled "Our common Future", stresses the factor of environmental degradation causing the violent relationship between states:

> Environmental stress is both a cause and effect of political tension and military conflict...nations have fought to assist or resist control over raw materials, energy supplies, land, river basin, sea passages and other key environmental resources. According to the report, such conflicts are likely to increase as these resources became scarcer and competition for them will increase (1987:290).

Environmental security as a concept encompassing non-military aspects was officially mentioned for the first time in the International Conference on the Relationship between Disarmament and Development convened by the UN General Assembly in New York from 24 August to 11 September 1987. The final document adopted by consensus states:

> Recently non-military threats to security have moved to the forefront of global concern. Underdevelopment and declining prospects for development as well as mismanagement and waste of resources, constitute challenges to security. The degradation of the environment presents a threat to sustainable development.... Mass poverty, illiteracy, diseases, squalor and malnutrition affecting a large proportion of world's population often become the cause of social strain, tension and strife (Fischer Dietrich, 1993:10).

Inadequacy of the conventional approach centring on state and its military apparatus as found prominent in realist parlance to meet the non-military and non-conventional threats stemming from environmental degradation led to a reschedule of security agenda. The illusion of a hermetically sealed and self reliant security founded on the dominant realist paradigm is felt to be naïve and dangerous. The question remains persistently nagging the arrogant security paradigm:

How can a nation launch fighter planes to resist global warming?

How can a nation dispatch tanks to counter advancing deserts?

How can a nation fire the smartest missiles against rising sea levels?

Non-military threats to security could not be perceived as concrete and tangible as the conventional threats find a central place in the security agenda of the states. But the environmental degradation has changed this archetypal security thinking saying the wrong end of a smokestack can be as much of a security concern to humans as the barrel of a gun. The growing number of people vulnerable to environmental hazards makes it clear that the security of a state well impregnated with modern and nuclear weapons is not coeval with that of individuals or human beings. America, representing the metaphor of the unipolar moment in the world at present demonstrated its utter inability to forestall the orgy of Katrina or Gustav, which wreaked havoc on its citizens recently. In mid April 2007 newspapers reported that the US Congress was poised to ask for a National Intelligence Estimate (NIE) on the 'national security implications' of human induced climate change. The Sydney Morning Herald stated that American politicians are so concerned about the threats posed by the effects of global warming, they are legislating to elevate it to an official defence issue. The fear appears to be that "climate change could trigger new humanitarian crises and force countries to go to war over diminishing water and energy resources" (Allard Tom etal. 2007:1). It testifies to the above fact that threats from environmental degradation are more dangerous than armed conflicts. Twenty million people have died each year because of lack of life supporting environment in sharp contrast to 20 million died in armed conflict in total since 1945. Between 1990-1999, 188 million people affected per year by environmental induced natural calamities six times more than 31 million annually affected by armed conflicts.

CRITIQUE OF ENVIRONMENTAL SECURITY

Though a number of studies have spawned up recently demonstrating the linkage between environmental stress and conflict, there has been some criticism of these findings as happens in other fields. Critics like Deudney argued that the language of security— a discourse marked by militarism, competition and secretiveness is incompatible with the ethos of modern environmentalism (Deudney Daniel H, 1990: 461-76; 1999). With the end of cold war and collapse of Soviet Union, the exposure of secretive nuclear installation to international scrutiny, and security being associated not with state, but with the individuals or people, the language of security is no more couched in terms of militarism, competition and secretiveness, rather in terms of demilitarization, nuclear free world and public democratic governance. The dominant geopolitical paradigm of national interest was based on realist parlance of US and its allies' interests overwhelming the entire globe since the Second World War. When environmental security because of environmental catastrophic consequences threatening the existence of human beings leapfrogs to the center stage of national security concern, it as assumed is not to be based on same dominant geopolitical paradigm of North's interests to acquire the status of national security. Rather it calls for redefining the very foundation of traditional outlook of national security based on geopolitical interests of the dominant players in the international realm. If it is to be just an appendage to the geopolitical interests of the dominant players defining the world order since the Second World War, then environmental security is not in any way different from conventional security based on secrecy, militarization and competition for dominance. It has climbed up to the top of the national security agenda not on the basis of realist paradigm, but on a different paradigm. That what cannot be described in old traditional languages lacks the raison detre to be called national security stands discredited in the face of new kinds of threats that are stemming from unprecedented environmental crisis. Advocacy of hesitancy to term environmental security as national security means advising to navigate the uncharted seas of environmental crisis with warped, discredited and conventional realist cartography. If in the words of old ideas of security, environmental security is tried to be defined, the very dilution of what it stands for, takes place, and the perpetuation of the geopolitical interests of the dominant North led by US continues to the perils of the people in the developing South. When the discourse of environmental security is defined in terms of old conventional idioms i.e. the unhindered right of dominant players to resource supply sources in the South, it merely 'extends the explicitly geopolitical understanding of security that were widespread during the cold war to maintain the current global division of wealth."(Dalby, 1999:160).

Another objection is that in the concept of environmental security the absence of "us vs. them" which is a cardinal part of traditional concept of national security, is like, according to Deudney, taking sex out of 'rocks and roll'. In his words, "rock and roll" was originally coined as a euphemism for sex (1990:467). Interstate or intrastate conflicts over environmental scarcity of renewable resources like water, and fish is a clear cut example of 'us vs. them' syndrome. There is no dearth of evidences to show that water sharing has been a major cause of conflicts between and among nations (Hatami Halch and Peter H Gleick, 1992). For example, despite a set record of tension and on being war path between Lebanon and Israel, recently they were on loggerheads with each other when Lebanon began a project to increase water supply from the Wazzani to its neighbouring village. Israel is opposed to the project as a major share of water for the nation's main water reservoir, the lake Tiberias comes from the river. Reacting to the project, the Prime Minister of Israel, Ariel Sharon said: it will create grounds for war between the two nations" (Down to Earth, 2002: 16). The very presence of Bangladeshi refugees in Indian North-eastern states and Assam due to environmental scarcity of land in Bangladesh has been an armed conflict involving the military forces of India and Bangladesh (Gaan N, 1998; Dixon Thomas F, 1999: 141-42).

Two distinct features of environmental security are: First, the environmental causes of conflict, i.e. environmental factors behind potentially violent conflicts; Second, the impact of environmental degradation on overall political economy, health and life of the people. If environmental degradation or deficiencies create the conditions that render conflicts, act as multipliers that aggravate core causes of conflict[36] or act as a catalyst factor in creating conflicts, then environmental degradation or scarcity of resources becomes a national security issue (Porter Gareth, 1995: 218).

There are some scholars who decline to accept the links between environmental degradation and national security threats (Deudney, 1990: 461-76; Finger Mathias, 1991; Moss Richard h, 1990 and Painchaud Paul ed., 1990). They argue that "taking the term security and using it to encompass anything that threatens our well-being, might really take the term and dilute it of any significance" (Deudney, 1990:12). The feeling is that defining environmental issues in terms of security threats may contribute more to the militarization of the environment than to the greening of the environment." (Bruyninckx Hans, 1993: 1-16). In other words, defining environmental issues in terms of security risk is in itself a risky operation ...We may end up contributing more to the militarization of the environmental politics than to the demilitarization of security politics"(Brock Lothar, 1992: 98). This kind of view is harboured only when environmental security is understood by the North as to include its unimpeded right to access to resources of the South. That means, environmental security is considered as mere an appendage to the geopolitical security interests of the North defined in terms of realist paradigm making a great departure from what the proponents of environmental security originally understand it, and shifting very conveniently the onus of environmental protection to the South, so that the flow of resources from the South remains unhindered. Thus, the relationship between resources and development should also form part of the security debate. From the cold war perspective, security issues were understood in terms of the right of access of the developed world to the resources of the South. The major problem in the current environmental crisis is the absence of equal access to resources (Lipschutz R.D and J.P. Holdren, 1990: 121-33). The world economic structure and major international financial institutions function in a way as to serve the economic interest of the developed North reinforcing the widening North-South economic disparities. They also facilitate the continued exploitation of the environment and natural resources of the South. With the perpetuation of this kind of unjust economy coupled with debt crisis, the environment will be seriously affected rendering those belonging to the poor nations more insecure.

There is almost unanimity among the scientists about their predictions of threats of environmental degradation to the security of the people. The worst affected will be the poor people in the South. But scientific inaccuracy, lack of certainty about the impact of environmental degradation region wise and lack of precision, associated with the environment are cited to argue against the environmental security. Neither the actual increased exposure to UV rays from the punching of the hole in the Ozone layer nor the degree of harm it will wreak on plants, animals and humans can be calculated to a mathematical accuracy. Neither the eventual increase in global average temperatures from a given level of greenhouse gas emissions nor the impacts on weather patterns, human health, crops or sea level rise on region or country-wise has been studied with a scientific precision. Similarly, the rate of land degradation on a global scale cannot be measured with accuracy and its impact on future food productivity can be predicted with any scientific precision. Thus, each of these environmental threats to global well being has been subject to significant empirical and scientific uncertainty and inaccuracy .All said does not any way denude environmental security of its significance. Such uncertainties highlighted to refute the basis of the concept environmental security are also found in case of military planning based on worst case contingencies which are most unlikely to occur. If the very fear of possible threats from the other states' use of weapons conventional or nuclear could be the basis of the realist framework of national security even without having the remotest chance of exercising military options, why the real dangers of environmental degradation cannot be held justifiably as threats to the national security of the people. Yet military preparations are justified for such future apprehended threats from other countries as an insurance against these unlikely threats (Porter Gareth, 1995:220). With threats of environmental degradations to the people looming large, the concept 'environmental security' stands the logic to replace the traditional realist framework of national security defined in terms of military insurance against future uncertain and unlikely threats.

There is a feeling among scholars that a rethinking of the concept of security keeping in mind environmental consideration could become a dangerous tool in the hands of the totalitarian left who could attempt environmental collectivism (Painchaud, 1990; Waever Ole, 1993). It is also argued that since the logic of ecology has religious dimensions, the handling of environmental issue carries the danger of eco fascism (Gorz Andre, 1993). The danger of environmental collectivism or eco fascism, however, seems exaggerated. For, a resolution of the ecological crisis requires a rethinking of the entire development strategy. Addressing the security concerns of the people taking into consideration all their dimensions rather than of the state alone, runs counter to the very rationale of relating security to the state military power. Where there has already been growing demands for more democratization, people's participation, diversification of state power, human rights and global governance and more transparency in decision making, the logic of eco fascism or totalitarian left sounds little credible. Since these regimes regard themselves as the arbiter of national security, they may oppose many international environmental movements, rules and regulation, on the pretext that these constitute sources of threat to national security (Dalby S, 1993: 512). But in the face of the deepening socio-economic crisis due to environmental scarcity or degradation of resources, these regimes may find the going tough. Since eco-geographical regions do not always coincide with territorial units, on many issues the priority cannot be given to strengthening state power but to environmental co-operation among states (Levy Marc A, Keohane Robert O and Peter M. Haas, 1993; Rogers Katrina, 1995:17-18; Hass Peter M, Robert O Keohane and Mark A Levy, 1993).

It is therefore not surprising that a strong feeling is growing that environmental security is a national security concern. Although many scholars think that environmental security is part of the economic agenda, the concept of national security has been tacked on to environmental debates, because it has a mobilization potential (Buzan Barry, 1993:13).

Indeed, if the predictions of scientists about climate changes in terms of global warming and greenhouse effects come true, then fears regarding the break-up of some Antarctic ice sheets could put "environmental security at the top of the global agenda very soon(Ibid, 1997:12).

ENVIRONMENTAL SCARCITY AND CONFLICT: THE DOMINANT PARADIGM

In spite of these criticisms, the most influential arguments in the field have concluded that environmental stress is linked to conflict indirectly, but significantly. While the precise character of the linkage varies from case to case, it is made possible environmental stress is supposed to overwhelm the adaptive capacity of some societies while simultaneously introducing and reinforcing forms of conflict and instability. While the field of environmental security is characterized by division and debate, there is a strong degree of theoretical consensus among researchers. The most prominent and dominant thread that runs through the entire environmental security literature is that the environmental stress simultaneously reduces adaptive capacity and engenders conflict.

The dominant paradigm in the environmental security

literature harks back to writers like Thomas Malthus, but it has obtained its contemporarily influential formulation in the work of Thomas Homer Dixon and Toronto Group. From a myriad of empirical case studies conducted by them on Haiti, Chiapas, Gaza, Pakistan and Bangladesh – India, they concluded that environmental scarcity of renewable resources viz., water, forest, fisheries and cropland give rise to a number of deleterious social effects including economic decline, social segmentation and human migration – these social effects in interaction with other political, economic and social factors, can generate conflict and instability. Central to their model was the notion of supply of ingenuity gap or a disparity between the solutions required to cope with environmental scarcity and the human, social and institutional capital that could be mustered to provide these solutions. This ingenuity gap essentially undermines human adaptive responses.

That means, according to their studies, resource scarcity and limited or inadequate adaptive capacity coalesce together to generate violent conflicts in various regions (Dixon, 1999; 1994; Dixon, Jessica Blitt, 1998).

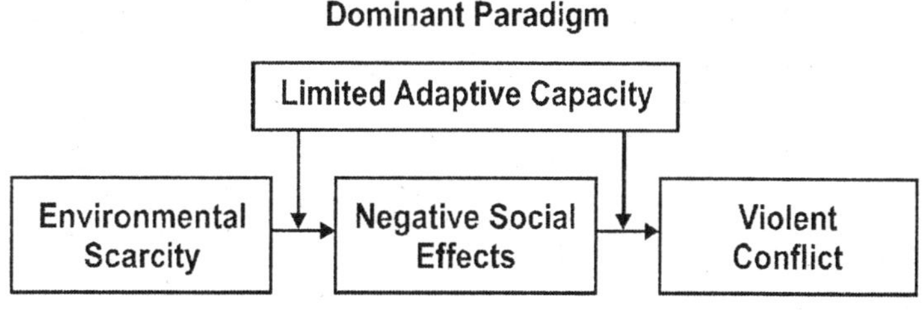

Dominant Paradigm

A theoretical representation is made in this figure (Ibid: 7) to understand the linkage between environmental stress and conflict.

Starting from 1st world war not only to the Falkland war as enumerated by Arthur H. Westing but to the latest

Gulf war all wars have been fought over access to natural resources such as minerals, fuels, fish stocks, products of the land and the land itself. The whole history of humanity has borne a testimony to the congeries of violent conflicts, contentions and wars that had taken place over access to and distribution of natural resources. In view of this, many scholars exhibit a tendency to interpret the linkage between environment and conflicts as a question of struggle for scare natural resources (Libiszewski, 1992: 6). Though environmental conflicts can manifest themselves as conflict over resources, in fact these multitude of wars are not really coming within what the term 'environmental' is understood. A human made environmental change does not simply mean any interaction between human beings and their environment. It means a destabilizing interference in the ecosystem's equilibrium. The pollution of atmosphere by emission of carbon dioxide, for example from fossil fuels based industries, overtaxes the ecosystem's absorption capability and causes the so called green house effects. This climate warming in turn changes among other things, the balance between ice sheets and liquid water on the earth's surface, causing a rise of the sea level. In a similar way, the process of desertification can be explained as consequences of the devegetation and overuse of the soil causes a decline of precipitation and soil erosion. As water supply is the prerequisite of nearly every ecosystem's functioning, serious manipulation in river flows is another example of human interference which often affects the ecological equilibrium in the concerned regions. The environmental degradation is only about these affected life supporting conditions, the negative impact on human beings and society. Environmental change can mean a loss of quality, degradation. Environmental degradation is thus, understood as a human made environmental change having a negative impact on human society. Gunther Bachler, in the place of degradation used the word 'transformation'. The term 'global human – ecological transformation' is meant the introduction of a heuristic concept in regarding those interactions between the three levels- nature, human beings and the economy in the regional context-which have led to conflicts between human communities and will increasingly lead to such conflicts (Bachler, 1993:5).

Resources are renewable because they provide both goods and services; forests supply timber (a good) while also maintaining regional hydrological cycles (a service).They are renewable because they are ecologically integrated in a feedback circle system which guarantees their replacement or the preservation of their quality. On the other hand, non-renewable resources as they are cannot be integrated in such an ecosystem. Therefore they can be depleted but they cannot be degraded. Their depletion causes degradation of the renewable resources. Further to distinguish, a non-renewable consists of a stock, which is the total quality of the resources available for consumption. A renewable resource has both a stock and flow which is the incremental addition to or restoration of the stock per unit of time. To draw an analogy between the stocks and flows of renewable resources and money in bank, a renewable resources' stock is the resource's capital or principal, which generates a flow of interests or income that can be tapped for human consumption and well-being.

A further characteristic of renewable resources is that they can be less substituted than non-renewable ones, and in several cases not substituted at all. Food, fresh water, clean air and life supporting climatic conditions are not just sources of wealth in an economic sense but also biological prerequisite of life. In addition to environment as a bank of material resources and a sink for wastes a third dimension of environment as a space of living should be considered. The loss of settlement areas due to the rise of the sea level, to desertification, or to industrial accident or project or dams, means more than just a shortage of resource 'land'. It includes an existential dimension and in certain dramatic cases of environmental degradation, it implies an aesthetic dimension of environment's impoverishment (Matthew Richard A.2001:9).

Environmental scarcity caused by environmental degradation means the resources that have traditionally been regarded as plentiful and naturally renewable but are becoming scarce now because of this failure of human beings to adopt sustainable methods of their management.

Unequal geopolitical and socio-economic distributions are often a source of degradation behaviour and the physical scarcity of a renewable resource can be a reason for the depletion of resource's capital stock. These are causally interrelated. Here the main focus is on the environmental scarcity of renewable resources that has the potential to seriously undermine human well- being. It can arise in three ways: through a drop in the supply of a key resource, through an increase in demands, and through a change in the relative access of different groups to the resource. Homer Dixon calls these respectively supply induced, demand induced and structural induced scarcities. Depletion and degradation produce a decrease in total resource supply or in other words a decrease in the size of the total resource stock. But population growth and changes in consumption behavior can also cause greater scarcity by boosting the demand for a resource. Thus, if a rapidly growing population depends on a fixed amount of cropland, the amount of cropland falls inexorably. Finally, scarcity is often caused by a severe imbalance in the distribution of wealth and power that results in some groups in a society getting disproportionately large slices of the total resources, where as others get slice that are too small to sustain their livelihoods. This is what is called structural scarcity.

Analysts and policymakers in the past have usually addressed these three sources of scarcity independently. Neo Malthusians and economic optimists have given importance to supply and demand induced scarcity while generally ignoring the political economy of resource distribution. According to Dixon, these three scarcities interact and reinforce each other in an extraordinarily pernicious ways (Dixon, 1999:114). One type of interaction is resource capture. The degradation and depletion of renewable resources can interact with population growth to encourage powerful groups within a society to shift resource distribution in their favour by manipulating laws and institutions governing resource access. These powerful groups tighten their grip on the dwindling renewable resources while subjecting the marginal groups to greater scarcity (Matthew Richard A, 2001:21).

Thus in Bangladesh, worsening land scarcities, partly caused by rapid population growth and human induced natural disasters, encouraged powerful landowners to exploit weakness in the state's land inheritance laws in order to seize lands from the poor farmers. These peasants have been forced to migrate to Indian territories for better livelihood. This happens also in Chiapas where the peasants were forced deeper into the state's lowland rain forest, farther away from the state's economic heartland, and deeper into poverty.

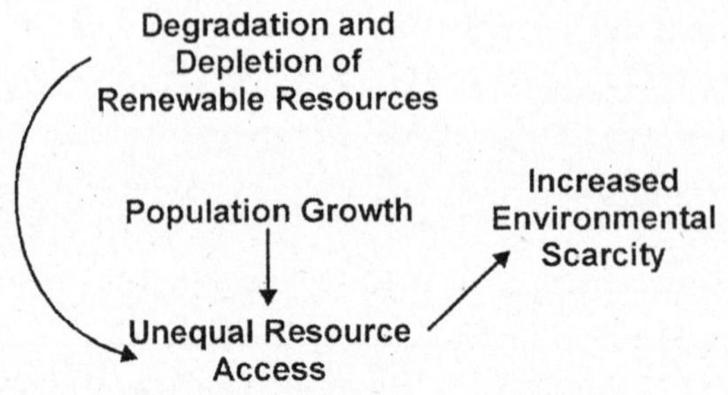

Process of Resource Capture

This figure is a representation of the process of resource capture as outlined by Homer Dixon (Dixon, 1999).

In the early 1990s, Israel's average annual supply of renewable fresh water was about 1950 million cubic meters against its demand including that of settlements in the West Bank and Golan Heights which was 2,150 cubic meters(Walzer Michael, 1992:). The annual deficit of about 200 cubic meters is covered by over-pumping aquifers which has already plummeted water tables in some parts of Israel and West Bank. This decline has caused the exhaustion of some wells and the infiltration of sea water from the Mediterranean (Matthew Richard A. 2001:24). At the same time Israel's population is expected to increase from the present 6.0 million to around 7.5 million in the 2020.Accordingly, the country's water demand by 2020 is estimated at 2,800 cubic metres.[61]

Ground water constitutes sixty percent or about 1200 cubic meters of annual sustainable supply of water. The rest comes from the river flow, flood water, and waste water cycling. Two of the three main aquifers on which Israel depends lie principally underneath the West Bank. About 475 cubic meters or about 40 percent of the ground water Israel uses originates in this territory. To protect its water interests Israel strictly restricted water use by Jewish settlers and Arabs on the West Bank. On a per capita basis in the early 1990s, settlers consumed four times as much as Arabs did. Of the 650 cubic meters only 125 cubic meters were allowed to be used by the Arabs. Israel also restricted the number of wells Arab could drill in the territory, the amount of water Arabs were allowed to pump, and the times at which they could draw irrigation water. During occupation after 1967 Arabs were not permitted to drill new wells for agricultural purpose, although the Mekorot, Israel Water Company drilled more than thirty wells for settler's irrigation. The area of irrigated Arab farmland on the West Bank dwindled from 27 percent of the total cultivated area to 3.5 to 6 percent. (Dixon, 1999). Arab agriculture in the regions got a setback because some Arab wells became dry or saline as a result of Israeli wells being drilled deeper nearby. These Israel water policies restricting water use to Arabs combined with the confiscation of agricultural land for settlers as well as Israeli restriction on Palestine agriculture propelled many West Bank Arabs to abandon farming and flee to towns to find either unemployed or become day labourers within Israel. No doubt many political, economic and ideological factors operate to explain the present conflagration in this region but the links between these processes and unrest in West Bank appears reasonable to conclude that water scarcity and its economic effects contribute to the present crisis in the region (Boge 1992:5). Rising frustration in Palestinian community due to this factor seems to lie underneath the long ongoing Israeli Palestine territorial war (Gleick Peter H. 1998).

ECOLOGICAL MARGINALIZATION

It is a process resulted out of a structural imbalance in resource distribution which in association with rapid population growth forces resource starved people into ecological marginal areas, such as upland hillsides.

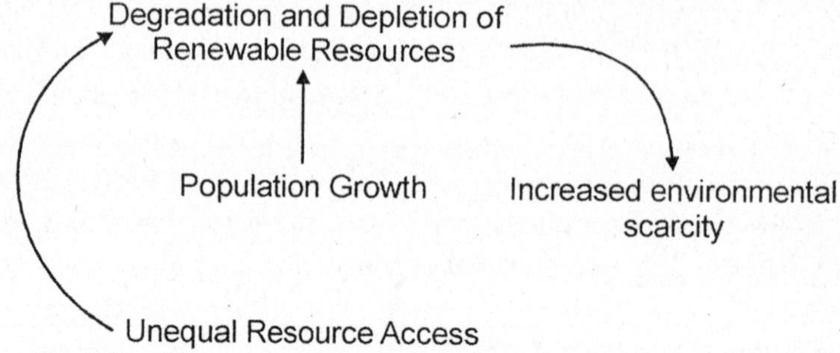

The Process of Ecological Marginalization

This figure as pointed out by Dixon represents the process by which poor people due to inequitable resource distribution, population growth and land degradation are forced to migrate to marginal regions (Dixon, 1999). As happened in Bangladesh, the people living in low lying areas affected by inequitable distribution of land, high density of population growth, soil erosion, and natural disasters such as cyclone, flood and storms have been settled in Chittagong Hill Tracts (CHT) which in turn, has not only caused massive deforestation because of slash and burn agriculture but also driven the indigenous tribal people Chakmas into Indian territories (Ibid).This process is visibly seen in the Himalayas, Indonesia, Central America, Brazil, Rajastan and the Sahel. Overtime the process "causes environmental degradation and intractable poverty to become more and more closely intertwined in particular geographic areas with fragile environmental degradation. The World's poorest people are thus increasingly clustered in two types of areas: remote and ecologically fragile rural areas and the edge of growing urban areas."(Ibid). A grossly unfair distribution of good cropland in lowland regions a colonial heritance bequeathed to Philippines by its former Spanish and American colonial rulers continues to be reinforced since independence by powerful landowning elite (Ibid). Introduction of green - revolution and modern technologies in agriculture from 1960s into the 1980s resulted in a hike not only in the lowland production of grain for domestic consumption but also in cash crops. The proceeds from the cash crops helped the country pay its huge external debt. This unusual increased production opened the prospects of demand for agricultural labourers in large farms but it was not enough to compensate for a population growth rate at over 2.5 percent. In combination with this population growth, unequal land access produced a surplus in agricultural unemployment. Daily wages demonstrated a downward slide with rural and urban industrialization lacking sufficient capability to employ the excess labour. Thus, economically impoverished millions of poor agricultural labourers and landless peasants migrated to urban areas such Mamila already overburdened with shanty towns, and millions others moved to the least productive and often ecologically vulnerable territories such as steep hill sides. In these upland areas the settlers used fire to clear the forested land for agriculture and to get charcoal for the cities. Thus, the slash and burn farming and procuring charcoal for the cities with little wherewithal to protect the fragile ecosystem resulted in horrendous environmental damage particularly water erosion, land slides and changes in the hydrological cycle. This damage caused a dismal fall in food production, and encouraged settlers to clear new forested land, thus ensuring massive land degradation. The often sought far marginally fertile land is no longer in sight in many places and economic conditions remain as desperate as before for many peasants.

SIGNIFICANCE OF CONTEXT

Not in all cases environmental scarcity or degradation has been a direct cause of conflict or violence. In cases of scarcity of renewable resources like water, fish, the conflict may be direct or where the environmental cause is found to be dominant. In case of environmentally induced migration the conflict is in association with social, political or economic contexts. These contexts are to be taken note of while studying the environmental causes of conflict. For example, some find behind the 1994 Rwandan genocide, the rapid population growth, severe land scarcity and the resulting food shortfalls- as the key factors. According to Washington Post in its editorial comment: while the Rwandan civil war was; military, political and personal in its execution", a key underlying cause was" a merciless struggle for land in peasant society whose birth rates have put an unsustainable pressure on it." (Washington Post 25 August 1994). On close scrutiny, the genocide in Rwanda was nothing but "a struggle among elites for control of the Rwanda state. Land scarcity played at most a peripheral role by reducing the regime legitimacy in the countryside and restricting alternatives for elite enrichment outside of government." (Dixon and Percival 1996: 270-91).

While putting a premium on contexts one should not swing to the opposite extreme saying the causal role of environmental scarcity is entirely subordinate to that of contextual factors. To some skeptics, scarcity is wholly a result of political, economic and social factors, such as failed institutions and policies and needs a little independent attention (Lipschutz, 1997: 35-50). Homer Dixon refutes this argument on the following grounds (Dixon 1999: 17-18).

First, environmental scarcity is not only influenced by social factors like institutions and policies, it can itself affect these institutions and policies in harmful ways. For example, the Mauritanian government built a series of dams along the Senegal river to avoid food shortages and drought, as a result the land prices hiked in these areas, given the critical land scarcities elsewhere in the regions.

Being controlled by Moors of Arab region, the government in order to get profit modified the existing laws relating to land ownership even abrogated the traditional right of black Mauritanians to farm, herd and fish along the river. This harmed the interests of a large section of the country's population.

Second, the environmental scarcity is not wholly a result of economic, political and social factors. It is also partly a function of a particular physical characteristic of society's surrounding environment. These characteristics are, in some respects independent of human activities. For example, the depths of soils in the Filipino uplands prior to land clearing and features that make Israel's aquifers vulnerable to salt intrusion are the physical givens of these environmental resources. Third, once environmental scarcity is irreversible, then the scarcity is an external influence on society (Haiti's top soil washes away into the sea). Even if new policies are undertaken to remove the underlying political and economic causes, the scarcity remains irreversible and remains a continuous burden on society. For example, chronic instability in Haiti and insurgency and violence elsewhere around globe such as in Filipino cannot be understood and remedied unless and until the independent causal role of environmental scarcity is understood and accepted not subordinate to contextual factors.

On the basis of preferential values, beliefs, social and political institutional behaviour, domestic and international arguments can be advanced in favour of not resorting to nuclear brinkmanship. These contexts are no doubt important and become effective in avoiding a nuclear holocaust but these do not in any way diminish the independent importance of possession of nuclear weapons on the part of a state as a security threat. Similarly, in some cases for example as argued, adaptation is a measure that people undertake by suffering a hardship in the form of starving, or death hazards in response to environmental stress, thus avoiding the slide into the loop of environmental conflict. Here, adaptation may not have resulted in a conflict as conceptualized by the dominant environmental conflict paradigm school of thought, but the threats posed by environmental degradation, say due to global warming or green house effect – the result of a policy and function of some governments remain irreversible, because scientific study on the causal role of nations on the region basis and their impact on nation wise has remained to a greater extent uncertain. For example, a scientific study is yet to be made out, pointing out what quality of emission of CO_2 from US to the atmosphere causes what amount of global warming, effects on agricultural, health, food etc on how many poor countries. This kind of scientific uncertainty and study in general has not been able to muster and organize the affected people politically against the cause nations. Even if there is adaptation or adjustment or surrender the threats to the people from the environmental degradation continue unabated. Thus environmental security is a broad and comprehensive spectrum which includes both the environmental causes of conflict and the adaptive measures, so that a review of policies, values and social and political preference of institutions can take place to ensure human security not in terms of adaptive suffering or resorting to conflict for resolution but in terms of an affirmative, positive proactive policy, renewed vision and new planetary ethics.

On theoretical ground it is criticized that even if resource scarcity plays a causal role in conflict, there are other more convincing explanations for conflict. Further, the prospects for adaptation, cooperation or resolution are not as completely bleak as is often presented. At the very prospects of an unlikely nuclear war, the fear of destructibility by the use of nuclear weapons has not any way diminished the universality of nuclear weapon as a main national security issue. It is that fear of destruction which may have brought many nuclear powers to negotiating table for cooperation or disarmament. The resultant cooperation should not be cited to underrate the holistic perception of nuclear weapons as being a national security concern. Similarly, environmental scarcity of resources with its disastrous social effects may not be everywhere a direct cause of violent conflict, sometimes in combination with other factors cause conflict. For example, sea level rise a consequence of global warming due to North's mindless pursuit of industrialization based on fossil fuel technology will affect low-lying areas such as of Bangladesh below the sea level turning millions of them as refugees fleeing to Indian territories that is likely to exacerbate the already infested ethnic conflict in North-Eastern states. That it would not affect other countries does not any way diminish the environmental causes of conflict not less than the universality of nuclear weapons as a security concern. The consequences of environmental scarcity of resources on political, economic and social life of a state or states may prompt states or nations to cooperate to avoid the negative effects of war on environment. So the environmental co-operation syndrome as argued by some should not be overrated to diminish the role of environmental scarcity of resources causing conflict or violence. No nuclear war has ever been fought in this world after American's dropping of hydrogen bombs on Japan's Herosima and Nagasaki during the course of Second World War. This would be as preposterous to say that nuclear weapon lack the potential or prospects for conflict as to say that the environmental scarcity of resources lacks the potential for conflict as it has not resulted in conflict in some areas or has resulted in cooperation. Adaptation means the involvement of all state apparatus, institutions, scientific community, even the social system and value structure including the affected to take steps that would obviate the negative effects of environmental scarcity. The poor developing countries may not have the economic and scientific wherewithal as argued by Dixon to cope with the situation. Even the developed countries will not find it a smooth sailing while responding to the environmental crisis. For example, in regard to stabilization of Co_2 in the atmosphere American steps to renege on its commitment agreed to at Kyoto were a capitulation to the petroleum, coal industrial lobby. What has threatened the world is the Western inordinate life style and pattern of development causing global warming, sea level rise and ozone layer depletion. To ensure environmental security what it requires is to make an overhaul of its pattern of life and development which is not possible with strong protestations from high class people. So Bush, American President caving in to the pressure of the industrial class justified his rejection of Kyoto protocol on the ground that countenancing the Kyoto commitment would hamper its economy and life style of its people (Levy David and Daniel Egan, 1998: 337-61; Gaan N.2001:89-112). Environmental security means overhauling the entire economic development pattern and existing social values related to liberal capitalism which is not possible without politico-socio-economic disruption. So the potential for conflict lies as much in the environmental scarcity of resources as in the very remedies and adaptive measures – a part of fulfillment of environmental security.

In spite of the criticisms above, the main thrust of the studies showing the linkage between environment and conflict, remains paramount: the environmental scarcity operates through a set of intervening variables, contexts or ideational factors that directly cause conflict, and that environmental social effects and stress, as such outstrip attempts to cope with the crisis.

Another study undertaken by Swiss Peace Institute's Environment and Conflicts Project (ENCOP) was in the direction of what the Toronto group suggests. Gunther Bachler belonging to this group in his study used the term transformation by which he meant "the introduction of a heuristic concept in recording those interactions between the three levels – nature, human beings and the economy in a regional context-which have led to conflicts between human communities and will ...increasingly, lead to such conflicts" (Bachler Gunther, 1993:5).

Degradation is used in this context as an indicator of the degree of environmental transformation. In the words of Kates et al,"the biosphere has accumulated or is on its way to accumulating such a magnitude and variety of changes that it may be said to be transformed" (Kates Robert W and Turner B.L and Clark William 1990). In other words, "transformation conflicts are caused by fundamental anthropogenic changes in the environmental media and by the interactions between the processes of change and their consequences in the eco-regional context" (Bachler, 1993:16).

Another authority Stephan Libiszewski belonging to ENCOP, making a distinction between traditional resource wars and environmental causes of conflict is of the view that 'an environmental conflict is a conflict caused by the environmental scarcity of a resource, that means: caused by a human made disturbance of its normal regeneration rate. Environmental scarcity can result from the overuse of a renewable resource or from the overstrain of the ecosystem's sink capacity, that is pollution. Both can reach the stage of destruction of space of living. Conflicts caused by physical, geopolitical or socio-economic resource scarcity are not environmental conflicts but traditional conflicts of resource distribution" (Libiszewski Stephan, 1992:6).

As found in the Toronto Group's research the ENCOP also walks on the same furrow that scarcity gives rise to conflict. Also it is alleged to be silent about human adaptation to resource scarcity. In these studies, it is mal-development, a condition similar to Homer Dixon's ingenuity gap that undermines human responses and enhances conflicts (Matthew Richard A, Gaulin Ted and Bryan McDonald, 2001:7). Though the ENCOP model is more complex than the Toronto group's general model, but the theoretical argument presented by both is very similar (Peluso Nancy and Michael Walts, 2001: 15-24).

In a 1999 NATO pilot study this dominant environmental conflict paradigm was found in the line with the other studies (1999: 232). According to this study," [i]t is not environmental stress in isolation that characterizes the nature of the conflict between groups but other factors" (Ibid: 22). Here too political, economic and social factors intervene between environmental stress and conflict.

The State Failure Task Force (SFTF), another research group marking the same dominant paradigm as with the preceding studies, reiterates the causal weight of environmental stress through intervening variables (Esty Daniel et al, 1999). While the researches did find that massive environmental damage in a short time frame could directly cause political collapse, the far more common scenario was that environmental stress operates through the intervening variable of quality of life to generate conflict.

Though highly critical of Toronto group, recent work by Gleditsch and de Soysa appears to have been co-opted by the dominant paradigm. According to their studies, resource scarcity, one component of a multifaceted development problem that they call "poverty" reduces agricultural production which in turn leads to conflict. That is, scarcity leads to a negative social outcome which becomes the proximate cause of conflict (Gauli Ted, 2000:9). Beyond this, however, the Gleditsch and de Soyasa model is similar to the Toronto Group in that there is little room for human adaptation to conditions of scarcity. Indeed, their key independent variable, poverty, is defined by a lack of social and human capital. "Like Homer Dixon's ingenuity gap, Gleditsch and de Soyasa's explanatory variable appears to lock in negative social outcomes, leaving little room for human adaptation (Matthew Richard et al: 2001:9).

There is some variation in these models and term presented by these research groups. But in each case the general theory linking resource scarcity and conflict is the same. Homer Dixon focuses on an "ingenuity gap", ENCOP on "mal-development" and Gleditsch and de Soysa on "poverty". Nevertheless, all these phrases describe a similar process- a limited capacity to respond to scarcity.

The model which is critical of all the above models adopted by Richard A Matthew et al finds flaws in current theory in environmental security on two counts. "First, it focuses on too short a time frame. Second, and relatedly it underestimates human adaptive capacity" (Ibid). They were averse to accepting the two extremes, Homer Dixon's lack of adaptive capacity in the poor countries, and Julian Simon and Herman Kahn's faith in the infinite capacity of individuals to adapt. To them, human adaptive capacity lies somewhere between these two extremes. Julian Simon writes, "there is no physical or economic reason why human resourcefulness and enterprise cannot forever continue to respond to impending shortages and existing problems with new expedients that, after an adjustment period, leave us better off than before the problem arose" (Simon Julian: 1996).

Homer Dixon responds to this saying, "while I acknowledge the extraordinary potential of human resourcefulness and enterprise, I nonetheless argue that some societies – especially poor societies – will not be able to supply the unprecedented amounts of ingenuity they will need to solve their emerging scarcity problems"(Dixon, 1999:114). This clearly demonstrates, Homer Dixon never maintains that all societies will not be able to cope with the situation. It is some poor societies because of various factors will be in dearth of required supply of ingenuity to adapt to the situation.

LACK OF INGENUITY SUPPLY AND ADAPTIVE FAILURE

According to Homer Dixon and his group the environmental scarcity of resources and its various social effects can make the developing societies vulnerable to the extent that they would not be able to adapt to the situation and find out solutions as they are plagued by lack of supply of ingenuity. What adds to their disadvantage is the very fact that many of them are not adequately endowed with the social institutions including the productive research centers, efficient markets and capable states which are necessary for an ample supply of both social and technical solution to environmental scarcity. As argued by this group, environmental scarcity sometimes diminishes these countries' ability to create and maintain such institutions (Romer, 1994: 3-22).But the proponents of new economic growth theory or endogenous growth theory, overlooking the fact that environmental scarcity can stymie the supply of ingenuity, argue that ideas are a factor of economic production in addition to capital, labour, and land (Dixon, 1999; 110). In their views scarcities will boost the supply of ingenuity. In other words necessity will often be the mother of invention. This will help alleviate scarcity's severity and social impacts. These economists focus mainly on ideas embodied in new technologies. Homer Dixon's concept of supply of ingenuity is not confined to mere technological and scientific innovations. That environmental scarcity and its social impacts need only the attention of scientists and engineers has been reviewed. According to Homer Dixon, "the supply of this technical ingenuity depends on an adequate supply of social ingenuity at many levels of society. Social ingenuity is the key to the creation, reform and maintenance of public and semipublic goods such as markets, funding agencies, educational and research organizations, and effective government" (Ibid). Social ingenuity is thus a precursor to technical ingenuity and key to adaptation strategies. Countries afflicted by environmental scarcity of resources need sophisticated and stable systems of markets, legal regimes, financial agencies, and educational and research institutions to promote the development and distribution of new grains adapted for dry climate and eroded soils, of alternative cooking technologies to compensate for the loss of firewood and of water conservation technologies. In the words of Dixon, "it is both an input to and output of the economic system" (Ibid). It is not that the ingenuity required to adapt to the crisis created by environmental scarcity is produced always at the top of the social hierarchy, it is also produced at the community and household levels.

Burgeoning population growth and increasing per capita resource consumption are causing a steady increase in the ratio of the consumption of resource per unit of time to the total amount of resource available. Thus the scarcity has in turn increased the requirement for ingenuity. The increased pace of resource depletion means that societies have less time to adjust their institutions and technologies. Since human beings are consuming a very broad spectrum of renewable resources at very high rates, serious scarcities can affect many resources simultaneously or in quick succession. This multiplicity of scarcities can make it harder to find relatively abundant resources to substitute for scarce ones. Further, the ingenuity requirement to compensate for scarcities of renewable is generally greater than that of non renewables. The difference between the two has been ignored by the economists. These can be no substitute for renewable resources. For example, nothing can substitute for water in the tissues of a living organism. Thus, the options for responding to scarcity of renewable resources are restricted and society's need for ingenuity rises. Even if the requisite is supplied, the systems will still be vulnerable to sudden shocks, because many environmental scarcities are interconnected and unpredictable. Further more, even if societies manage their resource systems exceptionally well, fundamental physical, biological, and social constraints may make it difficult to fully compensate for the effects of scarcity. These constraints include inescapable time lags that affect a society's ability to mitigate scarcities, like the time needed for a new forest to grow, for a new technology to be disseminated, or for cultural change to take place (Simon, 1981:345).

CONSTRAINTS ON SUPPLY OF INGENUITY

But optimists like Aaron Wildavsky, Todd La Porte, Dennis Avery, and Thomas Schelling ensconce faith in the ingenuity and resourcefulness of man to find solution to the crisis. As Julian Simon writes : " there is no physical or economic reason why human resourcefulness and enterprise cannot forever continue to respond to impending shortage and existing problems with new expedients that , after an adjustment period, leave us better off than before the problem arose" (Simon 1981: 345). Homer Dixon does not harbour a slightest doubt of the extraordinary potential of human resourcefulness and enterprise, but nonetheless argue that some poor developing societies will not be able to supply the unprecedented amounts of ingenuity required to solve the impending environmental scarcity. He has identified four factors that can limit the supply of social and technical ingenuity: market failure, social friction, shortage of capital, and constraints on science (Dixon, 1999).

MARKET FAILURE

Many resources especially renewable like hydrological cycles and productive seas cannot be physically controlled or divided into salable units for the exclusive use of specific consumers. It is therefore hard to assign clear property rights and they remain open access resources that are vulnerable to over exploitation. As Repetto notes, "Prices can guide market adjustment processes only if resources can be bought and sold which presupposes that they can be owned. Many important resources are not privately owned, usually because it is impossible to segregate one person's portion from another's and reserve it for exclusive use" (Repetto, 1987: 6-7). At best their scarcity is indirectly reflected in the prices of marketable resources that are dependent on them. For example, damage to ocean ecosystems can cause fish prices to rise.

Even if property rights are clear, market prices may still not fully reflect the costs of resource use. Resource extraction or use can produce negative externalities- such as river siltation from upstream deforestation- that are not incorporated in the resources price. The World Bank notes that "clear property rights may induce private users to adopt the correct pattern of timber extraction, taking into consideration the current and future benefits from logging, but give no incentive to take into account the costs of deforestation to those living outside the forests- for example, increased soil erosion or lost biodiversity" (World Bank, 1992: 70). Poor countries are particularly disadvantaged because they start with underdeveloped economic institutions. The state which is to play a key role in increasing ingenuity' supply through research, development, and extension services is very much stymied in developing societies because of economic and other constraints.

SOCIAL FRICTION

As analyzed above, environmental scarcity of resources produces frictions, cleavages and social segmentation among various groups. Mancur Olson's work (Olson, 1982) is cited by Dixon to understand his analysis. First, Olson shows that small coalitions can generally organize themselves more quickly and purse their interests with greater force than larger groups. They therefore have political power disproportionate to their size, and they can be more nimble, focused and effective in their lobbying. Second, this proportionate power will be particularly acute in unstable societies, because large coalitions need time and social stability to establish themselves and grow. The governments of unstable countries are therefore "systematically influenced by the interests, pleas and pressure "of small coalitions (Ibid). Third, small coalitions are always guided by their narrowly defined self interests in total disregard of the common well being. Olson writes, there is "no constraint on the social cost such an organization will find it expedient to impose on the society in the course of obtaining a larger share of the social output for itself" (Ibid).

It has been pointed out earlier that increased environmental scarcity of resources exacerbated social segmentation, sharpens cleavages among groups, and provokes action by group to protect their interests in terms of resource capture and rent seeking. Building on Olson's argument, Homer Dixon points out that the smaller groups purse their interests better than larger ones in developing countries, because their possession of wealth, power and status well informed by their position in the social order had made this minority well advantaged while pursing their narrow self interests, the small coalitions often impede the process of institutional building that reflect the broader interest of society. They hamstring all efforts to reform existing or establish new social institutions, laws and structural arrangements, if these effects run counter to coalition interests, as they often do (Dixon, 1999). This social friction arising out of environmental scarcity makes it harder to focus and coordinate social activities, talents, and resource in response to scarcity. As Olson points out, narrow coalitions "interfere with an economy's capacity to adapt to change and to generate new innovations" (Olson, 1982: 62). Thus, the coalitions provoked to action by scarcities will sometimes block solutions to the very same scarcities. Increasing social friction affects incentives for political entrepreneurs to produce and deliver the social ingenuity needed for new institutions. Ruttan and Hayani opine that "the supply of institutional innovations depends critically on the power structure or balance among vested interest groups in the society" (Ruttan et al, 1984: 213). As seen, scarcities of cropland and water in Bangladesh – scarcities arising from both skewed resource distribution and population growth – induce some agricultural innovation, but they also inflame existing distribution struggles among coalitions. These struggles in turn have obstructed reform of water control institutions and the deployment of irrigation technologies (Boyce, 1987). A society which is very much informed by a culture of selfishness will soon slip into narrow coalitions as scarcity worsens. For example, Filipino culture encourages cooperation within groups rather than among groups resulting in what is often remarked, clannishness of the society and undermining the concept of national welfare (Kessler, 1989: 18). To the contrary, a society where there is prevalence of culture of good will, reciprocity, civic mindedness, and trust can impede the rise of narrow coalitions as scarcity worsens.

Thus Homer Dixon cited these two contextual factors which will especially influence the degree of social friction caused by environmental scarcity and the extent to which this friction hamstrings the supply of ingenuity. In his words, "if narrow coalitions have already penetrated the state, social friction will have a particularly strong effect on society's capacity to reform and build institutions" (Dixon, 1999: 120).

CAPITAL AVAILABILITY

Capital both financial and human is necessary to respond to the environmental scarcity of resources. Availability of capital is generally lower in developing societies. To undertake any scientific and technological research in response to scarcity needs huge finance. Political entrepreneurs need financial capital to provide selective incentives and side payments to coalitions that block institutional change. The state needs capital to provide public goods like infrastructure and resource monitoring. Many societies afflicted by severe resource scarcity are poor; moreover, the often predatory behaviour of their elites further reduces general capital availability (Evans, 1992: 144). Dearth of adequate and required laboratory equipments, computers, journals and books impedes the efforts to build indigenous research capability in developing societies (Ibrahim, 1992). In addition to shortage of finance, lack of human capital also cripples the supply of ingenuity. For example, the United Nations reports that by 1987 nearly a third of Africa's skilled labour had left for Europe and that the continents as a whole lost sixty thousand middle and high level managers between 1985 and 1990 (United Nations Development Report 1992: 57).

CONSTRAINTS ON SCIENCE

As said above, the economic and technological optimists exude faith in humankind's ability to manage the resource scarcity. Homer Dixon outlines four constraints on science that will hinder ingenuity's supply (Dixon, 1999: 123-24). First are human cognitive limits. Humans do not have the infinite ability to understand and manage the complex, multivariate, nonlinear and often chaotic processes of ecological –social systems. The relationship in some of these systems are "simply too numerous and complex to be grasped , much less controlled, by the human intellect" (Wilson 1993: 29).Many natural, social systems are probably computationally intractable, which means they cannot be accurately modeled using any realistic amount of computational power (Traub etal, 1994: 102-7). Scientists are additionally handicapped because they cannot conduct controlled experiments with large scale natural and social systems.

The cognitive features of human brain evolved in ecological circumstances restrict human ability to supply ingenuity. Second is the escalating cost of research in the field of science and technology. To probe deeper into the labyrinthine nature has become a very costly affair. The poor societies afflicted by resource scarcity need the help of advanced science like molecular biology which they cannot afford, especially when faced with resource crunch. A third constraint arises from the cumulative nature of scientific knowledge: each new discovery must build on a host of earlier ones. "The pace of discovery is marked by jumps and lags as scientists make breakthroughs or lose time pursing fruitless leads. This pace cannot be easily forced, especially in basic science where the work's ultimate practical use is not clear" (Dixon, 1999:124).

A final constraint is science's vulnerability to social control. It needs a great variety and abundance of resource inputs, a non hierarchical institutional structure, a dense network of connections between like minded innovators, and a popular culture for promotion of science. For example, the development in former Soviet Union in 1990s crippled its vast research establishments and led to the rise in occult and anti science movements causing a decline in respect for analytical thought (Wright, 1991: 20-25; Kapitza, 1999: 32-38).

CONCLUSION

Many analysts and economists place undue faith in the infinite capability of human kind to produce ingenuity to deal with the environmental scarcity. So far as the developing societies are concerned, the supply of ingenuity will not be plenty because of factors and constraints analyzed above by Dixon and his group. There may be a mismatch between the severity of the crisis and the amount of ingenuity needed to adapt to the crisis. This ingenuity gap shall be a common phenomenon of developing societies where the scarcity of resources has been severe. This is the reason why the developing societies are more vulnerable to environmental scarcity than the developed world. The question is not about human adaptation to the environmental scarcity and its social effects whether by suffering, starving and bearing the amount of hardship. The fulcrum of the analysis lies on how to prevent the crisis. This is what comes within the broader ambit of environmental security. It is not that the environmental scarcity shall be allowed to bust into a crisis until a solution is to be found out putting boundless faith in the potential of human ingenuity, as the economists and critics suggest. Human ingenuity is not like a magic wand that unearths a solution out of its sleeve every time when we are spurred by necessity. The crisis shall not be kept on waiting till scientific investments and knowledge come out with a solution. The impact of social effects of environmental scarcity on future generations may have to be more severe and far reaching. Since the poor societies are afflicted by severe environmental scarcity, there will be more ingenuity gap and adaptive failure because of the constraints cited above. In that case the very onus and functions of maintaining intergenerational equity and responsibility may not be properly discharged. The scarcity if let go to be fully blown into a crisis, just keeping faith in the ingenuity of man to reveal a solution, the prospects for social friction and violent conflict not only in the present generation but also in future societies looms large. This analysis is not that of an apologist to put forth arguments linking environmental scarcity and conflict, or it is not that of an economic optimist to wait and see keeping undue faith in human ingenuity which is not available in plenty to the poor societies. It is about defining environmental security that includes a pro active preventive measure to avoid the prospects for conflicts as outlined by the dominant environmental conflict paradigm, and efforts to redefine the conventional wisdom about the security based on realist frame work, and the western pattern of development based on fossil fuel based industrialization taking into account the intergenerational equity and intergenerational responsibility.

This brings Homer Dixon closer to the position taken by Richard A. Matthew and his associates. If adaptation is a dynamic and continuous process, then there may be adaptation failure in some and adaptation success in others visited with trauma, travails and hardships. When such individual trauma, travails and ordeals while adapting to the environmental stress becomes a collective or group phenomena in a particular political context or in the face of growing incapability of state, the potential for violent conflict exists. Taking a departure from this, Matthew group holds that from a longer time perspective even if the adaptive failures through feed back will result in adaptive success, thus avoiding the prospects for environmental conflicts. Contrary to what Neo-Mathusians such as Paul Ehrlich, Robert Kaplan, and Thomas Homer Dixon contend, "adaptive mechanisms do not simply stall or become overwhelmed while levels of environmental stress continue to escalate" (Matthew Richard et al, 2001: 21).To quote Richard A Mathew further: "This is not to say that all forms of adaptation are socially desirable. Adaptation can mean people of the developing would going further and further into the hinterland to gather fuel, wood and water; parents sending their children to work in factories because of crop failure; and simple belt-tightening people eating less,"(Ibid) or as happened in Kalahandi district of Orissa people eating the dried up kernel of ripen mangoes died while adapting to food scarcity, or people in these tribal areas of Orissa are forced to sell their children as bonded labourers as a mark of adaptation to the environmental scarcity of crop land and food. These latter examples are certainly unsettling and portent of potential for violent behaviour in an organized form depending on the nature of political system prevailing. If to use the language of Matthew, these starvation, death, or going without food, or half fed situations are the genuine form of adaptation, then conflict arising out of these situations created by environmental scarcity in the form of collective or group behaviour or response can be a genuine version of adaptation with a view to develop new legitimate and representative political authority and institution and new value structure that would reinvent the political- economic thinking which so far has contributed to environmental scarcity. As Walzer argues, conflict is a normal and important aspect of social development (Walzer Michael, 1992; 1993; 1994; 1995). Then the portrayal of environmental crisis as an environmental conflict paradigm from a broader perspective does not lose its significance or acceptability, as a theoretical frame work as argued by Richard Matthew and his group. The conclusion that this group arrived at is not to deny the linkage between environmental scarcity and conflict but stresses on "longer term studies" that "might provide deeper understanding of the ways in which concerns about environmental stress and degradation are relevant not only to the those concerned with international security, but also those worried about human rights, social justice and sustainable development (Matthew Richard et al, 2001: 24).

On the one side, the economic deprivation, decreased agricultural production, health hazards, poverty, starvation or half fed or even death situation due to pollution and water scarcity- part of the adaptive success as propounded by Matthew – may cause indirect conflict in association with other factors as nuanced by Volker Boge(1992:5) or Homer Dixon(1999). The other side is the situation of direct conflict or violence arising out of the environmental scarcity of resources - a case of adaptive failure. Hence the conflict emanates directly from the overuse and or pollution / destruction of a renewable natural resource. For example, if a downstream riparian threatens to go to war against an upstream riparian, because the latter pollutes river water so gravely that it cannot be used by the inhabitants of the downstream riparian, who are highly dependent on this water, then the environmental character of conflict is evident(Boge, 1992). An array of evidences can be cited to show such threats of conflict over environmental scarcity of water all over the globe (Gleick, 1992; Haftendorn Helga, 2000: 51-68; Villiers Marq D, 1999). That in some cases it has led to cooperation to avoid war does not divest the environmental conflict of its theoretical appeal. Another example of direct violent conflict over environmental scarcity of resources like fish can be cited. The decline in fish catch due to environmental degradation all over the globe and in South Asian regions in particular could result in a series of violent conflict between Tamil Nadu fishermen of India, and Sri Lanka over fishing in waters of Kachchativu Island ceded by India to Sri Lanka as a gesture of friendship and good will ir 1974(Gaan N. 1997: 17-23).

The two aspects of environmental scarcity induced situation in terms of adaptive failure and adaptive success can dovetail together into what is called environmental security in a broader sense. What is called as adaptive success at micro level along with adaptive failure in terms of poverty, food scarcity, health hazards or suffering due to environmental degradation at macro level, for example the impact of global warming due to western pattern of development based on fossil fuel industrialization and inordinate life style, poses challenges to redefine development and the vision of and approaches to life. The findings of the latest study Living Planet Report 2000 measuring 151 nation states while distributing "earth share" in terms of consumption keeps at top the dominant economic players such as US numbering 75 countries who have over exceeded their legitimate share and below 76 countries such as Bangladesh, Afghanistan and Eritrea (Graham Kennedy, 2002:4). It is this over consumption and exorbitant life style of dominant North that has put the South poor people at the perils of environmental degradation. This shows the majority of humanity is living below earth share, a minority i.e. mere 21% of the humanity is living far above it and is responsible for the global "ecological overshoot" that constitute the threat not only to the present generation and the future generation's right to live. So the over consumption on the part of the North is normally and ethically indefensible. Are the people of US ready to come down to the levels of Cuba or Bangladeshis to ensure intergenerational equity? Are they ready to reinvent their established pattern of development and life style to ensure a sustainable world? Undoubtedly not – "the American life style," said the US President at Rio" is not subject to negotiation". But are they happier? Not necessarily, liberty and happiness are subjective pursuits and must answer to intergenerational equity. Put another way, the question is more different: Are Americans prepared to over consume in the knowledge that life for their children will be at a lower level? Probably not, if they would just think about it. Certainly, humanity cannot live at the North American level on prevailing technology; it would take many planets to sustain this. It is often claimed that, as in the past technological fixes applied by an ingenious species will overcome global resource constraint. But unlike in the past, the planet's natural resource base is now deteriorating rapidly. "Playing global roulette, with future generations as the stake, is a moral inequity of historic proportion."(Ibid). Answer to these questions remains pivotal to defining environmental security in a broader sense that will remove the causes of environmental conflict as well the causes of environmental scarcity that inflicts on the individuals in terms of health hazards, suffering, economic deprivation, poverty or starvation as undergone by them as a part of adaptation. Thus, at the confluence of the morally and ethically required nuance of sustainable development, economic rethinking, new planetary principles and new vision of and approach to life, stands the environmental security. Thus, the very basis of environmental security challenges the established frame of mind about what so far has been defined as development, pattern of life style, and geopolitical security of the sovereign state system. It is not the national security in terms of military but the planetary security that will be the foundation of environmental security on this confluence. What it needs a rethinking of western vision that gave birth to the modern political community-liberal, free, and capitalist, which inevitably carries the seeds of its destruction.

Paul Ehrlich and Anne Ehrlich's book, One with Nineveh: Politics, Consumption, and the Human Future (Ehrlich P. and Ehrlich A, 2004 : 8) shows how limitless consumption will lead to decimation of the present global civilization citing an illustration from history- the case of ruins of Assyrian capital of Nineveh and collapse of this ancient Mesopotamian civilization due to arrogance and pride. Similarly, the arrogance and hubris associated with the present high consumerism and exorbitant life style of the people of America and the West will signal the death knell of this civilization. If the whole world lived at U.S. per capita consumption levels, there would be a seven-fold increase in the use of minerals, two- fold in the case of metals, fivefold for wood products, eleven-fold for synthetics, and an overall increase of six-fold. Taking into account the consumption pattern of the people of Holland, it is said that Holland needs 10 Hollands to meet their consumption level. Quoting from Ehrlich and Ehrlich, Pirages observed:

> "Just as the Titanic's passengers partied into the night, confident that the ship was unsinkable, the rising tide of millionaires and near millionaires is caught up in a frenzy of consumption, supremely confident that their wealth and possessions will insulate them from any bad times to come" (Pirages D, 2004 : 84).

What is urgently required as sine qua non of sustainable development is to achieve a quantitative reduction in the use of materials and energy among other forms of dematerialization. Defining sustainable development Myers observes:

It is about the ways in which we can achieve an

acceptable quality of life for all in perpetuity, and exemplify it throughout our life styles. How can we achieve a better balance between work, leisure, and consumption? How can we prevent yesterday's luxuries becoming today's necessities and tomorrow's relicts? Sustainable development entails new approaches to economics, new technologies, new configurations of markets, new types of taxation, and whatever else fosters advances in our quality of life as well as quantity of livelihood. Tackling these fundamental factors will likely prove the most productive way ahead, even though it means addressing the basic structures as well as the processes of our economies (Myers, 2001).

CLIMATE CHANGE AND HUMAN SECURITY

The question how will changing climate patterns affect both inter-state relations and international and national security in a narrow, geo-strategic sense as well as the well-being and survival of human beings and humankind and thus human, water, health and livelihood security, comes to the fore with the findings of scientists about the imminence and impending danger of climate change looming large on the entire humanity. On 6 April, 2007, the Intergovernmental Panel on Climate Change (IPCC) released the second part of its Fourth Assessment Report demonstrating that the poor of this planet are most likely to suffer the worst effects of climate change. Human security takes on a broader meaning when one considers basic needs for food, water, health – in short, livelihood and a place to live – the issues addressed in the Millennium Development Goals.

> *Poor communities can be especially vulnerable, in particular those concentrated in high-risk areas. They tend to have more limited adaptive capacities, and are more dependent on clima-te-*

sensitive resources such as local water and food supplies (quoted from IPCC visited at http: // www.ipcc.ch/SPM6avr07.pdf.).

Furthermore, within the larger category of 'the poor' lies the frequently invisible (including within that IPCC summary document) group: women. Worldwide, seventy percent of those living below the poverty line are women (Ulrike Rohr.2006: 3-7) for whom climate change represents very specific threats to security. When the impacts of climate change are brought home, then women, in their roles as the primary managers of family, food, water and health, must deal very directly with the impacts.

While natural climate variations have existed for millennia, anthropogenic climate chan-ge has gradually emerged since the industrial revolution and especially after World War II due to western pattern of development based on the availability of cheap fossil fuels (coal, oil, natural gas) and the dramatic increase in its consumption first primarily in the industrialized countries but now increasingly also in the rapidly growing economies of the BRIC states (Brazil, Russia, India, China), especially of China and India.

CLIMATE CHANGE, SECURITY AND CONFLICTS

Ben Wisner and others have established the linkages between climate change and conflict having implications on national and international security (Wisner Ben et al). On 9 January 2004, David King, the UK Government's chief scientific adviser claimed that climate change is a far greater threat to the world than international terrorism. In February 2004, John Reid MP, then British Secretary of State for Defence and now Home Secretary, argued that climate change may spark conflict between nations. He forecast that violence and political conflict would become more likely in the next 20 to 30 years as climate change turned land into desert, melted ice fields and poisoned water supplies. He listed climate change alongside the major threats in future decades, including terrorism, demographic changes, and global energy demand. "As we look beyond the next decade, we see uncertainty growing; uncertainty about the geopolitical and human consequences of climate change. ...Impacts such as flooding, melting permafrost and desertification could lead to loss of agricultural land, poisoning of water supplies and destruction of economic infrastructure. ...More than 300 million people in Africa currently lack access to safe water; climate change will worsen this dire situation (Russell and Nigel Morris.2006). John Ashton, the UK Foreign Secretary's Special Representative for Climate Change, said at a conference on "Climate Change: The Global Security Impact", at the Royal United Services Institute on 24 January 2007: "There is every reason to believe that as the 21st century unfolds, the security story will be bound together with climate change(Vogel Ben. 2007). "Climate change is a security issue because if we don't deal with it, people will die and states will fail," Ashton concluded. Further he pointed out that defense and security planners must face a paradox when assessing their responses to the problem. Most security threats in today's world are amenable to some extent to a "hard power" or conventional reaction, he said, and demand will rise for such responses to climate change-related security problems. "But there is no hard power solution to climate change - you cannot force your neighbour to change its carbon emissions at the barrel of a gun (Littlecott Chris. 2007). Sir Crispin Tickell, the former UK Permanent Representative to the UN, highlighted the environmental factors behind societal collapse. Professor John Mitchell, the chief scientist at the UK Met Office, forecast that the coming decades will see a 30 per cent increase in severe drought. He added that Africa will experience increased desertification, water stress and disease (Tickell Crispin Sir.2003).

Besides the UK, other nations have begun to assess the security implication of climate change. In 2002, the German Ministry for the Environment, Nature Conservation and Nuclear Sa-fety published a commissioned report on climate change and conflicts raised the question whether climate change impacts can increase conflict potentials (Brauch.2002). n spring 2004 an internal report by Randall and Schwartz for the U.S. Department of Defense on the impact of Abrupt Climate Change on U.S. national security was leaked to the press(Brauch.2004).

The British initiative during its Security Council Security Council presidency to put cli-ma-te change on its agenda for 17 April 2007 has been the most recent attempt to "secu-ritize" clima-te change in the context of geo-politics (Press conference by Security Council President, 4 April 2007).

CLIMATE CHANGE AS A THREAT AND CHALLENGE TO INTERNATIONAL, NATIONAL AND HUMAN SECURITY

Climate change poses many new threats and challenges to national secu-rity and international stability as well as to human security at other scales. The concept of human security was introduced first by UNDP in 1994 and then developed further in a report by the Human Security Commission, co-chaired by Sadako Ogata and Amartya Sen, in its report *Human Security Now* (2003). The environmental dimension of human security has been addressed by an international team working on Global Environmental Change and Human Security (GECHS) and in several studies by the United Nations University Institute for Environment and Human Security (UNU-EHS) (Bogardi and Brauch, 2005).

In February 1999, during its presidency of the United

Nations Security Council, Canada, a founding member of the Human Security Network put human security on the agenda by addressing the impact of armed conflicts on human beings (Dedring Jurgen.2007). In March 2005, then UN Secretary General, Kofi Annan, in his report *In Larger Freedom*(Annan.2005) wrote of human security in a broad sense, the issue was placed on the agenda of the UN General Assem-bly in the fall of 2005.

UNDP will take up the relationship between human development and climate change in its *Human Development Report 2007* (HDR), to be launched in November. Over 17 years, UNDP has incrementally developed a sensitive measure of human development (the human development index – HDI). Earlier studies have shown that the HDI correlates well with measures of disaster risk such as UNDP's disaster risk index (DRI), especially for less developed countries (UNDP.2004). Preliminary analysis for this year's HDR suggests that climate change poses major obstacles to progress in meeting MDGs and maintaining progress raising the HDI: "There is a clear and present danger that climate change will roll back human development for a large section of humanity, undermining international cooperation aimed at achieving the Millennium Development Goals (MDGs) in the process (UNDP.2007).

Concerning the MDGs individually, UNDP states:

> *...[C]limate change may pose a threat to food security through erratic rainfall patterns and decreasing crop yields, contributing to increased hunger. Furthermore, adverse climate change impacts on natural systems and resources, infrastructure, and labor productivity may lead to reduced economic growth, exacerbating poverty. These effects threaten the achievement of MDG 1. Loss of livelihood assets, displacement*

and migration may lead to reduced access to education opportunities, thus hampering the realization of MDG 2. Depletion of natural resources and decreasing agricultural productivity may place additional burdens on women's' health and reduce time for decision-making processes and income-generating activities, worsening gender equality and women's' empowerment (MDG 3). Increased incidence of vector-borne diseases, increases in heat-related mortality, and declining quantity and quality of drinking water will lead to adverse health effects threatening the achievement of MDGs 4, 5, 6 and 7. In general terms, the realization of MDG 7 may be jeopardized through climate change negatively impacting quality and productivity of natural resources and ecosystems, possibly irreversibly, threatening environmental sustainability. Climate change, a global phenomenon, calls for a collective response in the form of global partnerships (Ibid).

From a state-centered international security perspective, the German Advisory council on Global Change (WBGU 2007/2008) reviewed the scientific research on Climate Change as a Security Risk'. The report argued that-

Without resolute counteraction, climate change will overstretch many 'societies' adaptive capacities with in the coming decades .This could result in destabilization and violence, jeopardizing national and international security to a new degree .However, climate change as a threat to humankind and soon sets the course for the avoidance of dangerous anthropogenic climate change will draw ever deeper lines of

> *division and conflicts between and within countries over the distribution of resources ,especially water and land ,over the management of migration, or over compensation payments between the countries mainly responsible for climate change and those countries most affected by its destructive effects...[this report] is based on the findings of research into environmental conflicts, the causes of war ,and of climate impact research. It appraises past experience but also ventures to cast a glance far into the future in order to asses the likely impacts of climate change on societies, nation-states regions and the international (WBGU.2007-2008website at:<http:// www.wbgu_jg2007_engl.html).*

The International Women Leaders Global Security Summit in November 2007 in New York in its report summarized the results stated on climate change:

> *Climate change poses significant security risks due to an increased occurrence of severe weather patterns, degradation of vital natural resources and threats to the livelihoods and threats to the livelihoods and safety of populations on every continent. Pressure on resources, natural disasters and humanitarian crises-including flooding, drought, desertification and loss of arable land, massive and rapid migration and refugee flows-have the potential to threaten economic, political and social stability while increasing the risk of internal civil unrest. Poor and underdeveloped communities and countries are particularly vulnerable and yet are marginalized in international negotiations on climate policy. An absence of political will on*

> *the part of developed nations to accommodate more comprehensive policy changes may meet with increasing resentment from those countries most vulnerable to the effects of climate change. Thus, it is imperative to take action now to decrease the momentum of climate change. Women's leadership must help increase political will at the national and global level, guide the private sector away from voluntary initiatives and toward legally required changes in practice, give voice to affected communities most in need of assistance to mitigate and cope with the effects of climate change. 'An integrated human, gender and environmental security approach is needed for dealing with the growing threat of climate change, in order to develop appropriate adaptation and mitigation strategies(Spring Ursula Oswald).*

The links between climate change, peace and war were analyzed a report by International Alert, an independent peace building organization; on: A climate of Conflict: The Links between Climate Change, Peace and War "consequences of consequences", i.e. The effects climate change has interacting with socio-economic and political problems in poorer countries. It highlighted four key elements of risk – political instability, economic weakness, food insecurity and large-scale migration (Smith/Vivekananda, 2007).

Margaret Beckett, the British Foreign Secretary in a speech in Berlin in late 2006 warned:

> *When people were faced with the stresses of overpopulation, including a lack of key resources such as water, energy and food," so we see the slide down the spectrum from stability to instability." A global temperature increase of just*

> *two or three percent would cut the crop yields in Africa, the Middle East and South Asia by up to 40 percent causing millions of people to be denied food even more than they are now. Climate change also affected issues such as immigration. A 50cm rise in sea levels would displace 25 million in Bangladesh." In short, a failing climate means more failed states. And that has implications for everything we want to achieve from conflict prevention and resolution to counter-terrorism."Ms Becktt said." By tackling climate change we can help address the underlying securities that feed and exacerbate conflicts and instability .By ignoring it we resign ourselves to the same crises flaring up again and again .And new ones emerging." She said the world was on the verge of "global irresponsibility of massive and irresponsibility of a massive and irreversible scale" by refusing to tackle climate change, but warned: "The greatest security threat we face as a global community would not be met by guns and tanks." It will be solved by investment in the emerging techniques of soft power -building avenues of trust and opportunity that will lead to a low-carbon economy. There is no backstop-politics and diplomacy has to work (British Embassy Berlin, 2006).*

In November 2007, the Human Development Report 2007/2008 stated:

> *It argues that the world is drifting towards a 'tipping point' that could lock the world's poorest countries and their poorest citizens in a downward spiral , leaving hundreds of millions facing malnutrition , water scarcity, ecological*

threats, and a loss of livelihoods. "Ultimately, climate change is a threat to humanity as a whole. But it is the poor, a constituency with no responsibility for the ecological debt we are running up, who face the immediate and most severe human costs," commented UNDP Administrator Kendal Derive(UNDP:2007/2008).

5

Women Deficit and Violent Conflict

The established notion in Political Science is based on the maxim that state is a territoriality or boundary inhabited by population. With the Westphalian thematic becoming a sine qua non of political theories about state, and its constitution, the multitudes i.e people not only formed the coping stone on which a supreme political entity rests, but also considered to be synonymous with state. Among a myriad of political and non-political institutions, state stands preeminent to become the sole identity/ security referent for the multitude and endows the title to what a people can be called. Paradoxically, if it is the people who constituted the state it is in reality the latter who gives identity, a political juridical title and a politically recognized existence to the people. In the absence of a state population is a just a multitude crowned with the supreme uncontested political and legal exclusivity, i.e sovereign power, state remains the symbol and provides the metaphor for the existence of collective identity transcending any other identity based on other denomination such as caste, class, religion, sex, population and other categories. State after the Westphalian convention provided the ontological foundation of nationalism –solely and exclusively identified with the state. All other distinctions remained either subservient or merged with the ultimate identity with the state. These distinctions remained important to mark the immediacy of their identity and later on with the distant state to distinguish their identity from other people and nations not to override the ultimate identity with the state as a whole.

To view the population as the whole not in terms of distinctions or categories and identified with the state as a nation is a constitutional desideratum for ushering in a political, legal and juridical order in the society. In other words, the foundation of people is state in the sense that a definiteness or particularity or an identity is thrown around a population to distinguish it from the multitude. State stands as a symbol of political catharsis for collectivity and assumes the rightness of authority to call a population a definite identifiable category to be entitled to come under a politico-legal, juridical order.

State is a political immediacy 'all sought for' political identity to bring an end to being permanently consigned to the category of what Machiavelli once portrayed of Italian people as a masterless men. It remains a permanent and prominent mainstream in the political lexicon protecting and at the same time dominating if need arises the other strands of different hues.

From outside or from an onlooker perspective the vast population or multitude with different distinctions or categories look cohesive and homogenous as like other distinctions, identity with the state is the sole and prominent distinction to be achieved by man to be what Rousseau says, instead of a stupid and unimaginative animal, he becomes intelligent and citizen". The existing plurality of identities does not have the legitimacy to challenge the ultimate identity with the state. It is insulated from the fear of distortion of particularities. If need arises, it even crushes these particularities to reinforce the identity with state.

Though state was a boundary and spatial distancing concept in relation to similar other states, it is considered a 'whole' or permanent from a cosmological perspective spanning beyond time and space into people's timeless culture or civilization. With the spindle of its own culture, values and hallowed views of civilization it was tried to be woven into a timeless cosmological tapestry. Instead of being confined to a political identity, it moves beyond to identify with a civilization. Huntington's clash of civilization is a nice metaphor to justify American hegemonic state. "Greatness of a civilization" is culled from history to justify a state. Even Hegel to make state a universal and cosmological concept identified it with the 'march of Gold on earth'.

These were the views about the prominent state providing identity to the people in an age where the monarchy controlled vast empires disintegrated and nations became free to constitute or consider themselves as separate identities on Westphalian thematic.

Thus said does not mean that this established notion about reification of the state's symbiotic relation with people as a collectivity was ideal and the pluralities of particularities in terms of individuals, sex, religion, class, caste or group completely lost in the whole. Understanding of state as the ultimate of refuge of the people can be plausible from a constitutive perspective in a specific historical context.

The development in the field of science and its application to social sciences heralded revolutionary change in the established thinking about state and it relation with people. Newtonian and Cartesian image of the universe as nothing but matter or particles in motion provided the ontological foundation to Hobbes and Locke's concept of possessive individualism. Individuals are seen simply as particles in motion for power, glory and wealth. Thus, people –the political reification of the collectivity state- were reduced to individuals as a category. In Hobbes's case complete individualism is complementary with absolute state. Locke seeing the contradiction between absolutism and individualism was of the view that limited state creates the condition for growth of individualism. A new identity in terms of individualism emerged to challenge the absolute state. What once were subordinate and at the periphery catapulted to the center stage to challenge the state- the only legitimate claimant to authority. These categories or distinctions got sharpened with the spread of democracy and liberal ideas for identity in their own distinctions not necessarily with the state. What was looking coherent, homogenous or a collectivity appeared divided, cleft and fractious on the basis of caste, class, sex, religion, group, environment, civilization. These searches for different identities other than with the state clash with each other with state becoming an intervening variable. These distinctive categories do not perceive as being interconnected or interrelated or as inseparable part of the whole rather think in terms of disjointed separateness or 'the other', needing preferential treatment. They prefer to define their identities in terms of their own distinction not necessarily with state. Paradoxically, the state is constantly asked to identity itself with a particular category's distinctions. The whole is to identity with the part or particularities. The conflicts in the state are understood as the consequences of these categories seeking identity in their own distinctions. Marx developed the category of class in terms of productive forces to challenge the false identity of the proletariat with the state. The wars or violent conflicts were understood in terms class struggle. Caste and religion came up in Indian societies as a category demanding preferential treatment from the state. Sex – the distinction between male and female has recently become a very distinguishable category demanding dismantling of male dominated political institutions.

The population no longer seems a conglomerate and homogenous unit looking alike. The whole seems to be fragmented into different categories – caste, class, sex, religion, environment and civilization etc. Unity or universalism is no longer the characteristic of state. Particularism and separateness at present define individuals' identity with state. Identity of individuals in terms of caste, class, gender etc religion reign supreme over identities with state. The root causes of conflict and motives in the state are found lying embedded in particularities like caste, class, sex and religion, etc. These particularities are today found more magnified than their identities with the state-the ultimate political organization. The consideration of 'people' as a whole – a homogenous unit is a constitutive desideratum when a state is to be formed and to survive as a viable political unit. "The voice of the people as the voice of God" is a holistic concept built around state to endow the later with stability, permanence and legitimacy to rule. It implies a euphemism for demonstrating legitimacy to the rule.

With rise of particularities in terms of caste, class, gender, religion, environment, civilizations or groups, 'the people' seems to be fractured and no longer holistic. The identities and security sought in terms of these particularities in the context of a state imply that the human beings are concerned with their immediate, intimate, or those that affect them than with the distance or beyond the immediacy to the far fetched state. Security which is basically understood as protector of identities of human beings both in materialistic and spiritual terms is no longer considered a monopolistic attribute of a state. The discrepancy between the security of state and security of the people came to the fore and occupied the center stage of security studies. Finding out the root causes of security threats or conflicts between states or even among individuals in particularities like caste, class, gender, environment, religion and civilization has become very common today. But demography, the difference in age structure and male/female dichotomy in population studies has become equally a security threat or a point of conflict within a state with destabilizing consequences. Studies on this demographic issue are very few. Like environment becoming a factor of conflict, demography and population age structure have raised in recent years the concern of policy makers, analysts, which have consequences upon security, stability and democratic structure of a state.

RELATIONSHIP BETWEEN POPULATION AND ENVIRONMENTAL CONFLICT

In the post-cold war security discourse demographic and environmental factors have occupied a predominant position. According to neo- Malthusians, rapid population growth will result in per capita scarcity of natural resources such as cropland, forests, freshwater and fisheries, soaring the risks of violent conflict over scarce resources. In contrast, the optimists claim that scarcity of agricultural land, caused by burgeoning population density, may lead to technological innovation, which could result in economic development and thus build peace over the long term. According to Thomas Homer Dixon, the most influential neo-Malthusian school, population growth is an important source of demand induced scarcity. If a resource base is constant, the availability of resources per person will diminish as an increasing number of persons share it, or as demand per capita soars. (Homer Dixon, 1999, p.48). Since the availability of these resources determines people's well being, their scarcity can, under certain conditions, cause violent conflict. The conflict over renewable resources like water or fisheries between and among nations may be direct or what is called simple scarcity conflict. Here, environmental causes of conflict are directly perceived to be primary and not subordinate to other factors. Group identity conflict occurs when the marginalized poor people migrate to other states or within a state in the context of demand induced scarcity of resources and population growth. The conflict is here indirect and occurs in combination with other factors. In case of failed or weak states, the environmental scarcity and population growth in combination with grinding poverty, ever widening economic disparity and growing unemployment may lead to insurgency or rebellion against the established political system (Homer Dixon and Blitt, 1998). Unlike some strict Malthusians, Homer Dixon drives home the point that population pressures do not increase the risk of conflict in isolation but they could in combination with environmental degradation and uneven wealth distribution.

This neo-Malthusian position on population and conflict linkage has been discounted. Colin Kahl criticizes neo-Malthusian writing for failing to identify the most important intervening variables. While state weakness is often cited as a necessary condition for environment related conflict, Kahl argues that conflict may also arise under conditions of state exploitation, when powerful elites exploit rising scarcities and corresponding grievances in order to consolidate power (Colin Kahl, 2002, p.265). In a similar vein, Richard Matthew criticizes the simple Malthusian thesis for understating the adaptive capability of many societies and for not adequately addressing the historical and structural dimensions of violence, such as globalization and colonial influence (Richard Matthew,

2002, p. 243) Making an empirical analysis of neo-Malthusian claims, Henrik Urdal reaches the conclusion that high population growth- by itself- is not associated with armed conflict. In addition, scarcity of productive land is associated with less conflict contrary to neo- Malthusian expectations. This relationship is neither strong nor robust (Henrik Urdal, 2005. pp.5-11).

POPULATION AGE STRUCTURE AND CONFLICT

Three months after the attacks of September 11, 2001, the New York Times asked, "Is the Devil in the Demographics". This paper examines the vulnerability of large cohorts of unemployed youth to extremist ideology and political recruitment. In the post-9/11 era, however there has been very little academic research on the relationship between youthful age structure and warfare. Literature on civil war, insurgency and terrorism has instead highlighted the role of other causal factors such as the scarcity of valuable natural resources, the degree of ethnic fractionalization, societal segmentation and the type of political regime while showing short shrift to the importance of population age structure. Saying this does not in any way denude these factors of their significant role in the onset of civil war but the importance of youthful age structure in insurgency based civil wars and terrorism should not be undermined.

History stands a witness to the linkage between young population and violence. Herbert Moller (1968) in his study established a close correspondence between the rise of Nazi party in Germany and the surges in proportion of young men in the population. Yale historian Paul Kennedy (1993) adduces that revolutions occur more often in countries with large populations of energetic and frustrated young men.

EXCESS YOUTH: A PERFECT VOLCANIC ERUPTION?

Some recent conflicts in Rwandan, Sierra Leone, Middle East and Pakistan sponsored terrorism in Kashmir lend credence to excess youth hypothesis. Philip Gourevirch (1998, p.93) describes how Rwandan genocidaires were recruited from among the jobless young men who were "wasting idleness and attendant resentments. Most of the men were motivated by the opportunity to drink, loot, murder and enjoy higher living standards than they were previously accustomed to". Similarly, Mastany in his work pointed out in Sierra Leone where young people comprised 95 percent of the fighting forces in a recent civil war. The youth are a "long neglected cohort; they lack jobs and training, and it is to convince them to join the fight." The recent terrorism in Palestine and the Democratic Republic of the Congo seems to have close correspondence with the fact that both areas have among the highest ratios of young adults (15-19) to older working age adults (30-54) anywhere in the world.

Population growth has slowed worldwide and will likely end within the next century. But high fertility rates in Africa, Middle East and Pakistan will continue to bring increasingly larger cohorts of young adults for the next few decades. As the statistics show, the ratio of young people to adults in the developing world will continue to remain well above the 1980 world peak for decades to come. The National Intelligence Council (2004) refers to these increasing youth cohorts as a part of perfect volcanic eruption- including failed states, poor economies, environmental scarcity and religious extremism- that will likely stoke the fire of violence in terms of terrorism and insurgency in certain parts of the globe for decades to come.

Youth Bulge is a misnomer which means literally, an irregular swelling visible in the young adult section of the age pyramid.

RELATIVE COHORT SIZE: A BETTER MEASURE OF AGE STRUCTURE

The main thrust of the argument is that the presence of young adults is not as important as the degree of alienation, frustration, and marginalization they experience. These factors are subjective and difficult to measure; one way might be to examine how much schools and the labour market must expand to accommodate the incoming cohort of teenagers. We can obtain a rough estimate by measuring the current group of young adults (ages 15 to 29) as a proportion of the number of older working adults (ages 30 to 54) to find a relative cohort size after a similar measure proposed by Richard Easterlin.

Relative cohort size can provide the missing link between the population of young men and the risk of insurgency based civil wars or terrorism. Easterlin's relative cohort size hypothesis explicates the relationship between youthful populations and the economic and psychological frustrations that enable political instability, and ultimately civil war, insurgency or terrorism. As a large relative cohort comes of age, the tension produced by lack of success in the job and marriage markets may in the presence of other factors render armed conflict, rebellion and insurgency a more appealing option. The relative cohort size may not be an immediate cause of civil war. But a large birth cohorts often strain the schooling system and labour market of a country, particularly a developing one, which can result in massive frustration, unemployment, reduced wages and dissatisfaction- and arguably create a potential army of young men who could be easily recruited in a rebellion or terrorist act like the Nepalese youth into the Maoist fold or the Tamils into the LTTE in Sri Lanka. Yet in most developing countries, where economic opportunities are not even sufficient for current youth cohorts, a rise in the population entering the labour force is likely to increase joblessness.

In countries with less economic opportunities and fewer channels for enacting social change, large cohorts of young adults may choose more violent means of protest and change.

RELATIVE MALE INCOME

One of the most important explanations of the importance of relative cohort size is what Easterlin calls relative male income, which is the standard of living a man's income can buy relative to his father's standard of living. Relative male income is inversely related to relative cohort size, other things being equal.

Not every society may respond the same way to low relative male income but large birth cohorts in any country -particularly males- must be accommodated by the school system and eventually by the labour market. In populations with many women of child bearing age, population momentum will cause overall population size to increase even after decades after fertility declines. The government will be required to increase expenditures on services such as roads, schools, and hospitals to accommodate each new cohort. When the large birth cohort reaches adulthood, they will require more jobs than vacated by previous cohorts. In deeply religious contexts where pre-martial sex is forbidden and men are expected to financially establish themselves prior to marriage, such a shortage of economic opportunities can be particularly frustrating, as the shortage can prevent even educated adults from entering into marriage and achieving cultural notions of adulthood. Imagine the following advertisement for Al Qaeda: "Wanted: Educated individuals preferably with a graduate degree in a technical field who have foreign language skills preferably fluency in English as well as a deep antipathy to their own and others' political leaders and must be comfortable with violence and available for training and important assignments in foreign countries." It shows that the terrorists of Al Qaeda were educated, and mostly from countries that have long graduated from the category of the world's poorest. What led them to such a path is perhaps disgust with their own often corrupt governments, a sense of humiliation by the West, religious fanaticism, boredom and alienation or perhaps dim prospects for a fulfilling career (Lancaster, 2003). Research on suicide bombers, for example, has shown that many are well educated and highly capable, yet lack the economic opportunities necessary to establish themselves (Sprinzak, 2000, Pape, 2005).

While testing the importance of relative cohort size in the probability of civil wars, the researchers have found that high infant mortality rates, lower per capita incomes, and larger population sizes consistently had a higher risk of civil wars onset (Staveteig, 2005). Infant mortality rate and per capita income were nearly strong predictors of civil war onset, and both measures were highly correlated to one another.

Calculating youth as a percentage of the entire population (non-relative cohort size) did not determine the onset of civil wars. On the other hand, comparing a specific population of youth to a specific population of adults (relative cohort size) and comparing a specific population of youth to all adults both strongly predicted the risk of civil war.

As found from the study, future relative cohort size could also be used to predict conflict. Relative cohort size can be measured up to 10 years in advance using current data on population age structure. For example, the ratio of future young adults (e.g., the current 5 to 19 year olds) to future older adults (the current 20-to 44 year olds) - combined with current information about infant mortality, population size, and governance- can predict whether conflict will occur 10 to 15 years from now almost as well as waiting 10 years to measure the actual cohort size. This finding could help develop conflict prevention policies; by identifying large relative cohorts up to 10 years before they reach young adulthood, policymakers and funders might devise better strategies for easing the transition, and thus reduce the chances of conflict.

MISSING WOMEN AND CONFLICT

Valerie M. Hudson and Andrea M. den Boer in their work Bare Branches: The Security Implications of Asia's Surplus Male Population (Hudson & den Boer, 2004) explicate how male deficits in Asia could drive the youths into the vortex of violence and terrorist activities. For example, the Indian government's estimate of its birth sex ration is approximately 113 boy babies born for every 100 girl babies, with some locales recording ratios of 156 and higher (India Registrar General, 2001. Valerie M. Hudson and Andrea M. den Boer explicate how male deficits in Asia could drive the youths into the vortex of violence. The Chinese government states that its birth sex ratio is approximately 119, though some Chinese scholars have gone on record to show that the birth sex ratio is at least 121 (China State Statistical Bureau, 2001). Similarly, countries such as Pakistan, Bangladesh, Nepal, Bhutan, Taiwan, Afghanistan and South Korea are examples of high female deficit.

Another indicator of gender imbalance is early childhood mortality. In some of the Asian nations mentioned above, early childhood mortality rates for girls are actually higher than boys (United Nations Population Division, 1998).

What forces drive the deficit of females in Asian nations such as India and China? Some scholars are of the view that hepatitis B disease and antigens of which have been associated with higher birth sex ratios, play a great role in preventing female births (Oaster, 2005). Supporting this thesis is another view that holds gender imbalance in Asia and elsewhere as man made phenomenon. It is through prenatal sex identification and female sex selective abortion or through relative neglect and abandonment in early childhood compared to male offspring, the females are eliminated. Another cause of gender imbalance is the ingrained preference for sons in Asian countries reinforced by religion and ancient culture and underrating of female life. The age old bias for boys, coupled with China's draconian one-child policy imposed since 1980, has produced what Gu Baochang, a leading Chinese expert on family planning, described as "the largest, the highest, and the longest" gender imbalance in the world (NBC News, September 14, 2004). For centuries, Chinese families without sons feared poverty and neglect. The male offspring represented continuity of lineage and protection in old age. The traditional thinking is best described in the ancient "Book of Songs" (1000-700B.C.):

When a son is born
Let him sleep on the bed
Clothe him with fine clothes,
And give him jade to play...
When a daughter is born,
Let her sleep on the ground,
Wrap her in common wrappings,
And give broken titles to play...

From a relatively normal ratio of 108.5 boys to 100 girls in the early 80s, the male surplus progressively spiralled to 111 in 1990, 116 in 2000, and is now close to 120 boys for each 100 girls. As it is reported, in eight to 10 years, China will have something like 40 to 60 million

Table 1. Number of Missing Women for Selected Asian Countries Using Census Data

Country	*Year*	*Actual Number of males*	*Actual Number of Females*	*Actual Sex Ratio*	*Expected Sex Ratio*	*Expected No. of Women*
Afghanistan	2000	11,227,000	10,538,000	106.5	96.4	11,646,266
Bangladesh	2001	65,841,419	63,405,814	103.8	99.6	66,646,266
China	2000	653,550,000	612,280,000	106.7	100.1	652,897,103
India	2001	531,277,078	495,738,169	107.2	99.3	535,022,234
Pakistan	1998	68,873,686	63,445,593	108.6	99.2	69,429,119
South Korea	2000	23,068,181	22,917,108	100.7	100	23,068,181
Taiwan						
Total	2000	11,386,084	10,914,845	104.3	100.2	11,363,357

Quoted from Valerie M. Hudson and Andrea M. Den Boer " Missing Women and Bare Branches: Gender Balance and Conflict" in Environmental Change and Security Program, The Woodrow Wilson International Center for Scholars, NW Washington, DC, Report, Issue 11, 2005, p.22.

missing women, which will have enormous implications for China's prostitution industry and human trafficking. According to a report by the International Planned Parenthood Federation, the vast majority of aborted fetuses, more than 70 percent, were female, citing the abortion of up to 750,000 female fetuses in China in 1999. A report by Zhang Qing, population researcher of the Chinese Academy of Social Sciences, said the gender imbalance is statistically related to the high death rate of female babies, with female death rate at age zero in the city or rural areas consistently higher than male baby death rate. Only seven of China's 29 provinces are within the world's average sex ratio, Zhang Qing's report cited eight "disaster provinces" from North to South China, where there were 26 to 38 percent more boys than girls. The hint of serious problems ahead can be seen in the increasing cases of human trafficking as bachelors try to purchase their wives. According to an estimate, over the next decade, some 40 million Chinese men will be unable to find wives due to the scarcity of females, thus the growing number of so called "bachelors' villages" in various parts of China (NBC News, 14 September 2004). While the 2001 census showed that India's countrywide sex ration for children under age six had risen to only about 108, it also revealed that the north-western states of Haryana and Punjab had reached ratios of 122 and 126 respectively. This practice of culling of girls is not confined to Asia; evidence for this practice can be found in every continent.

What effect will this deficit of females have on the security trajectory of nations? Anthropologist Barbara D. Miller 2001 has termed the preservation of a balanced sex ratio a "public good" that nations overlook at their peril. As studies show, by the year 2020, 12-15 per cent of their young adult males will not be able to tie the nuptial bond because the girls that would have grown up to be their wives were eliminated by their societies instead. With each passing year between now and 2020, both the proportion and number of young adult males that exceed the number of young adult females in China and India will increase (Hudson and den Boer, 2004). Chinese call it "guang gunner" "bare branches"- branches of the family tree that will never bear fruit, but which may be useful as "bare sticks" or clubs. This Chinese metaphor attests to the centrality of this above thesis that "men who are not provided the opportunity to develop a vested interest in the system of law and order will gravitate toward a system based on physical force, in which they hold an advantage over other members of the society". Further, this is compounded by the fact that in a society of too few women, the men who get the chance to marry are certainly of higher socio-economic status. Those men who are left out are poorer, less educated, less skilled and less likely to be employed. These left out unmarried adult males are likely to evince a predilection for establishing a system based on physical force in order to obtain by force what they cannot obtain legitimately. In such a spectre of remaining unmarried, their likely shift from potential threats to potential protectors of society can be stalled. The rate of criminal behaviour of unmarried men is many times higher than that of married men.; marriage is a reliable predictor of a downturn in reckless, antisocial, illegal, and violent behaviour by young adult males (Mazur and Michalek, 1998). If this shift or transition cannot be affected for a sizable proportion of a society's young men, the society is likely to become less stable.

Strong evidences establishing the linkage between gender imbalance and conflict are found by studies in India (Oldenburg, 1992, Dreze and Khera, 2000). This is not new. Historical case studies stand a testimony to this. The 19th

century Nien rebels came from a very poor region in China with a sex ratio of at least 129 men per 100 women. At first, relatively smaller groups of men coalesced to form smuggling and extortion gangs. Eventually, these gangs banded together to form larger armies wresting territory from imperial control. It took the emperor many years to subdue the rebellion.

From a sociological perspective, this thesis holds good. The scholars have studied the behaviour of unattached young males, noting their propensity to congregate with others like them and to engage in dominance displays in such groups. Sociologists have found that the risky shift in group behaviour, where a group is willing to take greater risks and engage in more reckless behaviour than an individual member of the group, is much more pronounced in groups comprised solely of unattached young adult males (Johnson, Stemler, and Hunter, 1977).

With rising sex ratio, the incidence of crime, violence, drug smuggling, trafficking, prostitution and weapon smuggling will increase (Hudson and den Boer, 2004). The question crops up how the governments respond to such a situation where the rate of sex ratio is on the increase. Aware of the negative consequences of bare branches, "most governments in the past tried to thin the number of bare branches, whether through fighting, sponsoring the construction of large public works necessitating dangerous manual labour, exporting them to less populated areas, or co-opting them into the military or police" (Hudson and den Boer, 2004). One 16th century Portuguese monarch sent his army, composed primarily of noble and non-noble bare branches, on one of the later crusades to avoid a crisis of governance; more than 25 per cent of that army never returned, and many others were seriously wounded (Boone, 1983, 1986). To control the rising instability caused by increasing bare branches, the governments are likely to favour more authoritarian approaches to internal governance and less benign international presences. As seen, gender imbalance does not cause war or conflict per se, but it can aggravate it. The potential for democracy in countries like India, China and other countries where gender imbalance is increasing, is likely to be affected by bare branches.

Thus, a youthful population age structure with the bare branches in combination with other factors like rising unemployment, environmental degradation and economic deprivation can increase the risk of the onset of civil conflict and political violence. Recent studies by Richard Cincotta and Elizabeth Leahy suggest that three- fourths of all countries with recent conflict will likely experience conflict in the next decade. One fourth of all non-conflict countries with 60 per cent young age structures under 30 years of age will likely experience a new civil conflict during the next decade (Cincotta and Leahy, 2006-2007, 55).

As the above studies show, the relative cohort size of youth population between the ages 15 to 29 is more vulnerable to the extremist ideology and insurgency. In the event of climate change and its disastrous impact on all aspects of human life, the linkage between youth age structure and violence becomes crystal clear.

CONCLUSION

In 2005, 1.9 billion people- nearly one third of the world's population- are under the age of 15. Ninety percent of these youth live in less developed countries. Even if fertility decreases, large birth cohorts in developing countries are unlikely to dwindle for a few decades. As these large birth cohorts enter adulthood, the risk of insurgent civil wars and terrorism increases. In the average least developed countries the ratio between the number of 15 to 29 year olds and the number of 30 to 54 year olds is expected to stay above one until 2035. The strain on school systems and labour markets in these countries will be profound. In absolute numbers, the increase in youth cohorts will be enormous. It is not likely that a high relative cohort size will be the inciting cause of conflict in least developed countries. A very youthful population is an important factor among others that flares up only under certain conditions or sparks. But at the same time, sparks can only trigger violent conflicts when contextual factors enable them. In such a situation relative cohort size is an important predictive factor for civil war, particularly insurgent based civil wars. The link between relative cohort size and civil war becomes stronger if attention is riveted at the sub national level, as insurgent groups often come from sub-populations with high relative cohort size. (For example, Chechens in Russia, Northern Irish in the United Kingdom, and Palestinians in Israel, Kashmir Muslims in India, Bodos in Assam). Recent suicide bombings in London and France are important reminders that developed countries are not immune to violent rebellions from youthful sub-populations. They signal the urgent need to improve integration and equality. Industrialized countries facing major pension shortfalls due to high ratio of retirees to workers could mitigate the problem by hiring young workers from the developing world though migration and integration are politically sensitive issues.

A better understanding of contextual factors leading to civil wars, insurgency and terrorism may improve policy maker's ability to prevent it in future. Research on the cause of civil wars, insurgency and terrorism should incorporate measures of relative cohort size. Unraveling the background factors that that put a country at risk for conflict is arguably more important than finding the immediate spark of conflict as policy is much better equipped to address structural problems than immediate factors. In many countries around the world, one cannot prevent large relative youth cohorts over the next two decades, but understanding the role of relative cohort size and planning wisely could help reduce the risk of future insurgency based civil wars.

With demographic imbalances in a society such as women deficit a state's prospects for democracy and peace looks bleak as increasing number of bare branches would likely to propel a government to prefer authoritarian approaches to internal governance. How this stands out in 21st century in Asia? As gleaned from the above study gender imbalance in a society does not trigger war or conflict per se, but it can amplify it. As studies show there will be 28 million bare branches in India- the same or more in China by 2020 raising the scope for more internal instabilities in these societies. The question crops up whether this substantial internal instability in these societies will overshadow external security concerns for the governments of these nations. In the context of the long blood stained history of Indo-Pakistan feuding over Kashmir and rise of Pakistan sponsored terrorism the burgeoning bare branches in India and Pakistan raises the spectre of some potentially unstable situations having great repercussions on the prospects for democratic governance and fostering of peace in the region. This is also evident more vividly in the case of Taiwan and China. Adding to this is the example of resource- rich Russian Far East which faces an influx of Chinese workers while Russia continues to be plagued by deficit of men. This will no doubt remain a fundamental problem for the policy makers how will gender imbalances affect the potential for democracy in China and evolution of democracy in India? This will not remain confined to these two countries alone as they constitute more than one- third of the world's population. The status of women in these nations could become a preponderant factor in both domestic and international security in Asia with possible implications for the entire international system. More researches and studies on the independent and causal impact of demography and gender imbalance on war and security of a state so far under researched and poorly understood will add new dimension to established and conventionally pronounced parlance on security studies.

6

Digital Age Security Threats: Challenges to International Relation Theories

Information and communication of ideas and opinions are like sensations carried through various agencies-sensory nerves to the brain- the state and back forth to the individuals. In democracy these become very important and played a key role in shaping and forming decisions. Information and communications set a dialogue between the governed and the rulers. When they were to modernize forms of communication and information as we find today such information and communication technology (ICTS), internet, television and mobile, there was a yawing gap between the state and the people and also among the people. States are biased, prejudiced and hamstrung in their perception, understanding and views of other states, people and culture. Time has fast changed and moved. The 21st century witnessed a great revolution in the field of information and communication. Geography and distance is no longer a barrier. It is said in the age of this tremendous change, that the present century is marked by the death of distance or geography. The states, which were earlier insulated from each other due to the communication barrier, are now interacting with each other more speedily and freely with every chances of their misperception and doubt being resolved by the use of and easy access to the available information technology. The world seems to be a global village. The information and communication technology have stacked all the markets of the world. But on the issue of their use and easy accessibility to the people the world witnessed a "digital gap" between the rich who have comparatively easy access and the poor who lack access to the technology. This is as truer of people within a state as of the people across the state boundaries.

The significance of information and communication technology has been widely felt not only within a state but also among and between the states in their multifarious day to day interactions. Information and communication technology can be rightly said as constituting the nerve center of both domestic and international politics. These have become the guiding metaphor for both domestic and international politics to maintain stability and political order, provide peace and security and protect people from natural catastrophes. Sovereign state systems are no longer impregnable, sacrosanct; the unhindered flow of information and the revolutionary exposure of the people irrespective of which state, security or culture they belong to, to the very sinews of information have made the entire world a melting pot of the absoluteness and arbitrariness of states. Earlier, issues confined to the boundary of the state or states have turned out to be global and mustered support from all sections, countries, nations and culture of the world. A new kind of threat from information and communication technologies seems to affect the states.

Some would argue walking on the conventionally trodden furrows that state is still the main player in international politics maintaining its supremacy in providing security even in cyberspace (Fountain, 2001). Others in a different vein maintain that the emergence of "virtual states" and network economies imply a decline of inter state violence and hence the predominant role "security" was playing in the past gets a plummeting. This optimistic undertone "sketches a future with an ever widening zone of international peace" (Rosencrance, 1999: 24). Still they are many who hold that the information revolution has spurred many firms, interest organizations, social movements, individuals and transnational relations into a network of activities and inter-connections. Hence these non state actors have become challengers to and provider of security (Arquilla and Ronfeldt, 2001; Castells, 1998: 376; Henry and Peartree, 1998; Nye, 2003, 2004a, 2004b).

In other words, the general observation is that the information revolution has bunked the established notion that security is the unrivalled monopolistic concern of states only, and distance security away from state into an increasingly important concern of all sectors of the society. Today, all modern societies are information societies. Taking into account Arnold Wolfers definition of security as "the absence of threat to acquired values" it can be said that a threat to information services can be equally considered a threat to the acquired value of the society.

The challenges of information revolution for both security and its apparatus state remain unexplored in terms of policy and substantive issues. In the past no effort has been made to apply and develop theory on this topic. No serious efforts have been made to apply international relation (IR) theory in analyzing the information revolution. It seems warranted to study the impact of information services on security and for development of international relation theory. John Eriksson and Giampiero Giacomello have made a commendable attempt at dovetailing the information revolution into the ambit of international relation.

During the post-second world war period the discipline of international relation was almost content with its Euro centric stance and putting on the western straight-jacket in analyzing the events in the world it tried to look at the world with its own glass. It claimed universality and parsimony on the ground of the events in the world being understood on western logic and idioms. This claim to universality and parsimony was at the expense of empirical applicability (Wight, 2002). That means, the empirical applicability requires a greater degree of complexity and contextually contingent thinking than has been provided by the dominant international relation theories (George and Bernet, 2005). For example, theories such as Kenneth Waltz's neo-realism and Keohane and Nye's theory of complex interdependence were considered either irrelevant or secondary to claims of internal validity (Keohane and Nye, 1977: vi; Waltz, 1979:6-7; Wight, 2002). Utter discontentment with this inward looking obsession with theoretical consistency appeared on the scene with the demise of cold war (Allan and Goldmann, 1995; Lebow and Risse-Kappen, 1995). The end of cold war signalled a major crisis for neorealism and international relation theories for having failed to predict and explain the turn of events.

THE DIGITAL AGE LITERATURE SILENT ON THE SECURITY ISSUE

Marxist Sociologist Manuel Castells was the fast proponent of the digital age. As early as the late 1980s, he noted that information had become the primary resource of material productivity in the newly emerging "knowledge economy" (Castells 1989). Information technology's influence was felt on banking, air travel, water, or energy distribution for their functioning. In the 1990s the network of information technology was all set to constitute an indispensable coping stone for modern and advanced societies. As pointed out by Castells, it was not long to see the dawn of global network society with nation states being stripped of their sovereignty and replaced by alternative identities and communities (Castells, 1996, 1997, 1998, 2000).

He pointed to the perspective of transnational crime as will rise becoming the greatest potential threat to global security. Hamid Mowlana, another international scholar worked in a similar vein and agreed with Castells' analysis. But their study is limited to the impact of ICTs on organized crime (Castells 1997, 1998, 2000), military strategic communication and the use of information was propaganda (Mowlana, 1997). According to Eriksson and Giacomello, Mowlana's work though insightful was weak in linking the information revolution to IR theory.

CONTROL OF INFORMATION BY GOVERNMENTS TO PRESERVE SOVEREIGNTY AND SECURITY

Before information revolution could affect the state, and reach out to the control of non state actors the main function to preserve national sovereignty and national security centered round state's ability to control information flows (Agnew and Corbriege, 1995, Anderson 1995; Krasner, 1995). The communication system was a one way flow through radio and television from the national government to the entire people with its own monitored, cooked and controlled message. Increasingly in recent years the state stranglehold over information flows has slackened due to professional media organizations, human rights organizations, non-governmental organizations and individuals having taken advantage of the same communication system to exercise control over flow of information, produce counter claims, independent views and non-governmental information. The ingrained impregnability of state sovereignty seems to be made porous by the uninterrupted international flow of information from one corner to another corner. The entire nation has been exposed to the outside world and the inviolability of its sovereignty has been peeled off one layer by another by the flow of information to the outside world under its very nose. The international flow of information has been taking place so rapidly that the capability of states to control and monitor the ingoing and outgoing information is utterly compromised. This network of information flows transcending the traditional boundary of states has resulted in reinforcing an integrated world communication system, which no longer remains captive to the control of state sovereignty (Camilleri and Falk 1992).

Not that the importance of information was unknown to the states or the latter were not vulnerable to the assaulting power of the information. A report to the Swedish government, the Tengelin Report (Tengelin, 1981) also emphasized the main risks of a networked society including dependence on foreign vendors and the threat of hackers' raids.

But at present most governments are very much aware and even affected by the fact that the uncontrolled information flows transcending the territorial boundaries of states. This cross-county information flows and the easy accessibility of individuals to new channels and sources outside the country about its own political and economic structures, are very likely to affect the attitude of its own citizenry vis-a-vis its political and economic structure. When the states had control over its radio and T.V. channel and other free flow of information was not possible and the information revolution was at its nascence, the extraordinary influence of information in forming the political attitude of the people vis-a-vis its state was subject to control and manoeuvrability. The difference is that what was once one-way traffic has became now a multiple traffic with multiple entry points making the entire sovereign state system look like a porous pot and emasculating it to block the penetration of that information (Eriksson / Giacomello : 224).

What has changed the concept of security is the prominence that the global information society has given to ICTs in human thinking and approach to life. With the industrial revolution and invention of machines, human beings put machines in the centrality of their security. Machines could communicate with each other and become provider of security with more accuracy and precision in a faster rate than the human beings would be able to do in the past. With it also grows the psychological effects of fear and the dehumanizing consequences of machines doing blunders. The solutions to the societal problems were found in the machines. More than these machines, the development of computers could herald optimistic visions of technical solutions to the societal problems or "technological fixes" as well as feelings of fear of (Volt 1995) these computers being turned evil. Too much dependence on computers as the vital decision maker and sole arbiter of well-being and development of human beings has marked a drastic change in human society thinking and at the same time exposed the human beings to the wrong or evil computers. Computers being the master of human destiny can escape into the hands of terrorist, and evil doers to wreck havoc on humanity on a larger scale than it was possible in the past. The entire world seems to be caught not in the network of human relations, but in a network of communications. Subject to intrigue manipulation, computers through its electronic gadgets can create revolutionary psychological dimensions of network.

The most famous computer network, the internet is at the same time an infrastructure and a communication medium. "On the same wires and with the same protocol, packets transport bytes that represent radically different information: an email to a friend, details on one's flight itinerary, online multiplayer gaming, statistics on a municipality's water consumption, or credit card numbers" (Eriksson and Giacomello: 225).

Most of the communication being public, anybody using the medium could read them. Earlier the computer networks were proprietary linking together a bank with its subsidiaries or US strategic command with nuclear missile silos was too expensive to be afforded by any other organizations and institutions. Further, they used protocols that authorized their legitimate users to be in the network. Today, the cost of networking has been comparatively less expensive and easily affordable with availability of multiple channels and unobstructed accessibility. The network of communication has been very simple making everybody completely nude before others. What was yesterday unnoticed, unwanted or undesirable or improper to intrude, has now become public. When man was the master and sole communicator the security of communication was fully insulated from others' intrusion. Today, Internet easily passing into every hand has taken away the security of communication at a higher price of providing sinews and opportunities to criminals and evil mongers to exploit the vulnerabilities of the network for their own narrow interest.

CYBER THREATS IN THE POST COLD WAR SECURITY THINKING: A THEORETICAL UNDERSTANDING

The end of cold war marked remarkably a downsize in the budgetary allocation for defense and military establishment. A shift of focus on conventional warfare to information security and cyber threats was perceived. Allusion to buzzwords like critical information, protection, information warfare, information operations, information assurance, cyber terrorism and Revolution in Military Affairs (RMA) became common among the analysts and policy makes in defense and military establishments.

The increased vulnerability of individuals, people, security and states to information revolution and loss of control over it has given rise to a fear resulting in what is termed as cyber threats. This has been due to the transformation of industrial society into an information society (Alberts, 1996a, 1996b, Albert and Papp, 1997, Henry and Peartree 1998, O'Day, 2004).

Images of cyber threats are found dominating in both public and private sphere, among both military as well as civilian actors. These became rampant with the world coming under the global computer network and communication. In the business community and within police cyber crime has become a salient threat image.

With the bureaucratic-military establishment perceived threats have been framed as information warfare, information operation, cyber terrorism and cyber war. Both state and non state actors can come within the targets and adversaries of image of cyber threats (O'Day 2004, Yourdon 2002, Polikanov, 2001).

According to Eriksson and Giacomello, "states are still typically seen as the single most important type of potential enemy, able to neutralize effectively the critical infrastructure of another country" (Eriksson and Giacomello: 226).

There is no dearth of literature to show the theoretical dramatization of the potential cyber threats and information security. A study by the National Research Council argues that "Tomorrow's terrorist may be able to do more with a keyboard than with a bomb" (Bendrath, 2001, Denning 2001a:282). Former US Homeland Security Director Tom Ridge (2002) observed that "Terrorists can sit at one computer connected to one network and can create world havoc – [they] do not necessarily need bombs or explosive to cripple a sector of the economy or shut down a power grid". The view doing the round is that the governments and societies are becoming more dependent on and comfortable with information technology, but at the same time are becoming increasingly vulnerable to all sorts of cyber threats being dramatized theoretically. The glaring example of cyber threats being theoretically dramatized is the electronic Pearl Harbor (Bendrath 2001, Everard 2000, Forno, 2002, O'Day, 2004, Smith 1998).

It is a dramatized apocalyptic vision of a situation where all governments' critical infrastructures and foundations totally depending on information technology would come to a grinding halt. Banks, phone system, subway cars would come to a standstill position putting thousands of people in jeopardy. This became the cynosure of many news papers and media in US, and its policy makers in certain circles started working on this. Former Deputy Defense Minister John Hamre argued that "we are facing the possibility of an electronic Pearl Harbor ... There is going to be an electronic attack on this country some time in the future" (CNN, 1997).

But there are critics who jibe at such rhetorical dramatization of potential cyber threats, castigating these are highly unlikely. Denning (2001 b) argues that cyber terrorism, defined as digital attacks causing physical destruction and human deaths is extremely unlikely. Even the US Naval War College in cooperation with the Gartner Group concluded that an "electronic Pearl Harbor", although theoretically possible was highly unlikely: "These are far simpler and less costly ways to attack critical infrastructure, from hoax phone calls to track bombs and hijacked airliners" (The Economist, 2002:19).

The major impact of information operations is the symbolic and the main effect is humiliation. Operating with online transactions, the firms incur a heavy financial loss. To a large degree cyber attacks are attacks with and against symbol and images. Denial of service attacks and the defacing of web pages certainly can have material consequences.

According to some analysts, the cyber attacks have been mostly transnational and network based (Deibert and Stein, 2003, Arquilla and Rofeldt 1999, 2001). Adversaries can be termed as network actors consisting of relatively independent nodes of individuals, groups, organizations or even states capable of quickly assembling and dispersing, even long before an attack has been discovered. These actors operating in loosely organized networks and using such means can resort to asymmetric warfare (Applegate, 2001, Arquilla and Ronfeldt, 2001, Goodman 2001, Herd 2000, Erbschloe, 2001). These warfares may not be conventional military conflicts, but are capable of wreaking serious damages by attacking and exploiting the vulnerabilities of information system by resorting to cyber attacks (Arquilla and Ronfeldt, 1999, 2001, Cordes man, 2002).

The conventional understanding of sovereign state system is premised on boundary making and spatial distancing. With the prospect of cyber attacks and information security the boundaries fencing off states against the other, demarcating the international sphere from the domestic sphere, the public from the private, peace from war and the military from the civil are dissolved. One of the major implications of the cyber threats is that the security of the information system on which the entire network of organization, individuals, groups and even states hinges is challenged. Besides, the very impregnability and invincibility of sovereign state system is challenged (Everard 2000, Fountain 2001, Giacomello, 2005). The very foundation of sovereign state system that it is solely capable of serving control of the national territory and the people residing within it is shaken. External sovereignty is also at stake due to easy accessibility to computer networks of all for manipulation and exploitation.

SECURITY STUDIES SILENT ABOUT INFORMATION SECURITY

Security studies resolve basically around two contending positions – traditionalists and the wideners. The traditionalists hold on to their ingrained stance that security is basically state centric and military oriented. Despite cataclysmic changes in the international realm in terms of the end of cold war, growing spate of ethnic and religious insurgence, global terrorism, transnational crimes and global warming, their age long stance on state centric security has not changed because of their preference for theoretical clarity and coherence (Ayoob 1997, Goldmann 1999).

The wideners in contrast to the traditionalists claim that the concept of security should be widened to include within its ambit the new challenges, threats even emanating not only from other states, but from the political, societal, economic and environmental sectors (Buzan, 1991, Deibert 1997, Muller, 2002, Stern 1999). Whereas in the traditionalists' view state was the center piece of security, in the widener's view state is not the only linchpin of security concern there are other non state actors like NGOs, social movements, terrorist organizations, private firms and individuals who pretend status equally with states in the security concerns. The traditionalists' focus is on the state, but distancing away from the state the wideners focus on individual under the rubric 'human security'. What is surprising is that in their broadened perspective no attention has been paid to the information revolution and its impact on security. While their concept of widened security incorporates everything spanning political, electronic, ecological and cultural issues but rarely addresses the emergence of Internet and information revolution and their impact on security. On the other hand, some traditionalists have tended to give importance to development of information technology to the extent it has been of immense utility to improvement of military capabilities (Lonsdale, 1999).

Enhancement of material capabilities has always been considered crucial to state centric and military oriented national security. Intelligence gathering and psychological warfare (a play of information operations) are also considered as elements of material capabilities of states and intrigue parts of warfare. The military and material aspects of states have evinced a greater interest in technological and information revolution as these would enhance their military capability and modernize the technology of warfare. The passage of state military apparatus from machine guns to radar and satellites demonstrates the interest traditionalists have shown in the utility of information technology to the enhancement and modernization of military capability of states. 'Electronic warfare' has been an established practice and concept within the military for several decades. But most traditionalists while sticking to their conventionally held stand on state centric security are of the view that "information technologies are merely a new fancy add on" (Eriksson and Giacomello : 228).

RELEVANCE OF INFORMATION SECURITY FROM THE PERSPECTIVE OF MAJOR INTERNATIONAL RELATION THEORIES ON SECURITY

The contemporary international relations is mainly dominated by three theoretical perspectives –realism, liberalism and constructivism, which are perceived and portrayed as separate perspectives, though these have linkages, overlaps and internal varieties. In the light of the digital age and information revolution, the relevance of each perspective can be examined.

REALISM

(1) Realism is founded on the basic assumption that the state is the cornerstone of any political system and the primary unit of analysis.

(2) It is state centric and military oriented and state is the sole determinant of what constitutes its national interest. It not only defines, but also satisfies its national interest by means of power.

(3) It is based on a pessimistic view of human nature and state is its reflection. So the relation as among states and between states is basically conflictual, and disputes arising among them are resolved by resorting to war (Morgenthau, 1965, 1985).

(4) Since international system is a compilation of independent sovereign states without having a central political structure and authority as found in case of states, the security and survival of state is based on self help strengthened by their respective military capabilities.

(5) The anarchical nature of international system tragically leads to "security dilemma". Power measured primarily in terms of military capabilities and the associated striving for security, is the main

driving force in world politics (Gilpin, 1986, Morgenthau, 1993, Schmidt, 2002).

Kenneth Waltz's 'The theory of International Politics' (1979) seeks to provide a scientific explanation of the international political system with foreign and security polices beyond its scope. Departing from the classical and neo classical realism, he ignores their normative concerns to provide a scientific international relation theory, being influenced by positivist models of economics. In so doing, he provided a universal and parsimonious explanation of how world politics functions. States are alike in all basic functional respects i.e. in spite of their different cultures or ideologies or constitutions or personnel, they all perform the same basic tasks. Waltz's neorealist approach does not provide explicit policy guidance to state leaders as they confront the practical problems of world politics (Jackson and Sorensen : 2008 : 77).

Despite information revolution in the digital age the realists have preferred to cling to their main thesis that state is the sole and main actor in both domestic and world politics with primacy on military power and process, denying the non state actors any power to play along with state. They would like to face the challenges of the information revolution in much the same way as they have tackled previous challenges of transnationalization, complex interdependence and globalization. These challenges may affect the policies of domestic politics and structure of the state but would not any way undermine the primacy of state as the supreme political unit and change their ingrained view about the anarchic international system.

The realist would like to treat the IT related security threats as coming under the rubric of economic issue not as security threats in themselves to penetrate into bastion of impregnability of states. There are some realists still inclined to define a narrow military centric definition of security, who are of the view that if widening of the concept of security is warranted, then it should incorporate the economic dimension without compromising its primacy (Buzan 1991, Walt, 1994). Interestingly they try to understand the new information warfare as new and digressing away from state but as a component in otherwise traditional interstate conflict (Lonsdale, 1999).

The case of electronic warfare such as the jamming of radio communication since the second world war for a much shorter time has been an element of inter state conflict. To realists this is not threat rather a change in the warfare within the state military apparatus presaging the greater change in the digital age warfare, which comes within the military apparatus of state as a part of its modernization process. The realists view the introduction of information warfare in strategic studies and military planning as a part of its modernization process. The realists view the introduction of information warfare in strategic studies and military planning as a continuation of its traditional military thinking not as a dramatic change envisaging the overhaul of the state centric security paradigm. The information revolution may have introduced new technologies into the warfare with new digital adversaries, "but the basic notion of attacking and defending information systems are as old as warfare itself-basically old wine in new bottles" (Eriksson and Giacomello, 2006: 229).

LIBERALISM

Realists are wont to understanding international relations as the relation between and among the governments of sovereign states. Rejecting this view as one sided and normally focused, the sociological liberalism holds that international relation is not only about state-

state relation, it is also about transnational relations that is relation between people, groups and organization belonging to different countries. State is not the only actor there are plurality of non-state actors. Transnational relations are considered by sociological liberals to be an increasingly important aspect of international relation. According to Rosenau, trans- nationalism marks "the process whereby international relations conducted by governments have been supplemented by relations among private individuals, groups and societies that can and do have important consequence for the course of events" (Resenau, 1980:1) . In a similar vein, Karl Deutsch argued that a high degree of transnational ties between societies leads to peaceful relations that amounts to what is called 'security community' (Deutsch, 1957). John Burton (1972) in his book 'World Society' purposes a 'cobweb model' of transnational relationships among different groups of people – religions, business, labour, with different types of external ties and different types of interests. In contrast, realist models' depiction of interstate relation is likened to a set of billiard balls i.e. a number of independent self sufficing and self contained units.

Rosenau studies transnational relation at the macro-level of human population coupled with those conducted at the micro-level by individuals. Perceiving a profound transformation of the international system, he is of the view that the state centric anarchic system has not disappeared but a new multi-centric world has emerged that is composed of diverse "sovereignty free" collectivities, which exist apart from and in competition with the state centric world of sovereignty-bound actors (Rosenau, 1992:282).

Interdependence liberalism is of the view that modernization increases the level and scope of interdependence between states. Under complex interdependence, transnational actors are increasingly important, military force is a less useful instrument, and welfare –not security-is becoming the primary goal and concern of states. According to Rosecrance, the end of cold war has made that the traditional option less urgent and thus less attractive. Consequently, the trading- state option is increasingly preferred even by very large states. David Mitrany (1960) put forth a functionalist theory of integration arguing that greater interdependence in the form of transnational ties between countries could lead to peace. Built on Mitrany's functionalism but rejecting his separation of technical experts from politicians, Ernst Haas enunciated the doctrine of neo-functionalist theory of international integration which is a process whereby "political actors are persuaded to shift their loyalties toward a new center where institutions possess or demand jurisdiction over the preexisting national states(Haas, 1958:16).

Robert Keohane and Joseph Nye, Power and Interdependence (1977, 2001) propounded a general theory of what they called "complex interdependence", which is qualitatively different from earlier and simpler kinds of interdependence. Under conditions of complex interdependence relations between states now a days are not only or even primarily relations between state leaders, there are relations on many different levels via- different actors and branches of government between individuals and groups outside of the state. Further, military force is a less useful instrument of policy under conditions of complex interdependence. In the words of Nye:

"The appropriate response to the changes occurring in world politics today is not to discredit the traditional wisdom of realism and its concern for the military balance of power, but to realize its limitation and to supplement it with insights from the liberal approach" (Nye 1990:177).

Institutional liberals differ from realists in that international institutions are mere scraps of paper and that they remain always hostage to the powerful states. International institutions are always of interdependent importance promoting cooperation between states (Keohane 1989a, Young 1989, Rittberger 1993; Levy et al, 1995).

One way to assess the institutional liberal view is to set it against that of neorealist analysis. Neorealists argue that the end of cold war is likely to bring the return of instability. But the institutional liberals (Keohane 1989a, Nye 1993: 38; Keohane et al 1993) are of the view that a high level of institutionalization significantly reduces the destabilizing effects of multi polar anarchy identified by Mearsheimer (Mearsheimer, 1993:148). While promoting cooperation between states, institutional liberalism can help alleviate the lack of trust between states and states' fear of each other, which are considered to be the traditional problems associated with international anarchy.

Having with it the normative element the republican liberalism advocates that democracies do not go to war against each other owing to their domestic culture of peaceful conflict resolution, their common moral values, and their mutually beneficial ties of economic cooperation and interdependence (Thompson 1996, Sorensen, 1992; Adler and Barnett 1996, Lipson, 2003).

In sum, it can be said that the development of increasingly complex and globally penetrating web of transnational relations and emergence of non- state actors has challenged the political, and economic stranglehold of the state and made it pregnable against the perforating penetration of transnational relations.

Both liberalism and realism having differential emphasis share a rationalistic epistemological approach aiming at interest based interaction (Buzan et al, 1998; Fearon and Wendt, 2002; Schmidt, 2002).

With shift of emphasis on state to other non- state actors and other transnational relations, liberalism has broadened the definition of what international relation is about, and regarded economic as much important as security. As a result, some liberals advocated a widened perspective of security, which includes economic, ecological and human security concerns. Joseph Nye and Robert Keohane, the advocates of theory of complex interdependence in the 70s have recently updated this to meet the challenges of the digital age (Keohane and Nye 1998, Nye 2003, 2004b). While treating the costs of interdependence in terms of vulnerability and sensitivity as new component of the theory and frame them purely in economic terms not portrayed as matters of national and international security, they have analyzed the impact of information revolution on international relations (Nye, 2003: 199-202, 2004b).

Nye is of the view that national security defined as the absence of threat to major values can be at stake. Within his theoretical framework is found absence of any elaborated analysis of critique of cyber security threats. Nonetheless, his concept of 'soft power' can be of relevance to this topic. Soft power is the "ability to get what you want through attraction rather than coercion or payments. It arises from the attractiveness of a country's culture, political ideals, and policies...Soft power rests on the ability to shape the performance of others" (Nye, 2004a: x, 5). Thus, modern liberalism seems to be greatly influenced by Kantian and Wilsonian idealism (Duncan et al, 2003: 21-2, 32- 4). Nye wants the spread of these ideals to other parts of the globe, through the exercise of this soft power. In his view, relevance of soft power is more highlighted than before in this digital age because of the ever increasingly evolution of multiple channels of global communication transcending the sovereign boundaries (Nye, 2004b: Ch 7).

It is mistaken to hold that the soft power and global ICTs that facilitate the opening of multiple channels of communication and interaction are only instruments of cooperation, democratization and peace, as Nye and other liberals would like to have it. These channels may exactly be the opposite instruments of deception, propaganda, threats and terror.

Casting aside its idealism and fear of treading on realist furrow of security analysis liberalism can be said as throwing insights into the nature of security threats in the digital age. In particular, this view is sustained and reinforced by the attention that the liberals pay to the growing emergence of non-state sovereignty free actors and the global complex interdependence in costs in terms of vulnerability and sensitivity. Eriksson and Giacomello cite two socio-economic trends that are found consistent with the dictum of liberal theory:

(1) expanding partnership between the public and private sector to provide services

(2) merging of the civil and military spheres (Eriksson and Giaconello, 231).

The very recognition of their growing incapability to meet the burgeoning demands of the modern societies, has led the governments to promote public –private partnership. The trends of privatization in the age of market economy quite evident in the sectors of health, education, transport and other services have been extended to national security. For example, in the United States, the National Strategy to secure cyberspace of the President's Critical Infrastructure Protection Board of September 2002 relies on public- private partnership, conceding that "Government alone cannot secure cyberspace" (PCCIP, 2000:5). This has resulted in what is called civilianization of the military or, perhaps, militarization of the society" (Eriksson et al, 231).

No sector is most apparently permeated by this integration and complex interdependence than the telecom sector. It has been always the practice with the military to use the help of civilian telecom networks. Now a days the dependence of vast majority of military communication on civilian networks for transmission has been profusely vast. Computer networks have been incorporated into the development of hard military powers and have formed the foundation of soft power (Fountain, 2001; Nye, 2002, 2004a).

It needs a critical analysis of the question whether a theory that was originally crafted to study actors and process in a political- economy context, can dovetail the impact of information revolution in a digital age into their theory. The question still remains unanswered whether the development of the ICTs in the age of globalization and modernization is a continuation of the process of transnationalization and complex web of interdependence.

Nevertheless, cyber threats and challenges of information revolution representing the current trends of development in the age of globalization appear to emasculate the sovereignty and security of the states. The non-state actors are numerically spawning and becoming powerful as found from their active participation and involvement in various domestic and international issues, because of information revolution. The emergence of Internet and network of communications and interaction with online groups may have facilitated integration, cooperation and liberation transcending the barricades of state sovereignty from a positive perspective, but certainly have brightened the prospect of terrorism, transnational crime and the destabilization of states.

The very recognition that beside state there are a plurality of non-state actors is the very valuable contribution by liberalism to theory building with regard to security in the digital age. But this remains still underdeveloped. Arquilla and Ronfeldt (2001) are among the few scholars who also study mainstream liberal notion of globalization and other challenges to state sovereignty and address explicitly the issue of actor plurality in the digital age.

CONSTRUCTIVISM

Much international theory and especially neo-realism is materialist: it focuses on how the distribution of material power such as military forces and economic capabilities, defines balance of power between states and explains the behavior of states. Rejecting such a one sided material focus, constructivists argue that the most important aspect of international relations is social not material. In their views, the social reality is not objective or external. The social and political world including the world of international relations is not a physical entity or material object that is independent of human consciousness. Consequently, the study of international relation must focus on the ideas and beliefs that inform the actors on the international scene as well as the shared understandings between them.

The end of cold war nullified the neorealist doctrine and its prediction about the future development in the international relation. The constructivist claim is that the neo-realist uncertainty is closely connected to the fact that the theory is overly spare and materialist. On the other hand, the constructivists argue that a focus on thoughts and ideas leads to a better theory of anarchy and power balancing.

Liberalism basically founded on neorealist assumptions as starting point is vulnerable to the diatribes directed against neo-realism by constructivists. After the end of the cold war some liberals begin to focus on the role of ideas. Fukuyama's End of History (1989) focused on the role of the ideas in spreading democratic and liberal values to all parts of the globe. Even if constructivists are sympathetic to several elements of liberal thinking, their focus is less on advance of liberal ideas, than on the role of thinking and ideas in general.

Constructivists maintain that the social world is in part constructed by physical entities or material reality. But it is the ideas and beliefs concerning those entities which are most important. The international system of security and defense, for example, consists of territories, populations, weapons and other physical assets, computers, ICTs and communication channels can be also included within its ambit. But it is the ideas and understandings according to which those assets are conceived, organized and used –that is most important. This can be called social reality. "The thought that is involved in international security is more important, far more important than the physical assets that are involved because those assets have no meaning without the intellectual component: they are mere things in themselves" (Robert Jackson and Georg Sorensen, 2008: 165). To quote Wendt:

The claim is not that ideas are more important than power and interest, or that they are autonomous from power and interests. The claim is rather that power and interests have the effects they do in virtue of the ideas that make them up (Wendt 1999:135-6).

In contrast to the materialist view held by neorealists and neoliberals, the constructivists propound their identical view. The core ideational element upon which constructivists focus is intersubjective beliefs and ideas that are widely shared among people.

Constructivists reject the notion of objective truth; social scientists cannot discover a final truth about the world, which is true across time and place. On the other hand, constructivists do make "truth claims about the subject they have investigated while admitting that their claims are always contingent and partial interpretation of a complex world" (Price and Reus-Smit 1998:272).

Constructivists are much more heterogeneous than realism and liberalism in that they advocate a very wide range of methodologies and an even wider range of particular international relation theories. On the issue of truth claims the view closer to above is represented by what is called conventional constructivists (Hopf 1998, Alexander Wendt 1999, Peter Katzenstein 19965, John Ruggie 1998, Emanuel Adler and Michael Barnett 1998, Ted Hopf 2002, Martha Finnemore 2003).

On the other hand, the critical constructivists argue that 'truth claims' are not possible because there is no neutral ground when we can decide about what is true. What we call truth is always connected to different, more or less dominant ways of thinking about the world. Truth and power cannot be segmented. The main task of critical constructivists is to unearth the relationship between power and truth and criticize those dominant versions of thinking that claim to be true for all (David Campbell 1998, Jim George 1994, James Der Derian 1987, R.B.J.Walker 1993, Ann Tickner 1992, Andrew Linklater 1998).

Further, some constructivists focus entirely on states and the inter state system (Wendt, 1999) while others study, for example, NGOs and transnational communities (Keck and Sikkink, 1998) and epistemic communities (Adler, 1992, Haas, 1990), Adler (2002:108, 110) is of the view that constructivists should focus more on the individual.

To understand constructivist theorem at the basic level it can be said that actors have a set of norms, belief and ideas about what is wrong and right. The norms shape identities-the separation of "we" from "them". In turn identities shape interests. If interests change, it is because there is an underlying shift in identities and norms. So in (Adler 2002:103-4) contrast to rationalism all these elements are seen inferently dynamic.

CONSTRUCTIVIST VIEW OF SECURITY

Realism focuses on violent actor based threats (interstate war); whole liberalism envisages a wider perspective including both non-state actors and structural threats. Constructivism, on the other hand, does not take a general stance as to what can be or cannot be framed as a security threat and how such threat can be dealt with. It focuses on the verb "become rather than can or cannot" (Adler, 2002:95). Constructivist security studies emphasize on identity and culturally related threats, which are downplayed in realist and liberal accounts of security (Buzan et al, 1998). The empirical amenability of constructivism to the widest possible range of perceived security threats makes it possible to address all kinds of threats. "In terms of threats to critical infrastructures, this would, for example, include not only digital attacks, but also technical collapses and bugs such as the infamous Y2K problem, as well as natural disaster such as earthquakes and violent eruption" (Eriksson and Giacomello, 2006 :234).

The constructive approach to security is the theory of "securitization" developed by the Copenhagen School. This is about how, when and with what consequences political actors construct something as a matter of security (Buzan et al, 1998, Waever, 1995, Williams, 2003). The emphasis is on speech acts i.e. political language and the implication this has for political agenda setting and political relations. Securitization implies that an "existential threat" is identified, and the "speech act" prioritizes the issue on the political agenda, legitimating extraordinary measures such as secrecy, the use of force and the invasion of privacy.

But on its advocacy of widening of security agenda, the Copenhagen School has lost sight of the information revolution.

Eriksson (2001a, 2001b) has pioneered the study of securitization of information technology in Swadeshi politics. His analysis demonstrates the impact of different frame of IT related threats on whom or what is blamed, and who is allocated responsibility for dealing with the problems. Framing an incident as "cybercrime" implies that criminals are to be blamed, and that the police are responsible for dealing with them. In contrast, the same incident can also be framed as an instant of 'information warfare' which implies that enemies to a given nation state, other states or non state actors are to be blamed, and that the military has a responsibility to respond to the threat (Bendrath, 2001; Eriksson, 2001a, 2001b).

In the current analysis of digital security threats the constructivists put emphasis on how information warfare challenges a multitude of boundaries, notably boundaries of identity. Everard (2000) argues that information warfare is a particular kind of "identity warfare" in which all kind of boundaries are challenged, including the classical domestic international divide. Hence the identity of nation-state is always threatened, although it may adapt to the constant penetration into the sovereign state by cyber threats, and to the emergence and articulation of new identities in cyber space (Saco, 1999).

In addition to material reality of computers and cables, the significance of images and symbols finds a peremptory place in the constructive analysis of power and security in a virtual world. Distancing of actors from the bloody war has been one of the many effects of war in the digital age (Der Derian 2000).

Due to Internet and Information Revolution from

anywhere in the world, a computer can be attacked in other distant places of the world. Having said this does not in any way undermine the significance of decreasing geographical distance. What is significant is here how virtuality affects the conduct and perception of the war? Digital war is akin to computer games to the extent that simulation is performed and perceived in the same way by using the mouse and keyboard of a computer. The boundary between the real and imagined is thus blurred. What is important here is to note that the film, tabloid and computer gaming industries with their effects, tactical tools and software have become an increasingly important source of inspiration and expertise for the military (Der Derrian 2000; Everard, 2000).

The use and abuse of symbols for manipulating political discourse and public opinion known as symbolic politics has assumed significance for studying digital age security. Long before the information revolution came into picture, the symbolic politics of approach for the first time laid by Murray Edelman can be held as a constructivist contribution in social science (Edelman, 1964, 1977, 1985, 1988; Merelman, 1993, Sears, 1993).

Defacing websites, a noteworthy practice of symbolic politics can be compared to the burning of an enemy's flag. What is important here is not the negligible cost involved in mending a website and securing a server. But the cost in terms of lost confidence, disparagement and feeling of vulnerability is immense. Assaults and counter attacks against U.S.A and Chinese Government websites by hackers from the respective countries are very much in the news. Similar digital wars are going on between Israeli and Arab hackers and between Indian and Pakistani ones. This symbolic politics approach very much practice in computers smacks of how and why these actions are seen as an insult and offense to national pride. The Internet has become the new global battle field for symbolic politics.

The function and impact of language in digital age security has been illustrated by the constructivist analysis. Frequent reference to bugs, viruses, worms and fire walls in computer with analogies to things familiar in the real or off-line world has rendered the abstract and technically complex world of cyber security intelligible (Eriksson and Giacomello 2006:235). Though the information warfare and electronic Pearl Harbor are constantly referred to as digital by nature, has nonetheless physical consequences equal to those of conventional war. Constructivist analysis can play a significant role in revealing and understanding the importance of rhetoric and symbolic actions in politics.

Eriksson and Giacomello have very succinctly attempted to demonstrate the need to develop middle range theories integrating liberalism, constructivism and realism for comprehending the impact of information revolution on security. As found out from the above analysis of various theories on security, short shrift has been paid to the security problems of the digital age by the scholars. Realism persists with its entrenched habit of putting emphasis on state and its military apparatus. On the other hand, liberalism and constructivism have widened the base of security and made a discursive approach to security. Liberalism denuded of its idealist and anti-realist pretensions entails within it many of the elements of the security in the digital age. The advocacy of multiplicity of non-state actors with transnational capacity, network economics, vulnerability, interdependence and consequent perforation of formally sovereign boundaries have enabled it to grasp the impact of information revolution on security. In a similar vein, constructivism has analyzed the symbolic, rhetorical and identity based aspects of digital age security. Realism has tried to understand the impact of information revolution and digital age security by subsuming it under state as it was wont to understanding globalization and other challenges by relating it to political economy or domestic politics under the rubric "state".

Even in the classical realist formulation of security information warfare is held as mere the technological continuation of classical forms of psychological warfare and more recently of electronic warfare. In this classical perspective the developments in the information technology in the digital age are seen as nothing but an unfolding of technological change in the military warfare within a military centric state. The foregoing analysis demonstrates how the international relations theories on security are plagued by the dichotomy between theory and practice in the digital age. All current theories are inherently weak so far as the theoretical adoption and application in analyses of the complexities of the emerging information revolution in the digital world is concerned.

Adopting a pragmatic approach founded on bridging the gap between theory and practice taking insights from methodological pluralism and theoretical complementarities and tolerance of a diverse range of international relations theories, seems to be the desideratum to incorporate digital security into the corpus of international relation theories.

7

Feminist Perspectives on Security in International Relation

Feminism theory of international relations is a broad term given to works of those scholars who have sought to bring a concern with *gender* into the academic study of *international politics*. In terms of *international relations* (IR) theory it is important to understand that feminism is derived from the school of thought known as reflectionism. Feminist International Relations has expanded, and built on the work of feminist political and economic theory to examine the masculinist framing of politics and economics and associated institution, including notably the state and its key military and governmental components, as well as the discourses through which these institutions operate and are reproduced over time. In the course of this work, feminist analysis has highlighted three major related phenomena:

- The state and market, in theory and practice, are gendered by masculinist assumptions and structures.

- The dominant conceptualization of political and economic agency in male dominated terms ignores both women's realities and their active contributions to political and economic life.
- Lack of attention to the analytical category of gender obscures the interrelated social construction of male and female identities and roles (Youngs Gillian, 2004: 75).

Feminist International Relations has stressed that the mainstream International Relations theory has been malestream in its epistemological foundation and discourses, which have resulted in perpetuation of a distorted and partial portrayal of world view that reflects the disproportionate power of control and influence that men hold and exercise. Its view of the social reality comprising the lives of women, children and men is not at all comprehensive and all encompassing. Thus this theory is more reflective and expressive of historically established male power than it is an open and comprehensive exploration of the political and economic processes in which all members of societies are engaged. The malestream International Theory has accepted the male dominance as given without giving due attention to how power works, including its gendered, racialized and socio-economic dimensions, or to situate individuals and groups differently in terms of contrasting levels of capacity, control, influence and freedom. What has been fundamental to feminist international relations and international political economy is to adduce both deconstructive and reconstructive approaches focusing on identifying through critique the masculinist limitations of mainstream approaches, but also, crucially, traversing beyond those limitations and investigating political and economic processes in which women and men are engaged. Where women have been largely ousted from mainstream international relations, it has been essential to develop increasing corpus of theoretical and substantive research related to them. The concept of gender keeps to the fore the relational nature of categorizations of male and female and signals the importance of not taking either as given or necessarily natural. Both women and gender have therefore been identified by feminist analyses as problematically absent from mainstream approaches and essential to understanding international relations. Feminism vouchsafes for an ontological revisionism: a recognition that it is necessary to go behind the appearance and examine how differentiated and gendered power constructs the social relations that form that reality.

One of the most influential works in feminist IR is *Cynthia Enloe's Bananas, Beaches and Bases* (London: Pandora Press 1990). She dwelt upon how the realms of International Relations have been dominated by masculine assertion of power in military and conflict to show their deeper gendered realities. Her work has turned out to be a vitriolic critique of established notion that made gender and women almost absent in the practice and theory of International Relations, and where masculinity had the ultimate deciding and defining moment. This text sought to chart the many different roles that women play in international politics - as plantation sector workers, diplomatic wives, sex workers on military bases, etc. The important point of this work was to emphasize how we look at international politics from the perspective of women; we are forced to reconsider what we think international politics is 'all about'. However, it would be a mistake to think that feminist IR was solely a matter of identifying how many groups of women are positioned in the international political system. From its inception, feminist IR has always shown a strong concern with thinking about men and, in particular, masculinities. Indeed, many IR feminists argue that the discipline is inherently masculine in nature. For example, in her article "Sex and Death in the Rational World of Defense Intellectuals" Carol Cohn identified how a highly masculinised culture within the defense establishment contributed to the divorcing of war from human emotion (1987: 687-718).

Ann Tickner is of the view that the continuing dominance of masculine character in International Relations still persists, even though America in recent years recruited women into its military establishment. With Rice Condolezza being the first woman Secretary of State, the foreign and military policy making in most states remain male dominated (Tickner Ann, 2001: 1-2). In another work a decade earlier she threw gauntlet to the malestream international relations by asking questions: why women are kept aloof from the subject matter of international relations more so conspicuously absent in the military and foreign policy decision making (Tickner, 1992).

These questions thus posed to malestream international relations have not in any way denuded it of its masculinity but have prompted answers to reason its being male dominated. To bring an end to the unequal gender hierachies that have perpetuated the androcentric biases remains the greatest challenge. The overriding maleness of international relations in practice has so far remained impervious to the analytical relevance of feminist international relations. This may partly explain the strong opposition and unresponsiveness of malestream international relations to the arguments of feminists for decimating the masculine character of international relations. The concerns of feminist international relations about gender and women remain always on the fringe and runs subsidiary to the state conducted international relations with men becoming the key players and decision makers.

Feminist IR emerged largely from the late 1980s onwards. The end of the Cold War and the re-evaluation of traditional IR theory during the 1990s opened up a space for gendering International Relations. Because feminist IR is linked broadly to the critical project in IR, by and large most feminist scholarship has sought to problematize the politics of knowledge construction within the discipline - often by adopting methodologies of deconstructivism associated with postmodernism and poststructuralism. It should be noted however, that the growing influence of feminist and women-centric approaches within the international policy communities (for example at the World Bank and the United Nations) is more reflective of the liberal feminist emphasis on equality of opportunity for women. Members of the feminist theory and gender studies section seek to rectify that oversight by exploring "how we think, or do not think, or avoid thinking about gender" (Flax, 1987: 622) when we think about IR. The many of us who are feminist focus on how "we" ignore the activities of people called women when we think about IR. Specialists in this field have avoided thinking of men and women as embodied and socially constituted subject categories in three ways: by subsuming them in the "more relevant" categories of statesmen, decision makers, soldiers, refugees, prisoners of war, earthquake victims, and publics; by too readily accepting into scientific analyses the common social assumption that women are located inside the separate sphere of domestic life, where they engage in activities that have nothing to do with the usual activities International Relations chronicles and theorizes- war, crisis decision making, regime formation, trade and so on; and by retreating to abstractions (the state) that mask a masculine identity (as competitive, rational, egoistic, power-seeking). Indeed, the theoretical diversity of this field seems to belie a common disinterest in the question of how the usual activities of some people come to be excluded from realist, neorealist, world systems, decision making, neoliberal institutionalist and other theoretical frameworks while other people's idealized traits, if not their daily activities, seem to inspire the models, concepts, and processes. Gender-minded analysts seek to move from suspicion of officially ungendered IR texts to their subversion and to replacement theories. This process, however, does not rely on a single and steady course. Feminist IR in particular, like the broader field of feminist theory, features conversations and disagreements across epistemologies (Sylvester, 1990). Feminist empiricists, for instance, are comfortable using the standards of science to investigate masculine activities in officially gender-blind IR and unacknowledged women's activities in various sectors of the field, e.g., in wars, on global assembly lines, in the peace movement (Stiehm, 1989; Schwartz-Shea and Burrington, 1990). Feminist standpointers argue that people in positions of social subordination — in this case women in IR — develop different and more accurate insights on how the world and its "rules" work (Hartsock, 1983; Mies, 1986). Feminist postmodernists suspect "men" and "women" are invented subject categories that function to maintain specific relations of inequality and to hide instances of unanticipated insurrections by people whose existences are straight-jacketed by labels, e.g., women volunteering for the war, and women peace campers refusing to feel protected and secure by medium-range nuclear missiles in Europe (Elshtain, 1987). There have been three recent streams of gender-attentive research into IR:

The first stream destabilizes the field's core, often from a base of feminist standpoint thinking. Christine Di Stefano (1983) and Carol Pateman (1988), for instance, suggest ways to reevaluate Thomas Hobbes' vision of the state of nature — the key metaphor for the international state system- vis-a-vis the "civilized" conditions associated with legitimately governed nation-states. Di Stefano (1983:639) depicts the social contract as an agreement forged by male "orphans who have reared themselves, whose desires are situated within and reflect nothing but independently generated movement." Pateman (1988) speaks both of the state of nature and of the state of lawful domestic order as underwritten by a sexual contract: women were conquered in the wars of nature, owing to the handicap of having to defend themselves while also defending their children, and were turned into family-members-as-servants who, thereafter, have had a notoriously troubled relationship with public citizenship (also Jones, 1990). Nancy Hartsock (1983:283) suggests that orderly domestic politics have, in fact, been "defined in opposition to dangerous, disorderly, and irrational forces... consistently conceptualized as female," and this is what limits women citizenship at home. In *Public Man, Private Woman* (1981), Jean Bethke Elshtain takes a more postmodernist route to reinterpret the philosophical core of the idea that women are mostly nonpublic creatures. Her journeys through Plato, Aristotle, the Christian philosophers, Machiavelli, Rousseau, Hegel, Marx, and the contemporary women's movement lead her to appreciate "[b]oundary shifts in our understanding of `the political' and hence of what is public and what is private... throughout the history of Western life and thought" (p. 201).

There is also postmodernist interest in "how questions of gender, along with all other questions about political identity are resolved, in an historically specific way, by the seemingly solidly established principle of state sovereignty" (Elshtain, 1987). V. Spike Peterson (reviewed in Runyan and Peterson, 1991) draws attention to the early foundations of sovereign politics in the Athenian polis, pointedly arguing that:

"It was in the Athenian context that specifically Western constructions of the state, security, representation, sovereignty, and the "sovereign subject," public and private, and "what constitutes the political" were established; these constructions — and the metaphysics they presuppose — profoundly shaped modern state formation, and they continue to "discipline" IR (p. 91).

Her discussion of the "sovereign subject" and of public/private distinctions of ancient times has implications for continuing fixations on sovereign authority today, whether the authority is the state or the leadership of men in the public activities of politics. As Robert Keohane (1989:245) puts it, the usual way sovereignty is discussed "seems to reflect traditionally male thinking, with its emphasis on control and its penchant for absolute and dichotomous categories." Arguing that IR builds on an analogous distinction between domestic and international politics, R.B.J. Walker suggests that the task at hand is not simply to add the historically excluded voices of domestic-sphere people to IR, but to challenge the grounds on which IR has been constructed as an instance of sovereign boundary-drawing authority. While the realm of international relations between sovereign entities is denied to women, there may be room in the more ambivalent concept of "world politics" for people and activities excluded from ancient and modern sovereign specifications (also Ashley, 1989).

Cynthia Enloe (1989) returns to a feminist standpoint interpretation to argue that women are always inside international relations through their work in the practice of its politics — as diplomats' wives and secretaries, as assemblers of commodities for export, as tourists bringing foreign exchange to the nearly empty tills of third world countries and dirty laundry for poor handmaids to wash, as consolers of soldiers based far from home, and wearers of khaki (1983) — if we choose to see them there. She states the problem as learning "how the conduct of international politics has *depended* on men's control of women..." (1989:4). Whether that dependence is a sign of the taming powers of public/private images or of specific sovereignties at work is less the issue for Enlow than the complex relationship between continuities in IR -- "seemingly new trends are likely to be gendered, just as past international events were" (p. 200) — and her sense that every time a woman explains how her government is trying to control her fears, her hopes and her labor, a fresh, more realistic approach to international politics is being made (p. 201).

Related critiques of foundational IR thinking reveal gender biases in Hans J. Morgenthau's realist principles (Tickner, 1988), discuss gender relations as the quintessential elements of human history, including the history of IR (Windsor, 1988), and proffer the view that "the proper object and purpose of the study of international relations is the identification and explanation of social stratification and of inequality as structured at the level of global relations" (Brown, 1988: 461). There is also the assessment that an unacknowledged convention of "cooperative autonomy" keeps IR theory free of women-gendered activities while simultaneously subverting the prevalent identification of IR with anarchy. "Strange" subversions of and complicities with cooperative autonomy emanate from communities usually trivialized in IR, such as women's peace camps and lobbying associations of diplomats' wives (Enloe, 1989).

John Ruggie (1989:32) tells us that "what we look for obviously has an effect on what we find" and "we," understood as most members of the mainstream community of IR scholars, have not looked for signs of gender within IR's core premises, perhaps because "our" boundaries rely too heavily on "objective" readings of gendered foundational philosophies. When one reads with an awareness of gender, those texts tell of worlds differently constituted and maintained from the world recounted in official IR.

WAR AND PEACE

Of the many topics IR calls its own few have elicited as much interest by gender-aware researchers as war and peace. From Lourdes Baneria's and Rebecca Blank's (1989) feminist empiricist discussion of "Women and the Economics of Military Spending" to Elshtain's (1987) postmodernist explorations of gendered war narratives; from Judith Stiehm's (1989) empirical research on women in the U.S. military to the epistemologically varied essays that form Adrienne Harris' and Ynestra King's (1989) volume on how feminists think about peace and the parallel volume edited by Sharon MacDonald, Pat Holden, and Shirley Ardener (1988) on images of women in war and peace, a stream of efforts has been made to consider who owns, accepts, challenges, and rejects IR's wars and peaces.

This enables one to consider different gender receptivity to violence, warfare, and peace. Some argue that women's biology and/or habitual social assignments as mothers and caretakers position women against the violence of war as a means of settling disputes (e.g. Brock-Utne, 1985; Ruddick, 1989), and help them to develop a politically viable standpoint on wars, peaces, insecurities, and militaristic taming in the lives of women (Reardon, 1985; Enloe, 1983). Nancy Hartsock (1989) and Carol Cohn (1987) respectively, see links between masculinity and the appeal of war-making and war preparations by soldiers and defense intellectuals, while Zala Chandler (1989) and Barbara Omalade (1989) study lessons on conflict-management taken from the experiences of black women who routinely survive the double violence of racism and sexism.

Feminist postmodernists think of the constitution of identifiable selves in relation to war-making, war-resisting, and war-supporting as less rigid than it is thought; for example, some women seek out various battlefields to escape the stultifying peaces of protected lives (Elshtain, 1987). For this reason the postmodernists implicitly warn against "natural" feminist mergers with peace politics (Harris, 1990); Sylvester, 1989); and against ignoring the presence of women in third world revolutions and in historical warrior positions (MacDonald, 1988; Urdang, 1979). Some seek to bring ecological issues into the study of security and some would insecure gender in general as a way of questioning usual understandings of secure identities and places (Dinnerstein, 1989; Morgan, 1989; Mack, 1986; Elshtain, 1987).

Because the war/peace territory of IR is now well-marked with gender-aware signposts and warnings, it is increasingly apparent that mainstream ways of conceptualizing war and (non-speaking of peace as) national security or international stability are partial and problematic. Projecting war as the dangerous bottom line of anarchic politics and peace as the hardnosed "world of ongoing equilibrium, harmony, and perfect order," is something Elshtain (1988:447) encourages feminists to eschew and Cohn (1987:711) encourages women to surmount by "creating compelling alternative visions of possible futures."

GENDER PERSPECTIVE ON NATIONAL SECURITY

According to International Relations scholar Kenneth Waltz, the state conducts its affairs in the "brooding shadow of violence", and therefore war could break out at any time. In the name of national security, states have justified large defense budgets, which take priority over domestic spending, military conscription of their young adult male population, foreign invasions, and the curtailment of civil liberties. The security of the state is perceived as a core value that is generally supported unquestioningly by most citizens, particularly in time of war, while the role of the state in the twentieth century has expanded to include the provision of domestic social programmes, national security often takes precedence over the social security of individuals. When feminists think about the provision of national security they enter into what has been, and continues to be, and almost exclusively male domain. While most women support what they take to be legitimate calls for state action in the interests of international security, the task of defining, defending, and advancing the security interests of the state is a man's affair, a task that, through its association with war, has been especially valorized and rewarded in many cultures throughout history (Waltz, 1979: 102).

The best contribution the discipline of international relations can make to national security is to investigate the causes of war and thereby help to design "realistic" policies that can prolong intervals of peace. Realists counsel that morality is usually ineffective in a dangerous world: a "realistic" understanding of amoral and instrumental behavior, characteristic of international politics, is necessary if states are not to fall prey to others' ambitions. In looking for the explanations for the causes of war, realists as well as scholars in other approaches to international relations, have distinguished among three levels of analysis: the individual, the state, and the international system. The way in which realists describe the individual, the state, and the international system is profoundly gendered; each is constructed in terms of the idealized or hegemonic masculinity.

NATIONAL SECURITY IN REALIST PARADIGM

Using Hobbes' anarchical state of nature metaphor the realists argue that the security of states is 'self help security' as there is no common agreed international government capable of enforcing rules for regulating states' behavior, states must take matters of security into their own hands even if it is not in the best interests of the system as a whole. Given the problematic nature of national security and the international anarchy in the absence of an international government, the rationality demands that states will act in a spirit of mutual cooperation. Waltz cited Rousseau's metaphor of a stag hunt to describe the self seeking security behaviour of states. Five hungry men agreed to trap and share a stag, but when a hare passes by one of them in total disregard of the agreed common goal grabs it and thereby letting the stag escape. This man sacrifices the long term cooperative interests of the group for his own immediate and short term interest (Waltz, 1959: 167). Since men are self seeking, politically ambitious and not always rational, states reflective of this human nature are not cooperative and will resort to war to settle issues and preserve their security. The net result is setting in motion a vicious cycle of an ever increasing race for armaments among states with the ingrained belief that war could break at any time.

Given the classic security dilemma in realist parlance the very non-attainability of perfect security in an imperfect world could prompt states to optimize their security through preparation of war. For Hans J Morgenthau, the security of the state is attained and preserved through the maximization of power, particularly military power. Elements of national power include secure geographical boundaries, large territorial size, the capacity for self sufficiency in natural and industrial resources, and a strong technological base, all of which contribute to a strong military capability (Morgenthau,1973: 113). On the other hand, in an anarchical international system Waltz finds a better prospective for enhanced security in the self help security, which they can do by building their capabilities necessary to create bulwarks against the aggressive acts of others than in dependence on others. According to him, the greatest rewards for a state flow, not from an increase in wellbeing, which might be achieved through heightened interdependence, but from the maintenance of autonomy. It is the enhancement of power through self help that constitutes the most dependable criteria to judge whether a state is successful or failure because power busts a wide range of actions and leads to new sinews of strength (Waltz, 1979: 106-7).

The question crops up what is the prospects for peace and security in an uncertain, dangerous, imperfect and anarchical international system given Morgenthau's prescriptions for power maximization and Waltz's ambiguously defined notion of self help? In the realist explanations of the behaviour of states in the international system, the prospects for peace and security rest on the operation of balance of power. In Morgenthau's analysis, peace and security rest on balance of power and international law though to depend solely on the latter is unrealistic given its lack of enforceability in an anarchical international system. Peace will be maintained by balance of power although imperfectly. He seems to be ambivalent as to whether states intentionally engage in power balancing. On the other hand, Waltz claims that even if it is not the intention of any one state, balances will form as states act either alone or in alliances with others to counter the power of others. Since power configuration changes, the alliances also change and make power balance fragile, which tend toward instability. Given these uncertainties Waltz claims that bipolar balance of the cold war period was more stable than the multipolar systems. During the cold war what most observers pointed out that it was balance of terror resulting in vast array of nuclear weapons possessed by both the United States and the Soviet Union that created stability in international relations. From the 1960s until the end of the cold war, the notion of mutual deterrence characterized the strategic relationship between them. It was a nuclear form of bipolar balancing, which depended upon second strike capability, the ability of both sides to destroy each others' homeland with nuclear weapons after either side has launched a first attack.

Realists believe that the states' behaviour can be described in terms of laws that are objective, universal and timeless having roots in human nature. Therefore, it is possible to discover a rational theory that reflects these objective laws. Morgenthau claims that political man must be abstracted from other aspects of human behaviour in order to build an autonomous theory of political behaviour. Neorealists developed system level explanations rejecting the reductionist theories in order to insert more scientific rigour into the field. Waltz asserts that it is not possible to understand states' behaviour simply by looking at each individual unit; one must look at the structure as a whole and see how each state's capabilities stand in relation to others'. Focusing his explanations at the level of the international system, Waltz claims that it is possible to observe regularities in the power balancing behaviour of states that can be explained in terms similar to those of equilibrium theory in microeconomics (Waltz, 1979: Ch 6).

A GENDERED PERSPECTIVE ON NATIONAL SECURITY

Morgenthau, Waltz, and other realists claim that it is possible to develop a rational, objective theory of international politics based on universal laws that operate across time and space. In her feminist critique of the natural sciences, Evelyn Fox Keller points out that most scientific communities share the "assumption that the universe they study is directly accessible, represented by concepts shaped not by language but only by the demands of logic and experiment". The laws of nature, according to this view of science, are beyond the relativity of language. Like most contemporary feminists, Keller rejects this positivist view of science that, she asserts, imposes a coercive, hierarchical and conformist pattern on scientific inquiry. Since most contemporary feminist scholars believe that knowledge is socially constructed, they are skeptical of finding an unmediated foundation for knowledge that the scholarly claims about the neutral uses of language and about objectivity must continually be questioned (Tickner, 1992). What is claimed to be universal view comes out of a Western centered historical worldview that is exclusively based on the experiences of men. "Underneath its claim to universality this worldview privileges a view of security that is constructed out of values associated with hegemonic masculinity" (Ibid).

POLITICAL MAN

Morgenthau's "political man" is a social construct based on a partial representation of human nature abstracted from the behavior of men in positions of public power. He suggests that, while society condemns the violent behavior that can result from this struggle for power within the polity, it encourages it in the international system in the form of war. His "political man" has been criticized by other international relations scholars for its essentializing view of human nature, the social construction of hegemonic masculinity and its opposition to a devalued femininity has been fundamental to many established and prevalent discourses in international politics. In western political theory from the Greeks to Machiavelli, traditions upon which contemporary realism relies heavily for its analysis, this socially constructed type of masculinity has been projected onto the international behavior of states. The violence with which it is associated has been legitimated through the glorification of war. Warrior-citizenship concept translated into Machiavelli's idealization of warrior prince is a gendered construction of personality. Feminist political theorist Wendy Brown suggests that Machiavelli's representation of the political world and its citizenry is profoundly gendered; it is dependent on an image of true manliness that demands qualities that are superior to those that naturally inherent in men (Brown Wendy, 1988 : Chapter 5). Hannah Pitkin claims that for Machiavelli triumph in war, honour and liberty in civic life, and independent critical thought and manliness in personal relationships are all bound together by a central preoccupation with autonomy, a characteristic associated with masculinity (Pitkin, 1984 : 22). Machiavelli's construction of the citizen- warrior required a devalued other against which true manhood and autonomy could be set. In his writings this feminine other is fortuna originally a Roman goddess associated with capriciousness and unpredictability (Tickner, 1992). Hannah Pitkin claims that in his writings fortuna is presented as the feminine power in men themselves against which they must continually struggle to maintain their autonomy (Pitkin, 1984 : chapter 6). In Machiavelli's own words, " Fortune is a woman, and it is necessary if you wish to master her, to conquer her by force" (Machiavelli, 1940 : 94). He makes it clear that he considers women to be a threat to the masculinity of the citizen-warrior.

THE MASCULINE STATE

Charlotte Hooper's influential book, Manly states: masculinities, international relations and gender politics' reflects the two levels of ontological revisionism. 'Manly states' is a description both of the masculinist nature of states, traditionally the central actors in international relations, and of the general conditions of manliness, otherwise the problem of masculinity and masculine subjectivity. The nature of the state has been male defined and male dominated from a long masculinist historical perspective. The mainstream International Relations has tended to treat the state largely as a coherent male controlled unit. It has traditionally defined politics and economics as predominantly public spheres of male influence and identification. Private spheres were defined in terms of home, family and social reproduction and as predominantly spheres of female influence and identification. Feminist International Relations is strongly critical of this private-public dichotomy, which is male dominated and gendered to the exclusion of women (Youngs, 2004: 81). The history of state formation and identity is therefore one of gendered (and other forms of) oppression. "As a historical matter, early, state formation marked the effective centralization of political authority and accumulation process, institutionalization of gender and class exploitation, and ideological legitimation of these transformations" (Ibid). At least since Aristotle, "the codification of man as 'master' [subject] and woman as 'matter' [object] has powerfully naturalized/de-politicized man's exploitation of women, other men, and nature" (Peterson,,1992:14). The mainstream International Relations has been accused by feminists of understanding the political power of states not in terms of relational gendered dynamics but in terms of masculinist actors. Ignoring women from the malestream framing of power has resulted in depoliticizing the exploitation of women by men. Thus, in their critical assessment, the feminists are of the view that the historically masculinist construction of power should not be understood as given; the state as the seemingly supreme representation of collective power is nothing but historically and socially constructed male power, which can needs be explained in dynamic gender terms and not taken as given. What it appears as collective at the state or individual level is masculine superficially and beneath it lie the fuller dynamics of political and economic power relations (Youngs, 2004:81-82). A reflection by Steve Smith emphasizes, in this context, the importance of gender as a relational concept: " the most productive focus is on gender, not women or feminism, because only this focus allows in IR that shape what happens to actual women and men in IR" (Smith Steve (54-72, 62). "It is essential to add to this that, historically, feminist theory and analysis have been the spheres of critique and knowledge building that have led the way in championing, explaining and validating attention to gender as a category" (Youngs, 2004: 82).

As Charlotte Hooper has successfully summarized: "One of the achievements of feminist contributions to international relations has been to reveal the extent to which the whole field is gendered. The range of subjects studied, the boundaries of the discipline, its central concerns and motifs, the content of empirical research, the assumptions of theoretical models, and the corresponding lack of female practitioners both in academic and elite political and economic circles all combine and reinforce each other to marginalize and often make invisible women's roles and women's concerns in the international arena" (Hooper, 2001:1).

The neorealist depiction of the state as a unitary actor is grounded in the historical practices of the western state system: neorealist characterization of state behavior, in terms of self help, autonomy, and power seeking, privilege characteristics associated with the western construction of masculinity. "Since the beginning of the state system, the national security functions of states have been deeded to us through gendered images that privilege masculinity" (Tickner, Man, the State and War).

SOVEREIGNTY, SECURITY AND MILITARISM

Sovereignty is a core concept in International Relations because it defines the pre-eminent role of states as political actors, and by implication also defines political identity (citizenship) in state –centred terms, binding 'authentic' politics exclusively within territorially-bound communities'. For feminist International Relations there are ways in which sovereignty can be regarded as a foundational problem in the masculinist distortions of the nature of politics and political agency. Masculinist dominance is institutionalized by the 'sovereignty contract' and the 'sexual contract' of modern European state-making, which is simultaneously – and not coincidentally- the making of rational man, the sovereign subject and political agency. In this historical context, politics as concept and action is rendered definitely masculine and political identity is gendered both conceptually (in terms of how we think about political agency, subjectivity and subjective relations) and empirically (in terms of how we organize political activities, structures and objective relation).

The public over private (male over female) social hierarchy leads to the gendering of political agency and influence in profound ways. Radical thinkers such as John Hoffman argue for the reconstruction of the political concept of sovereignty as emancipatory, for 'a sovereignty beyond the state'. States are an expression of patriarchal power. "Empirically, states are (mostly) run by men, defended by men and advance the interests of men... Logically, state sovereignty is gendered by its assertion that leadership is monolithic, hierarchical and violent. These principles are all "masculinist" in character since the idea of concentrating power so that the few rule by force over the many is associated with the domination of men" (Hoffman, 2001 :6). Hoffman explores the problematics and complexities of the characteristic of the state as the sole legitimate user of force in the interests of maintaining internal and external order, a legitimacy deriving in the liberal tradition from the social contract (Ibid: 83-90). This characteristic of the state and issues of violence associated with it are central to the concept of security in International Relations. Feminists have examined extensively the degree to which mainstream concepts of security in the field have been traditionally constrained by masculinist blinkers, failing to take account of security issues women confront daily that are associated with their unequal or oppressed conditions of existence in relation to men, for example domestic violence. They also fail to take account of the specific ways in which women and children are affected by war, military occupation, militarization, (forced) migration, human trafficking, sexual and other forms of slavery and (forced) prostitution (Pettman, 1996). As Ann Tickner has explained.

> "Whereas conventional security studies have tended to look at causes and consequences of wars from a top-down, or structural, perspective, feminists have generally taken a bottom-up approach, analyzing the impact of war at the micro level. By so doing, as well as adopting gender as a category of analysis, feminists believe they can tell us something new about the causes of war that is missing from both conventional and critical perspectives. By crossing what many feminists believe to be mutually constitutive levels of

> analysis, we get a better understanding of the interrelationship between all forms of violence and the extent to which unjust social relations, including gender hierarchies, contribute to insecurity, broadly defined" (Tickner,2001: 48-9).

Feminist International Relation has broadened the definition of security, and gone deep inside state boundaries as well as across them, to get behind the masculinist warrior/protector mythology that tends to depict war and conflict in archetypal (gendered) and frequently nationalist terms, and to reveal the increasing suffering that women and children have endured through death and injury, rape, displacement and deprivation, as well as the many roles women have forged in peace- and community building (Ibid:49-51). Cynthia Enloe has studied diverse areas such as sex tourism, women in the military, military wives, militarized prostitution, domestic service and export processing zones with the multi level, bottom up approach that distinguishes feminist work in international politics. She has unravelled the myth of the dichotomy between 'home front' and 'battle front' by giving a depiction of gendered militarism (Cynthia Enloe, 1988: xxxi). She like others demonstrates how militarism and masculinity go cheek by jowl linking the collective patriarchal system to individual masculine identities. In her words "The military plays a special role in ideological structure of patriarchy because the notion of combat plays such a role in the construction of concepts of manhood and justifications of the superiority of maleness in the social order" (Ibid: 12-13).

THE ANARCHICAL INTERNATIONAL SYSTEM: HOBBES' MASCULINE METAPHOR

The most common metaphor that realists employ to

describe the anarchical international system is that of the seventeenth-century English philosopher Thomas Hobbes' depiction of the state of nature. Although Hobbes did not write much about international politics, realists have applied his description of individuals' behaviour in a hypothetical pre-contractual state of nature, which Hobbes termed the war of everyman against everyman, to the behavior of states in the international system. Although Hobbes did suggest that women as well as men could be free and equal individuals in the state of nature, his description of human behavior in this environment refers to that of adult males whose behavior is taken as constitutive of human nature as a whole by contemporary realist analysis. According to Jane Flax, the individuals that Hobbes described in the state of nature appeared to come to full maturity without any engagement with one another; they were solitary creatures lacking any socialization in interactive behavior. Any interactions they did have led to power struggles that resulted in domination or submission. Suspicion of others' motives led to behavior characterized by aggression, self-interest, and the drive for autonomy (Flax: 245-281). In a similar vein, Christine Di Stephano uses feminist psychoanalyst theory to support her claim that the masculine dimension of atomistic egoism is powerfully underscored in Hobbes' state of nature, which she asserts, is built on the foundation of denied maternity (quoted in Tickner Man, the State and War). An international system that resembles Hobbes' depiction of individuals in the state of nature is a dangerous environment. Driven by competition for scarce resources and mistrust of others motives in a system that lacks any legitimate authority; states, like men, must rely on their own resources for self – preservation. Machiavelli offers advice to his prince that is based on similar assumptions about the international system. Both Pitkin and Brown note that Machiavelli's portrayal of fortuna is regularly associated with nature, as something outside the political world that must be subdued and controlled. Pitkin refers to "The golden Ass", a long unfinished poem by Machiavelli, based on the legend of Circe, a female figure who lives in the forest world and turns men into animals (Pitkin,1984:127)

Just as the image of waging war against an exterior other figured centrally in Machiavelli's writings, war is central to the way International Relations is understood. Wars are fought for many reasons, yet frequently, the rationale for fighting wars is presented in gendered terms such as the necessity of standing up to aggression rather then being pushed around or appearing to be a sissy or wimp. As Sara Ruddick states, while the masculinity of war may be a myth, it is one that sustains both women and men in their support for violence (Ruddick, 1989:152). War is a discourse of militarism and masculinity permeates the whole fabric of society. Colonized peoples were often described as being effeminate, masculinity was an attribute of the white man, and colonial order depended on Victorian standards of manliness. Cynthia Enole suggests that the concept of "ladylike behavior" was one of the mainstays of imperialist civilization. Like sanitation and Christianity, feminine respectability was meant to convince colonizers and colonized alike that foreign conquest was right and necessary. Masculinity denoted protection of the respectable lady; she stood for the civilizing mission that justified the colonization of benighted peoples (Enloe, 1989: 48-49).

C.D Jackson, an adviser to President Eisenhower and a patron of western development theorists in the 1950's evoked these feminine characteristics when he observed that "the Western world has somewhat more experience with the operations of war, peace, and parliamentary procedures than the swirling mess of emotionally supercharged Africans and Asiatics and Arabas that outnumber us" (Hunt, 1987: 164). Further he stated that Eisenhower himself regarded the English speaking people of the world as superior to all the rest; thus they provided a model for right behaviour in the international system. This idea is consonant with contemporary realism dominated by white Anglo-Saxon men, which prescribed the behaviour of states throughout the international system. In the words of Tickner: " If systems-oriented realists criticize reductionist causal accounts focused only on human nature, feminists might equally well object that scientific causal analyses of state and system- level phenomena distract our attention from the role of responsible individuals and groups in the construction and maintenance of state- level and systemic relationships. Power- oriented statesmen have a vested interest vis-a-vis their domestic supporters in painting a picture of the world around them as threateningly anarchic; anarchic international systems are reproduced by individuals who believe no alternatives exist" (Tickner, Man, the State and War).

FEMINIST PERSPECTIVES ON NATIONAL SECURITY

Critics of realism argue that a more global vision of security is necessary. The extent to which realism has been able to justify its distinction between domestic order and international anarchy depends on its focus on the major actors in the international system. Thinking about security from a global perspective must take into account that 90 percent of the military conflicts of the 1970s and 1980s took place in the Third World; many were domestic, some international and some, particularly when the great powers were involved, blurred the distinction between the two. Security threats have traditionally been defined as threats to national boundaries, but since the end of the process of decolonization, relatively few cross-border wars and changes in international boundaries have occurred in spite of the large number of military conflicts. Acknowledging these multiple sources of insecurity, various new thinkers have come up with very different definitions of security. In the introduction to the Report of Independent Commission on Disarmament and Commission defines what it calls "common security" in terms that extend well beyond nuclear strategic issues. It looks at security in North-South as well as East-West terms; focusing on military conflict in the Third World, new thinking points to possible contradictions between the military security of states and the economic well-being of their citizens. The Palme Report notes that a growing militarization of the Third World has drained resources that might otherwise be used for economic development.

Feminist reformulations of the meaning of security are needed to draw attention to the extent to which gender hierarchies themselves are a source of domination and thus, an obstacle to a truly comprehensive definition of security. It is difficult to find definitions by women of national security. While it is not necessarily the case that women have not had ideas on this subject, they are not readily accessible in the literature of international relations. When women speak or write about national security, these are often dismissed as being naïve or unrealistic.

Recent debates have also focused on 'hegemonic masculinity', conveying the sense of dominant forms of masculinity among other, contested forms. This is an important development because it facilitates exploration of power dynamics among men as well as between men and women. It allows for socio-economic, racial and other inequalities among men, recognizing overtly that 'men' are not a homogenous group but a highly diversified collection of different identities and power positions. Charlotte Hooper explains that the 'bourgeois rationalist' model of masculinity tends to be 'less aggressive, more egalitarian and democratic' than the 'heroic warrior-citizen' model, which is oriented towards conquest of women, and the 'patriarchal' model, which 'ignores women'.

At the Women's International Peace Conference in Halifax, Canada, in 1985, a meeting of women from all over the world, participants defined security in various ways depending on the most immediate threats to their survival; security meant safe working conditions and freedom from the threat of war or unemployment or the economic squeeze of foreign debt. Discussions of the meaning of security revealed divisions between western middle- class women's concerns with nuclear war, concerns that similar to those of Jane Addams and her colleagues, and Third World women who defined insecurity more broadly in terms of the structural violence associated with imperialism, militarism, racialism, and sexism. Yet all agreed that security meant nothing if it was built on others' insecurity (Runyan, 1988: ch 6).

The final document of the World Conference to Review and Appraise the Achievements of the United Nations Decade for Women, held in Nairobi in 1985, offered a similarly multidimensional definition of security. The introductory chapter of the document defined peace as "not only the absence of war, violence and hostilities at the national and international levels but also the enjoyment of economic and social justice" (quoted in Pietila, Hilkka and Vickers,1990: 46-47). According to Tickner, "All these definitions of security take issue with realists' assumptions that security is zero sum and must therefore be built on the insecurity of others" (Man, the State and War). Feminist peace researcher Elise Boulding stated that women peace researchers were the first proponents of this contemporary redefinition of security, although, like Jane Addams at the beginning of the century, their work did not receive the attention it deserved. It is often the case that new ideas in any discipline do not receive widespread attention unless they are adopted by significant numbers of men, in which case women's work tends to become invisible through co-optation. Boulding claims that the one area in which women are not in danger of cooptation is their analysis of patriarchy and the linkage of war to violence against women.

RETHINKING REALIST'S ANARCHY/ORDER DISTINCTION

The growing realization that security of state is not synonymous with security of individuals, and the spiraling internal violence within the state have called into question the realist assumption about the anarchy/order distinction. Critics of realism have also questioned the unitary actor assumption that renders the domestic affairs unproblematic and insulated when talking about their international behaviour. Strongly adducing that militarism, sexism and racism are interconnected, most feminists would agree that the bahaviour of individuals and the domestic policies of states cannot be viewed as separated from states' behaviour in the international system (Reardon, 1985: ch1). Feminists draw attention to the particular vulnerabilities of women within states, vulnerabilities that grow out of hierarchical gender relations that are also interrelated with international politics. Calling into question the notion of the "protected", the National Organization for Women in their "Resolution on Women in Combat" of September 16, 1990 estimated that 80-90 percent of casualties due to conflict since World War II have been civilians, the majority of whom have been women and children.

Feminist theories draw attention to another anarchy/order distinction – the boundary a public domestic space protected, at least theoretically, by the rule of law and the private space of the family where, in many cases no such legal protection exists. In most states domestic violence is not considered a concern of the state and even when it is law enforcement officials are often unwilling to get involved. Domestic assaults on women, often seen as "victim precipitated", are not taken as seriously as criminal assaults. Maria Mies argues that the modernization process in the Third World, besides sharpening class conflict, has led to an increase in violence against women in the home as traditional social values are broken down. While poor women probably suffer the most from family violence, a growing women's movement in India points to an increase in violence against educated middle class women also, the most extreme form of which is dowry murder.

Recent studies of family violence in the United States and Eastern Europe have brought to light similar problems. When the family is violence –prone, it is frequently beyond the reach of the law ; citing a 1978 report of the California Commission on the Status of Women, Pauline Gee documents that in 1978, one – quarter of the murders in the United States occurred within the family, one – half of these being husband – wife killings. Much of this family violence takes place outside the sanction of the legal system; it has been estimated that only 2 percent of men who beat their wives or female living partners are ever prosecuted. Feminist perspectives on security would assume that violence, whether it be in the international, national, or family realm, is interconnected (Pietila, Hilkka and Vickers, 1990: 46-47). Family violence must be seen in the context of wider power relations; it occurs within a gendered society in which male power dominates at all levels (Breines and Gordon, 1983 : 492-93). If men are traditionally seen as protectors, an important aspect of this role is protecting women against certain men (Stiehm, 1989: 228). According to Tickner, "Any feminist definition of security must therefore include the elimination of all types of violence, including violence produced by gender relations of domination and subordination. The achievement of this comprehensive vision of security requires a rethinking of the way in which citizenship has traditionally been defined, as well as alternative models of describing the behaviour of states in the international system" (Tickner, Man, the State and War).

FEMINIST PERSPECTIVE ON STATE'S SECURITY-SEEKING BEHAVIOR

The use of Hobbesian analogy in international relations theory is based on a partial view of human nature that is stereotypically masculine; a more inclusive perspective would see human nature as both conflictual and cooperative, containing elements of social reproduction and interdependence as well as domination and separation. Generalizing from this more comprehensive view of human nature, a feminist perspective would assume that the potential for international community also exists and that an atomistic, conflictual view of the international system is only a partial representation of reality. Liberal individualism, the instrumental rationality of the marketplace and the defector's self –help approach in Rousseau's stag hunt are all, in analogous ways based on a partial masculine model of human behavior (Ibid).

These characterizations of human behavior, with their atomistic view of human society, do not assume the need for interdependence and cooperation. Yet states frequently exhibit aspects of cooperative behavior when they engage in diplomatic negotiations. As Cynthia Enole states, diplomacy runs smoothly when there is trust and confidence between officials representing governments with conflicting interest. Many agreements are negotiated informally in the residences of ambassadors where the presence of diplomatic wives creates an atmosphere in which trust can best be cultivated (Enloe,1989: Ch 5). As Enole concludes, women, often in positions that are unremunerated or undervalued, remain vital to creating and maintaining trust between men in a hostile world.

Given the interdependent nature of contemporary security threats, new thinking on security has already assumed that autonomy and self-help, as models for state behavior in the international system, must be rethought and redefined. For many feminists would agree with this, but given their assumption that interdependence is as much a human characteristic as autonomy, they would question whether autonomy is even desirable (Tannen,1990:25-26). Autonomy is associated with masculinity just as femininity is associated with interdependence: in her discussion of the birth of modern science in the seventeenth century, Evelyn Keller links the rise of what she terms a masculine science with a striving for objectivity, autonomy, and control (Keller,1985: ch3). Perhaps not coincidentally, the seventeenth century also witnessed the rise of the modern state system. Since this period, autonomy and separation, importantly associated with the meaning of sovereignty, have determined our conception of the national interest. Betty Reardon argues that this association of autonomy with the national interest tends to blind us to the realities of interdependence in the present world situation. "Feminist perspective would thus assume that striving for attachment is also part of human nature, which, while it has been suppressed by both modern scientific thinking and the practices of the Western state system, can be reclaimed and revalued in the future" (Tickner, Man, the State and War).

In realist parlance power is masculine and synonymous with domination. Hannah Arendt defines power as the human ability to act in concert or action that is taken with others who share similar concerns

(Arendt,1969: 44). Compatible with this view is that of David McCllelland who portrays female power as shared rather than assertive (McCllelland, 1975, ch.3). Jane Jaquette argues that, since women have had less access to the instruments of coercion, women have more often used persuasion as a way of gaining power through coalition building (Jaquette, in Stiehm, 1984, ch. 2). From feminine perspective power is understood as mutual enablement rather than domination. Power is frequently used in international relations in coercive forms. Power as conceptualized by feminists leads to devising the cooperative solutions necessary for solving the security threats.

Feminist perspectives on national security go beyond realism's statist representations. The realist view of national security is constructed out of a masculinized discourse, which is not only partial but is taken as universal. Women's definitions of security are multilevel and multidimensional. Women have defined security as the absence of violence whether it be military, economic, or sexual. Not until the hierarchical social relations, including gender relations, that have been hidden by realism's frequently depersonalized discourse are brought to light can we begin to construct a language of national security that speaks out of the multiple experiences of both women and men.

8
Conceptualizing Human Security: Toward Shifting Paradigm

The very genesis of the concept of security understood in an institutional or organized form harks back to the day human beings first got sensitized to fear, inadequacy of self help against adversaries or thinking of self or cohorts as different and threatened from others. The very search for security which materialized first in the family in an inchoate and non-political form evolved through a network of institutions to find ultimately its accentuation and conceptualization in the state. Thus, security was identified with and remains crucial to state. Security of individuals is held as synonymous with state. Distancing, boundary making or fencing one off against others by exercise of military force constitutes the cornerstone of classical formulation of security. It implies threats to territorial integrity, sovereignty, autonomy and domestic political order as threats to individuals thus, legitimizing state as the ultimate and sole political instrument to use force it deems adequate to meet the impending challenges to its existence. State is the only identity and referent object of security to which all other rival claimants must remain subservient. In this classical formulation, security has been considered as both a prerogative and a responsibility of states. The evolution of threats during the last decade has considerably altered this conventional understanding. Under the stentorian voice of cold war sabre rattling, while the states were busy stockpiling arms and ammunitions, the other voices deserving attention for referent objects of security could not be heard. The end of cold war facilitated the unheard voices to be heeded more forcibly and urgently and catapulted them into the centre stage of security. As pointed by Francois Fouinat, "Even if the danger of a nuclear apocalypse is more remote, the life of millions is threatened by violent conflict, often within borders and with outside interferences, and with little concern for the victims"(Francois Fouinat, 2004 : 289).

To some critics the classical formulation of security laying primacy unilaterally on force would not hold good in a world where nations are tied with each other in a network of interdependence, and possession of weapons of mass destruction is no longer the monopoly of the few. This one-dimensional view of security must give way to cooperative security. To another band of critics the classical formulation of security holds states as the only referent point of security and threatened militarily by other states. This classical formulation confining the scope of security to state military was too narrow to account for the threats other states pose to its political and territorial integrity not in military terms but in environmental, economic and cultural terms. Besides, threats also emanate not just from other states but from non-state actors and even natural calamities. Thus, widening of the sources and instruments of security beyond the state military has led to the enunciation of comprehensive security. The third school of thought challenges the classical notion that the security of state is synonymous with the security of the individual. A state well equipped with most sophisticated and modern weapons may not be able to provide security to individuals against health hazards, global warming, sea level rise and other catastrophes. Even when a state is secure from external threats or internal instabilities, security for its people is not guaranteed. The classical state security does not answer the issues of gender, human rights and identity which have been central factors in political instability and social tensions. No state can protect its citizens against these realities by strengthening traditional state control mechanisms alone. Further, the primacy of state security is very closely associated with the notion of sovereignty. In its historic meaning, sovereignty implied the security of the sovereign, or the Prince. The emergence of democratic polity and transfer of primacy from the Prince to the citizenry implies a shift in the notion of security so far strewn around state and broadening it to include the security not only of the Prince but also of the everyday survival of the Citizen. Thus, primacy on security of the individual as central to the conceptualization of security along with the state is defined as human security.

GENEALOGY OF HUMAN SECURITY

The increasing disenchantment with the prevailing notions of development and security and utter inadequacy of the state apparatus to address the challenges from not only military sector but from economic, cultural, environmental and societal sector in the 1960s, 1970s and 1980s, and the growing discrepancy between security of state and security of the individuals created an intellectual upheaval to redefine security and trace back the origin of human security. The concern for individual well being and safety occupied a central position in the multinational World

Order Models Project to envisage and construct a new just world order (Saul B. Mendowitz, 1975).

Among the most prominent protagonists of the idea of human security was in the 1970, the Club Rome group, which produced a series of volumes on the world problematique which were premised on the idea that there is "a complex of problems troubling men of all nations: poverty; degradation of the environment; loss of faith in institutions; uncontrolled urban spread; insecurity of employment; alienation of youth; rejection of traditional values; and inflation and other monetary and economic disruption"(Donnela H. Meadows, Dennis L. Meadows, Jorgen Randers and William W. BehrensIII, 1972 : 10). The report noted that:

Every person in the world faces a series of pressures and problems that require his attention and action. These problems affect him at many different levels. He may spend much of his time trying to find tomorrow's food.... He may be concerned about personal power or the power of the nation in which he lives. He may worry about a world order...or a war next week with a rival clan in his neighbourhood (Ibid: 17-18).

Accelerating industrialization as an ideal type of development, burgeoning population growth, widespread malnutrition, depletion of non-renewable resources and degradation of renewable resources did not come under the rubric of traditional state centric security and need to be understood in their disastrous impact on individuals. This implies that there are alternative ways of redefining development and security. As the report envisions, "a state of global equilibrium could be designed so that the basic material needs of each person... are satisfied, and each person has an equal opportunity to realize his individual human potential" (Ibid: 21).

In the 1980s two other independent commissions contributed to the changing thinking on development and security. The first was the Independent Commission on International Development Issues chaired by Willy Brandt, which in 1980 issued the North South report. In his introduction Brandt wrote: - "Our report is based on what appears to be the simplest common interest that mankind wants to survive and one might even add has the moral obligation to survive. This not only raises traditional questions of peace and war, but also how to overcome world hunger, mass misery and alarming disparities between the living conditions of rich and poor (The Independent Commission on International Developmental Issues, North-South: A Programme for Survival,1980 : 13).

The second commission of 1980s, the Independent Commission on Disarmament and Security Issues authored the famous Common Security report, which also turned attention to alternative ways of thinking about peace and security, while it focused on military issues and the nuances of national security, it acknowledged that in the Third World security was also threatened by "poverty and deprivation, by economic inequality". The report also noted: "Common security requires that people live in dignity and peace, that they have enough to eat and are able to find work and live in a world without poverty and destitution (The Independent Commission on Disarmament and Security Issues. 1982: xv and 172).

The end of cold war witnessed a spurt of intellectual activity demonstrating the glare failure of neorealism and realism to account for these upheavals and urging upon the imperatives for redefining security. In 1991, the Stockholm Initiative on Global Security and Governance stressing upon "Common Responsibility in the 1990s' alluded to "challenges to security other than political rivalry and armaments" and to a wider concept of security, which deals also with threats that stem from failures in development, environmental degradation, excessive population growth and movement, and lack of progress towards democracy" (The Stockholm Initiative on Global Security and Governance, 1991: 17-18). Four years later the Commission on Global Governance's report, our Global neighborhood, was resonant with the sentiments of the Stockholm initiatives: "The concept of global security must be broadened from the traditional focus on the security of states to include the security of people and the security of the planet" (The Commission on Global Governance, 1995: 338). These reports' stress on paramountcy of individual security and welfare of the people over and above the state centric security added new impetuses to the intellectual efforts in the 1990s to articulate explicitly human security with some rigour and candour.

The Pakistani development leader and thinker, Mahbub ul Haq, championed the concept of 'human security' as a supplement to his 'human development' concept in the 1993 Human Development Report with considerable impact in the 1994 Human Development Report. Central to the formulation of human security is the notion that development thinking and policies must hinge on the welfare of individuals rather than simply the macro economy. He added six types of security to a conventional concern with security from physical violence: income security, food security, health security, environmental security, community/identity security, and security of political freedoms. In the words of Des Gasper, "Just as human development for him[Haq] was more than a humanizing addition of health and education concerns to economic growth, so human security meant securing what is humanly central, not only humanizing an existing state security discourse by a concern for the physical security of persons (Des Gasper, 2005 : 223).

The second important intervention on human security was that of Canadian Government and various Canadian academics which launched a middle powers initiative. To understand the difference between human security and traditional national security conceptions, it is necessary to refer to the Political Scientist Baldwin who has argued that in order to evaluate the debate over the conception of security, it is vital to define the term more closely. This requires at the very least two things: agreement on the root meaning of security, for whom security of which values, how much security, security from what threats and security by what means (David Baldwin, 1997: 12-18). Baldwin takes as a starting point – Arnold Wolfers' famous discussion of security as "the absence of threat to acquired values" and modifies this to read a low probability of damage to acquired values" (Ibid : 13). To understand the UNDP and Canadian Schools' approach to Human Security, to answer the four key questions: Security for whom, security of which values, security from what threats, and security by what means remains important.

Haq answers the question of "security for whom" by holding that human security is not about states and nations, but about individuals and people. Thus, he argues that the world is "entering a new era of human security." In which "the entire concept of security will change dramatically. In this new conception, security will be equated with the "security of individuals, not just security of their nations, or put it differently, a security of people, not just security of territory". He says "We need to fashion a new concept of human security that is reflected in the lives of our people not in the weapons of our country." Whereas the traditional conception of security emphasizes territorial integrity and national independence as the primary values that need to be protected. Human security pertains above all to the safety and well being of "all the people every where in their homes, in their jobs, in their street, in their communities, in their environment."(Mahbub ul Haq, 1994: 1). Haq listed a myriad of threats to human security out of which drugs, disease, terrorism and poverty are pertinent. Besides, an unequal world order scripted by the Bretton Woods system and the dominant development conception and practices, the yawning gap between the North and the South, and the reliance on arms for security poses the greatest threat to human security. Haq outlines a long list of truly far reaching proposals for global human security. These include:

1) **Developmentally :** Sustainability; equity of opportunities, better distribution of productive assets, including land and credit, open access to market opportunity, job creation, social safety.

2) **Militarily :** Reducing arms expenditures, closing all military bases, converting military aids to economic aid, stopping arms transfer, eliminating arms export, subsidies and retraining workers in defence industries.

3) **North :** South restructuring: - Equitable access to global markets for the poor countries built on the removal of trade barriers. Financial compensation from the rich countries in return for immigration controls and for over-use of global environment resources.

4) **Institutionally :** The resuscitation and restructuring of the IMF, World Bank and UN to focus more on Human Development; Economic adjustment that target the rich more than the poor; new governance patterns every where such as a world control bank, a global taxation system, a world trade organization, an international investment trust and a world treasury.

5) **The evolution of a global civil society :** All of the above would require grassroot participation and a change from authoritarian to democratic government (Ibid: 3-17).

UNDP AND HUMAN SECURITY: A SHIFTING PARADIGM

UNDP's Human Development Report of 1994 called "Redefining Security: The Human Dimensions" begins with providing an alternative to traditional security and a necessary supplement to human development. It answers the question of "security for whom" by referring to traditional notion of security, which is premised on protecting the territorial states from external aggression, or protection of national interest in foreign policy and provision of global security from the threat of nuclear catastrophe. What this traditional concept of security ignored was the legitimate concern of ordinary individuals for security in their daily lives. The referent object of security is not the state but the individuals or people. It writes:

> Human security is a child who did not die, a disease that did not spread, a job that that was not cut, and ethnic tension that did not explode in violence, a dissident who was not silenced. Human security is not a concern with weapons – it is concern with human life and dignity. It is concerned with how people live and breathe in a society, how freely they exercise their many choices, how much access they have to market and social opportunity and whether they live in conflict or in peace (UNDPa: 1995:229).

Along with a sense of choice and surety about the future, people should be efficacious and empowered enough to be "able to take care of themselves: all the people should have the opportunity to meet their most essential needs to earn their own living" (Ibid: 230). Similarly, the Commission on Human Security conceptualized human security in terms of protecting people's vital freedoms from severe threats, in ways that empower people to fulfill their strengths and aspirations. The focus was on people, considered both as individuals and as communities. To advance the goals of human security, the Commission proposed a framework based upon the protection and empowerment of people. Neither protection nor empowerment can be dealt with in isolation as they are mutually reinforcing. Protection refers to norms, processes, and institutions that are required to shield people from threats. Empowerment allows people to act and develop their capacity (Fouinat, 2004 : 290-91). The report lists seven components or specific values of human security:-economic security, food security, health security, environmental security, personal security, immunity security and political security on the basis of which localized threats can be understood (UNDPa, 1995: 230-234). They are as follows:

1. Threats to economic security : Lack of productive and remunerative employment, precarious employment, and absence of publicly financed safety nets.

2. Threats to food security : Lack of food entitlement, including insufficient access to assets, work and assured incomes.

3. Threats to health security : Infectious and parasitic diseases of the circulatory system and cancers; lack of safe water; air pollution; and lack of access to health care facilities.

4. Threats to environmental security : Declining water availability; water pollution; declining arable land; deforestation, desertification; air pollution and natural disasters.

5. Threats to personal security : Violent crime, drug trafficking; and violence and abuse of children and women.

6. Threats to community security : Break down of the family ; collapse of traditional languages and cultures; ethnic discrimination and strife and genocide and ethnic cleansing.

7. Threats to political security : Government

repression; systematic human rights violations and militarization.

The report also mentions a myriad of global or transnational threats that have effects beyond territorial boundaries grouped into six areas:

1. Population growth, which increases the pressure on non-renewable resources and is linked to global poverty, environmental degradation and international migration.
2. Growing disparities in global income leading to over-consumption and over-production in industrialized countries, and poverty and environmental degradation in the developing world.
3. Increasing international migration as a function of population growth, poverty and the policies of the industrial countries, which have contributed to the flow of international migrants, as also an increase in refugees and internally displaced persons.
4. Various forms of environmental decay (that among other things cause acid rain, skin cancer and global warming) as well as reduced biodiversity, and the destruction of wetlands, coral reefs and temperate forests as well as tropical rainforests.
5. Drug trafficking, which has grown into a global, multinational industry.
6. International terrorism, which has spread from Latin America in the 1960s to a global phenomena.

The question crops up whether the traditional concept of security founded on state and its military apparatus both nuclear and conventional, military alliance and balance of power could be the right response to the congeries of values to be shielded against and the multifarious threats to humans and living beings to be combated. The missiles cannot plug the ozone hole, nuclear weapons cannot halt the ongoing global warming and weapons of mass destruction cannot check the expansion of desertification. The state equipped with all advanced military weapons and technology cannot remove food insecurity, heath hazards and stall sea level rise and Tsunami like catastrophes. Given the above compendium of threats to living beings and values, a new kind of security agenda is to be designed with new instrumentalities, cooperation between and among a vast range of non state actors including the state to face the crisis. The place of conventionally entrenched military based force in this new security agenda seems wholly inadequate and irrelevant. The Report advocates the concept of human security with changes in national and international policy focusing on fulfillment of basic human needs, productive and remunerative employment and human rights, preventive diplomacy, and preventive development and the reform of global institutions (Ibid : 236).

THE CANADIAN AND MIDDLE POWERS' APPROACH TO HUMAN SECURITY

The Canadian led middle powers approach to human security having some points common with the UNDP approach, has tried over the years to maintain a distinct stand of its own. Canada has made two major statement of its position and along with Norway organized a middle power's conference in Lysoen in Norway (1999), which largely affirmed its viewpoint. Both approaches stress on individual security as the basis of human security, which is nothing but a people centred view of security. As stated by Lloyd Axworthy, the Foreign Minister of Canada, it "includes security against economic privation, an acceptable quality of life, and a guarantee of fundamental human rights" (DFAIT: 1).

Human security addresses the question 'security for

whom' and "security of what values", as noted above. Human security values include "an acceptable quality of life and a guarantee of fundamental rights." Minimally, it implies basic needs...., sustained economic development, human rights and fundamental freedoms, the rule of law, good governance, sustainable development and social equity. (DFAIT: 1)

What are the threats to these key values? The Canadian paper is less systematic than the UNDP report, but nevertheless presents a rather impressive list of threats. The 1997 paper cites among others the income hiatus between the rich and poor countries, internal conflict and state failure, transnational crime, the proliferation of weapons of mass destruction, religious and ethnic discord, environmental degradation, population growth, ethnic conflict and migration, state repression, the widespread use of anti personnel land mines, child abuse, economic underdevelopment and an unstable protectionist international trading system (Axworthy, 1997a: 183-84, 187, 189, 190). The 1999 paper also alludes to dangers posed by civil conflicts, large scale atrocities and genocide. Globalization is another factor, which has brought in its wake "violent crime, drug trade, terrorism, disease and environmental deterioration, internal war fought by irregular forces of ethnic and religious groups equipped with small arms (DFAIT: 2).The decline of state control and relatedly the growth of warlordism, banditry, organized crime, drug trafficking and private security forces have all increased violence against individuals (DFAIT: 2). Besides, "a broadening range of transnational threats renders individuals more vulnerable: economic globalization and better communications and transportation increase pollution, disease vectors and economic instabilities world wide (DFAIT: 2).

In 1997 Canada suggested the instrumentalities to

carry out the new complex security agenda, which includes peace building, peacekeeping, disarmament, safeguarding the rights of the children and economic development through rules-based trade. To move the agenda further, Canada emphasizes increasingly on the role of soft power defined as "the art of disseminating information in such a way that desirable outcomes are achieved through persuasion rather than coercion" (Axworthy, 1997a: 185-91).

The 1999 Canadian paper amplifies the 1997 approach by listing six broader principles that might guide action. All these can be condensed to three major principles: - first- the international community must consider coercion, including the use of sanctions and force if necessary. Second- national security policies themselves must be alerted to give due consideration to the promotion of human security goals. Integral to the new security policy agenda must be the promotion of norms/institutions and the use of development strategies- norms/institutions would set standards of conduct and development strategies would presumably, bring about conditions within which it would be easier for states and non-state actors to observe those norms (DFAIT: 3-4).The Lysoen declaration enumerates ten areas in which norms were required: anti- personnel land mines, small arms, children in armed conflict, international humanitarian and human rights law, international criminal court proceedings, exploitation of children, safety of humanitarian personnel, conflict prevention, transnational organized crime and resources for development. (Axworthy, 1997a: 192-196) For effective implementation, internal democratization of states coupled with a more effective UN structure and construction of a coalition of states, international organizations and NGOs that would promote development and help enforce agreed upon norms to secure human rights (DFAIT).

THE UNDP AND CANADIAN APPROACHES: A COMPARISON SECURITY REFERENT

Whereas the traditional paradigm of security focuses on state as the main referent object of security, both Canadian and UNDP focus on individual. That does not derogate from the primacy of state security in certain circumstances. The cold war super power rivalry, production of nuclear weapons and the emerging differences among the newly independent countries in Asia and Africa led to the realism's portrayal of international relations as a situation of inter state war. The dominance of the traditional paradigm of security focusing on state was never entirely justified. The security of the individuals no doubt depends on state security. But the state security is not always synonymous with individual security. The realists' cold war justifiability of inter state violence does not mean that the threats to human beings and values on which the proponents of human security give primacy were nonexistent. Rather, in the thunderous sabre rattling of cold war these threats either remained unheeded or tried to be understood in realist parlance as subordinate to state security.

The dramatic and unpredictable end of the cold war in 1991 belied the realist and neorealist understanding and interpretation of international relations, and receded the apocalypse of a nuclear holocaust. What was stonewalled and remained underneath came to the surface and occupied the centre stage of policy making. The concern for individual and human security replaced the conventional concern for state security. The ingrained view that state security was coterminous with individual security was considered anachronistic and simply inadequate to meet the new challenges to humanity. Having put a premium on human security does not mean to Canadian government that traditional national security concerns are irrelevant. They remain important, but they are no longer adequate for "stability and peace" (Axworthy, 1997a: 183-184).

VALUE THREATS: SHIFTING SECURITY

In the traditional conception of security the immediate and ultimate identity of individuals and people living within a definite territory and space was with state sovereignty to enjoy absolute security. Inside identity with state was the legitimacy given to sovereignty to protect the insiders' identity from the outsiders' threats. It meant the body, or organization or person in whom the sovereignty is ensconced as the identity and security referent point has the exclusive control over some space and territory and it is free to choose friends and enemies outside and establish relations with other states without remaining captive to any other authority. In the traditional paradigm exclusive territorial control, impregnability, indivisibility political independence and spatial distancing and boundary making remained the key values and constituted the referent objects for identity of people with the state. Thus, the primacy of state security is very closely associated with the notion of sovereignty. In its historic meaning, sovereignty implied the security of the sovereign or "Prince". "The emergence of democratic polity and the transfer of primacy from "Prince" to the "Citizen" call for not only a transformation of the understanding of traditional security and but also transfer of sovereignty from Prince to the Citizenry. With sovereignty now residing in the Citizenry rather than just the Prince, the notion of security must also be broadened to include security not only of the Prince (i.e. state) but the everyday survival of the Citizen" (Adil Najam, 2003 : 61.)

Such a conceptual shift does not undermine the importance of state security, but it does amplify the desideratum to broaden the concept. It is no longer sufficient to define the security of the state in terms of territorial exclusiveness and boundary making because the state is no longer defined simply by the sovereign i.e. the Prince or the territoriality. Rather, the state security must now also secure the well-being and livelihoods of the Citizen, who is the ultimate custodian of sovereignty in the modern state. As Elliot (2001: 449) recognizes, the human security paradigm "turns the conventional security aphorism- secure state means secure people- on its head."

In consonance with this changing perspective, both the UNDP and Canadian view the safety and well being of the individual in physical terms, and individual freedom. As stated by UNDP: "Human security is not a concern with weapons- it is a concern with human life [physical safety and well-being] and dignity [freedom]." As noted earlier, the UNDP enumerates personal, economic, food, health and environmental security, all of which relate to the overarching values of individual safety and well-being. The Report also suggests that the capacity of individuals to make choices, a sense of surety about the future, feelings of personal efficacy and empowerment, and community and political security are important human security values, which for the most part relate to the freedom/dignity of the individual in social and political life. Similarly, in Canadian approach human security implies "an acceptable quality of life", which connotes physical safety and well-being minimally; and "a guarantee of fundamental human rights", which connotes a basic charter of political freedoms (Axworthy, 1997a: 184).

There is a parallel, therefore, between national security values and human security values. When individuals sought identity with state, the traditional values in terms of sovereignty were the value referent objects. Security becoming discursive and diversified away from state, individual values in terms of their own identity and dignity become important. Broadly, if sovereignty of the state is at the heart of the traditional national security conception, so sovereignty of the individual is at the heart of human security. If national security is at base about territorial integrity or protection of the body politic, human security is basically about physical integrity or protection of the individual human body from harm. Human security is about political freedom of an individual to associate with others as well as the freedom to lead a private life without undue interference from fellow citizens and state authorities (Kanti Bajpai, 2003: 209).

SECURITY THREATS

According to Galtung, violence is not merely the "international use of force... against one or more others"... to inflict injury or death". It is not necessary "goal oriented" and intended "to achieve some particular or general purpose (Kathleen M. Weigert, 1999: 432). He distinguishes between direct violence and structural or indirect violence both of which result in a difference between the potential and the actual:

> We shall refer to the type of violence where there is an actor that commits the violence as personal or direct, and to violence where there is no such actor as structural or indirect. In both cases individuals may be killed or mutilated, hit or hurt in both senses of these words, and manipulated by means of stick or carrot strategies, but whereas in the first case the consequences can be traced back to concrete persons as actors, in the second case this is no longer meaningful. There may not be any person who directly harms another person in this structure. The violence is built into the

structure and shows up as unequal power and consequently as unequal life chances (Ibid).

Harm or damage can be traced back most usefully in this view to social relations or structures. Structures, according to Galtung, in this context allude in turn to "the settings within which individuals may do enormous amounts of harm to other human beings without ever intending to do so.... Structural violence was then seen as unintended harm done to human beings... as a process, working slowly in the way misery in general, and hunger in particular, erode and finally kill human beings" (Ibid: 433).

An array of the threats cited by the UNDP and Canadian Government papers mostly relate to personal security and well being. Both depict about indirect and direct threats. Direct threats cover everyday violent crime, child abuse and abuse of women including government repression, terrorism and genocide. It also refers to other kinds of direct violence that endangers personal safety, including the existence of private security forces, banditry, warlordism, internal war and ethnic violence. Thus Canada refers to the violence caused by transitional crime, world wide narcotics trafficking and proliferation of small arms, all of which endanger personal safety and well- being. Finally, there is international/ global violence, which also harms the individual- inter state war, weapons of mass destruction and, in the Canadian conception in particular, anti personnel land mines.

INDIRECT THREATS AT THE SOCIETAL LEVEL

So far as indirect threats are concerned, both approaches conceive of disease as a key indirect threat to personal safety and well- being. In the UNDP scheme there is a recognition that the type of diseases at issue differ by economic development levels – infectious diseases in the developing world and cancers and cardiopulmonary ailments in the developed world. At a more expanding societal level, the extent of poverty (UNDP) and economic underdevelopment (Canada) in developing societies constitute the indirect threats. Lack of remunerative and sustained employment is important for both developing and industrially developed countries. In the developing countries lack of employment opportunities is considered a matter of life and death, whereas in the developed countries they may lead to psychological anxieties and debilities that threaten individual health and happiness.

According to Kanti Bajpai, "neither the UNDP nor the Canadian paper note the other side of the coin: - namely that slow population growth or even population decline are threats to other societies..." (K. Bajpai, 2003: 210). Richard Easterlin's relative cohort size hypothesis which is obtained by measuring the current group of young adults (ages 15-29) as a proportion of the number of working adults (ages 30-54) delineates the relationship between youthful populations and economic and psychological frustrations that enable political instability and, ultimately, civil war (Richard Easterlin, 1968,1978,1987). As a large relative cohort comes of age, the tension produced by lack of success in the job and marriage markets may, in the presence of other contextual factors, render armed conflict a more appealing option. While relative cohort size is unlikely to be an immediate cause of civil war, large birth cohorts often strain the schooling system and labour market of a country, particularly a developing one, which can result in massive frustration, unemployment, reduced wages, and dissatisfaction- and arguably create potential army of young men who could be easily recruited in a rebellion. (Sarah Staveteig, 2005:12-19). Recent studies suggest similarly that a large youth bulge- a youthful population age structure can increase the risk of the onset of civil conflict and political violence (Urdal,2006, Cincotta et al; 2003). Another recent study shows how the missing women in developing countries more particularly in Asia and Africa due to the result of son preference and devaluation of female life could lead to violent conflict in the event of many young marriageable males not finding brides to marry. The men unable to marry are poorer, less educated, less skilled, and less likely to be employed. These men are already at risk for establishing a system based on physical force in order to obtain by force what they cannot obtain legitimately. Without the opportunity to establish a household, they may not transition from potential threats to potential protectors of society (Valerie M. Hudson and Andrea M. Den Boer, 2005: 20-24). The rate of criminal behaviour of unmarried men is many times higher than that of married men; marriage is a reliable predictor of downturn in reckless, antisocial, illegal, and violent behaviour by young adult males (Mazur and Michalek, 1998). Thus, the increasing number of bare branches i.e. missing women has serious security implications in countries where the number of females is plummeting. The onset of civic violence and internal instability and conflict challenging the established political system will certainly overshadow the external security concerns of these governments. The link between population age structure and onset of civic conflict can be another challenge to human security, which finds no mention in both UNDP and Canada papers.

INDIRECT THREATS AT THE INTERNATIONAL AND GLOBAL LEVEL

In addition to indirect threats at the societal level, indirect threats at the global and international level include population growth, migration, global environmental degradation in terms of ozone depletion, emission of carbon dioxide, global warming, sea level rise, desertification, deforestation, acid rain, loss of biodiversity and highly unequal worldwide pattern of consumption. The issue of inordinate life style and profligate consumption of the global rich becoming contentious of both the North and South countries is at the root of environmental deterioration and consequent threats to human life. Good life defined in terms of exorbitant consumption in America and other North countries has led to deprivation of millions now in South and also in future and heavy pressure on scarce resources of the Earth. The political economy of the North based on Hobbesian and Lockean possessive individualism deriving the ontological metaphor from Newtonian mechanistic view of the universe has led to the proliferation of not only millionaires in America and other North countries but destitute in South. Thus, the unsustainable consumption and concentration of wealth of the rich and ultra- rich in North at the cost of the poor and the future generations has turned out to be threat to human life. Paul Ehrlich and Anne Ehrlich, 2004, in their book One with Nineveh: Politics, Consumption, and the Human Future taking the title from Rudyard Kipling's poem "Recessional" about the fallen Assyrian capital of Nineveh, the ruins of which lie near the contemporary Iraqi city of Mosul observe that just as pride and arrogance led to the collapse of ancient Mesopotamian societies, similar hubris derived from profligate consumption, inordinate life style and concentration of wealth could lead to the downfall of today's global civilization. "One of its consequences is the catastrophic climate change having disastrous implications on human life. Just as the Titanic's passengers partied into the night, confident that the ship was unsinkable, the rising tide of millionaires and near millionaires is caught up in a frenzy of consumption, supremely confident that their wealth and possessions will insulate them from any bad times to come" (Dennis Pirages, Review article on Paul Ehrlich and Anne Ehrlich' book One with Nineveh, in ECSP Report, Woodrow

Wilson International Center for Scholars, Issue 10, 2004, 84).

Both the UNDP and Canadian reports while putting the blame on global market economy for what has been wrought to the environment and to human life have never forgotten to cite global economy as an opportunity to both rich and poor alike. They are of the view that protectionist economy has been a threat to individual safety and well-being. In Canadian view economic crises and shocks in one part of the globe have their repercussions on other parts constituting an array of indirect threats.

One may allege that both the UNDP and Canadian writings while have been prolific in their description of threats to personal safety and well-being have shown parsimony in their treatment of threats to other core values of human security and individual freedom. But a little reflection will demonstrate that many of the direct and indirect threats to personal safety and well-being are also threats to basic and civic freedom. Thus, unorganized threats such as physical abuse of children and women as well as the more organized societal level threats such as ethnic conflict, genocide, warlordism, internal war and government repression are threats to both personal safety/well-being and individual freedom. Similarly, indirect threats such as economic deprivation, underdevelopment, extreme poverty, unemployment, gross deprivation of basic needs and growing inequality may emasculate individuals to participate in political and social affairs rendering their basic rights mere untranslatable letters in a constitutional parchment.

Human rights violations and government suspension of rights may not be physical threats but are certainly constraints on enjoyment of civic and basic human rights and freedom. Suspension of the constitution and rule of law constitute direct threats to freedom. Discriminatory policies and rules relating to ethno-religious groups are also direct threats. The UNDP also points out that the communities being the sources of identity and security can curtail one's freedom. Decimation of one's culture, tradition and customs is a threat to one's identity. At the same time imposition of traditional customs and archaic practices on people against their wishes is as serious threat as the government's abridgement of one's rights. Finally, the UNDP argues that the militarization of social and political life is itself potentially a threat to freedom.

DIFFERENCES BETWEEN UNDP AND CANADIAN APPROACHES

First, both approaches suggest that direct and indirect violence threaten personal safety and well being and basic and civic freedom. The two approaches identify many of the same threats. Second, the UNDP approach, on balance, places greater emphasis on indirect threats, where as the Canadian approach puts greater stress on direct threats. This is no where more evident than in the stress that Canadian writings put on traditional national security threats and organized internal violence such as banditry, warlordism, ethnic violence, genocide, internal war. In criticizing the UNDP approach, Canada explicitly notes that – "in emphasizing the threats associated with under development the Report largely ignores the continuing human insecurity resulting from violent conflict" (DFAIT: 2). Third, both approaches peg threats to personal safety and well being at the centre of their analysis.

INSTRUMENTS OF HUMAN SECURITY

In the traditional view, states are self help and self sufficing sovereign entities always in a Hobbesian state of war with other states in a supposedly anarchical international system. An ever increasing and perpetuating military strength either through balance of power or alliance is considered necessary to protect one against the other and put an end to security dilemma.

Since human security approaches consider traditional security concept inadequate and anachronistic to meet the threats by the exercise of unilateral use of force, it is obvious that both the UNDP and Canadian "view of security" and "security by what means" must be obverse of the national security view. First of all, in the UNDP and Canadian view force is a secondary instrument. In the UNDP schema there is virtually no room for the use of force because the main instrumentality in achieving goals is development. In the Canadian schema force remains an instrument, but one that is only a last resort and not very effective in dealing with the multifarious threats to personal safety and freedom. Force if at all is to be used, is to be used for cosmopolitan not solely for national goals. Another qualification for use of force is that it is to be used if required under the aegis of international institutions or regional organizations for protecting human security.

Second, both the UNDP and Canadian view stress on long term co-operation, which is both possible and necessary in an increasingly interdependent world. In an age when there is already death of distance, it is very difficult to assume that what happens in a distant place will not affect the other people. So states must come together and reach out to international organizations, NGOs and other agencies in civil societies to meet the myriad of challenges to human security. Canada ekes out a particular role for countries like itself, which dispose of soft power, the power of persuasion. This power would play a significant role in disseminating information and ideas in order to awaken others to the need for co-operation and collaboration on the means to be used.

Third, states, international organizations and NGOs can coalesce to foster norms of conduct in various areas of human security. The spreads of norms must be accompanied by the strengthening of global institutions. Fundamentally, in the UNDP view, global society itself must be restructured to bring about a condition in which both direct and indirect threats will disappear. That restructuring should basically be a developmental one. Thus the UNDP urges that a new human development paradigm must be evolved with an accent on equity, sustainability and participation. A rethinking of established pattern of development, dominant economic view and structures needs to take prioritization in human security paradigm.

In contrast to the UNDP approach, Canada offers a more pragmatic approach in that it is more "a shift in perspective or orientation...an alternative way of seeing the world" (Ibid). On the question of policy formulation or commitments Canada is of the view that practice might better lead the formulation of norms. Thus, it notes: "As is so often the case in public policy, practice has led theory" (Axworthy, 1999. Foreword in DEAIT: 1).

As is seen, the UNDP and Canadian approaches on the referent values and threats of security do not differ in any great measure. Canada's real concern is over the policy implication of the almost revolutionary agenda offered by the UNDP: "The very breadth of the UNDP approach made it unwisely as a policy instrument" (DFAIT: 2). While Canada insists that" vigorous action in defense of human security objectives will be necessary", the programme of action it recommends is modest in comparison to that of the UNDP. For example, it considers protection of human rights is crucial to human security but in terms of actions it merely suggests that "security policies must be integrated more closely with strategies for promoting human rights, democracy and development" (Ibid:3).

Haq and the "left of the center" UNDP approach is

more concerned about economic underdevelopment as leading to deprivation and violence, with the implication that greater development, equity and intervention would remedy the problem. But in the Canadian formulation the breakdown of states, societies and governance- mostly in the developing world- or political underdevelopment is the cause of deprivation and violence. The remedy in the Canadian approach is not so much the UNDP's interventionary developmentalism, but 'protection' (K. Bajpai, 2003: 214).

It is important to note that the Canadian paper of 1999 dose not rule out the more developmentalist agenda of the UNDP approach. But attention to development was very scant. The 1997 paper by Axworthy argues that after the end of the cold war "the international community... would turn its attention to global problems, such as poverty, the environment, and population growth" (Axworthy, 1997a:183). The 1999 paper recognizes that "the widespread social unrest and violence that often accompanies economic crises demonstrates that there are clear economic underpinnings to human security" (DFAIT, Human Security: 3). Further, it notes that poverty and insecurity are interlinked "in a vicious circle" and "breaking the cycle requires measures to promote human development, through access to reliable employment, education, and social services". Human development and human security are "mutually reinforcing" and "development assistance" can complement "political, legal, and military initiatives in enhancing human security" (Ibid: 3).

Disenchantment with the traditional instruments of security- force, deterrence, alliance, balance of power- has been the common denominator that finds both the UNDP and Canada in agreement on "security by what means." While the UNDP prefers to put greater emphasis on economic development, Canada relies on political development to meet the challenges to human security. The similarities on many aspects of human security between the two schools outstrip the differences that exist.

APPROPRIATION FOR SECURITY

Where the 1994 Human Development Report nods at freedom from fear before going on to emphasize the necessity for human development policies, the Canadian approach does the opposite. The Canadian Foreign Ministry's concept paper devoted to the term criticizes the UNDP approach for being broad and unwieldy, and for largely ignoring human insecurity resulting from violent conflict. It defines human security as "safety for people from both violent and non-violent threats... a condition or state of being characterized by freedom from pervasive threats to people's rights, their safety, even their lives" (DFAIT, 1999). It stops short of excluding economic deprivation from the definition, but blithely claims that "over the past two years the concept of human security has increasingly centred on the human cost of violent conflict". After acknowledging that poverty and insecurity are linked in a vicious circle, it goes on to highlight "measures to promote human security by offering protection from crime and political violence, respect for human rights including political rights, and equitable access to justice. "The absence of such guarantees of human security constitutes a powerful barrier to human development. Thus, it focuses on precisely the opposite causal relation to that emphasized by UNDP" (Marlies Glasius, 2008 : 42). In its subsequent usage Canada has dropped the developmental element entirely. In Canadian government's human security website, poverty alleviation, social justice or even humanitarian aid do not find any entry under the rubric of human security.

The Canadian approach has placed considerable emphasis on international law as an instrument of human security, specifically mentioning the UN Charter, the Universal Declaration of Human Rights and the Geneva Conventions (DFAIT, 1999). But it is precisely from this angle that it lays open to attack. "The international rule of law is conceptualized as something to be brought to insecure people in conflict zones, much less as something that should govern the behaviour of would be providers of human security" (Marlies Glasius, 2008 : 43).

HUMAN SECURITY: THE CONCEPT AND DISCOURSE

The question crops up whether human security is what has been described in the UNDP and Canada approaches. Human security literature often reads like an uneasy merger of human development and peace themes, via the bridge of the term 'security': "human security joins the main agenda items of peace, security and development" (Commission on Human Security, 2003 : 4). In fact, the human security discourse does more. Various answers are given as to why we need a concept of human security.

First, human security concerns the stability of the effective (i.e. attainable), valued opportunities that are the currency of evaluation in Sen's capability approach. In particular, it concerns downside risks (Sen., 2003). That means, 'human security' could then concern also the degree of stability with which the super- rich possess super- riches. Sen intends something more here by securing than merely stability; such as removal of intolerable risks. A down turn in income for a rich man and for a poor person is not the same experience. If security is equated to stability, his phrase 'downturn with security' introduced to partner the conventional aspiration of 'growth with equity', might not avoid this danger. So two augmented phrases, 'growth with equity and security' and 'downturn with security and equity' are required unless it is assumed that equity entails security. As pointed out by Gasper, "the first answer focuses only on the noun 'security' and neglects the adjective' human'. It is an answer from the side of human development discourse: the human security concept is seen as an addition that concerns stability of human development as opposed to its level or trend" (D Gasper, 2005 : 224)

The second answer is that 'human security' concerns freedom from fear in addition to 'freedom from want' to use the terms of the US Secretary of State in 1945 (cited by Haq, 1999, p.190). The physical security was incorporated from the mid-1990s into the definition of human development (UNDP : 56). This can be done "as part of bringing down to earth of the human development concept- back to substantiate specified priority aspects of human life- from the abstracted capability heights of attainable valued opportunities" (D.Gasper, 2005 : 224). It does not reduce human security to physical security alone.

The third answer is based on the fact that human security concerned with the security of persons is opposed to the security of states. It connects to the idea that state security will be precarious, expensive and even empty unless founded on and consistent with the security of individuals. As seen above, Canadian/ Norwegian government definition of human security corresponds to personal security and reacts against both the UNDP notion of human security being too broad and the traditional concept of security becoming increasingly misleading or insufficient in an era when most violent conflict is intra-national and, overwhelmingly, most casualties are civilian. It means the Canadian school reduces human security to physical security of individuals.

The fourth answer traversing beyond the freedom

from fear and want deals with what are the requirements of being human in addition to sheer existence. With a broader attention to the adjective human, it includes freedom from humiliation and indignity. Mary Robinson, the former UN Commissioner for Human Rights, highlights also freedom from despair (Robinson, 2003). 'Freedom to' is understood in the potential capability sense to act or attain, and is differentiated from 'freedom from' which concern definite absences not just potential absences. Some also are inclined to include within the list of human security the right of future generations to inherit a healthy natural environment.

In the words of Sabina Alkire, who was senior researcher to the Commission on Human Security, "the objective of human security is to safeguard the vital core of all human lives from critical pervasive threats, without impeding long term human fulfillment.... The term 'vital core' is not meant to be precise; it suggests a minimal or basic or fundamental set of functions related to survival, livelihood and dignity" (Alkire, 2003 : 24). The Commission on Human Security largely adopting this view defined human security as: "to protect the vital core of all human lives in ways that enhance human freedoms and human fulfillment (Commission on Human Security, 2003 : 4). Drawing from Hampson et al. (2002) this approach prompted Haq to state: "Human security is not a concern with weapons- it is a concern with human life and dignity" (UNDP, 1994 : 22).

As seen from the various types of answers regarding the purpose of human security concept, it can be stated in sum that human security complements the human development concept by a concern with the stability of whatever goods are highlighted within human development. It broadens the scope of human development concept by including the physical security of persons. It also takes away the scope of security studies and the concept of security beyond state and military security and/ or shifts the focus to a concern with the physical security of persons. Finally, it narrows down the scope as compared with human development concept by concentrating on the basics i.e. types and level of goods required for securing humanity.

BRIDGING HUMAN SECURITY AND BASIC HUMAN NEEDS APPROACH

If human security is defined "as the preservation and protection of the life and dignity of individual human beings (Takasu, cited in Harvard Human Security Project, 2002) or about "The task of carving out a certain subset of material and political needs around which to form a consensus for concerted action" (Alkire, 2003 : 28), is it worthwhile to say that human security is same as basic human needs? Or in the words of D.Gasper, "is this not simply the good old wine of basic human needs, rebottled and relabelled for a new generation? In many respects they share the same bed but not in all. The label and the concept/bottle are indeed new. Alkire is of the view that "the term 'vital core' is not yet claimed by any approach" (Alkire, 2003 : 25).

Human security discourse is distinguished from basic human needs approach in that the former includes a style of analytical integration or open system analysis and some normative insistence on the inviolability of basic human needs, their status as human rights. On the question of whether human security concept and discourse contain anything new, Galtung stated: "Very much of what has been mentioned [in Human Security Now] is in the basic human tradition... [But] No doubt human security is... developing that approach further" (Galtung, 2004 : 7).

Alkire frequently talks of "what people valued or needed at a very basic level" (2003 : 24), "a minimal or basic or fundamental set of functions" (2003 : 24), "basic capabilities" (2003 : 36). According to her the basic human needs concept is distinguished from human security concept in that the latter is always couched in the idioms of freedoms: of capability not functioning (Alkire, 2003 : 27). Various formulations of basic needs theory have, however, involved capability (Gasper, 1996, Doyal and Gough, 1991). While comparing human security with other policy frameworks- state security, human development, and human rights, Alkire "tends to conflate basic human needs work with the basic material needs approach of some 1950s-1980s planning agencies and development banks, which reduced human needs to only material needs or considered that those have exclusive priority. This conflation is commonly linked to equation of basic needs work to a simplified representation of needs theory of Abraham Maslow." (Gasper, 2005 : 230). In his schema of hierarchy of needs, physiological needs are felt most intensely until they are fulfilled, followed by safety needs and so on. He recognized in his late work the central importance of non-material needs at all stages though the needs are active concurrently. While bringing out a sustainable contrast between much human security work and some needs approaches, which concern aggregation, Gasper notes:

> Much needs-based planning concerned itself with a broader range of goods than those measured by money but shared the readiness of money- metric approaches to aggregate across people. This brings the risk, in practice, of some people being sacrificed 'for the greater good': even that some people's basic needs will be sacrificed for the fulfillment of less pressing needs or wants of a large number of other people. Much human security work now adopts

> a human rights stance: the basic requirements of no individual are to be sacrificed (Gasper, 2005 : 230).

Gasper is of the view that human security is the human rights conscious child of the basic human needs approach. Human beings are entitled to the enjoyment of human rights because they are humans. Human rights can be seen as rights to the fulfillment of, or ability to fulfill, basic human needs. "Behind human rights are freedoms and needs so fundamental that their denial puts human dignity itself at risk" (Goldewijk and Fortman, 1999 : 117). Gasper is of the view that " Basic human needs are whatever people require to be able to achieve a level of functioning that satisfies a given ethical conception of the acceptable minimum; such conceptions include, for example, human dignity, or the avoidance of serious harm" (Gasper, 2005 : 231).

In a better refinement of basic human needs approach, Galtung warns that the traditional human rights approach connects better to survival needs and freedom needs- "needs that are more clearly threatened by deliberate acts of evil actors"- and for which we can more readily state norms in the form of rights that imply duties by specific actors. In contrast, identity needs and some other needs "are more often impeded by wrong structures" (Galtung, 1994 : 69). Stressing on the need for a post-traditional approach, he further avers that "needs rather than rights direct us to look for causal factors rather than evil actors" (Galtung, 1994 : 55).

In a similar vein Francois Fouinat (2004: 293-294) is of the view that there is a case in human security for establishing a 'social minimum' for all human beings. Traditionally, social protection has been defined in terms of a range of public measures that support society's poorest and most vulnerable members and help individuals, households, and communities to manage risks better. While fulfilling most of the aspirations of the beneficiaries, social protection is a very sophisticated system requiring huge resource flows that even advanced societies find difficult to maintain. Social protection sits at the upper end of a spectrum of policies that shield individuals from all forms of vulnerabilities. At the lower end of the same spectrum, emergency handouts of food or basic health services are included in what are known as social safety nets. A possibility between these two extremes can be the provision of a limited social minimum that focuses on protecting the vital core of all human lives, enhance human freedom, and is realistically adapted to the limited resources of the concerned societies.

BRIDGING BETWEEN THE CONCEPTIONS OF HUMAN RIGHTS AND NEEDS

The connection between the conceptions of human rights and needs has long been acknowledged but not absorbed as a standard formulation. "The two ideas have been primarily located in different disciplines and fora: rights more in the worlds of law, social movements and 'humanitarian intervention', needs more within social and economic policy and planning and 'humanitarian relief'. Added to this have been confusions around needs discourse, attacks on it by many libertarians and free market advocates, and antagonism by some socialists and economists to rights formulations" (Gasper, 2005 : 232). Recent years have witnessed a modification in the stringency of these stands and a connection between the two.

Rights are "justified claims to the protection of persons' important interests" (Gewirth, 1995 : 776). In other words, human rights are legitimated claims/entitlements "grounded in basic needs" (Goldewijk and Fortman, 1999 :

120). Prioritization in the capabilities/human development language now begins to often use the label 'human security.' Nussbaum (2000) proposes similarly that many human rights are best seen as rights to basic needs, seen in turn as basic capabilities to function (Gasper, 2005). For Leaning (2004), human security means ability to secure basic material and psycho-social needs. Thus, Galtung can conclude that human security is the fulfillment of basic human rights that are in turn the fulfillment of basic human needs. In his model these are survival, wellness, freedom and identity (Galtung. 2003 : 7). In the words of Alkire, "human security does bridge a number of previous concepts" (Alkire, 2003 : 25). The human security concept " tries to combine human development discourse's broad focus and stress on reasoned freedoms, basic human needs discourse's stress on prioritization, and human rights discourse's unwillingness to sacrifice anyone" (Gasper, 2005 : 234). One advantage is that while human rights concept generates specific claims in the language of Gewirth, it also emphasizes on specific duties and accountability (St Clair, 2004b). Alkire states this emphatically: "the human rights approach holds the notion of obligation and duty centrally" (2003 : 26) and it entails an "automatic sense of moral obligation" (2003 : 39). Secondly, human security work acknowledges more fully than the human rights tradition the necessity often for prioritization. Human rights concepts are often too absolutist (Commission on Human Security, 2003 : 28). Alkire hopes that human security discourse can take over strengths of the human rights language while avoiding some of the old disputes and connotations (2003 : 39).

BRIDGING SECURITY AND DEVELOPMENT: A PARADIGM SHIFT

The most unexplored potential of the human security paradigm is to weave together 'want' and 'fear' dimensions into one framework. The interrelatedness of poverty and violence is widely acknowledged. But the exact nature of the relationship between the two in different crisis situations is under-populated. Relative poverty, job insecurity and a subjective sense of inequity may be much more closely related to a resort to violence than absolute poverty. The interplay between socio-economic conditions and the use of violence in situations of escalating human insecurity has been too elusive to be crafted into policy framework that would tackle both simultaneously as neither researchers, activists, NGOs and policy makers are well equipped for this.

Moreover, a legacy of ingrained suspicion and competition between the developmental and the military realms exists, both at the policy design level and on the actual ground of operation. Schulze (2006:11) describes how profound mutual distrust impinged on the relief effort after the Tsunami in Aceh, Indonesia: "Civilian relief workers were skeptical of soldiers' involvement in humanitarian aid as they did not believe a military role could or should be combined with relief work. Conversely, the militaries saw the NGOs as ineffective, uncoordinated and self promoting "do – gooders" who ...wanted to use the militaries' equipment- helicopters, trucks, and ships- but preferably without the soldiers" What is needed for a holistic and realistic human security policies is a fierce dialogue between security and development realms about their approaches to situations of human insecurity.

Human security also bridges the distance between traditional security policies and other non-traditional threats that are not easily reduced to either the fear or the want dimensions: disease, environmental disasters and organized crime, including trafficking in drugs and people (Liotta, 2002; Newman, 2001:245-246). The indivisibility between these sources of insecurity, on the one hand, and poverty and violence, on the other has primarily touched more a rhetorical height than having got into the real policy making.

BRIDGING REALISM AND ETHICS: HUMAN SECURITY AS A BOUNDARY OBJECT

Human security concept has been castigated as a ragbag of concepts. Amartya Sen's inclination for integration through freedom formulation and adoption of the 'security' label "is perceived by some as drinking from a poisoned chalice rather than as its purification; even as acceptance now of a fearful American agenda marked by fantasies of invulnerability. The approach is attacked as too broad to be operational or have policy value; as too individualistic, even too Christian...as old wine in an unhelpful new bottle" (Gasper, 2005 : 234).

Asuncion St Clair views "human security as an intellectual 'boundary object': a conceptualization that attempts to bridge between different intellectual and professional worlds, notably between the worlds of science and policy" (2004a, 2004b). As argued by Bernstein (2004 : 3), the human security approach coupled with normative and theoretical organizing principles in the human security discourse, contains "all the right bells and whistles". 'Boundary objects' are practices, ideas or sets of ideas that are employed for the inter-community interchange (Star and Griesemer, 1989). As opined by Gasper: " Boundary objects must be malleable enough to be used by diverse parties, while robust enough to keep sufficient shared meaning across the range of users" (Gasper, 2005 : 235). Taking into account St Clairs' (2004b) views, Gasper states: "Boundary work at the borders of theory and policy in national and international development circles is particularly complex. Multi-national, multi-disciplinary, multi-agency contexts bring special demands for participation, trust and equity.

International development agencies have typically not adequately theorized the boundary work in which they engage, because of rosy myths such as that economic growth will bring all good things and that everyone agrees on the value content of development" (Gasper, 2005 : 235). Along with human development, human security had the function of bringing ethical concerns into the economistic frameworks of traditional development bulwarks like the World Bank or USAID (St Clair, 2004, Gasper, 2005). Under the stewardship of Mahbub ul- Haq, various Human Development Reports sought a deliberate role as purveyors of such boundary objects based on a realization of " the importance of vivid concepts to mobilize support, and ...organizational autonomy in order to elaborate, defend and disseminate alternative ideas" (Gasper, 2005 : 236-237).

While deliberating on factors for successful intellectual 'boundary objects' that contribute to ethically intervention in these contexts, St Clair "argues that propounding ethical claims alone is not very effective. We need rather to embody conscious ethical meanings into boundary objects that frame and regulate boundary work. Boundary objects with embodied ethical concerns survive better the rough- and-tumble of policy debate where power pressures, disciplinary habits and other forces enter. Ethical concerns should be embedded in a policy/ planning approach rather than left as disembodied words, detached from action and power" (Cited in Gasper, 2005 : 236).

The UNDP played a great role in preserving and presenting moral concepts in its policy discourses by maintaining an intellectual influence. "Its boundary objects have directed attention to people's lives, local situations and learning paths. The human development language centers on attainable options, thus retaining a strong connection to economists; but it is not easily co-opted and reduced for it is so explicit on its values and on including all of life beyond only the monetized and monetizable. Its impact on policy has been less than on prose, yet positive and unexpected" (Gasper, 2005 : 237).

Some pilloried Human development's partner, 'human security discourse' for being a hotchpotch of different incoherent and vague concepts. This is not so because it has left enough space for those areas, situations, contexts and ideas not yet foreseen to be conceptualized into the framework. Alkire argues that the generality of the human security concept is a virtue. It appropriately allows human security to encompass many variants and to reflect different priorities in different times and places, including according to "the comparative advantage of the implementing institution" (Alkire, 2003 : 10) while putting still a unified prioritizing focus.

But Gasper only depicts the influence of human security as a boundary object on established development thinking. This is nothing compared to its impact on established security thinking. In conventional security studies ethical concerns tended to be treated as frivolity and security of the state sovereignty was the only ethics. What was conducive to its national interest constituted moral precepts for it. "The human security paradigm, on the other hand, treats formerly realistic concerns for the security of one's own polity and formerly ethical concerns for human beings elsewhere as inseparable, and has found a fair measure of acceptance for this view point" (Marlies Glasius, 2008 : 39). This is not to buttress that the entrenched tension between foreign policy making and ethical consideration has been resolved entirely by the human security discourse. Some radical foreign policy critics are averse to the idea of human security entering into the vocabulary of governments. Bellamy and McDonald (2002: 374) contend that "if states are often agents of human insecurity rather than security, then the co-option of human security into a statist policy framework risks limiting the emancipatory potential of this security discourse." They would like to see 'human security' operate less as a policy agenda within existing political structures and discourses than as a radical critique of those practices. There is one argument, which adduces that narrowing down usually in'violence' rather than the poverty direction is required in order to come out with an operational concept that can guide policy (Krause, 2004; Mack, 2004; Thomas and Tow, 2002a). Another stand contends that the concern for 'narrowing' and 'operationalizing' is really code for adapting and co-opting the concept so as to fit the current practices of states (Bellamy and McDoald,2002; Grayson,2004).

ROLES OF HUMAN SECURITY DISCOURSE

Human security discourse is not a buckle that joins together the different aspects concerning human beings across the disciplinary and national boundaries or simply additive yet plays a significant boundary role such as integration, prioritization, motivation, and operationalization.

It provides a convenient working hypothesis and mechanism to find all issues interconnected and integrated in a loop of analytical examination for more insights and policy guidance starting from " postcolonial structures and world economic power balances to debt crises, to economic regimes imposed in poor countries, to social conflicts, to armed conflict, to economic collapse, to banditry as a profession and from economic, social and military crises to health pandemics, the global drugs trade, domestic conflicts and changing gender roles". It ensures a "realistic understanding" of "causes, costs and other effects of violent conflict" (Gasper, 2005 : 238).

As mentioned by Uvin, the four traditionally

separated fields of "humanitarianism, development, human rights, and conflict resolution" are found integrated in the human rights discourse including the highly flaunted national security (Uvin, 2004 : 353).

In St Clair's language, the human security discourse provides a boundary object that is imbued with ethical concerns for equity. "In a world where equity in participation remains remote, it is particularly important to embed equity concerns in the conceptualization of policy issues" (Gasper, 2005 : 238).

All the above issues find getting attraction in human development approach but human security discourse puts accent on these without strong distinctiveness. Compared with human development approach, it prioritizes its focus on human needs with more immediate policy relevance.

Human security discourse plays a great role in motivating action by focusing on individual human beings, their vulnerability and on their basic needs. As mentioned by Gasper, "The human development approach broadened and re-cast the attention to the meaning and ends of development, but provided no clear guarantee for individuals. Many could still be sacrificed in the course of bringing the broad range of good things to the majority, by governments who warmly adopted the language of human development" (Gasper, 2005 : 239). Human security discourse aims at looking beyond the territorial, political, geographical and psychological confinement of being portrayed as the other. In that sense it is both cosmic and cosmopolitan in terms of addressing the issues concerning the security of humanity at large without any distinctiveness not only of the present but also generations of the future. It has the potential to cross the limitations of time and space. It looks at the individuals as not mere objectified versions of security but as subjectivities assured psychological satisfaction of being secured physically and assured of being not plagued by any wants or basic needs. Jennifer Leaning (2004) defines human security as "psycho-social well-being over time", and anthropologists Winslow and Erikson (2004) link it to notions of identity and community. It "looks at people as agents, across the 'vital core' of their lives, not only at isolated dimensions of nutrition, longevity or violence. "The language of fear and of central aspirations conveys more, about people who strive and feel. Thus, vitally for a policy framework, the exercise of integration extends to include the emotions too" (Gasper and Truong, 2005).

Finally, it connects to an accountability structure- the UN system, and its other institutions setting goals and monitoring for implementation at national, global and local level- Millennium Development goals, human rights, international conventions, peace keeping etc. If accountability is understood within the established UN system, the discourse is at its limitations because these institutions have not moved beyond reified notions of the state and national sovereignty yet dominated by political and economic genie of the rich North who played a major role in drafting the Bretton Woods institutions for the entire globe. What Srgian Kerin, the President of the 62nd session of the United Nations General Assembly said is worth being excerpted:

> We need a new kind of internationalism that caters to a new global society based on principled pragmatism and shared responsibility... This new paradigm must not be built around another illusory 'world order'. What we need instead is a new culture of internationalism, a new way of thinking about our shared fate and our shared responsibilities. It should be fluid and flexible enough to cope with our changing world, and should have the

> wellbeing of the individual at its center... However, our present international structures are too rigidly anchored in an international system where preeminence is given to the state as the primary interlocutor and agent of change.... We need a fundamental renewal and radical rethinking of what we expect from the United Nations, the Bretton Woods institutions as well as from other international and regional bodies (Srgian Kerim, quoted in The Hindu, April 15, 2008 : 9).

SHIFTING AWAY FROM HUMANITARIAN INTERVENTION

The question sometimes is raised over the human security being caught in the debate over the rights and wrongs of humanitarian intervention. The justifiability of intervention in Kosovo, Iraq, Afghanistan has been of great ethical interest to both supporters and opponents. Opponents of the 'freedom from fear' concept of human security argue that once the concept of ' humanitarian intervention' began to lose credibility, human security became just the latest phrase for legitimating military intervention, with or without sanction by international law (Woodward, 1999, Galtung, 2004). This finds its resonance in what Canadian Foreign Minister Lloyd Axworthy claimed during the NATO campaign against Kosovo that "the crisis in Kosovo, and the Alliance's response to it, is a concrete expression of the human security dynamic at work" (Axworthy, 1999, as quoted in Newman, 2001: 244). In a critique of this Johan Galtung (2004:7) stated the report legitimizes the word 'security' by giving it the connotation 'human'. What then happens is beyond the pages of the report. We would expect the state system with its monopoly on the violent means of security to use this legitimation, justifying intervention inside other states in the name of 'human security'....Since the security discourse tends to see the solution to violence in terms of counter- violence, 'security' is essentially a euphemism for 'combat'.

"If Galtung is right, then 'human security' has been entirely absorbed and emasculated by the state security concept it was designed to contest" (Marlies Glasius, 2008: 43). This contention can be tested, as Galtung suggests, by examining the use of the term 'human security' in relation to the war in Iraq. The term 'human security' has been widely used to critique the war in Iraq. Just before the war, Amnesty International (2003) called on the EU to accord higher priority to human security- that is, the risks of civilian casualties, disruption to food supplies and refugee flows. Prominent people associated with 'Canadian style human security' such as former foreign minister Lloyd Axworthy (2003) and Nobel Prize winner Jody Williams (2004), have used the term in denouncing the intervention. The much publicized 'Iraq body Count' project also identifies itself as a human security project. Thus, it is said, "while a narrow Canadian 'freedom from fear' interpretation does suffer from myopia as much as the narrow developmentalist interpretation, it cannot be argued that 'human security' has now been stretched to legitimize military intervention in general" (Marlies Glasius, 2008: 44).

There has been a shift away from 'humanitarian intervention'. Key to this shift was the foregrounding of the concept of human security in the report of the International Committee on Intervention and State Sovereignty, The Responsibility To Protect (ICISS, 2001).This report while challenging the untrammelled state sovereignty builds on the concept of human security- not a right to intervene, but a responsibility to protect within and if necessary beyond borders. "The focus on 'sovereignty as responsibility' implemented through all kinds of policy, rather than on a right to intervene, allowed the debate to proceed beyond preoccupation with the legality of troop deployment" (Marlies Glasius, 2008: 36).

CONCLUSION

The above discussion is demonstrative of the utter poverty of realism and neorealism to comprehend violence and threats other than those caused by interstate war or violence. Glued to Westphalian straight jacket, these traditional security concepts have shown unrealistic proclivity to study security in state centric terms. The vast array of threats as pointed above to human life and values not arising always necessarily from state and its military apparatus but diversifying from other sources could not deserve being christened under the rubric ' security' in traditional idioms. Besides, these orthodox theories remained averse to a clearly acknowledgment of the new threat challenges to the entire collective capacity to respond, and of the heralding of a new world of interdependence and multilateralism impinging on us to chart out new ways and insights to meet the inadequacy of state centrism. The shifting of security away from state paradigm to the individuals and people has been the sine qua non of human security. Edward Newman (2004: 358) has expressed this trenchantly: "Traditionally, state sovereignty and sovereign legitimacy rest upon a government's control of territory, state independence and recognition by other states. The role of citizens is to support this system. The human security approach reverses this equation: the state- and state sovereignty- must serve and support the people from which it draws its legitimacy." This means the indivisibility, inseparability and all inclusive transnational nature of security across borders. "The consequences of this insight are on the one hand, to bring the idea back down to the security of the individual citizen and, on the other hand, to extend it (in rhetoric at least) beyond one's own citizens to every human being" (Marlies Glasius, 2008 : 36). What is most important, often overlooked, is that the means and instruments of providing or restoring human security have to be fundamentally different from those employed to provide state security (Kaldor and Salmon, 2006). This has spurted the critics and skeptics of the human security to ask whether it is helpful to include these values and threats within the conception of security. The theoretical objection to human security is most stringently raised by neorealist security analysts who agree that lumping together such a disparate set of threats causes the term security to lose all theoretical utilities (Florini and Simmons, 1998: 29-33). The policy objection to human security is that by positing so many different forms of violence there is little hope of framing a coherent response.

Human security is a response to the urge to know better what one should care about what it is one's power to do and what crises are looming. According to Kanti Bajpai (2003: 226), its concerns are both consequentialist and deontological. Human security concern with personal safety and freedom is consequentialist in that it regards inter state war as frequently the end product of direct and indirect violence against individual. It acknowledges that inter-state violence may arise from international anarchy but it regards threats to individual life and liberty as equally a cause of international violence". Its " concern with personal safety and freedom is deontological because it affirms that individual life and liberty are values that require protection not so much because of the consequences that may flow from their non-protection, but rather because these are morally worthy values that must be upheld for their own sake."

Recent years have witnessed a surge of interest in human security in both academic and policy realms. The continuing concerns for human security have occupied the space between developmental and military appropriations, as well as between actual foreign policies and radical critiques. To advance the goal of human security the Commission on Human Security (2003) has turned the development- security connectivity into a double mandate of protection and empowerment. "Protection refers to the norms, processes, and institutions that are required to shield people from threats. Empowerment allows people to act and develop their capacity. People enjoying protection can make choices and people who are empowered can make choices... It combines a 'top down' approach- which includes establishing the rule of law, accountable institutions, and social protective policies- with a' bottom up' approach, in which democratic practices emphasize people as actors in defining and implementing their essential freedoms" (Francois Fouinat, 2004: 291). In the orthodox concept of national security the people are at the receiving end. But here the people are both the object and subject of security.

The proponents of human security claim that human security discourse addresses the issues plaguing humanity and endangering its life with indispensable motivating concerns. But it is said, like its predecessors, it is much more concerned with the promotion of an idea, with "shifting the vision" (DFAIT, 1999), than with concrete policy precepts. "As a result, it lacks the edge that might provoke governments and international organizations into actually changing current practices" (Marlies Glasius, 2008: 44). It gives policy makers somewhere to hide, to say 'we' are already doing human security (Kaldor, Martin and Selchow, 2007: 274). Mamphela Ramphele sees it as "taking the sting out of the national security preoccupation", using and directing its energy (Ramphele, 2004: 3). Security like well-being has both subjective and objective aspects. It makes no sense to ignore either. Thus Leaning and Arie's definition of human security (in Harvard Human security Project, 2002) concerns psychological security. Studies indicate that felt insecurity is often unrelated to objective insecurity; indeed, sometimes it is inversely correlated. "The danger arises that a human security agenda could be hijacked by the fears of the rich" (Gasper, 2005: 241). Caroline Thomas (2004) concludes that the key test is whether the integrative analytical agenda of the human security discourse really will focus the attention of the powerful on the connections between freedom from fear and freedom from want, indignity, humiliation and despair.

A concern with physical security of the people is not novel in human security discourse, for that is present in human development. What is novelty is its added focus on basic human needs and stability. In the scintillating words of Gasper (2005: 242): " The human security discourse includes, besides the concept, strong attention to the interconnections between conventionally separated spheres, which helps it to link diverse organizational worlds; and a motivating focus on human vulnerability and human rights that flow for every human being from basic human needs. The 'human security' label for the concept and discourse well matches their contents and purpose, but carries risks: there are other contenders for the label, coming from national security studies and possible distorting forces from the psychological insecurities of the rich". To move toward a holistic practice what is needed is the translation of the precepts and priority concerns of human security discourse into policy frameworks at the national and international level. But the precepts still remain stuck in the compartmentalization between developmental policies and security policies. In the words of Gasper (2005: 242), the human security discourse and label " serves as a promising framework for the 'boundary work', intellectually, emotionally, ethically and politically, that is required in connecting different disciplinary and organizational worlds, and embedding priority human concerns into analytical and policy agendas." It sets the goal post and paves the groundwork for it. Each and every person's state of being 'secure' from inside and outside in political, economic, social, cultural and ethical sphere is the crucible for human security discourse's adoptability in policy making.

The scourge of insecurity, which afflicts many people has already spurted a moral upsurge in the world. Once a moral and philosophical construct, human security as a concept and discourse has touched every human being in transcendence of Westphalian territorial straight- jacket in an interdependent word and has become the main tenets in international politics. "What is most urgently needed now is to develop proposals for translating these ideas into policy practice, to contrast them with current practices, and to nudge policymakers into going beyond the rhetoric of human security" (Marlies Glasius, 2008: 51). Human security provides a grand theoretical vision and design taking different strands of security understood conventionally in terms of sectoral narrowness but as distinguished parts to be woven into a holistic tapestry. It acts as a critical mirror for the governments to study the impacts of their holistic policies in the name of human security on the lives and security of the people. It functions as a political leit motif that can serve as coordination/action oriented guidance for governments.

9
Conclusion

Plagued by deepening crises in terms of environmental catastrophe, climate change, global warming, increasing number of people below poverty line, spread of infectious diseases, death of children, women and poor people out of malnutrition and lack of environmental sustained condition, food insecurity, migration and ever flattening military budget at the cost of other human needs, terrorism and alarming drug and women trafficking, the world has now felt the justifiability of moving many strides away from adhering to the realist paradigm of security defined on Westphalian thematic some centuries ago that security revolves round the state and its military apparatus. The inadequacy of realist or neorealist paradigm of security to meet the multifaceted threats to individual human beings and non human beings has impelled one to move beyond even the most influential arguments of Stephen Walt in 1991 that security studies "should focus on the threat, use and control of military force" (Walt, 1991:211-39). The multifarious nature of security threats and their diverse sources and severity signalled a broadening and deepening phase of conceptualizing security in non-statist terms.

THE WELSCH SCHOOL

The Welsch School of critical security studies

promoted by scholars such as Ken Booth, Richard Wyn Jones and Andrew Linklater and drawn on a tradition of political theory from Immanuel Kant and Karl Marx through to the Frankfurt School theorists such as Adorno, Horkheimer and Habermas began one important alternative line of approach to broadening security in realist terms. "What is most distinctive and valuable about their approach is their desire to radically re-conceive security as the emancipation of individuals and communities from structural constraints" (Burke Anthony, 2007:6). Considered as epochal Booth's article in 1991 on security as emancipation nuanced on a holistic and non-statist approach to security discarding realist emphasis on use or threat of force. His approach aims at:

> the freeing of people (as individuals and groups) from those physical and human constraints which stop them carrying out what they would freely choose to do. War and the threat of war is one of those constraints, together with poverty, poor education, [and] political oppression (Booth, 1991:319).

In consonance with cosmopolitan ideals he argued that "the concept of emancipation shapes strategies and tactics of resistance, offers a theory of progress for society, and gives a politics of hope for a common humanity" (Booth, 2005:181). These postulates seem to have struck a concordant note with feminists' vision of a security founded upon the "the elimination of unjust social relations, including unequal gender relations" and for a reformulation of international relations in terms of the "multiple insecurities" stemming from environmental degradation, poverty and structural violence, rather than the abstract threats to the integrity of states, their interests and "core values" (Tickner, 1992: 127-8). Both these critical theorists and feminists joined the same chorus with an inspirational note for reformulating security in more positive ways.

These pronouncements on reinventing security found a common chord with the idea of human security enunciated by the United Nations Development Programme (UNDP) in 1994 arguing for a shift of the referent object of security from the state to the individual human being. In Booth's view the state is simply a means not an end of security. More radical, revolutionary and significant than is available in most underpinnings of human security is their "insistence on understanding insecurity and achieving security as complex, holistic processes that require not merely the amelioration of particular needs, or the defence of humans against discreet threats contained by time and place, but ongoing structural transformation based on ideas of emancipation, social justice and human progress" (Burke, 2007:7). While Booth stressed on security as a means for emancipation, Wyn Jones argued that "even if a more emancipated order is brought into existence, the process of emancipation remains incomplete. There is always room for improvement..." (Booth, 2005:182). While setting the milestone for emancipation in their intrinsically important conceptualization of security they launched a broadside against those proponents of human security who evince strong predilections for cooption of human security to statist agendas- such as those of Canada, which have reiterated their insistence on return of the state to the primacy of providing the metaphor for national identity and international citizenship, and a liberal governance intervention into the issues of intra-state conflict. At present the human beings remain vulnerable to a compendium of security threats, practices and processes- poor governance, political oppressive regimes, civil conflicts, terrorism, global economy, malnutrition, health hazards, corruption, human rights abuse, gender violence and discrimination, environmental degradation and natural calamities. If these be the referent security objects, "securing them requires work at all these levels including the most systemic and apparently immovable. In turn, security is merely a way-station to something grander and more inspiring" (Burke, 2001:215-39).

The critical security project looks revolutionary to the hilt as it aims at complete transformation of the existing system. But Wyn Jones turns conservative in his enunciation of 'concrete utopias' that his proposal for political transformation must be based on the 'immanent possibilities' for change in the political order. That means, transformation remains half way as it is contingent upon the identification of real possibilities inherent in the system. The crux of the problem is whether the utopias sought are in reality realizable. In his words:

> descriptions of a more emancipated order must focus on realizable utopias...If [critical theorists] succumb to the temptation of suggesting a blueprint for an emancipated order that is unrelated to the possibilities inherent in the present...[they] have no way of justifying their arguments epistemologically. Furthermore, it is highly unlikely that a vision of an emancipated order that is not based on immanent potential will be politically efficacious (Jones Richard Wyn in Booth, 2005: 230).

Booth's is a two pronged vision: first a movement of radical questioning and opening drawing on Horkheimer and Robert Cox where the aim is to avoid the "negative consequences of problem solving theories, particularly the legitimizing and replicating of the regressive aspects of prevailing situations". To Cox the aim of these theories is that they take the world as they find it, with the prevailing social and power relationships and the institutions into which they are organized, as the given framework for action. Without envisaging any change the general aim of the problem solving theory is to make these relationships and institutions work smoothly by dealing effectively with particular sources of trouble. It is like giving importance to the treatment of symptoms not the root causes of diseases. Booth's task "begins with critique: a radical rethinking of the theories and practices that have shaped political life is an essential foundation for the reinvention of human society" (Booth, 2005:263). Second, in resonance of what Wyn Jones envisages in his 'concrete utopias', Booth states that "in the strategic action undertaken to attempt to bring change about" the "latent potentials in situations on which to build political and social progress", must be unravelled. "This means building with one's feet on the ground, not constructing castles in the air" (Ibid).

The task of identifying potentials remains crucial to critical security project. But the question crops up in case the latent potentials do not exist or in the process of actively dying out, what will be the fate of the project? Whether it will lead to denuding the project of its purpose or disabling it or catapulting it to new impetus and imperatives to own responsibility for carrying out the change? In an age when the pores for unearthing the latent potentials are shut down and the clamours for normative change are muzzled, the importance of critical security project remains distinct. "In the face of such obstacles the critical project must think and conceive the unthought and its limiting test ought not to be realism but responsibility" (Burke, 2007: 9). Burke invokes George Orwells'1984 as a metaphor to describe how political party has reduced the scope for human thought and action by removing the concepts from the language until English disappeared in favour of Newspeak. What strikes him "is whether the concept of 'security' itself has not become a form of 'Newspeak' whose hold on people's minds drives away other possibilities of conceiving and enabling human existence on this planet" (Ibid).

A paradoxical note seems to strike the critical security project of this school when realism inveighing which has been its main plank, seeps through to make purpose of the project stuck in the very discovery of immanent potentials for transformation. In a critique of this approach, Burke stated:

There is a residual ontological realism at work in their thinking here that works against the constructivist basis of their theorizing, and it runs the risk of being both disabling and disingenuous. It could be disabling because it risks forcing an emancipatory politics to choke off its efforts of critique and imagination prematurely, to accept the boundaries of the given at some level (Ibid).

The Welsh school understanding of agency and action while aiming at creation of a greater humanistic scope for them has been subject to criticism. For Booth, human agency is a concern of individuals who are constrained and repressed by power, who if secured properly might exercise their agency freely and be "more fully human" (Booth, 2005:183). Power prevents and emancipation frees. Burke objected to this alluding to Foucauldian ideas of power, which is understood as productive of selves, institutions, concepts and social relations and which does not preclude the fact that power can be repressive and take on the form of major dominations. It is a fact of modernity that the thoughts and actions are not free or do not belong to the self. It is important that a space for individual agency and resistance –hence responsibility exists. In the words of Burke, "the focus then shifts to the webs of discourse, concepts and institutional power that shape and constrain the individuals that enable their development, existence or thoughts. Security is such a web, and in this way it is much more than either an end or a means: it is a socio-political field within which life takes form" (Burke, 2007:10). In Foucauldian understanding even as action and thought are limited by a pre-existing system of thought and power, action is, as Hannah Arendt recognized, also radically contingent and creative (Arendt, 1998:231).

This creates scope for positive political transformation. As Arendt views action has no end, which lays upon the individuals a burden of irreversibility and unpredictability. "Given the vast powers of life and death, mobilized in security policy.... The burden it lays upon us is responsibility- not merely for actions in their immediacy and possible consequences, but for the entire political field that they derive from, resist and potentially transform" (Burke, 2007:10).

SECURITIZATION AND DESECURITIZATION: THE COPENHAGEN SCHOOL

The understanding of security and securitization as gleaned from the writings of the Copenhagen school represented by Waever, Jaap de Wilde and Barry Buzan in Schmittian terms is a response to existential threats to survival, the 'special nature' of which 'justifies the use of extraordinary measures to handle them. As Waever argues," traditionally, by saying security, a state representative declares an emergency condition, thus claiming a right to use whatever means are necessary to block a threatening development" (Waever, Jaap de Wilde and Barry Buzan,1998:21). The security discourse and policy often assumes this ontological foundation of security. As Giorgio Agamben and many others have argued, Carl Schmitt's political ontology is a deeply anti-democratic one which reifies sovereignty as the supreme anchor in politics, conceives politics in terms of a stark ontological division between friend and enemy, and legitimates the suspension of the rule of law to facilitate what Schmitt calls the decision, a process in which the sovereign assumes" unlimited authority" to meet "a danger to the existence of the state" (Schmitt Carl, 1985:5).

Holding on to this 'state of exception' while defining security has serious implications and may be used as carte blanche by a state to cross the limits of its authority in the name of security. As Agamben, Judith Butler and Arendt have argued, such approaches have their roots in processes that systematically dehumanized their victims producing lives that were 'bare', 'ungrievable' 'unlivable' and 'superfluous' (Agamben, 1998; Butler,2004). It raises serious doubts as to how securitization theory can be helpful in resignifying security as emancipation. Advocacy of environmental or human security in terms consistent with democratic political processes in a state of normalcy can be stymied. As Roxanne Lynn Doty and Karin Fierke have argued, the Copenhagen School's conceptualization of security blocks the way to human security (Doty Roxanne Lynn, 1998-99:80; Fierke Karin, 2007:110). This is implicit in the way Waever tries to provide an ontological copingstone to what he defines security in his 1995 article. There he states that "as concepts, neither individual nor international security exists":

National security, that is the security of a state, is the name of an ongoing debate, a tradition, an established set of practices... there is no literature, no philosophy, no tradition of security in non-state terms... the concept of security refers to the state (Waever,1995:48-49).

In his view security is to be seen through the lens of national security. He reiterates it when he said that it is the survival of the unit as a basic political unit- the sovereign state-that is the key. Those issues with this undercutting potential must be addressed prior to all others because, if they are not, the state will cease to exist as a sovereign unit and all other questions will become irrelevant. This, then, provides us with a test point, and shows us what is lost if we 'de-compose' the state by individualizing security... even if the challenges can operate on the different components of the state they must still pass through one focus: Do the challenges determine whether the state is to be or not to be (Ibid: 53).

In Burke's view security historically has taken "the form and promise of a metaphysical discourse: an overarching political goal and practice that guarantees existence itself, that makes the possibility of the world possible" (Burke, Beyond security, 2007: 28-9). In Waever's analysis what is clear "is that such a space of possibility is limited to the nation state, precluding the emergence of alternative conceptualizations of political community and existence such as cosmopolitanism or what we might call 'non-ontologies' of primally interconnected being, such as can be found in the philosophy of Emmanuel Levinas and Martin Buber" (Ibid: ch3).

In furtherance of his arguments Waever states that security is a "speech act" that "does not refer to something more real; the utterance is the act" (Waever, 1995: 55). Successful securitization occurs when an audience accepts it as such (Waever, de Wilde and Buzan, 1998: 25). When it is averred that "something is a security problem when elites declare it to be so" (Waever 1995: 55) it means that the meaning of security is contingent, contested and subject to the play of power (Burke, June 2007: 13). Following Foucauldian path Waever argues that "the way to study securitization is to study discourse and political constellations. The relevant question is: When does an argument with this particular rhetorical and semiotic structure achieve a sufficient effect"? (Waever, de Wilde and Buzan, 1998:25). This contradiction in Copenhagen school has prompted Booth to characterize it as "a curious combination of liberal, post-structural and neorealist approaches", which gathers "a bundle of conceptual problems and political issues" (Booth, 2005:271). What remains prominent in the main thrust of arguments about security in Copenhagen school's approach is that nation-state is the ultimate referent and ontological ground for security even if dangers lurk in securitizing some issues.

Dwelling upon societal security as a new referent of security on issues of immigration, intra- state cultural competition, and identity "the Copenhagen School reify claims to collective identity as legitimately securitisable. They do grant that minorities may feel such threats also, but, given their overarching statist ontology, this ultimately reinforces a broadening agenda in which migration and identity issues become read as threats to national security and dealt with coercively" (Burke June 2007: 14). As Bill McSweeney points out Waever et, al. offer "no basis or criteria on which to adjudicate between competing identity claims" which he argues should involve" moral judgments to arbitrate between the competing moral decisions which underlie all claims to collective identity and all security policies which flow from them" (McSweeney Bill,1999:75). Michael Williams also recognizes the ethical danger inherent in the somewhat amoral idea of securitization as "an objective process and possibility" rather than "a normative question" but wishfully hopes that casting security as a speech act enables us to see it as more than "a tool of social explanation", placing "that act within a framework of communicative action and legitimation that links it to a discursive ethics that seeks to avoid the excesses of a decisionist [Schmittian] account of securitization" (Williams Michael C, 2003:521-2).

From the reconstructive end, Booth has been sharply critical of some poststructuralist work on security which he thinks fails to acknowledge, or create space for, an agenda which resignifies security in terms of social justice or emancipation. In his words:

> the poststructuralist approach seems to assume that security cannot be common or positive sum but must always be zero-sum, with somebody's security always being at the cost of the insecurity of others.[Hence] security itself is questioned as desirable goal... They also tend to celebrate insecurity, which I regard as a middle-class affront to the truly insecure (Booth, 2005:270).

While challenging the realist discourses of security based on Orwellian metaphor that sacrifices the security of others, Burke likened the critical security project to human security agenda. The power of statist ontologies of security has led him to say that "it might be better to speak of the human needs and priorities named by security in their specificity". His "concern was and remains, that security's perversion into a metaphysical canopy for the worst manifestations of liberal modernity has been too final and dangerous" (Burke, in fear of security: 308-9).

Further making a dig into the critical security studies project as outlined above, Burke stated his move was not to part with but to provide "alternative critical idioms". In the first place, envisioning security from a holistic perspective needs space, which challenges "the continuing power of political ontologies that connect security, sovereignty, belonging, otherness and violence in ways that for many appear like enduring political facts". This is based "on a suffocating ontology of political subjectivity and community in which all the bodies of citizenry merge with that of the sovereign, with whom they form a body-politic or general will" as conceived by the social contractualists- Hobbes, Locke, and Rousseau. "Such an image of political community ... constitutes an overarching technology of identity and subjectivity that presupposes sameness and is intrinsically hostile to difference. This image seems clear in Hobbes's analogy of the body with society, in which the sovereignty is an artificial soul, concord is health, sedition is sickness, and civil war death (Burke, 2007: 36-41). This seems to provide a basis for the later Schmittian vision of collectivities of friends and enemies engaged in an existential struggle for survival in the international realm. Schmitt also argues that the political is authentic "when a fighting collectivity of people confronts a similar collectivity" (Schmitt Carl, 1996: 28). This is built on Georg Hegel and Clausewitz's views that nations can be strongest "if national character and familiarity with war fortify each other by continual interaction" (Hegel, 1967: 210). Finding this political ontology put human beings in a dangerous space, Burke opines that "security dilemmas, then, are no mere accidents of military competition; they are coded into our very being' (quoted from Burke, June 2007: 18).

In the second move Burke argues for shifting security as an end or metaphysical promise to security as a set of practices and technologies. He depicts " security as a 'political technology' which combines two linked modes of power: totalizing power that works at the level of states and populations, where discourses of national identity and purpose, and systems of macroeconomic management, join with foreign and strategic policy; and individualizing power which works on people's bodies and minds" (Burke, June 2007: 18).

COUNTER-ARGUMENTS MOUNTED AGAINST CRITICAL THEORISTS

The first objection is the argument that critical theorists understate, ignore or wish away the importance of state. But in no way does the claim that the principal institutions of world politics are socially constructed imply this. Many critical scholars recognize that the state has reached a historical high point, and that it presents a powerful object of loyalty and aspiration that needs perhaps to be taken more seriously (Walker, 1990, Ayoob, 1997). Others have put emphasis on examining the way in which the substantive and normative content of the concept of 'state sovereignty' may have changed and be changing (Barkin and Cronin, 1994; Biersteker and Weber, 1996).

According to Krause, "a focus on identities and identity formation does not mean that critical theorists believe identities are infinitely malleable, and can be changed like sets of clothing" (1998: 318). As Mearsheimer puts the charge: "the key...is to alter state identity radically or more specifically, to transform how states think about themselves and their relationship with other states... states must stop thinking of themselves as solitary egoists, and instead develop a powerful communication ethos (Mearsheimer, 1994/95: 39, 41). The most extreme version of this is the accusation that critical approaches represent pure idealism- the belief that ideas are the driving force of history, and that if our ideas are simply changed, so too will be the world. "This misinterprets the argument that the process of constituting political subjects (such as states) endows them with identities and interests that are not just given. The only claim advanced is that interest must be endogenized[Wendt's term] in our theories: that the interest of political subjects such as states are not given by structures, but are generated by social processes of interaction between them" (Krause,1998; Wendt,1994).

A third attack on critical methodology accuses it of 'subjectivism', colloquially presented as the 'anything goes argument'. Mearsheimer quotes Ashley to the effect that "there are no constraints, no fixed meanings, no secure grounds, no profound secrets, no final structures or limits to history...there is only interpretation" (Mearsheimer, 1994/95:41). As argued by James Der Derian, that to acknowledge that " meaning endlessly differs and is deferred" does not lead one "to claim that there is no truth, no values, no reality" (Der Derian,1992:6). " The acceptance that our knowledge (as scholars) of the subjects, structures and practices of world politics is not objective, does not even lead all scholars to a rejection of naturalist models for science. Some, such as Wendt, Barnett and Katzenstein, " fully endorse the scientific project of falsifying theories against evidence", and argue that " the research practices of scholars like Ruggie, Kratochwit and others identified with constructivist or interpretative approaches converge substantially with those advocated by mainstream scholars... [and] methodological differences appear to be small' (Wendt, 1995:75, Jepperson et al., 1996:67-8). Krause states that "a critical methodology does not imply rejection of the idea that these are arbitrated against some external reality rather than against social actors' understanding their world" (Krause, 1998: 320).

The fourth argument concerns critical theorists' contextual understanding and practical knowledge. Knowledge of historical facts of some centuries back has all embedded interstate interactions in a complex web of ideas that gives practical and shifting content to understandings of interests, and to the identities of states themselves (Barkin and Cronin, 1994; Hall and Kratochwil, 1993, Ruggie, 1993, Biersteker and Weber, 1996). Since human agents and political actors are engaged in constructing their world and their future, scientific models of explain- predict-control are at best misguided, and at worst pernicious (Fay,1975). Robert Cox's rejection of prediction is not to be misunderstood. In his framework of problem- solving theory, he takes the political order as fixed and works within this with a determinist if- then logic that denies much scope for human agency (Cox, 1986). To claim then that his failure to make predictions is a weakness of critical theory is to miss the forest for the wood.

The final argument points to the central assumptions of a critical approach, which do not commit any individual scholar to a particular political position. But the acceptance that world politics is not static, and that its structures and identities are constructed, and is subject to possibility of change remains the mainstream of critical theorists. One cannot disagree with this that socially constructed structures are deeply entrenched and unlikely to change rapidly. In this 'unlikeliness of change' syndrome how the emancipation project of critical theorists is to be translated remains the greatest challenge to them as "the state presents a compelling resolution to modern political problems that should not be transcended or consigned to the dustbin of history" (Krause,1998:322). In a similar vein Ronald Jepperson, Alexander Wendt and Peter Katzenstein note, " because states remain the predominant legitimated 'actors' in the current world system, theories of national-security-in-international-anarchy remain dominant, building around world-cultural reifications of state sovereignty and actorhood" (Jepperson et al., 1996:72). While redefining security whether it is possible on the part of the critical theorists to downplay the imperatives of the metaphorical presentation of state of nature and its contractarian account of world politics remains crucial to their emancipatory project. "The challenge for critical scholarship, however, is to ensure that our theoretical conceptions of what is possible and desirable are not bound within rigid intellectual straight-jackets that place us far behind policy makers' and political actors' appreciation of the complexities and potential of the contemporary world, or that prevent us from thinking creatively and seriously about how to resolve complex contemporary problems of war and peace" (Krause, 1998:323).

If Critical Theory is the most serious intellectual challenge to realism and even more significant than idealism or postmodernism, and, considers "extending community beyond the nation-state as its most important problem", then it is inconceivable how reconstruction of society or carrying the nation-state beyond border and recognizing community or group as new referents alternative to state, could take place without paying sufficient attention to ecology or the impending environmental crisis- which challenges the dominant established frame of mind about security, social way of life, economic and political thinking and state. It is not that the critical theorists have failed to mention the ecological crisis or the environmental movement as sources of emancipatory change they have not yet incorporated the many insights offered by ecological thought into their theory.

The debate controverted over the acceptability of the preponderant role of environmental scarcity and degradation causing violence continues and has not been built into a theoretical framework challenging the established International Relation, let alone accepted by the emancipatory theorists. The logic, reason, explanation and findings of the proponents of 'environment and conflict' paradigm could have provided new grist to the emancipatory theorists' overall design to bring liberation to mankind. How is that possible without looking into nature which is intrinsically woven with human's way of thinking and living? This lacuna could be well bridged and environmental security could be well accepted into the mainstream of emancipatory change.

Environmental crisis accentuated predominantly by the western way and style of life, pattern of development and economic thinking is also highly related to future generations' right to the resources of the planet, to the problem of intergenerational and interspecies equity and accountability. That means concern for environmental security challenges the very way and style of life, pattern of development and economic thinking. The realist paradigm of security confined to the spatial and temporal limits comes in for questioning, because it has excluded the others (not only the present generation, but also the future generations, nature, living and non living) as the external fixated on a zero sum syndrome of pursing self-interests. Recognition of this problematiq as a priority concern for solution could be a starting point and resources of emancipatory theory.

ECOLOGICALISING EMANCIPATORY MISSION

An ecological approach to International Relation Theory and global governance rests on alternative ontologies, epistemologies, and ethical/ political prescription. The mechanical view of nature and the attribution of the 'Other' to it need to be reconsidered. Nature is finite, whole, an interdependent body connecting all living matter in a cyclical and non-hierarchical manner. It is more often a function of cooperation within and between species. Diversity and timelessness are the other attributes of nature. Diversity allows nature to withstand the demise of individual life forms while maintaining its grandeur, beauty and bounty. Timelessness shows life is not imposed or spontaneously created but is undissociable from time. It is a long, slow and cumulative process. Recognition of longevity supports the assumption of mutual aid in nature. Thus it rejects the traditional utilitarianism, and mechanical view of nature, and ontologies of conflict. What Pope John Paul II said in the Conference of Roman Catholic bishops in the Philippines and Dominican Republic in 1988 deserves excerption: "... One cannot use with impunity the different categories of beings, whether living or inanimate – animals, plants and natural elements-simply as one wishes, according to one's economic needs. On the contrary, one must take into account the nature of each being and its mutual connection to an ordered system, which is precisely the cosmos" (Origins: NC Documentary Quoted in Engel Ronald J. 1990:4). It advocates a harmonization with physical surroundings admonishing against imposition of structures of domination. The principle of classical theory of democracy, freedom, individual fulfillment and equal treatment are vindicated by ecological ethics. Instead of looking the world of nature as the other, a more coordinated view of the world embracing both the world of nature and the world of humanity (Toulmin Stephen.1982:255-56) is what the ecological approaches insist on. "To deny moral value to ecosystem because they are not integrated in the same way as centralized individual organisms is to make a category mistake. In thinking about the value of social and biotic communities we should be concerned for a matrix of interconnections between centers, not for a single center" (Rolston Holmes,1988:174).

Thus, the mechanical view of the world and nature must be replaced by an organicistic one (Merchant Carolyn, 1980), which reads the world not as a soulless machine subjected to cause and effect, and repetitive patterns – sine qua non of scientific investigations, positivism and behaviouralism. To confine the study to the limitation of cause and effect syndrome means to fall short of understanding the complexity of nature and its inextricable connections with the evolution of life in a timelessness frame. Not that these scientific investigations, assumptions and methods are not helpful, but should not constitute the principal means of understanding or attributing meaning without organicism being attached with mysticism (Biehl Janet,1991:89-90). The ecological project calls for a rejection of the detached object of study, objectivity and mechanism forming the core of the Cartesian – Newtonian dominance in social sciences in favour of subjectivity.

The ecological teleology points to the significance of historicity and dialecticism in understanding the current human conditions as the dynamic ebb and flow and product of synergistic forces through time. This means to get rid of Westphalian straightjacket (Buzan and Little,2001:25) -the prevalence of ahistorical bias in formulating the concept of international system reinforced by the dominance of an economist, natural science based understanding of the social world.

"A silent acceptance of this cultural bias" the imposed dominant economic and political thinking of western paradigm—" is virtually universal, not only within the context of a Western centered parochialism, but also among IR scholars who have tragically abandoned their own quite different historical and cultural traditions" (Ibid: 26). Seducing all cultural diversities, civilisational essences, regional specificities and bioregimes' particularities and their coordinated interconnections woven into the warp and woof of cosmos, into wearing the western straitjacket is to block communication of the mainstream International Relations with other disciplines and snap man's eternal chord with the cosmos. It calls for a multi disciplinary and multidimensional approach that will travel beyond microeconomic analogies, handling forces that are much more elusive and much less amenable to behavioural manipulation than the heavily magnified state. Awakening it from the Westphalia Procrustean bed, it should be studied as an historical action and a social actor among many. Thus, the ecological vision includes a system cosmology, a theory of democracy of global structure of governance, a new scientific epistemology supplementing behaviouralism and Newtonian objectivity, a strategy for global peace and security on the basis of cooperation and a recognition of intergenerational equity and accountability, and interspecies responsibility.

Given the sources of many of the new threats stemming from complex systems both natural and human made, and diversifying away from the state into diverse, regional and local in character, the monolithic statist westphalian approach quite familiar with realist paradigm seems to outstrip the solution. "Global environmental governance emerges because the spatial scale of the state is inadequate in dealing with the scales of environmental change, and thus, the practices of governance move towards regional and global levels and at the same time towards local levels in response" (Paterson Matthew, 1999: 795).

The ecological project of governance envisions a world of small interacting communities, what, as mentioned earlier, Bookchin named it municipal confederalism or what Karliner termed it as 'grassroots globalization' (Karliner Joshua, 1997: ch7), which means a myriad locally organized, but transnationally networked, social movements and NGOs are becoming increasingly mobilized to resist the dominant practices of TNCs and states. To create alternative forms of the western dominated political economy the most common phrase used is the 'commons'. It is defined as a site of ecologically sustainable and socially just political economy. This means the construction of a myriad small scale societies organized around commons regimes through resistance to the globalizing practices of TNCs, states and international development agencies (Paterson M. 2000).

The western picture of human beings as selfish, atomistic, individualistic, acquisitive, profligate, aggressive and conflictual always in quest for a commodious living, inordinate life pattern needs to be redefined. "The excessive use of nature and its resources in the North is a principal block to greater justice in the world... A retreat of the rich from the over consumption is thus a necessary first step towards allowing space for improvement of the lives of an increasing number of people (quoted in Guha Ramachandra.2000: 370). To reorient society and its economy towards a more sustainable path is necessary recognizing the future generations' right to life and without severing the organic bond between the present and future generation and the living and non-living. As mentioned earlier, about the speech situation by the critical theorist, the ecological ethics emphasizes engaging the sectorised 'Other' in democratic dialogue which requires "abandoning the notion that nature and social are distinct. The social and natural are inextricable. We constitute nature through our practices at the same time we constitute the social world. Thus, an ecologically informed political discourse will be one that recognizes the environmental ethics embedded in all political worldviews" (Barkdull John.2000:362). What will define the individual is not acquisitive individualism and consumerism. Springing from the limitless and profligate acquisitiveness of market political economy driven way of life–contribution of both science and the liberal possessive individualism of Hobbes and Locke–the concomitant decline in human beings' sensibility to other humans, living and non-living beings, the human beings have been on a rapacious rampage that cuts at the very root of the common organic bond with the whole of creation and the very survival of all. Acceptance of ecological ethics and enlargement of self that includes all will certainly usher in an atavistic change in human approach, vision and way of life. As Aldo Leopold has pointed out, ethics is the recognition of constraints put on an individual as a member of the community, and the ecological ethic simply enlarges the boundaries of the community to include soils, waters, plants and animals or collectively the land (Leopold Aldo. 1966:262).

The Critical theorist should take note of the need for an overhaul of the western pattern of development, way of life and social philosophy based on acquisitive individualism and consumerism–a wrong notion of providing happiness. So far as restructure of a society remains uppermost to the critical theorist, different from the dominant western universalized one, the question is not just about a technocratic, or expertise response because these technocratic or expertise knowledge emanate from the some rich North powers. "Ecologists along with Critical Theorists cannot escape the fact that law and knowledge, rules and technicity, are mere expression of power over nature, power over men and women"(Laferriere Eric.1996:72). Critical theorists while emphasizing the significance of studying historicity should not be oblivious of the fact that science and liberal political theory share the same ontological foundation when "Newtonian image of particles in motion was the guiding metaphor in the emerging liberal conception of possessive individualism" (Litfin KarenT.2000:130).

As mentioned earlier, the emancipatory goal of the Critical Theory was to deconstruct and expose the imposition of dominant hegemonic discourse of the mainstream of International Relation and suggest the possibilities of new ones different from the existing one. Apart in all the approaches such as dependency theory, feminism, world order model projects and postmodernism, is the resistance theory against the cultural hegemony and western straitjacket of the mainstream International Relation. The Critical Theory as seen in Cox's approach travels beyond the limits of problem solving and embraces an historical approach to contemporary hegemony based on Gramscian notion of historic bloc (Cox).

Equally evident in dependency theory and in the

literature on structuration is the significance of a genuinely global approach to order, recognizing the fluidity of space and evolutionary character of time. The insistence on reproductive social structure and the ontological skepticism in the latter case is quite evident in critical theory.

Postmodernism's anti foundationalism and relativism led by Foucault stress on historically specific conditions in which knowledge is generated. The dominant perspective in IR is socially constructed by the people (Foucault Michael,1970). Ecological theory's deconstructed study of nature as it is in terms of biological imperatives can add to the Critical theory's revolt against the established pattern of thinking.

Ecological approach addresses all those normative positions and contains all elements required by an emancipatory theory of International Relation. Ignoring the organic relationship that exists between human beings and nature to go ahead toward the emancipatory goal the critical theory unwittingly endorses the mainstream view of human nature. The construction of identity with the mainstream of IR so far as the realist and liberal view of human being's nature is concerned, the critical theory cannot get rid of this if ecological approach is not taken into consideration. It will remain halfway in its emancipatory mission.

In this sense ecological approach gets at the very foundation of emancipatory theory by pointing to the relationship between control of nature and the control of man/woman. It does not keep itself limited to defense of any constituency or identity. Freedom is no longer confined to any group at the cost of nature. The 'Other' is no longer the external, or spiritless matter–whether living or non-living but the enlarged itself. In other words, the emancipatory approach cannot be emanicipatory without the vision of an enlarged or universal self as suggested earlier by the ecological theory. The identity with the dominant mainstream of International Relation against which Critical Theory rises in revolt can be dissipated only when emancipatory approach puts stress on a moral reconstruction of human beings that will see in its enlarged self the existence of the nature–the vision of 'Basudheiva Kutumbakam' the whole world is a family – the vision required of humanbeings. Constancy, fixity, superiority of culture, clash of civilization or permanence, and spatial exclusion associated with the mainstream of International Relation are considered irrational. Ecological approach addresses a different kind of essentialism that is divested of linearity, hierarchy and elitism evoking the notion of natural law. Everything is in constant flux in this timelessness frame into which both human beings and nature are woven with the warf and woof of cooperation, and coordination. Thus, the political project for human kind is built on the foundation of these ecological imperatives, as outlined above. Nature is not mere a bundle of lifeless raw materials and the sacredness and holism attached to it by ecological epistemology can emanate from a renewed vision and perspectives- at present lacking in emancipatory approaches of Critical Theory. Ecological theory subsumes the critical theory offering the vision of an enlarged self, timelessness of evolutionary process, subjectivity existence in diversity and democratic global governance on the basis of Bookchin's municipal confederalism or grassroots globalization. Emancipatory theory seems to have jettisoned the concept of peace aware of its hegemonic and ordering connotations. The non-military threats diversifying away from state and stemming from environmental degradation can be addressed by ecological approach, by ensuring environmental security. It is not synonymous with environmental conflict. It is founded on the confluence of sustainable development, recognition of future generations both living and non-living' s right to life and ecological ethics of enlarged self, renewed vision and an overhaul of the dominant view of inordinate and profligate life style. That nonmilitary threats can be addressed by non-military means can herald positive peace, which is not mere absence of intra state or interstate conflict or violence. It is creation of positive conditions born of ecological ethics, renewed vision about life and universal self without sacrificing the freedom and subjectivity of any whether men, women, future generations or nature. This is what the ecological approach stresses on to be the guiding metaphor for the emancipatory mission of Critical Theory.

The dominant paradigm of environmental security and conflict as conceived by Homer Dixon and his colleagues from an array of empirical data that will occur among and between and within states due to environmental scarcity of resources seems to appeal more to traditional security and its military apparatus. "In general, many scholars sense that environmental degradation will ratchet up the level of stress within national and international society increasing the likelihood of many different kinds of conflict and impeding the development of cooperative venture" (Dixon, 1991:3). "It recognizes sovereignty as legitimate and accords an important role to the state. The focus on war and conflict is consistent with traditional understanding of security" (Smith Heather A.2000:4). A secret report commissioned by influential Pentagon defence adviser Andrew Marshall and obtained by the Observer "predicts that abrupt climate change could bring the planet to the edge of anarchy as countries develop a nuclear threat to defend and secure dwindling food, water and energy supplies. The threat of global stability eclipses that of terrorism". According to the other members of the secret report, Peter Schwartz,

CIA consultant and Doug Randall, "By 2020 catastrophic shortages of water and energy supply will become increasingly harder to overcome, plunging the planet into war" (The Observer, New York Sunday, 22 February 2004). Not only that newspapers in mid-April 2007 reported that the US Congress was poised to ask for a National Intelligence Estimate(NIE) on the 'national security' implications of human –induced climate change. A group of retired US army and naval leaders in their 'write up' for CNA Corporation stressed on a call for an NIE on climate change and security (CNA Corporation.2007). The Sydney Morning Herald stated that "American politicians are so concerned about the threats posed by the effects of global warming, they are legislating to elevate it to an official defence issue". It expresses the fear that "climate change could trigger new humanitarian crises and force countries to go to war over diminishing water and energy resources" (Allard Tom, Mark Forbes and agencies. April 2007:1). These reports are emblematic of and consistent with the narrow and traditional concept of US national security founded on Hobbes and Clausewitz.

The wide ranging ramifications of environmental change on entire humanity transcending the traditional borders and sovereignty point to the utter inadequacy of state as a guarantor of human beings. National security defined in narrow terms seems to be of little use. In a landmark article Jessica Tuchman-Mathews recommends that national security be broadened to include "resource, environmental, and demographic issues" because the assumptions and institutions that have governed international relations in the postwar era are a poor fit with these new realities... The once sharp dividing line between foreign and domestic policy is blurred, forcing governments to grapple in international fora with issues that were contentious enough in the domestic arena (Tuchman-

Mathews Jessica, 1989:162).

In a speech at the London School of Economics in November 1995, Robert McNamara, another former United States Secretary of State for Defense said " The international system that relies on the national use of military force as the ultimate guarantor of security, and the threat of its use as the basis of order, is not the only possible one. To seek a different system (based on collective security) is no longer the pursuit of an illusion, but a necessary effort towards a necessary goal" (McNamara, quoted in Parkin Sara, 1999: 43). If environment remains as the potential source of conflict in the whole context of security, defense and foreign policy and comes as the greatest threat to human beings, it will form the ground among the nations for meeting satisfactorily the challenges through concerted collective action. In the scintillating words of Sara Parkin: "The environment would make an ideal diplomat. Whatever the colour of your skin, whatever god you worship, whatever hideous wrong you or your ancestors may have done to me or my ancestors, each single person on this earth has more or less identical requirements when it comes to air to breath, water to drink and food to eat. What could be more fundamental ground to meet on that that?" (Ibid: 44).

The nature of many global environmental problems such as climate change that defies artificial boundaries reflects the challenges to the established notion of sacrosanct sovereignty. "Climate change cannot be assimilated to realist security paradigm based on the social contract, and we can imagine a nightmarish future in which not only are mitigation efforts stillborn but states become garrisons against the unpredictable" (Burke, June 2007:19). The multifarious security threats from climate change making the realist theory anachronistic must look to deconstructive critical approaches to security for advocating cosmopolitan discourses and institutions and at the same time must promote reconstructive approaches to grapple with the unequal but shared burden of responsibility with a new look at the Newtonian- Cartesian view of the universe for the planet that the emancipatory vision of critical theory fails to capture. Thus, the traditional and critical security studies get a profound challenge from the climate change.

COMPREHENSIVE/HUMAN SECURITY

Human security and comprehensive security are multifaceted conceptions of security that include environmental issues without privileging them. They recognize interconnectedness between the numerous sources of insecurity. Comprehensive human security according to Arthur Westing:

> has two intertwined components: political security on the one hand (with its military, economic, and social/humanitarian sub-components); and environmental security on the other (with its protection-oriented and utilization-oriented sub-components). To achieve comprehensive security requires the satisfaction of both the political and the environmental sub-components – neither of these two major sub-components being either attainable or sustainable unless the other is satisfied as well (Westing, 1989: 129).

In Westing's conceptualization of security the role of state is not undermined. It is assumed "that the states have the obligation to protect their citizens not only from military threats to their security, but also from the threats of socially unjust and environmentally unhealthy living conditions" (Ibid: 129-130). In the Canadian Government vision, human security is intertwined with state security.

The proponents of human security are divided over its dichotomous broad versus narrow conceptualization. Krause, Mack and Macfarlane represent the narrow focus of human security. All three argue forcefully for the inclusion of violence into traditional security thinking and point to the normative success of violent based human security initiatives. Mack launches a broadside against realism's failure to recognize the state as a possible internal aggressor, as well as its inherent inability to explain the 95% of all warfare that is now within rather than between states.

In their broad conceptualization of security, Learning, Alkire, Thakur, Axworthy, Bajpai, Hampson, and Winslow and Eriksen all suggest that human security means something more than safety from violent threats. They have included in their conceptualization a wider range of issues such as poverty, disease and environmental disasters. While shifting the referent of security they have included all these issues threatening individuals under the canopy of human security. Learning in his analysis includes the social, psychological, political and economic aspects of vulnerability under the rubric of human security. Wilson and Erikson moving beyond the broad-versus-narrow debate pointed to the social and cultural contexts in which people experience insecurity and how this is dealt with through social institutions.

As seen from these conceptions of human security the proponents are not concerned with definitional or theoretical clarity. To many, human security has utility only if it can be catered to address policy problems. Hampson adds that by refocusing our attention on the issues affecting the most people, human security gives political voice to the otherwise politically marginalized. This puts emphasis on addressing the broader context of vulnerability. Acharya sees human security as a rational response to the 'globalizing' of international policy. Apart from economic growth, political stability, and invasion by external powers, the governments at various scales must look at a wider mandate. Human security is nothing but the underlying rationale for this new mandate.

Most importantly, many proponents like to address human security as a framework or working hypothesis in which to revaluate the traditionally established understanding and norms of sovereignty. Newman points out that human security reverses our common understanding of how to link the citizen to the state. Traditional security sees state legitimacy looking outward to the international system for power, recognition, and independence. Human security forces the state to look inward to the 'people from where it draws its legitimacy'. Thus, human security is an inward looking approach to address the internal problems within a state affecting individuals. Hubert suggests that any conceptualization of human security must have a response to genocide, the necessary consequence of which is rethinking of sovereignty. Mack questions the sanity of clinging to principles of sovereignty in the face of 'legitimate' genocidal regimes.

Critiques pounced upon human security in two forms: theoretically based and policy oriented. From a theoretical angle it is simply the shifting of referent from state to the individual. By this it "proliferates the concept without analytic value- the more harms that are labelled security threats, the harder it is to study the relations between them" (Owen Taylor, 2004: 378).

The second line of criticism dwells upon the potentially unmanageable policy consequences of human security. The first charge is that labelling all potential harms to the individual security threats makes prioritizing political action impossible. Krause, Buzan, Macfarlane, and Mack rightly point out that 'security' is the label given to the highest priority issues-again, making everything a security threat in effect prioritizes nothing.

The second critique points to the consequences of securitizing development and humanitarian assistance. Krause asks whether making education a security issue facilitates more effective action, or instead leads to militaristic solutions for problems of social welfare.

Third, the consequence of linking suffering in other countries to our own national security was raised. "Many critics, however, most notably from the humanitarian relief community, warn that the policy consequences of such a connection are potentially devastating. Making this connection could mean, for example, that poverty alleviation in likely 'terrorist breeding grounds' would be prioritized over aid to our ideological allies. Moreover, it could also further the militarization of humanitarian assistance that we have seen in Afghanistan and Iraq" (Owen, 2004:379).

Other critiques raised the claim that 'security' is inextricably linked to violence (Paris, 2001), and Thomas points to the Marxist perspective that human security is simply a repackaging of a liberal humanitarian order.

Thakur and Mack in their rebuttals in the guise of attacks against realism are of the view that "the principle that absolute faith in the state is the only weapon against the 'mean enemies of the international jungle', is antiquated and grossly out of step with the reality of the globalized threats we face" (Ibid). In addition, the military focus of 'national security' is used to divert massive funds to an industrial complex that is not capable of addressing nonviolent harms.

On analytic perspective both Mack and Paris argue that preparing a broad list of socioeconomic conditions under the umbrella of human security conflates independent and dependent variables, making causal analysis impossible. "Measuring human security as a unified concept is indeed plagued with analyzed capturing the same phenomenon on both sides of the equation. However, neither the narrow conception of human security nor the traditional conception of security is immune from such critique; both are susceptible to the similar problem of endogeneity" (Ibid: 380).

On policy utility: Too much is made of the implications of 'securitizing everything'. Shifting the focus away from the state, as Mack points out, was simply a means of dealing with harms that may not threaten the state as an identity but do threaten the lives of its citizens. Second, nobody is suggesting that securitizing necessarily means militarizing. In fact, it is the very assumption that security is solely a militaristic endeavor that human security attempts to challenge.

A THRESHOLD BASED DEFINITION

Owen provides a hybrid definition making a compromise between both broad and narrow proponents. "Instead of being pre-chosen, threats would be included on the basis of their actual severity. All would be considered, but only those that surpass a threshold of severity would be labeled threats to human security" (Owen, 2004: 382). Such a threshold-based definition has two parts:

First, human security must recognize that there is no difference between deaths from floods, communicable disease, or war, as all preventable harms could potentially become threats to human security. A complete coverage of a vast array of threats by which people are affected is analytically and practically impossible. The definition must be selective without limiting harms that threaten a large number of people. This is in consonant with what the Commission on Human Security (2002) defines human security as "the protection of the vital core of all human lives from critical and pervasive threats". Thus making the referent object 'all human lives' puts the focus on the individual while at the same time indicating a universalism in the mandate. Reference to 'critical and pervasive threats' establishes severity, immediacy, and scope.

The second part of the definition addresses the issue of conceptual clarity. A definition must be able to separate and categorize all possible threats for meaningful analytic study.

Regardless of the exact wording used, the idea of a threshold-based conceptualization of human security requires a degree of sacrifice from both narrow and broad proponents. Narrow proponents have to recognize that violence falls into only one of the six human security categories, personal security.

At the other end of the spectrum, broad proponents have to recognize that, while important, not all development concerns should be labelled threats to human security. When they do, we must have both a monitoring system that can identify them and a security infrastructure that can effectively mitigate the threat. In the words of Owen:

> By recognizing that the point of human security is to bring the resources and prescience of the security infrastructure to a new set of issues, it limits the issues that are raised to this top-priority level. For analytic clarity, it delineates these threats in disciplinary categories. It is naïve to believe that any one definition of human security will become the norm, as there are already so many. However,

> the idea of human security as a threshold beyond which a wide range of issues become something similar, something requiring the unified policy response granted to security threats, can be applied to any of the existing conceptualizations (Owen, 2004: 384).

Bibliography

REFERENCES

CHAPTER 1 : SECURITY AND SECURITIZATION

Abrahamsen, Rita& Michael C.Wiiliams, 2006. "Privatization, Globalization and the Politics of Protection in South Africa" in jef Huysmans, Andrew Dobson& Raja Prokhovnik, eds, The Politics of Protection: Sites of Insecurity and Political Agency. London: Routledge (34-37).

Acharya, Amitav (1992) "Regionalism and Regime security in the Third world: Comparing the Origins of the ASEAN and the GCC," In Brian job (ed). The Insecurity Dilemma. Boulder: Lynne Rienner, pp. 143-164.

Adams, W.M. (1990) Green Development: Environment and Sustainability in the Third World. London: Rutledge.

Adams, John, 1995. Risk. London: University of College London Press.

Adler, Emanuel (1992) "The Emergence of Cooperation: National Epistemic Communities and the International Evolution of the Idea of Nuclear Arms Control, "International Organization, 46:2, pp. 101-146.

______ (1995) "Seizing the Middle Ground," unpublished manuscript.

Adler Emanuel and Michel j. Barnett (1996) "Governing Anarchy: A Research Agenda for the Study of Security Communities, "Ethics and International Affairs, 10, pp. 63-98.

Agamben, Giorgio, 2005. State of Exception. Chicago, IL: University of Chicago Press.

Allison, Graham (1971) The Essence of Decision: Explaining the Cuba Missile Crisis, Boston: Little, Brown

Anderson, Benedict (1983) Imagined communities-Reflections on the Origins and Spread of Nationalism. London: Verso Publishers.

Anderson Kim, and Richard Blackhurst (1993) Regional Integration and the Global Trading System. Hemel Hempstead: Harvester Wheatsheaf.

Appiah, Kwame Anthoony (1994) "Identity, Authenticity, Survival: Multicultural Societies and Social Reproduction "in Amy Gutmann (ed) Multiculturalism: Examining the Politics of Recognition. Princeton: Princeton University Press, pp. 149-163.

Arendt, Hannah (1958). The Human Condition. Chicago: University of Chicago Press.

______ (1959) "On Humanity in Dark Times: Thoughts About Lessing "an address on accepting the Lessing Prize of the Free City of Hamburg (originally in German), Reprinted in Men in Dark Times. New York: Pelican Books, 1973.

Arriff, Mohammed (1996) "Institutionalization of Economic Cooperation in the Asia – Pacific Region with special reference to APEC," Dokkyo International Review, 9, pp. 177-192.

Armstrong, David (1993) Revolution and World order: The Revolutionary State in International Order. Oxford: Clarendon Press.

Austin, J.L (1975[1962] How To Do Things with Words. 2d ed. Oxford: Oxford University Press.

Ayoob, Mohammed (1995) The Third World Security Predicament: State Making, Regional Conflict, and International System. Boulder: Lynne Rienner.

Baker, Tom,2000. "Insuring Morality", Economy and Society 29(4): 559-577.

Baldwin, David A "The Concept of Security" Review of International Studies 23:1 (1997), pp. 5-26.

Balzacq, Thierry, 2005. "The Three Faces of Securitization: Political Agency, Audience and Context", European Journal of International Relations 11(2).

Barnett, Michael (1995) "Sovereignty, Nationalism, and Regional Order in the Arab States System." International Organization 49:3, pp. 479 – 510.

Barnett, Robert W. (1984) Beyond War: Japan's Concept of Comprehensive National Security. Washington, D.C.: Pergamon / Brassey's.

Baudrillard, Jean (1994[1992]) The Illusion of the end (translation of L' Illusion dela fin: ou La greve des evenenments .Paris: Galilee, 1992), translated by Chris Turner. Stanford: Stanford University Press. (An alternative translation by Charles Dudas , York University , Canada ,was made available chapter by chapter during 1993-1994 on the internet through CTHEORY .)

Beck, Ulrich, 2002. "The Terrorist Threat: World Risk Society Revisited", Theory, Culture and Society 19(4): 39-45.

Beck, Ulrich, 2003. "The Silence of Words: On Terror and War", Security Dialogue 34(3).

Benedic, Richard Elliot (1991) Ozone Diplomacy – New Direction in Safeguarding the Planet. Cambridge: Harvard University Press.

Berdal, Mats& David Malone, eds, 2000. Greed and Grievance: Economic Agendas in Civil Wars. London: Lynne Rienner.

Bernstein, Peter,1998. Against the Gods: The Remarkable Story of Risk. New York: John Wiley and Sons.

Bigo, Didier (1994) "The European Internal Security Field Stakes and Rivalries in a Newly Developing Area of Police Intervention," in Malcolm Anderson and Monica den Boer (edt), Policing Across National Boundaries. London: Pinter Publishers, pp. 161-173.

______ (1996) Polices en reseaux : I ' experience europeene, Paris: Presses de science Po.Blaikie, Piers,Terry Cannon,Ian Davis, and Ben Wisner (1994) At Risk: Natural Blaikie, Piers, Terry Cannon, Ian Davis, and Ben Wisner (1994) At Risk : Natural Hazards, People's vulnerability and Disasters, London : Routledge.

Bigo, Didier, 2000. " When Two become One: Internal and External Securitizations in Europe", in Morten Kelstrup& Michael C. Williams, eds, International Relations Theory and the Politics of European Integration, Power, Security and Community. London: Routledge.

Bigo, Didier, 2002. "Security and Immigration: Toward a Critique of the Governmentality of Unease", Alternatives 27(1).

Boge, Volker (1992) "Proposal for an Analytical Framework to Grasp Environment Conflicts, "Zurich, ENCOP (Environment and Conflicts project) Occasional Paper.

Bonditti, Philippe, 2004. "From Territorial Space to Networks: A Foucaldian Approach to the Implementation of Biometry", Alternatives 29(4).

Booth, Ken (1979) Strategy and Ethnocentrism, London, Croom Helm.

——— (1991) "Security and Emancipation, "Review of International Studies, 17.4., pp.313-327

____ (1994) "Dare Not to Know: International Relations Theory Versus the Future "in Ken Booth and Steve Smith (eds.) International Political Theory Today. London Polity Press, pp 328-350.

______(1995) "Human Wrongs and International Relations" International Affairs, 71:1, pp 103-122

______(2004). "Realities of Security: Editor's Introduction", International Relations 18(1).

_______(2005a). Critical Security Studies and World Politics. London: Lynne Rienner.

Bourdieu, Pierre (1991 [1982] Language and Symbolic Power, Cambridge: Harvard University Press (mostly a translation of Ce que parler veut dire.) Paris: Libreire Atheme Fayard, 1982.

———— (1996) Response at seminar on "Fin-de-Siecle Power, Cambridge: Harvard University Press (mostly a translation of Ce que Parler veut dire).Paris: Libreire Artheme Fayard, 1982.

______ (1996) Response at seminar on "Fin-de-Siecle Intellectuals: Looking Back, Looking Forward," University of California at Berkeley, April.

Brauch Hans Gunter. 2008. "Reconceptualizing Security: Global Environmental and Climate Change as New Security Dangers and Concerns", paper presented at the 49th ISA Annual Convention". San Francisco, March 26th -29th 2008.

Brock. Lothar (1991), "Peace Through Parks: The Environment on the Peace Research Agenda," Journal of peace Research, 28:4 pp-407-422

Brown Lester R. et al (1993) State of the World 1993: A Worldwatch Institute Report on Progress Toward a sustainable Society, New York – W.W.Norton

Brown Neville (1989) "Climate, Ecology ad International Security", Survival, 31:6 pp. 519-532

Bull, Hedley, and (1977) The Anarchical Society: A Study of Order in World Politics.London, Macmillan.

Bull, Hedley, and Adam Watson (eds.) (1983). The Expansion of International Society: Oxford: Clearendon.

Bureau of the Census (1996) "U.S. Population Projections" Washington, D.C., U.S.Department of Commerce.

Butler, Judith (1996a) "Perfomativity's in Theodore R. Schatzki and Wolfgang Natter (eds). The Social and Political body. New York: Guilford Press.

____ (1996b) "Anti- Intellectualism" Presentation with pierre Bourdieu at semi- nar"Fin-de- siecle Intellectuals: Looking back, Looking forward, "University of California at Berkeley, April.

————1997. Excitable Speech. A Politics of the Performative. London: Routledge.

Butterfield, Herbert (1965) "The Historic States-Systems", unpublished paper for the British Committee for the Theory of International Politics.

____ (1975) " Raison d'Etat," Martin Wight Memorial Lecture, University of Essex.

Buzan Barry (1983) "Regional Security as a Policy Objective: The Case of South and South West Asia," in A.Z Rubinstein (ed). The Great Game: The Rivalry in the Persian Gulf and South Asia. New York: Praeger, chapter10.

____ (1984) "Economic Structure and International Security: The Limits of the Liberal Case," International Organization, 38. 4, pp.597-624.

______ (1987) An Introduction to Strategic Studies: Military Technology and International Relations. London: Macmillan.

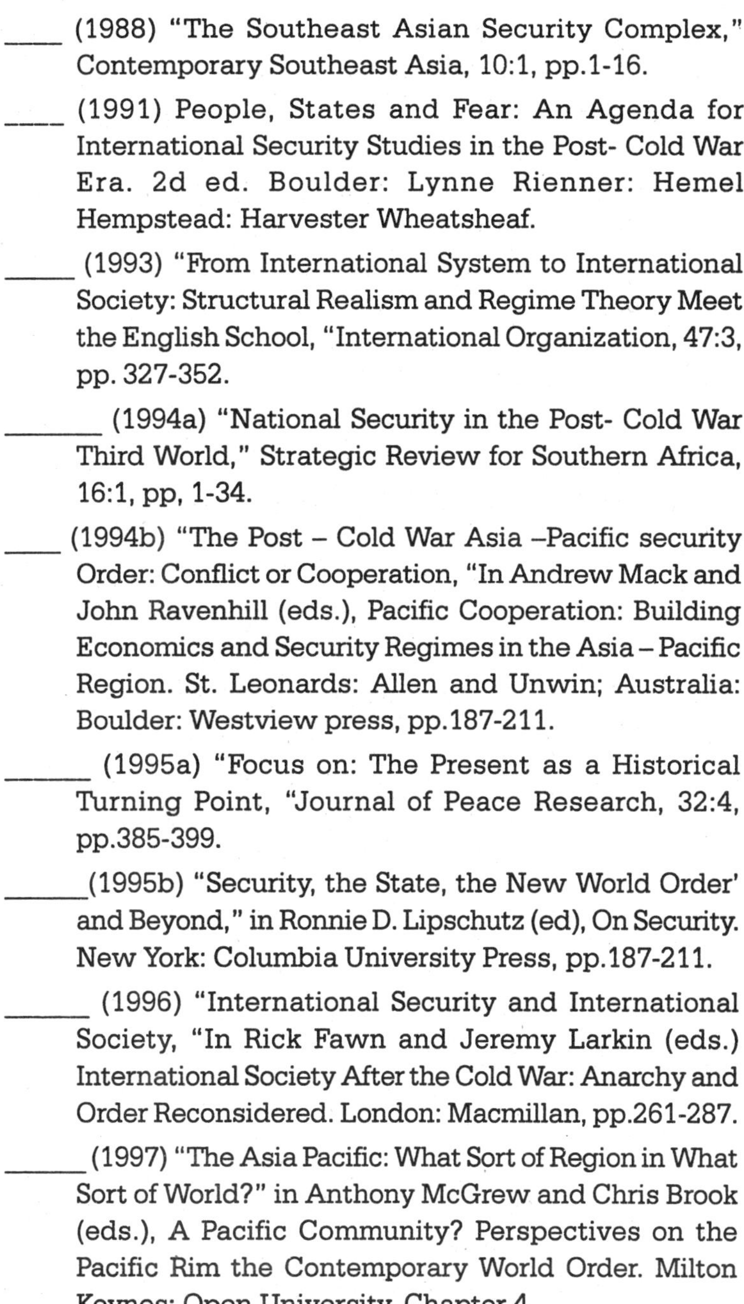

____ (1988) "The Southeast Asian Security Complex," Contemporary Southeast Asia, 10:1, pp.1-16.

____ (1991) People, States and Fear: An Agenda for International Security Studies in the Post- Cold War Era. 2d ed. Boulder: Lynne Rienner: Hemel Hempstead: Harvester Wheatsheaf.

_____ (1993) "From International System to International Society: Structural Realism and Regime Theory Meet the English School, "International Organization, 47:3, pp. 327-352.

_______ (1994a) "National Security in the Post- Cold War Third World," Strategic Review for Southern Africa, 16:1, pp, 1-34.

____ (1994b) "The Post – Cold War Asia –Pacific security Order: Conflict or Cooperation, "In Andrew Mack and John Ravenhill (eds.), Pacific Cooperation: Building Economics and Security Regimes in the Asia – Pacific Region. St. Leonards: Allen and Unwin; Australia: Boulder: Westview press, pp.187-211.

______ (1995a) "Focus on: The Present as a Historical Turning Point, "Journal of Peace Research, 32:4, pp.385-399.

______(1995b) "Security, the State, the New World Order' and Beyond," in Ronnie D. Lipschutz (ed), On Security. New York: Columbia University Press, pp.187-211.

______ (1996) "International Security and International Society, "In Rick Fawn and Jeremy Larkin (eds.) International Society After the Cold War: Anarchy and Order Reconsidered. London: Macmillan, pp.261-287.

______(1997) "The Asia Pacific: What Sort of Region in What Sort of World?" in Anthony McGrew and Chris Brook (eds.), A Pacific Community? Perspectives on the Pacific Rim the Contemporary World Order. Milton Keynes: Open University, Chapter 4.

Buzan Barry, Gowher Rizvi, et al. (1986) South Asian Insecurity and the Great Powers. London: Macmillan.

Buzan, Barry, Morten Kelstrup, Pierre Lemaitre, Elzbieta Tromer and Ole Waever (1990) The European Security Order Recast: Scenarios for the Post- Cold War Era. London: Pinter Publishers.

Buzan, Barry, And Gerald Segal (1992) "Introduction: Defining Reform as Openness", in General Segal (ed.) Openness for Foreign Policy Reform in Communist States. London: Routledge, pp.1-17.

Buzan, Barry, and Ole Waever (1992) "Framing Nordic Security-European Scenarios for the 1990s. Options in the Changing Europe, London, Pinter Publishers, pp. 85-104.

Buzan, Barry, Charles Jones, and Richard Little (1993) The Logic of Anarchy: Neorealism to Structural Realism, New York: Columbia University Press.

Buzan, Barry, and Gerald Segal (1994) "Rethinking East Asian Security" Survival 36:2, pp.3-21.

Buzan, Barry, and Richard Little (1996) "Reconceptualising Anarchy: Structural Realism Meets World History, "European Journal of International Relations 2.4, pp. 403-438.

Buzan, Barry, and Gerald Segal (1997) Anticipating the Future. London: Simon and Schuster.

Buzan, Barry and Ole Waever (1997) "Slippery? Contradictory? Sociologically Untenable? The Copenhagen School Replies," Review of International Studies 23:2, pp.143-152.

Buzan, Barry and Eric Herring (1998) Pandora's Box, Military Security: Technology, and World Politics, Boulder: Lynne Rienner.

Buzan, Barry&Ole Waever, 2003. Regions and Powers: The

Structure of International Security. Cambridge: Cambridge University Press.

Buzan, Barry; Ole Waever& Jaap de Wilde,1998. Security: A New Framework for Analysis. Boulder, CO: Lynne Rienner.

Cable, Vincent (1995) "What is International Economic Security?" International Affairs 71:2 pp. 305-324.

Campbell: David (1993) Writing Security: United States Foreign Policy and the Politics of Identity, Manchester: Manchester University Press.

Campbell, David, 1998. Writing Security: United States Foreign Policy and the Politics of Identity, rev.edn. Manchester: Manchester University Press.

Carr, E.H (1939) - The Twenty Years' Crisis 1919-1939- An Introduction to the Study of International Relations. London and Basingstoke: Macmillan.

Carrol, John E (ed.): (1988) International Environmental Diplomacy: The Management and Resolution of Transfrontier Environmental problems. Cambridge: Cambridge University Press.

Carson Rachel (1962) Silent Spring. Harmondshire: Penguin, 1991.

Cerny Phil (1995) "Globalization and Structural Differentiation"., unpublished paper, European Consortium for Political Research-Standing Group on International Relations (ECPR-SGIR) Conference, Paris.

Chipman, John (1992) " The Future of Strategic Studies: Beyond Grand Strategy". Survival 34:1 pp-109-131.

Clausewitz, Karl von (1983(1832) Vom Kriege. Berlin: Verlag Ullstein.

Conze, Werner (1984) "Sicherheit, Schutz" in Otto Brunner, Werner Conze, and Reinhart Koselleck (eds,)

Geschichtliche Grundbegriffe: Historisches Lexicon zur politisch-sozialen Sprache in Deutschland, vol-5 Stuttgart: Klett-Cotta.

Cox.Robert (1994): "Global Restructuring: Making Sense of the Changing International Political Economy." in Richard Stubbs and Geoffrey Underhill (eds.) Political Economy and the Changing Global Order, Toronto: McClelland and Stewart, PP-45-59.

Crawford, Beverly (1993), Economic Vulnerability in International Relations- The Case of East-West Trade, Investment and Finance, New York. Columbia University Press.

—— (1995) "Hawks, Doves, But No Owls: International Economic Interdependence and Construction of the New Security Dilemma" in Ronnie D. Lipschutz (ed.) On Security, New York, Columbia University Press, pp. 149-186.

Crawford, Neta C. (1991) "Once and Future Security Studies", Security Studies, 1:2 pp 283-316.

Critical Approaches to Security in Europe : A netorked Manifesto, C.A.S.E. Collective, 2006. Security Dialogue, Vol. 37(4) : 443-487.

Dalby, Simon (1988) "Geopolitical Discourse: The Soviet Union as Other", Alternatives, 13:4, pp- 415-443.

______ (1990) Creating the Second Cold War: The Discourse of Politics, New York: Guilford.

Daston, LorraineJ., 1995. Classical Probability in the Enlightenment. Princeton, NJ: Princeton University Press.

den Boer, Pim (1993) "Europe to 1914: The Making of an Idea." In Pim den Boer, Peter Bugge, and Ole Waever, The History of the Idea of Europe. Milton Keynes: Open University (republished by Routledge, 1995). pp.13 – 82.

Dean, Mitchell, 1999. Governmentality: Power and Rule in Modern Society. London: Sage.

Delumeau, Jean (1986) Rassurer et proteger: le sentiment de securite dans l' Occident d' autrefois, Paris: Fayard.

Deng, Francis M. (1995) War of Visions: Conflict of Identities in the Sudan. Washington, D.C.: Brooking Institution.

Der Derian, James (1987) On Diplomacy .Oxford: Basil Blackwell.

______ (1992) Anti – Diplomacy: Spies, Terror, Speed and War. Oxford: Basil Blackwell.

_______ (1993) "The Value of Security: Hobbes, Marx, Nietzsche and Baudrillard," in David Campbell and Michael Dillon (eds.), The Political Subject of Violence. Manchester University Press, pp.94 – 113.

Derrida, Jacques (1977a [1972]) "Signature Event Context." Glyph, I, pp. 172-197.

_______ (1977b) "Limited Inc a b c," Glyph, 2, pp. 162-254; reprinted in Derrida, Limited Inc. Evanston, III.: Northwestern University Press, 1988, pp.29 – 110.

_____ (1988) "Afterword: Toward an Ethic of Discussion," in Derrida, Limited Inc. Evanston, III. Northwestern University Press, pp.III – 154.

_____ (1992[1991]) The Other Heading: Reflections on Today's Europe. Bloomington: Indian University Press.

Dessler David (1989) "What's at Stake in the Agent – Structure Debate?" International Organization, 43:3, pp. 441 – 473.

Deudney, Daniel (1990) "The Case against Linking Environmental Degradation and National Security," Millennium, 19:3, pp.461 – 476.

______ (1995) "The Philadelphian System: Sovereignty, Arms Control and Balance of Power in the American

States Union, circa 1789-1861" International Organization, 49:2 pp. 191-229.

Deutsh, Karl, et al (1957) Political Community and the North Atlantic Area, Princeton: Princeton University Press.

De Wilde, Jaap (1991) Saved for Oblivion: Interdependence Theory in the First Half of the 20th Century: A Study in the Causality between War and Complex Interdependence, Dartmouth: Aldershot.

_______(1994) : " The Power Politics of Sustainability, Equity and Liveability", in Phillip B, Smith, Samuel E. Okoye, Jaap de Wilde, and Priya Deshingkar(eds) The World at the Crossroads : Towards a Sustainable. Liveable and Equitable World, London, Earthscan: pp- 159-176.

_______ ((1995) "Security Levelled Out: The Dominance of the Local and the Regional", in Pal Dunay. Gabor Kados, and Andrew J Williams (eds.) New Forms of Security, Views from Central, Eastern and Westerns Europe. Dartmouth: Aldershot. Pp. 85-102.

_________ (1996) "The Continuous (Dis) Integration of Europe: A Historical Interpretation of Europe's Future" in Jaap de Wilde and Haken Wiberg (eds.) Organized Anarchy in Europe: The role of States and Intergovernmental Organizations, London: I.B. Taurus pp- 85-106.

Dibb Paul (1995) "Towards a New Balance of Power in Asia" Adelphi Paper 295, London: International Institute for Strategic Studies (IISS).

Dieren, Wouter van (ed.) (1987) Taking Nature into Account, Towards a Sustainable National Income: A Report to the Club of Rome. (Dutch translation: De natuue tel took mee. Naareen duurzaam national inkomen.) Utrecht: Spektrum.

Dillon, Michael, 1995. "Sovereignty and Governmentality: From the Problematics of the New World Order to the

Ethical problematic of the World Order", Alternatives 20: 323-368.

Dillon, Michael, 2005. "Global Security in the 21st Century: Circulation, Complexity and Contingency", Chatham House ISP/NSC Briefing Paper 05/02: 2-3. London: Chatham House.

Dose, Rene A. H. and Andre W.M. Gerrits (1994) "Eurazie: millieu als casus belli. Over ecologie nationalisme en national veilligheid in het GOS." Transaktie, 23:4, pp.399-429.

Dorff, Robert H. (1994) "A Commentary on Security Studies for the 1990s as a Model Curriculum Core," International Studies Notes, 19:3, pp.23-31.

Ehrlich, Anne(1994) " Building a Sustainable Food System," In Philip B. Smith, S. E. Okoye, Jaap, de Wilde and Priya Deshingkar(eds), The World at the Crossroads: Towards a Sustainable Liveable and Equitable World. London: Earthscan, pp. 21-38.

Elbe, Stefan, 2005." AIDS, Security, Biopolitics", International Relations19: 403-419.

Elias, Norbert (1978[1939] The Civilizing Process, vols. 1 and 2.New York: Urizen Books.

Ember, Carol, Melvin Ember, and Bruce Russett (1992) "Peace between Participatory Polities: A Cross Cultural Test of the 'Democracies Rarely Fight Each other 'Hypothesis," World Politics, 44:4, pp.573-599.

Fawcett, Louise and Andrew Hurrell (eds). (1995) Regionalism in World Politics. Oxford: Oxford University Press.

Feshbach, Murray and Alfred Friendly, Jr. (1992) Ecocide in the USSR: Health and Nature Under Siege. New York: Basic Books.

Flavin, Christopher, and Odil Tunali (1995) "Getting

Warmer: Looking for a Way out from the Climate Impasse, "World watch paper, pp.10-19.

Foucault, Michel (1979) Discipline and Punish: The Birth of prison. New York: Vintage Books.

____ (1991[1978] "Governmentality," In Graham Burchell, Colin Gordon, and Peter Miller (eds.), The Foucault Effect: Studies in Governmentality. Chicago: University of Chicago press, pp.87-104.

Furet, Francois (1995_) "Europe After Utopianism," Journal of Democracy, 6:1 pp79.89.

Galtung, Johan. 1969. " Violence, Peace, and Peace Research", Journal of Peace Research 6(3): 167-191.

Galtung, Jonhan (1971) "A Structural Theory of Imperialism" Journal of Peace Research, 8:2, pp.81-118.

Gilpin, Robert (1981) War and Change in World Politics. Cambridge: Cambridge University Press.

____ (1987) The Political Economy of International Relations. Princeton: Princeton University Press.

Goldgeier, James M. and Michael McFaul (1992) "A Tale of Two Worlds: Core and Periphery in the Post-Cold War Era," International Organization, 46:2, pp. 467-491.

Gong Gerrit W. (1984) The Standard of "Civilization" in International Society. Oxford: Clarendon Press.

Gordon, Colin (1991) "Government Rationality: An Introduction," in Graham Burchell, Colin Gordon, and Peter Miller (eds.) The Foucault Effect: Studies in Governmentality. Chicago University Press. Pp.1-52.

Gorz, Andre(1977) Ecologie et liberte Paris: Editions Galilee.

Gowa, Joanne S. (1994) Allies, Adversaries and International Trade. Princeton: Princeton University Press.

Gray, Colin S. (1992) "New Directions for the Strategic Studies: How can Theory Help Practice?" Security Studies, 1:4, pp.610-635.

_____ (1994a) "Global Security and Economic Wellbeing: A Strategic Perspective, "Political Studies, 42:1, pp.25-39.

Gray, Colin S. (1994b) Villains, Victims and Sheriffs: Strategic Studies and Security for and Inter- War Period. Hull: University of Hull Press.

Gutmann, Amy (1994) "Peace and Acknowledgment" and "Introduction," in Gutmann (ed.) Multiculturalism: Examining the Politics of Recognition. Princeton: Princeton University Press, pp. ix-xv, 3-24.

Haas, Peter M. (1992) "Introduction: Epistemic Communities and International Policy Coordination, "International Organization, 46:1, pp.1-35.

Haas, Peter M; Robert O. Keohane, and Marc A. Levy (eds.) (1993) Institutions for the Earth-Sources of Effective International Environmental Protection. Cambridge, Mass: MIT Press.

Hacker, Andrew (1992) Two Nations: Black and White Separate, Unequal, and Hostile. New York: Scribners.

Hacking, Jan, 1990. The Taming of Chance. Cambridge: Cambridge University Press.

Haftendorn, Helga(1991) "The Security Puzzle: Theory Building and Discipline Building in International Security, International Studies Quarterly, 35:1,pp.3-17.

Halliday, Fred (1990) "The Sixth Great Power: On the Study of Revolution and International Relations," Review of International Studies, 16:3, pp.207-222.

Hansen, Lene (1994) The Conceptualization of the Security in Poststructuralist IR Theory. M.A. thesis. University of Copenhagen, Institute of Political Science.

Hansen, Lene, 2006. Security as Practice: Discourse Analysis and the Bosnian War> London& New York: Routledge.

Hansenclever, Andreas, Peter Mayer, and Volker Rittberger (1996) "Interests, Power, Knowledge: The Study of International Regimes, "Mershon Hart, Thomas G. (1978) "Cognitive Paradigms in the Arms Race: Deterrence, Détente and the 'Fundamental Error' of Attribution, "Cooperation and Conflict, 13:3, pp.147-162.

Hassner, Pierre (1996) La violence e la paix. De la bombe atomique au nettoyage ethnique. Paris: Editions Esprit.

Healey, Denis (1989) The Time of My Life, London Michael Joseph.

Helleiner, Eric (1994a) "From Bretton Woods to Global Finance: A World Turned Upside Down," in Richard Stubbs and Geoffrey Underhill (eds). Political Economy and the Changing Global Order. Mc Clelland and Stewart, pp.163-175.

Helleiner, Eric(1994b) Regionalization in the International Political Economy: A Comparative Perspective, East Asia Policy Papers no.3 University of Toronto York University, Joint Centre for Asia Pacific Studies.

Herz, John H. (1950) "Idealist Internationalism and the Security Dilemma, "World Politics, 22, pp.157-180.

______ (1959) International Politics in the Atomic Age, New York: Columbia University Press.

Hirsch, Fred, and Michael Doyle (1977) "Politicization in the World Economy: Necessary Conditions for an International Economic Order," in Fred Hirsch, Michael Doyle, and Edward L. Morse (eds.), Alternatives to Monetary Disorder. New York: Mc Grew-Hill, [[.11-66.

Hirscham, Albert O. (1991) The Rhetoric of Reaction: Perversity, Futility, Jeopardy: Cambridge: Belknap Press of Harvard University Press.

Holzgrefe, J.L. (1989) "The Origins of Modern International Relations Theory," Review of International Studies, 15:1, pp.11-26.

Homer Dixon, Thomas (1991) "On the Threshold: Environmental Changes and Acute Conflict, "International Security, 16:2, pp.76-116.

Horsman, Matthew, and Andrew Marshall (1995) After the Nation State: Citizens, Tribalism and the New World Disorder, London: Harper Collins.

Huntington, Samuel P. (1993) "The Clash of Civilizations?" Foreign Affairs, 72:3, pp.22-49.

_____ (1996) The Clash of Civilizations and the Remaking of World Order. New York: Simon and Schuster.

Hurrell, Andrew, and Benedict Kingsbury (1992) The International Politics of the Environment- Actors, Interests and Institutions. Oxford: Oxford University Press.

Huysmans, Jef,1998c. "The Question of the Limit: Desecuritization and the Aesthetics of Horror in Political Realism", Millennium: Journal of International Studies 27(3).

________2006. The Politics of Insecurity. London: Routledge.

Jackson, Robert H. (1990) Quasi-states: Sovereignty, International Relations, and the Third World. Cambridge: Cambridge University Press.

Jahn, Egbert, Pierre, Lemaitre, and Ole Waever (1987) Concepts of Security: Problems of Research on Non – Military Aspects. Copenhagen Papers no. 1. Copenhagen: Centre for Peace and Conflict Research.

Jervis, Robert (1976): Perception and Misperception in

International Relations. Princeton: Princeton University Press.

________ (1978) "Cooperation under the Security Dilemma," World Politics 30:2, pp—167-214.

__________ (1982) "Security Regimes", International Organization", 36:2, pp-357-378

Joenniemi, Pertti (ed.) (1993) Cooperation in the Baltic Sea Region, New York: Taylor and Francis.

_________ (ed.) (1997) Neonationalism or Regionality? The Restructuring of Political Space Around the Baltic Rim. Stockholm, Nordrefo.

Joenniemi, Pertti, and Ole Waever (1992) Regionalization Around the Baltic Rim – Background Report no 1992:521, Stockholm, Nordic Council.

Kakonen, Jyrki (ed,) (1992) Perspectives on Environmental Conflict and International Politics: London: Pinter.

_____(ed.) (1994) " The Coming Anarchy", Atlantic Monthly, February, pp.44-76

Katzenstein, Peter J (1996a) Cultural Norms and National Security: Police and Military in Postwar Japan, Ithaca, N.Y. Cornell University Press.

_______ (ed.) (1996b) The Culture of National Security: Norms and Identity in World Politics, New York: Columbia University Press.

Kaldor, Marry.2001. New and Old Wars. Cambridge: Polity.

Kelstrup, Morten (1995) "Societal Aspects of European Security", in Birthe Hansen (ed.) European Security - 2000, Copenhagen: Copenhagen Political Studies Press.pp-172-199.

Kennedy, Paul (1989) The Rise and Fall of the Great Powers, London, Fontana.

Keohane, Robert O (1980) " The Theory of Hegemonic Stability and Changes in International Economic

Regimes," in Ole Holsti, R. Siverson, and A.L. George (eds.) Change in the International System , Boulder, Westview Press.

_____ (1984) After Hegemony: Cooperation and Discord in the World Political Economy, Princeton: Princeton University Press.

Keohane, Robert – O. and Joseph S, Nye (1977) Power and Interdependence, Boston: Little Brown.

Kindleberger, Charles P. (1973) The World in Depression 1929-39, London: Allen Lane.

______ (1981) "Dominance and Leadership in the International Economy", International Studies Quarterly, 25: 2/3, pp-242-254.

Kissinger, Henry (1957) A World Restored: From Castlereagh, Metternich and the Restoration of Peace, 1812-1822. Boston: Houghton Mifflin.

Klein, Bradley (1990) "How the West Was Won: Representational Politics of NATO "International Studies Quarterly, 34:3 pp-311-325.

_____ (1994) Strategic Studies and World Order: The Global Politics of Deterrence: Cambridge: Cambridge University Press.

Knudsen Olav F. 2001. Post-Copenhagen Security Studies : Desecuriting Securitization. Security Dialogue, Vol. 32(3) : 355-368.

Kostecki, Wojciech (1996) Europe After the Cold War: The Security Complex Theory: Warsaw: Instytut Studiow Politycznych PAN.

Krause, Keith (1992) Arms and the State: Patterns of Military Production and Trade. Cambridge: Cambridge University Press.

_____ (1993) "Redefining Security? The Discourses and Practices of Multilateral Security Activity," Paper presented at British International Studies, Association (BISA) Conference December, University of Warwick (Coventry).

Krause, Keith, and Michael C. Williams (1996) "Broadening the Agenda of Security Studies: Politics and Methods," Mershon International Studies Review, 40, supplement 2, pp. 229-254.

______ (1997) "From Strategy to Security: Foundations of Critical Security Studies," in Krause and Williams (eds.), Critical Security Studies. Minneapolis: University of Minnesota Press.

______ (1998). "Critical Theory and Security Studies: The Research Programme of Critical Security Studies", Cooperation and Conflict 33(3).

Laclau, Ernesto (1990). New Reflections on the Revolution of Our Time, London: Verso.

Lake, David A. (1992) "Powerful Pacifists: Democratic State and War," American Political Science Review, 86:1, pp. 24-37.

Lasswell Harold (1965[1935]) World Politics and Personal Insecurity. New York: Free Press.

Leander, Anna, 2005. "The Power To Construct International Security: On the Significance of Private Military Companies', Millennium: Journal of International Studies 33(3): 803-826.

Leander, Anna, 2006. 'Privatizing the Politics of Protection: Military Companies and the Definition of Security Concerns', in Jef Huysmans, Andrew Dobson & Raia Prokhovnik, eds, The Politics of Protection: Sites of Insecurity and Political Agency. London: Routledge (19-33)

Lebow, Richard N. (1998) "Interdisciplinary Research and the Future of Peace and Security Studies," Political Psychology, 9:3, pp. 507-543.

Lefort, Claude (1986) The Political Forms of Modern Society: Bureaucracy, Democracy, Totalitarianism. Cambridge: Polity.

Levy, Marc A. (1995a) "Is the Environment a National Security Issue?" International Security, 20:1, pp. 35-62

_____ (1995b) "Time for a Third Wave of Environment and Security Scholarship," in P.J. Simmons (ed.), Environmental Change and Security Project Report, no. Princeton: Woodrow Wilson Center, pp. 44-46.

Lodgaard, Sverre (1992) "Environmental Security, World Order and Environmental Conflicts Resolution," in Nils Petter Gleditsch (ed.), Conversion and the Environment. Oslo: International Peace Research Institute (PRIO), pp. 115-136.

Lodgaard, Sverre, and Anders H. af Ornas (eds.) (1992) "The Environment and International Security," PRIO Report, 3.

Luciani, Giacomo (1989) "The Economic Content of Security," Journal of Public Policy, 8:2, pp.151-173.

Luhmann, Niklas, 1993. Risk: A Sociological Theory. New York: Walter de Gruyter.

Luke, Timothy (1989) "What's Wrong with Deterrence? A Semiotic Interpretation of National Security Policy," in James Der Derian and Michael Shapiro (eds.) International /Intertextual Relations. Lexington Books, pp. 207-229.

MacNeill, Jim, Pieter Winsemius, and Taizo Yakushiji (1991) Beyond Interdependence: The Meshing of the World's Economy and the Earth's Ecology. New York: Oxford University Press.

Mann, Michael (1986) The Sources of Social Power: A History of Power from the Beginning to AD 1760. Cambridge: Cambridge University Press.

Manning, C .A .W. (1962) The Nature of International Society. London: London School of Economics.

Mansfield, Edward D. (1994) Power, Trade and War. Princeton: Princeton University Press.

Maoz, Zeev, and Bruce Russett (1993) "Normative and Structural Causes of Democratic Peace," American Political Science Review, 87:3, pp. 624-638.

Matthew, Richard A. (1995) "Environmental Security: Demystifying the Concept, Clarifying the Stakes," in P.J. Simmons (eds), Environmental Change and Security Project Report, no. 1. Princeton: Woodrow Wilson Center, pp. 14 – 23

Mathews, Jessica Tuchman (1989) "Redefining Security", Foreign Affairs, 68:2, pp.162-177.

Mattingly, Garett (1955) Renaissance Diplomacy. Boston: Houghton Miffin.

Mayall, James (1991) "Non Intervention, Self – Determination and the 'New world Order", International Affairs, 67:3, PP.421-430.

____ (ed.) (1996) The New Interventionism 1991-1994: United Nations Experiences in Cambodia press.

McKinlay, R.D and Richard Little (1986) Global Problems and World order, London: Pinter.

Mc Sweeney, Bill (1996) "Buzan and the Copenhagen School", Review of International Studies, 22:1 pp.81-93.

McSweeney, Bill, 1996. 'Identity and Security: Buzan and the Copenhagen School', Review of International Studies 22(1): 81-93.

_________1998. "Durkheim and the Copenhagen School: A Response to Buzan and Waever" Review of International Studies 24(1): 137-40.

_________1999. Identity and Interests: Sociology of

International Relations. Cambridge: Cambridge University Press.

Meadows, Donella H. Dennis L. Meadows, and Jorgen Randers (1992) Beyond the Limits: Confronting Global Collapse, Envisioning a Sustainable Future. Mills, Vt: Chelsea Green Publishers.

Meadows, Donella H. et al. (1972) The Limits to Growth A Report for the Club of Rome Project on the Predicament of Mankind. New York: Potomac Associates.

Mintz, Alex and Nehemia Geva (1993) "Why don't Democracies Fight Each Others? An Experimental Study, "Journal of Conflict Resolution, 37:3, pp.484-503.

Moller, Bjorn (1991) Resolving the Security Dilemma in Europe: The German Debate and Non- Offensive Defense. London: Brasseys.

Morgenthau, Hans J. (1996) "Introduction," in David Mitrany (eds.) A Working Peace System. Chicago: Quadrangle Books, pp. 7-11.

Mouritzen, Hans (1980) "Selecting Explanatory Levels in International Politics: Evaluating a Set of Criteria, "Cooperation and Conflict, 15, pp. 169-182.

____ (1997) "Kenneth Waltz: A Critical Rationalist Between International Politics and Foreign Policy, "in Iver B. Neumann and Ole Waever (eds.) The Future of International Relations: Masters in the Making? London: Routledge, pp. 66-89.

Myers, Norman (1993a) Ultimate Security- The Environmental Basis of Political Stability. New York: W.W. Norton.

______ (ed.) (1993b [1984]) The GAIA Atlas of Planet Management. London: Gaia Books.

Nardin, Terry, David R. Mapel (1992) Traditions of International Ethics. Cambridge: Cambridge University Press.

Nierope, Tom (1994) System and Regions in Global Politics: An Empirical Study of Diplomacy, International Organization and Trade, 1950-1991. Chichester, N.Y. John Wiley and Sons.

Nye Joseph S. Jr (1989) The Contribution of Strategic Studies: Future Challenges," Adelphi Paper no 235. London: International Institute for Strategic Studies (IISS).

Nye, Joseph S; Jr and Sean M. Lynn-Jones (1988) "International Security Studies, International Security, 12:4, pp.5-27.

Ohlsson, Leif (ed.) (1995) Hydropolitics: Conflicts over Water as a Development Constraint. London: Zed books.

Olsson, Christian, 2003. 'Vrais process et faux debates: perspectives critiques sur les argumentaries de legitimation des enterprises de coercition para-privees' [True Trials and False Debates: Critical Perspectives on the legitimizing Discourses of Para-Private Military Companies], Cultures & conflicts 52: 11-48.

Onuf, Nicholas J. "Levels," European Journal of International Relations, 1:1, pp.35-58.

Owen, John (1994) "How Liberalism Produces Democratic Peace," Journal of International Relations. , 19:2, pp.87-125.

Paye, Jean- Claude (1994) "Merciless Competition: Time for New Rules?" International Economic Insights, 5:1, pp.113-122.

Pena, Flex (1995) "New Approaches to Economic Integration in the Southern Cone," Washington Quarterly, 18:3, pp.113-122.

Petersen, Karen, 2006. 'Terrorism: When Risk Meets Security', paper presented at the 46th Annual Convention of the International Studies Association, San Diego, CA, 23 March.

Polanyi Karl (1957[1994]) The Great Transformation. Boston: Beacon Press.

Ponting, Clive (1991) A Green History of the World. London: Sinclair Stevenson.

Porter, Gareth, and Janet W. Brown (1991) Global Environmental Politics, Boulder: Westview Press.

Poulsen-Hansen, Lars, and Ole Waever (1996) "Ukraine," in Hans Mouritzen, Ole Waever, and Hakan – Wiberg (eds.) European Integration and National Adaptations: A Theoretical Inquiry. New York: Nova Publishers, pp, 231-260.

Power, Micahael, 2004. The Risk Management of Everything: Rethinking the Politics of Uncertainty. London: Demos.

Prescott, J.R.V (1987) Political Frontiers and Boundaries. London : Unwin Hyman.

Prins, Gwyn (ed.) (1993) Threats Without Enemies: Facing Environmental Insecurity. London: Earthscan.

Rasmussen, Mikkel V., 2002. 'A Parallel Globalisation of Terror: 9-11, Security and Globalisation', Cooperation and Conflict 37(3): 323-349.

Rasmussen, Mikkel V., 2004. 'It Sounds Like a Riddle: Security Studies, the War on Terror and Risk', Millennium: Journal of International Studies 33(2): 381-395.

Reich, Robert (1991), "What is a Nation?" Political Science Quarterly, 106:2, pp. 193-209.

____ (1992[1991]) The Work of Nations: Preparing Ourselves for 21st Century Capitalism (with a new afterword).

New York: Vintage Books.

Rex, John, (1995) "Multiculturalism in Europe and America". Nations and Nationalism, 1:2, pp-243-260.

Roberts, Adam (1995-1996) – "From San Francisco to Sarajevo: The UN and the Use of Force", Survival, 37:4, pp-7-28.

Romero, Federico (1990)"Cross-Border Population Movements", in William Wallace (ed.), The Dynamics of European Integration, London, Pinter, pp. 171-191

Rosenau, James N (1989) "Subtle Sources of Global Interdependence: Changing Criteria of Evidence, Legitimacy, and Patriotism," in James N. Rosenau and Hylke W.Tromp (eds.) Interdependence and Conflict in World Politics. Aldershot- Avebury, pp.31-47.

_____ (1990) Turbulence in World Politics, A Theory of Change and Continuity. New York: Harvester Wheatsheaf

Rosenberg, Emily R. (1993), "The Cold War and the Discourse of National Security" Diplomatic History, 17:2, pp.277-284.

Rothschild, Emma (1995) "What is Security?" Doedalus, 124:3, pp- 53-98.

Ruggie, John G (1982) "International Regimes, Transactions and Change: Embedded Liberalism in the Postwar Economic Order, "International Organization, 36:2, pp. 379-415.

_____ (1983) "Continuity and Transformation in the World Today" Toward a Neo- Realist Synthesis," World Politics' 35:2, pp. 261-285.

_____ (1993) "Territoriality and Beyond: Problematizing Modernity in International Relations "International Organization", 47:1, pp.139-175.

Rytkonen, Helle (1995) "Securing European Identity-

Identifying Danger" paper presented at the annual conference of the International Studies Association, Chicago, April.

Santer, Jacques (1995a) " Speech to the European Parliament- January 17, 1995", Debates of the European Parliament, no.4- 456, Luxembourg, Office-4, Official Publication of the European Community, pp.13-20.

______ (1995b) "Speech to the European Parliament" Presentation of the Work Programme of the Commission – February 15, 1995" Debates of the European Parliament, no.-4-457, pp105-107.

______ (1995c) "State of the Union" speech by the president of the European Commission, Debates of the European Parliament, 15 November, no.4-470. pp.137-140.

Schmitt, Carl, [1992] 1985. Political Theology: Four Chapters on the Concept of Sovereignty, trans. George Schwab. Cambridge, MA: MIT Press.

Schulz, Michael (1995), "Turkey, Syria and Iraq: A Hydropolitical Security Complex" in Leif Ohlsson (ed.) Hydropolitics: Conflicts over Water as a Development Constraint, London, Zed Books, pp.91-122.

Scheweller, R (1992) "Domestic Structure and Preventive War: Are Democracies More Pacific"? World Politics. 44:2.

Segal, Geralad (1994) "China Changes Shape: Regionalism and Foreign Policy", Adelphi Paper No. 28, London: IISS.

Sheehan, Michael, 2005. 'International Security: An Analytical Survey. Boulder, CO: Lynne Rienner.

Singer, Max, and Aaron Wildavsky (1993) The Real World Order: Zones of Peace/ Zones of Turmoil, Chatham:

Chatham House Publishers.

Sjostedt, Gunnar (ed.) (1993) International Environmental Negotiation, London: Sage.

Skocpol. Theda (1979) States and Social Revolution, Cambridge: Cambridge University Press.

Skodvin, Tora (1994) "Structure and Agent in Scientific Diplomacy: Institutional Design and Leadership Performance in the Science Politics Interface of Climate Change," Working Paper 1994:14, Oslo: Centre for International Climate and Energy Research (CICERO).

Smith, Phillip B.S., E Okoye, Jaap de Wilde , and Priya Deshingkar (eds.) (1994) The World at the Crossroads : Towards a Sustainable, Liveable and Equitable World, London, Earthscan.

Spence, Jack (1994) "Entering the Future Backwards: Some Reflections on the Current International Scene" Review of International Studies, 20:1, pp. 3-13.

Strange, Susan (1984) "The Global Political Economy, 1959-84". International Journal, 39:2, pp. 267-283.

_____(1994) "Rethinking Structural Change in the International Political Economy, States, Firms and Diplomacy", in Richard Stubbs and Geoffrey Underhill (eds.) Political Economy and the Changing Global Order, Toronto: McClelland and Stewart, pp.103-115.

Stritzel Holger (2007). "Towards a Theory of Securitization: Copenhagen and Beyond". European Journal of International Relations, 13(3).

Stubbs, Richard, and Geoffrey Underhill (1994) " Global Issues in Historical Perspective" in Stubbs and Underhill (eds,), Political Economy and the Changing Global Order, Toronto: McClelland and Stewart, pp-145-162.

Tanaka, Akihiko (1994) "Japan's Security Policy in the 1990s," in Yoichi Funabashi (ed.) Japans' International Agenda. New York: New York University Press, pp- 28-56.

Taylor Charles (1992) Multiculturalism and "the politics of Recognition", Princeton: Princeton University Press.

Taylor Paul, (1993) International Organization in the Modern World: The Regional and the Global Process, London, Pinter.

Thomas, Caroline (1992) The Environment in International Relations, London: Royal Institute of International Affairs.

Thompson, Janice E., 1994. Mercenaries, Pirates and Sovereigns: State-Building and Extra-Territorial Violence in Early Modern Europe. Princeton, NJ: Princeton University Press.

Tickner, J.Ann (1992) Gender in International Relations: Feminist Perspective on Achieving Global Security: New York: Columbia University Press.

Tilly, Charles (1990) Coercion, Capital and European States: AD 990-1992. Oxford: Basil Blackwell.

Tromp Hylke (1996) "New Dimensions of Security and the Future of NATO" in Jaap de Wilde and Haken Wiberg (eds.) Organized Anarchy: The Role of Intergovernmental Organizations. London: I.B, Tauris, pp. 323-338.

Ullman, Richard (1983), "Redefining Security" International Security, 8:1, pp. 129-153.

Underhill, Geoffrey (1995) "Keeping Governments Out of Politics: Transactional Securities, Markets, Regulatory Cooperation, and Political Legitimacy, "Review in International Studies," 21:3, pp.151-278.

UNRISD (United Nations Research Institute for Social

Development) (1995) States in Disarray: The Social Effects of Globalization, March, New York: UNRISD.

Van Munster, Rens, 2004. 'The War on Terrorism: When the Exception Becomes the Rule', International Journal for the Semiotics of Law 17(2): 141-153.

Vayrynen: Raimo (1984) "Regional Conflict Formations: An Intractable Problem of International Relations" Journal of Peace Research, 21:4, pp337-359.

_____ (1988) "Domestic Stability, State Terrorism, and Regional Integration in the ASEAN and the GCC", in Michael Stohl and George Lopez (eds.) Terrible Beyond Endurance, New York: Greenwood Press, pp. 194-197.

Waever Ole (1988) "Security, the Speech Act," unpublished manuscript.

_____ (1989a) "Conceptions of Detente and Change: Some Non-Military Aspects of Security Thinking in the FRG." In Ole Waever, Pierre Lemaitre, and Elzbieta Tromer(eds.) European Polyphony, Perspectives Beyond East- West Confrontation, London, Macmillan, pp.186- 224.

______ (1989b) "Conflicts of Vision: Visions of Conflict" in Ole Waever, Pierre Lemaitre, and Elzbieta Tromer (eds.), European Polyphony: Perspectives Beyond East- West Confrontation, London: Macmillan, pp283-325.

______ (1990) "Politics of Movement: A Contribution to Political Theory in and on Peace and Movements" in Katsuya Kodama and Unto Vesa (eds.) Towards a Comparative Analysis of Peace Movements, Aldershot, Dartmouth 1990, pp.15-44.

_______ (1994) "Resisting the Temptation of Post Foreign Policy Analysis" in Walter Carlsnaes Perspectives in Europe. London, European Consortium for Political

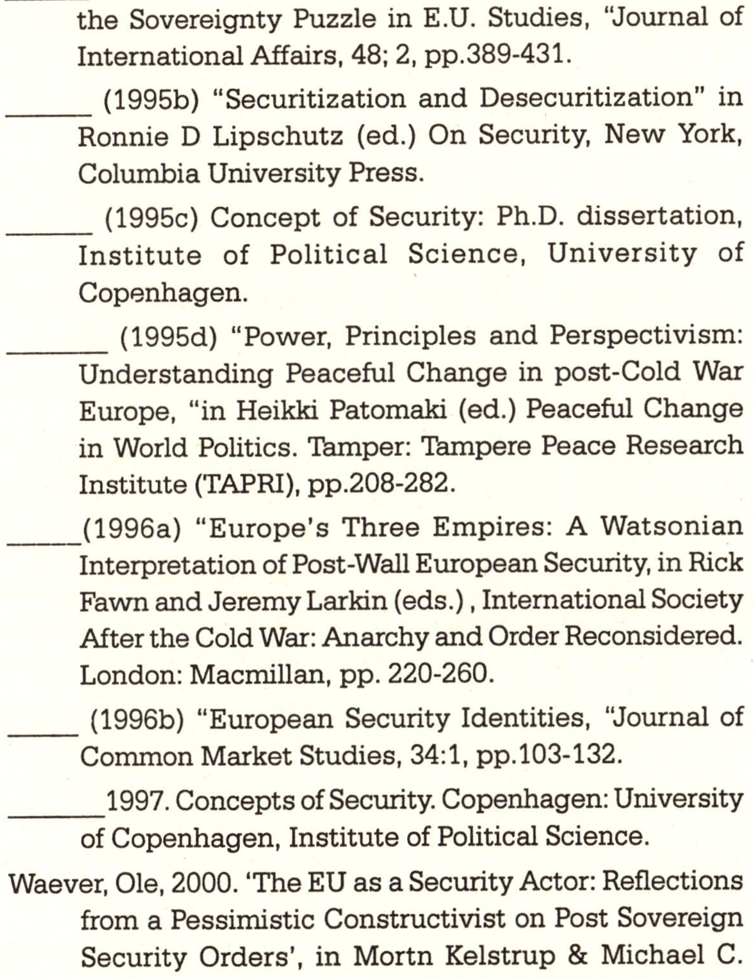

Research/Sage. pp.238-273.

______ (1995a) "Identity, Integration and Security: Solving the Sovereignty Puzzle in E.U. Studies, "Journal of International Affairs, 48; 2, pp.389-431.

______ (1995b) "Securitization and Desecuritization" in Ronnie D Lipschutz (ed.) On Security, New York, Columbia University Press.

______ (1995c) Concept of Security: Ph.D. dissertation, Institute of Political Science, University of Copenhagen.

_______ (1995d) "Power, Principles and Perspectivism: Understanding Peaceful Change in post-Cold War Europe, "in Heikki Patomaki (ed.) Peaceful Change in World Politics. Tamper: Tampere Peace Research Institute (TAPRI), pp.208-282.

_____(1996a) "Europe's Three Empires: A Watsonian Interpretation of Post-Wall European Security, in Rick Fawn and Jeremy Larkin (eds.) , International Society After the Cold War: Anarchy and Order Reconsidered. London: Macmillan, pp. 220-260.

_____ (1996b) "European Security Identities, "Journal of Common Market Studies, 34:1, pp.103-132.

_______1997. Concepts of Security. Copenhagen: University of Copenhagen, Institute of Political Science.

Waever, Ole, 2000. 'The EU as a Security Actor: Reflections from a Pessimistic Constructivist on Post Sovereign Security Orders', in Mortn Kelstrup & Michael C. Williams, eds, International Relations Theory and the Politics of European Integration. London: Routledge (250-294).

Waever, Ole, 2004a. 'Aberystwyth, Paris, Copenhagen: New "Schools" in Security Theory and Their Origins Between Core and Periphery', paper presented at the 45th Annual Convention of the International Studies

Association, Montreal, Canada, 17-20 March.

Waever, Ole, 2004b. 'Peace and Security: Two Concepts and Their Relationship', in Stenfano Guzzini & Dietrich Jung, eds, Contemporary Security Analysis and Copenhagen Peace Research. London: Routledge (53-65).

Waever, Ole, Barry Buzan, Morten Kelstrup, and Pirre Lemaitre (1993) Identity, Migration and the New Security Order in Europe. London: Pinter.

Walker, R.B.J. (1988) One World, Many Worlds: Struggles for a Just World Peace. Boulder: Lynne Rienner.

_____ (1990) "Security, Sovereignty, and the Challenge of World Politics Alternatives, 15:1, pp.3-28.

_____ (1993) "Inside / Outside: International Relations as Political Theory. Cambridge: Cambridge University Press.

Wallerstein, Immanuel (1993) "The World System After the Cold War," Journal of Peace Research, 30:1, pp.1-6.

Walt, Stephen M. (1991) "The Renaissance of Security Studies," International Studies Quarterly, 35:2, pp.211-239.

Waltz. Kenneth N. (1979) Theory of International Politics. Reading, Mass: Addison- Wesley.

Warner, Jeroen (1996) "De drooglegging van de Jordaanvallei, "Transakite, 25:3, pp.363-379.

Watson, Adam (1992) The Evolution of International Society. London: Routledge.

WCED (World Commission on Environment and Development) (1987) Our Common Future. Oxford: Oxford University Press.

Weart, Spencer R. (1994) "Peace Among Democratic and Oligarchic Republics. " Journal of Peace Research, 31:3, pp.299-316.

Webb, Michael (1994) " Understanding Patterns of Macroeconomic Policy Coordination in the Postwar Period" in Richard Stubbs and Geoffrey Underhills (eds.), Political Economy and the Changing Global Order, Toronto: McClelland and Stewart, pp. 176-189.

Weber. Max (1972[1922]) Wirschaft and Gesellschaft Tubingen: J.C.B, Mohr.

Wendt, Alexander (1987) "The Agent – Structure Problem in International Relations Theory," International Organization, 41:3, pp. 335 – 370.

______ (1992) "Anarchy is What States Make of It: The Social Construction of Power Politics," International Organization, 46:2, pp. 391 – 425.

Wendt, Alexander, 1999. Social Theory of International Politics. Cambridge: Cambridge University Press.

______ (1994) "Collective Identity Formation and the International State," American Political Science Review, 88:2, pp. 384 –396.

______ (1995) "Constructing International Politics," International Security, 20:1, pp. 71-81.

Westing, Arthur H. (ed.), (1988) Cultural Norms, War and the Environment. Oxford: Oxford University Press.

_____ (ed.) (1990) Environmental Hazards of War: Releasing Dangerous Forces in an Industrialized World. London: Sage (International Peace Research Institute Oslo [PRIO], United Nations Environment Program (UNEP).

Wheeler, Nicholas (1996) "Guardian Angel or Global Gangster: A Review of the Ethical Claims of Internationals Society", Political Studies, 44:1, pp.123-135.

White, N.D. (1996) The Law of International Organization, Manchester: Manchester University Press.

Wilberg, Hakan (1993) " Societal Security and the Exploison

of Yugoslavia" in Ole Waever, Barry Buzan, Morten Kelstrup, Pierre Lemaitre, et al, Identity, Migration and the New Security Agenda in Europe, London, Pinter, pp. 93-109.

Williams, M.C., 1998. 'Modernity, Identity and Security: A Comment on the "Copenhagen controversy", Review of International Studies 23(3): 435-440.

Williams, M. C., 2003. 'Words, Images, Enemies: Securitization and International Politics', International Studies Quarterly 47(4): 511-532.

Wight, Martin (1978) Systems of State. Leicester, Leicester, University Press.

_______ (1986) Power Politics, 2d rev. ed. London, Penguin.

Williams, Marc (1993) "Re- Articulating the Third World Coalition: The Role of the Environment Agenda," Third World Quarterly, 14:1, pp.7-29.

Williams Michael C. (1996) "Hobbes and International Relation: A Reconsideration," International Organization, 50:1 pp. 213-236.

Williams, Michael C. (2003) "Words, Images, Enemies: Securitization and International Politics", International Studies Quarterly 47(4): 511-31.

Wills, Garry (1995) "The New Revolutionaries", New York Review of Books, 10 August, pp. 50-54.

Wolfers, Arnold (1962) Discord and Collaboration: Essays on International Politics, Baltimore: Johns Hopkins University Press.

Wolfson, Ze'ev, and Henry Spetter (1991) "Ecological Aspects of East-West World Integration Trends", Environmental Policy Review, 1, pp. 14-20.

World Bank (1993) World Development Report 1993: Investing in Health World Development Indicators, New York: Oxford University Press.

Wriggins W.Howard (ed.) (1992) Dynamics of Regional Politics: Four Systems on the Indian Ocean Rim. New York, Columbia University Press.

Wynn Jones, Richard (1995) "Message in a Bottle? Theory and Praxis in Critical Security Studies, "paper presented at the annual conference of the International Studies Association, Chicago, April.

Wyn Jones, Richard, 1999. Security, Strategy, and Critical Theory. London: Lynne Rienner.

Wyn Jones, Richard, 2005. 'On Emancipation: Necessity, Capacity and Concrete Utopias', in Ken Booth, ed., Critical Security Studies and World Politics. London: Lynne Rienner (215-235).

CHAPTER 2 : NEOREALIST AND NEOLIBERAL VIEW OF SECURITY

Alt, James, and Kenneth Shepsle,1990. Perspectives on Positive Political Economy. Cambridge : Cambridge University Press.

Art Robert and Robert Jervis. International Politics, 3rd ed. Boston : Harper Collins.

Axelrod Robert. 1984. The Evolution of Cooperation. New York : Basic Books.

Axelrod and Robert Keohane. October 1988. "Achieving Cooperation Under Anarchy," World Politics 38 : 226-54.

Baldwin,David. Ed. 1993. Neorealism and Neoliberalism : The Contemporary Debate. New York : Columbia University Press.

____________, 1995. Security Studies and the End of the Cold War. World politics 48 : 117-41.

Brolie Bernard, 1959. Strategy in the Missile Age. Princeton : Princeton University Press.

Brooks Stephen G. Summer. 1997. "Dueling Realisms (Realism in International Relations)", International Organization, Vol. 51, no. 3.

Brown M. E., S.M. Lynn- Jones and S.E. Miller, eds.1995. The Perils of Anarchy : Contemporary Realism and International Security. Cambridge, Massachusetts : MIT Press.

Bueno de Mesquita, Bruce.1981. The War Trap. New Haven, Conn. : Yale University Press.

Buzan,Barry.1993. "Rethinking System and Structure". In The Logic of Anarchy : Neorealism to Structural Realism, by Barry Buzan, Charles Jones, and Richard Little, 1993. New York : Columbia University Press.

Chatterjee Shibasis. 2003. " Neo-realism, Neo-Liberalism and Security," International Studies.vol.40.no.2 : 125-44.

Christensen Thomas J. 1997. "Perceptions and Alliances in Europe, 1865-1940," International Organization, no.51 (winter) : 65-97.

Christensen Thomas J. and Jack Snyder. 1990. " Chain Gangs and Passed Bucks : Predicting Alliance Patterns in Multipolarity," International Organization.

Desch, Michael.1996. Why Realists Disagree About the Third World (and Why They Shouldn't). Security Studies 5 : 358-84.

Deudney, Daniel. 1993. Dividing Realism : Structural Realism and Security Materialism on Nuclear Security and proliferation. Security Studies 2 : 7-36.

Dunn Martin, "Realism in International Relations" available at http://www.geocities.wm/virtualwarcollege/ir_realism.htm.

Farnham, Barbara. 1994. Avoiding Losses/Taking Risks : Prospect Theory and International Conflict. Ann Arbor : University of Michigan Press.

Fischer, Markus.1992.Feudal Europe, 800-1300 : Communal Discourse and Conflictual Practices. International Organization 46 : 427-66.

Frankel, Benjamin. 1996.Restating the Realist Case : An Introduction. Security Studies 5 : ix-xx.

Friedberg, Aaron.1989.The Political Economy of American Strategy. World Politics 41 : 381-406.

Fudenberg Drew and Eric Maskin, "The Folk Theorem in repeated games with Discounting or Incomplete Information", Econometrica 54, October 1986, pp. 533-54.

Gaddis,John Lewis.1982.Strategies of Containment : A Critical Appraisal of Postwar American National Security Policy. New York : Oxford University Press.

___. 1987. The Long Peace : Inquiries into the History of the Cold War. New York : Oxford University Press.

Gilpin, Robert. 1975. U.S. power and the Multinational Corporation. New York : Basic Books.

___.1977. Economic Interdependence and National Security in Historical Perspectives. In Economic Issues and National Security, edited by Klaus Knorr and Frank Trager,1966. Lawrence Kans. : Regents Press of Kansas.

____. 1981. War and Change in World Politics. Cambridge : Cambridge University Press.

____. 1984. The Richness of the Tradition of Politics Realism. International Organization 38 : 287-304.

____. 1996. No One Loves a Political Realist. Security Studies 5 : 3-28.

Glaser, Charles. 1994-95. Realists as Optimists : Cooperation as Self-Help. International Security 19 : 50-90.

Gowa, Joanne. 1994. Allies, Adversaries, and International

Trade. Princeton, N.J. : Princeton University Press.

Grieco, Joseph. 1988. "Anarchy and the Limits of Cooperation, Realist Theory and the Problem of International Cooperation," Journal of Politics 50 : 600-624.

__________, 1990. Cooperation Among Nations : Europe, North America, and Non-Tariff Barriers to Trade. Ithaca, N.Y. : Cornell University Press.

__________, 1993. "Anarchy and the Limits of Cooperation : A Realist Critique of the Neoliberal Institutionalism" in Baldwin, ed., Neorealism and Neoliberalism : The Contemporary Debate. New York : Columbia University Press.

____. 1995. The Maastricht Treaty, Economic and Monetary Union, and the Neo-realist Research Programme. Review of International Studies 21 : 21-40.

____. 1997. Realist International Theory and the Study of World Politics. In New Thinking in International Relations, edited by Michael Doyle and G. John Ikenberry. New York : Westview Press.

Grieco Joseph, Robert Powell and Duncan Snidal. September 1993. " The Relative Gains Problem for International Cooperation," American Political Science Review 87 : 729-43.

Grunberg, Isabelle, and Thomas Risse-kappen. 1992. A Time of Reckoning? Theories of International Relations and the End of the Cold War. In The End of the Cold War : Evaluating Theories of International Relations, edited by Pierre Allan and Kjell Goldman, 104-46. Dordrecht, Netherlands : Martinus Nijhoff.

Haggard, Stephan. 1991. Structuralism and Its Critics : Recent Progress in International Relations Theory. In Progress in Postwar International Relations, edited by Emanuel Adler and Beverly Crawford, 403-37. New

York : Columbia University Press.

____. 1995. Developing Nations and the Politics of Global Integration. Washington, D.C. : The Brookings Institution.

Hirschman, Albert. 1980. National Power and the Structure of Foreign Trade. Berkeley : University of California Press.

Huntington, Samuel. Spring 1993. Why International Primacy Matters. International Security 17 : 68-83.

Huth, Paul,and Bruce Russett. 1984. What Makes Deterrence Work : Cases from 1900-1980. World Politics 36 : 495-526.

Jervis, Robert. 1977. Perception and Misperception in International Politics. Princeton, N.J. : Princeton University Press.

______, 1978. Cooperation Under the Security Dilemma. World Politics 30 : 167-214.

_______,1988. "Realism, Game Theory, and Cooperation," World Politics 40 : 324-25.

___. 1993. International Primacy : Is the Game Worth the Candle? International Security 17 : 52-67.

Kang, David. 1995. South Korea and Taiwanese Development and the New Institutional Economics. International Organization 49 : 555-87.

Kapstein, Ethan. 1995. Is Realism Dead? The Domestic Sources of International Politics. International Organization 49 : 751-74.

Kause Keith. 1996. "Broadening the Agenda of Security Studies : Politics and Methods," Mershon International Studies Review, no.40.

Kaysen, Carl. 1990. Is War Obsolete? International Security 14 : 42-64.

Kennedy, Paul. 1983. Strategy vs. Finance in Twentieth

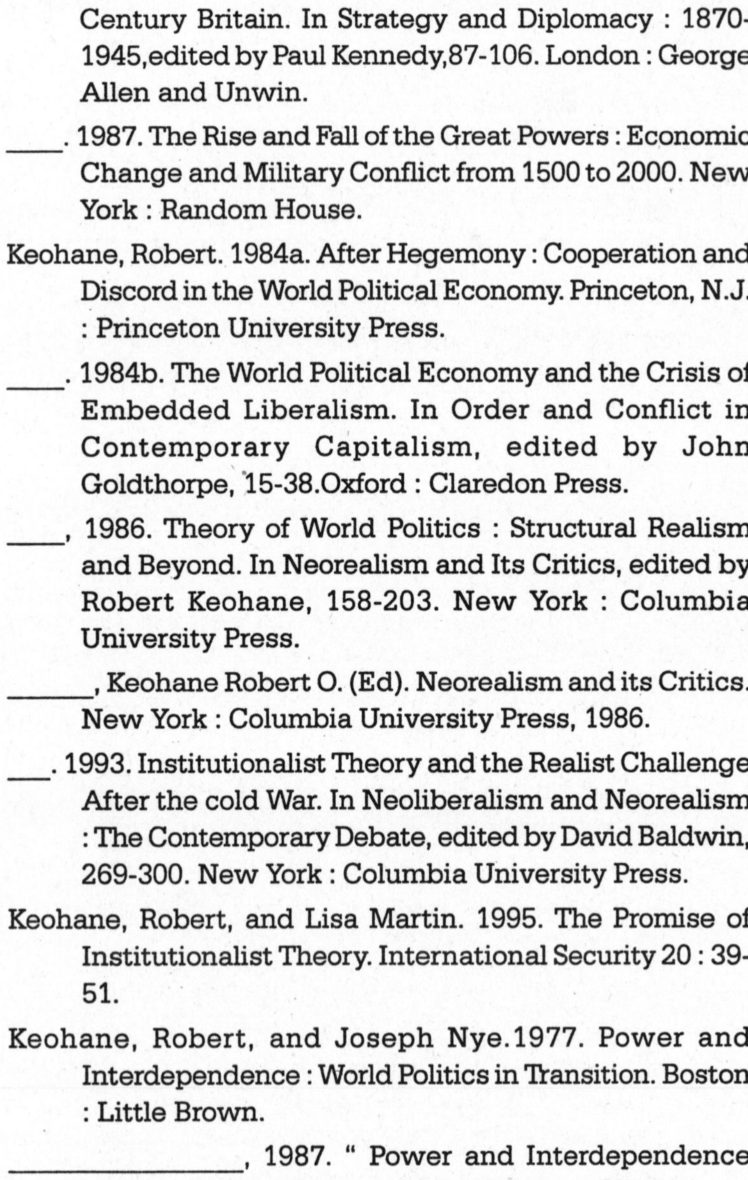

Century Britain. In Strategy and Diplomacy : 1870-1945,edited by Paul Kennedy,87-106. London : George Allen and Unwin.

____. 1987. The Rise and Fall of the Great Powers : Economic Change and Military Conflict from 1500 to 2000. New York : Random House.

Keohane, Robert. 1984a. After Hegemony : Cooperation and Discord in the World Political Economy. Princeton, N.J. : Princeton University Press.

____. 1984b. The World Political Economy and the Crisis of Embedded Liberalism. In Order and Conflict in Contemporary Capitalism, edited by John Goldthorpe, 15-38.Oxford : Claredon Press.

____, 1986. Theory of World Politics : Structural Realism and Beyond. In Neorealism and Its Critics, edited by Robert Keohane, 158-203. New York : Columbia University Press.

______, Keohane Robert O. (Ed). Neorealism and its Critics. New York : Columbia University Press, 1986.

___. 1993. Institutionalist Theory and the Realist Challenge After the cold War. In Neoliberalism and Neorealism : The Contemporary Debate, edited by David Baldwin, 269-300. New York : Columbia University Press.

Keohane, Robert, and Lisa Martin. 1995. The Promise of Institutionalist Theory. International Security 20 : 39-51.

Keohane, Robert, and Joseph Nye.1977. Power and Interdependence : World Politics in Transition. Boston : Little Brown.

________________, 1987. " Power and Interdependence Revisited," International Organization : 725-53.

Krasner, Stephen. 1976. State Power and the Structure of International Trade. World Politics 28 : 317-43.

___. 1978. Defending the National Interest : Raw Materials Investments and U.S. Foreign Policy. Princeton, N.J. : Princeton University Press.

Lake, David.1984. Beneath the Commerce of Nations : A Theory of International Economic Structures. International Studies Quarterly 28 : 143-70.

___. 1996. Anarchy, Hierarchy, and the Variety of International Relation. International Organization 50 : 1-34.

Layne, Christopher. 1994. Kant or Cant : The Myth of the Democratic Peace. International Security 19 : 5-49.

____. 1995. The Unipolar Illusion : Why New Great Powers Will Rise. In The Perils of Anarchy : Contemporary Realism and International Security, edited by Michael E. Brown, Sean M. Lynn-Jones, and Steven E. Miller, 130-76. Cambridge, Mass. : MIT Press.

Levy, Jack. 1994. An Introduction to Prospect Theory. In Avoiding Losses/Talking Risks : Prospect Theory and International Conflict, edited by Barbara Farnham, 7-22. Ann Arbor : University of Michigan Press.

Liberman, Peter. 1993. The Spoils of Conquest. International Security 18 : 125-53.

Lipson, Charles. 1984. International Cooperation in Economic and Security Affairs. World Politics 37 : 1-23.

Lipschutz Ronnie D (ed). 1995. On Security. New York : Columbia University Press.

Luce, R. Duncan, and Howard Raiffa.1957. Games and Decisions : Introduction and Critical Survey. New York : John Wiley & Sons.

Lynn-Jones, Sean M., and Steven E. Miller. 1995. Preface. In The Perils of Anarchy : Contemporary Realism and International Security, edited by Michael E.Brown,

Sean M. Lynn-Jones, and Steven E. Miller, ix-xxi. Cambridge, Mass. : MIT Press.

Mastanduno, Michael.1991. " Do Relative Gains Matter? America's Response to Japanese Industrial Policy", International Security, no.16(summer) : 73-113.

_____________, 1996. Security Engagement and Economic Competition : Realism and United States Strategy After the Cold War. Unpublished Manuscript, Dartmouth College, Hanover, N.H.

_____________, 1997. " Preserving the Unipolar Moment : Realist Theories and U.S. Grand Strategy after the Cold War," International Security, no.21(spring).

Mastanduno, Michael, David Lake, and G.John Ikenberry. 1989. Toward a Realist Theory of State Action. International Studies Quarterly 33 : 457-74.

Mearsheimer, John. 1990. Back to the Future : Instability in Europe After the Cold War. International Security 15 : 5-56.

____, 1992. Disorder Restored. In Rethinking America's Security : Beyond Cold War to New World Order, edited by Graham Allison and Gregory F. Treverton, 213-37. New York : W.W. Norton.

____. 1993. The Case for a Ukrainian Nuclear Deterrent. Foreign Affairs 72 : 50-66.

____. 1994-95. The False Promise of International Institutions. International Security 19 : 5-49.

Miller, Benjamin. 1996. Competing Realist Perspectives on Great Power Crisis Behavior. Security Studies 5 : 309-58.

Miller, Steven. 1993. The Case Against a Ukrainian Nuclear Deterrent. Foreign Affairs 72 : 67-80.

Morgenthau, Hans. 1946. Scientific Man vs. Power Politics. Chicago : University of Chicago Press.

Morrow James, "Social Choice and System Structure," World Politics 41, October 1988 : 75-97.

North, Douglass. 1990. Institutions, Institutional Change, and Economic Performance. Cambridge : Cambridge University Press.

Nye, Joseph. 1988. Neorealism and Neoliberalism. World Politics 40 : 235-251.

Nye Joseph and Robert Keohane, 1987. "Power and Interdependence Revisited", International Organization 41 : 725-53.

Ordeshook, Peter, and Emerson Niou.1991. Realism vs. Neoliberalism : A Formulation. American Journal of Political Science 35 : 481-511.

Oye Kenneth A. October 1985. " Explaining Cooperation under Anarchy : Hypothesis and Strategies," World Politics, XXXVIII, no.1 : 1-24.

Pollins, Brian. 1994. Cannons and Capital : The Use of Coercive Diplomacy by Major Powers in the Twentieth Century. In Reconstructing Realpolitik, edited by Frank Wayman and Paul Diehl. Ann Arbor : University of Michigan Press.

Posen Barry. 1993. "Nationalism, the Mass Army and Military Power," International Security, no.18 : 80-124.

__________, 1984. The Sources of Military Doctrine : France, Britain and Germany between the World War. Ithaca : Cornel University Press.

Powell, Robert. 1991. Absolute and Relative Gains in International Relations Theory. American Political Science Review 85 : 1303-320.

____. March 1993. Guns, Butter, and Anarchy. American Political Science Review 87 : 115-32.

____. 1994. Anarchy in International Relations Theory : The Neorealist-Neoliberal Debate. International

Organization 48 : 2, 313-344.

Putnam, Robert. 1988. Diplomacy and Domestic Politics : The Logic of Two Level Games. International Organization 42 : 427-60.

Quester, George. 1977. Offense and Defense in the International System. New York : John Wiley and Sons.

Reiss, Mitchell. 1995. Bridled Ambition : Why Countries Constrain Their Nuclear Capabilities. Baltimore, Md. : Johns Hopkins University Press.

Rosecrance, Richard. 1981. International Theory Revisited. International Organization 35 : 691-713.

____. 1982. Reply to Waltz. International Organization 36 : 682-85.

Ruggie, John Gerard. 1983. Continuity and Transformation in the World Polity : Toward a Neorealist Synthesis. World Politics 35 : 261-85.

Russett, Bruce. 1993. Grasping the Democratic Peace : Principles for a Post-Cold War World. Princeton : Princeton University Press.

____. 1995. The Democratic Peace : "And Yet It Moves." International Security 19 : 164-75.

____. 1996. Counterfactuals About War and Its Absence. In Counterfactual Thought Experiments in Worm Politics : Logical, Methodological, and Psychological Perspectives, edited by Philip Tetlock and Aaron Belkin,171-'87. Princeton : Princeton University Press.

Schweller, Randall. 1992. "Domestic Structures and Preventive War : Are Democracies more Pacific"? World Politics, no.44 : 235-69.

__________,1994. Bandwagoning for Profit : Bringing the Revisionist State Back in. International Security 19 : 72-107.

_________, December, 1997. " New Realist Research on Alliances : Refining Not Refuting Waltz' s Balancing Proposition", American Political Science Review, no.91 : 927-30.

SIPRI (Stockholm International Peace Research Institute). 1995. SIPRI Yearbook 1995 : Armaments, Disarmament, and International Security. Oxford : Oxford University Press.

Smyser, W. R. 1994. Dateline Berlin : Germany's New Vision. ForeignPolicy 97 : 140-57.

Synder, Jack. 1991. Myths of Empire : DomesticPolitics and International Ambition. Ithaca, N.Y. : Cornell University Press.

Stein, Arthur. 1990. Why Nations Cooperate : Circumstance and Choice in International Relations Ithaca, N.Y. : Cornell University Press.

Tversky, Amos and Daniel Kahneman. 1986. The Framing of Decisions and the Psychology of Choice. In Rational Choice, edited by Jon Elster,123-41. New York : New York University Press.

Van Evera, Stephen. 1990-91.Primed for Peace : Europe After the Cold War. International Security 15 : 7-57.

_________________, 1986. "Why Cooperation Failed in 1914," World Politics, vol.38 : 80-117.

_______________, 1994. " Hypothesis on Nationalism and War," International Security, no.18 : 5-39.

Vasquez, John. 1983. The Power of Power Politics : A Critique. New Brunswick, N.J. : Rutgers University Press.

________,1998. The Power of Power Politics : From Classical Realism in Neotraditionalism. Cambridge : Cambridge University Press.

Walt, Stephen. 1987. The Origins of Alliances. Ithaca, N.Y. : Cornell University Press.

____. 1992. Alliance, Threats, and U.S. Grand Strategy : A Reply to Kaufman and Labs. Security Studies 1 : 448-82.

__________, 1988. " Testing Theories of Alliance Formation : The Core of Southwest Asia", International Organization, vol.42, no.2(spring) : 275-316.

Waltz, Kenneth. 1959. Man, the State, and War. New York : Columbia University Press.

____. 1979. Theory of International Politics. Reading, Mass. : Addison-Wesley.

____. 1986. Reflections on Theory of International Politics : A Response to My Critics. In Neorealism and Its Critics, edited by Robert Keohane, 322-45. New York : Columbia University Press.

____. 1989. The Origins of War in Neorealist Theory. In The Origin and Prevention of Major Wars, edited by Robert Rotberg and Theodore Rabb,39-52. Cambridge : Cambridge University Press.

____. 1991. America as a Model for the World : A Foreign Policy Perspective. Political Science and Politics 24 : 667-70.

____. 1993. The Emerging Structure of International Politics. International Security 18 : 44-79.

____, 1990. " Realist Thought and neorealist Theory," Journal of International Affairs 44 : 21-37.

______, 1990. " The Balance of Power in International Politics" in Paul R. Viotti and Mark V. Kauppi, eds, International Relations Theory : Realism, Pluralism and Globalism. New York : Macmillan, 1990.

Wayman, Frank, and Paul Diehl. 1994. Realism Reconsidered.In Reconstructing Realpolitik, edited by

Frank Wayman and Paul Diehl, 3-29. Ann Arbor : University of Michigan Press.

Wendt, Alexander. 1987. "The Agent-Structure Problem in International Relations Theory," International Organization 41 : 335-70.

______,1992. Anarchy Is What States Make of It : The Social Construction of Power Politics. International Organization 46 : 391-425.

____. 1995. Constructing International Politics. International Security 20 : 71-81.

Wendt, Alexander, and Daniel Friedheim.1995. Hierarchy Under Anarchy : Informal Empire and the East German State. International Organization 49 : 689-721.

Wohlforth, William. 1993. The Elusive Balance : Power and Perceptions During the Cold War. Ithaca,N.Y. : Cornell University Press.

____. 1994-95. Realism and the End of the Cold War. International Security 19 : 91-129.

Zakaria, Fareed. 1992. Realism and Domestic Politics. International Security 17 : 177-98.

CHAPTER 3 : POSTSTRUCTURALIST VIEW OF SECURITY

Ashley, Richard k, (1987) 'The Geopolitics Of Geopolitical Space : Towards A Critical Social Theory Of International Politics', Alternatives 12(4) : 403-34.

Baudrillard, Jean (1983) Simulations. New York : Semiotext(e)

Buzan, Barry (1997) 'Rethinking Security After The Cold War', Cooperation and Conflict 32(1) : 5-28.

Buza, Barry and Ole Waever 1997) 'Slippery? Contradictory? Sociologically Untenable? The Copenhagen School

Replies'. Review of International Studies 23(2) : 241-50.

Campbell, David(1992) Writing Security : United States Foreign Policy and Politics of Identity. Manchester University Press.

Dalby, Simon (1990) Creating The Second Cold War : The Discourse of Politics. London : Pinter.

Dalby, Simon(1992) 'Security, Modernity, Ecology : The Dilemmas Of Post-Cold War Security Discourse', Alternatives 17(1) : 95-134.

Der Derian, James (1987) On Diplomacy : A Genealogy of Western Estrangement. Oxford : Basil Blackwell.

Der Derian,James (1992) Antidiplomacy : Spies, Terror, Speed, and War, Oxford : Basil Blackwell.

Der Derian, James(1995) 'The Value Of Security : Hobbes, Marx, Nietzsche, And Baudrillard', In Ronnie D, Lipschutz (ed.) on Security. New York : Columbia University Press, Pp. 24-45. An earlier version was published in David Campbell and Michael Dillon (eds). The Political Subjects of Violence. Manchester : Manchester University Press, 1993

Dillon, Michel(1995) ´Security, Philosophy and Politics', in Mike Featherstone, Scott Lash and Roland Robertson (eds) Global Modernities. London : Sage, pp.155-77.

George, Jim(1994) Discourses of Global Politics : A Critical(Re) Introduction to International Relations. Boulder : Lynne Rienner.

Gregory, Donna U. (1989) 'Foreword', in Der Derian and Shapiro (1989), pp. xiii-xxi.

Hansen Lene (1997) A Case for Seduction? Evaluating the Poststructuralist Conceptualization of Security, Nordic Journal of International Studies, Vol. 32(4), December 1997.

Huysmans, Jef (1997) 'James Der Derian : The Unbearable Lightness of Theory', in Neumann and Waver (1997),pp. 337-58.

Keohane, Robert O.(1989) International Institutions and State Power : Essays in International Relations Theory. Boulder : Westview.

Keohane, Robert O.(1991) 'International Relations Theory : Contributions of a Feminist Standpoint', in Rebecca Grant and Kathleen Newland (eds) Gender and International Relations. Buckingham : Open University Press, pp. 41-50.

Klein, Bradley S. (1994) Strategic Studies and World Order : The Global Political of Deterrence. Cambridge : Cambridge University Press.

Lawler, Peter (1995)A Question of Values : John Galtung's Peace Research. Boulder : Lynne Rienner.

Luke, Timothy W. (1991) 'The Discipline of Security Studies and the Codes of Containment : Learning from Kuwait', Alternatives 16(3) P : 315-44.

Shapiro, Michael J. (1988) The Politics of Representation : Writing Practices in Biography, Photography, and Policy Analysis. Madison, Wisconsin : University of Wisconsin Press.

Shapiro, Michael J. (1990) 'Strategic Discourse/ Discursive Strategy : The Representation of "Security Policy" in the Video Age', International Studies Quarterly 34(3) : 327-39.

Walker, R.B.J.(1987) 'Realism, Change and International Political Theory', *International Studies Quarterly* 31(1) : 65-86.

Walker, R.B.J.(1990) 'Security, Sovereignty, and the Challenge of World Politics', *Alternatives* 15(1) : 3-27.

Walker R.B.J. (1993) Inside/Ouside : International Relations as Political Theory. Cambridge : Cambridge University Press.

Walker, R.B.J.(1994) 'Social Movements/World Politics', Millennium 23(3) : 237-46.

Waltz, Kenneth N. (1979)Theory of International Politics. New York : Mc. Graw-Hill.

Waever, Ole (1995a) 'Securitization and Desecuritization', in Ronnie D. Lipschutz (ed.) On Security. New York : Columbia University Press, pp. 46-86.

Waever, Ole, Buzan, Barry, Kelstrup, Morten and Lemaitre, Pierre with David Carlton et al. (1993) Identity, Migration and the New Security Agenda in Europe. London : Pinter.

Williams, Michael C (1997a) 'The Institutions of Security : Elements of a Theory of Security Organisations', Cooperation and Conflict 32(3) : 287-307

Williams, Michael C. (1997b) 'Identity and the Politics of Security', paper presented at the Annual Meeting of the International Studies Association, Toronto, Canada, 18-22 March, 1997.

Wolfers, Arnold (1962) Discord and Collaboration. Baltimore : Johns Hopkins University Press.

CHAPTER 4 : ENVIRONMENTAL SECURITY

Allard Tom, Mark Forbes and agencies, " US braces for global warring", Sydney Morning Herald, 10 April 2007, p.1.

Annan Kofi. March 2000. We the Peoples : The Role of the United Nations in the 21st Century.

Annan Kofi (2005) *In Larger Freedom: Towards Development, Security and Human Rights for All*. United Nations: New York *http://www.un.org/largerfreedom/*

Gunther Bachler. 1993. Conflict and Cooperation in the Light of Global Human- Ecological Transformation, ENCOP, occasional paper 9 (October).

Barnett.W. 1986. Beyond War: Japan's Concept of Comprehensive National Security (Washington: Pergamon Brassey's).

Boge Volker.1992. Proposal for an Analytical Framework to grasp Environmental Conflict ", ENCOP, occasional paper no. I (July), Swiss Peace Foundation.

Booth K. 1991. "Security and Emancipation," Review of International Studies, Vol.17, pp. 313-26.

Boyce James.1987. Agrarian Impasse in Bengal: Institutional Constraints to Technological Change. Oxford: Oxford University Press.

Brock Lothar.1992. "Security Through Defending the Environment: An Illusion in E. Boulding, ed. New Agendas for Peace Research: Conflict and Security Reexamined (Boulder Co: Lynne Rienner See: Brauch Hans Gunter (2002) "Climate Change, Environmental Stress and Conflict," In: Federal Ministry for the Environment, Nature Conservation and Nuclear Safety, ed. *Climate Change and Conflict*, pp. 9-112. Federal Ministry for the Environment, Nature Conservation and Nuclear Safety: Berlin *http://www.afes-press.de/pdf/Brauch_ClimateChange_BMU.pdf*

Brauch Hans Gunter (2004) "*Abrupt Climate Change and Conflicts: Security Implications from a European Perspective - Hobbesian vs. Grotian Analyses*," *Friedrich Ebert Foundation* and Carnegie Endowment for International Peace, Washington, DC, 29 March *http://www.afes-press.de/pdf/Brauch_Climate Change.pdf* .

On the narrow and broad definitions of 'security', see:

Brauch Hans Gunter: *Environment and Human Security*," InterSecTions, 2/2005 (Bonn: UNU-EHS); at: *http://www.ehs.unu.edu/file.php?id=64*; and Hans Günter Brauch: *Threats, Challenges, Vulnerabilites and Risks in Environmental and Human Security. Source 1/2005* (Bonn: UNU-EHS) *http://www.ehs.unu.edu/file.php?id=63* and Commis-sion on Human Security (2003) Human *Security Now*. Commission on Human Security: New York *http://www.humansecurity-chs.org/* .

Brauch Hans Gunter.2008. " Reconceptualizing Security: Global Environmental and Climate Change as new Security Dangers and Concerns", Paper presented at the 49th ISA Convention, San Francisco, March 26th-29th, 2008: 1-39.

British Embassy Berlin: "Speech given by Foreign Secretary, Margaret Beckett, at the British Embassy, Berlin,24 October 2006"; at: *http://www.britischebotschaft.de/ennews/items/061024htm*; the quotes are from " Climate change, serious threats to global security"; at:<http://www.polotics.co.uk/news/foreign-policy/international-development/debt-and-debt-relief-in-developing-word/climate-change-serious-threat-global-security-$455615.htm>.

Bruyninckx Hans. 1993. "Environmental Security: An Analysis of the Conceptual Problems Defining the Relationship between Environment and Security ", paper presented at Budapest on the Workshop on Environment and Security organized by the European Peace Research Association, 11-16 November: 1-16.

Buzan Barry. "Environment as a Security Issue", pp.1 and 24 f, quoted in Ole Waever," Securitization and Desecuritization", p.13.

___________, 1997. "Rethinking Security after the Cold

war", Nordic Journal of International Studies, Vol.32, no.I, March.

Committee on the Challenges of Modern Society, NATO. 1999. "Environment and Security in an International Context", NATO Report 232.

Cooke P. 1980. "National State, Modernity," in R. Preet and N. Thrift, eds., New Models in Geography, Vol. I (London: Unwin, Hyman): 267-91.

Dalby S. 1990. "American Security Discourse: The Persistence of Geopolitics," Political Geography Quarterly, 9, pp.171-88.

__________, 1999. 'Threats From the South? Geopolitics, Equity, and Environmental Security," in Daniel H. Deudney and Richard A. Matthew, eds, Contested Grounds: Security and Conflict in the New Environmental Politics (Albany: State University of New York Press): 164-65.

__________, 1992. "Security, Modernity, Ecology: The Dilemmas of Post-Cold War Security Discourse," Alternatives, Vol.17, pp.95-134.

Dessler David, 1999. "Review of Environmental Scarcity and Violence", Environmental Change and Security Project Report 5 (1999), pp.100-101.

Dedring Jurgen (2007) "Human Security and the UN Security Council", In: Hans Günter Brauch, John Grin, Czeslaw Mesjasz, Pal Dunay, Pal Chadha, Navnita Pal, Béchir Chourou, Ursula Oswald Spring, Ursula, P.H. Liotta, Patricia Kameri-Mbote, eds. (2007) *Globalisation and Environmental Challen-ges: Reconceptualising Security in the 21st Century.* Chapter 48. Hexagon Series on Human and Envi-ronmental Security and Peace, vol. 3. Springer: Berlin.

Deudney Daniel H. 1990. "The Case Against Linking Environmental Degradation and National Security ", Millennium 19, pp. 461-76.;

_____________, 1999. "Environmental Security: A Critique", in Dan Deudney and Richard A. Matthew, eds., Contested Grounds: Security and Conflict in the New Environmental Politics (Albany: State University of New York Press, 1999)

Dixon Thomas F. Homer. 1999. Environment, Scarcity, and Violence, Princeton / New Jersey: Princeton University Press, 1999, pp.95-96, 141-42

Dixon Thomas F. Homer and Jessica Blitt. 1998. Evidences: Links Among Environment, Population, and Security. New York: Rowman and Littlefield.

_____________, 1994. "Environmental Scarcities and Violent Conflict: Evidence from Cases", International Security, vol.19, pp.5-40.

Down to Earth, Vol.II, No.10, October 15, 2002, p.16

Ehrlich Paul and Ehrlich Anne. 2004. One with Nineveh : Politics, Consumption and the Human Future. Washington, D.C. : Island Press.

Enlee C, 1989. Bananas, Beaches and Bases: Making Feminist Sense of International Politics, London: Pandora.

Esty Daniel et. al., "The State Failure Task Force Report: Phase II Findings", Environmental Change and Security Project Report 5, 1999, p.63.

Evans Peter.1992. "The State as Problem and Solution: Predation, Embedded Autonomy, and Structural Change" in Stephan haggard and Robert Kaufman. Princeton, N.J.: Princeton University Press.

Finger Mathias.1991. "The Military, the National State and Environment", The Ecologist, vol.21, no.5.

Fischer Dietrich. 1993. Nonmilitary Aspects of Security: A system's Approach, United Nations Institute for Disarmament and Research (UNIDIR), Aldershot: Dartmouth Publishing Company Ltd, p.10.

Gaan N. 2001. "Politics of Governance of Global Climate Change: Not on Equity but on North's Interests", India Quarterly, vol. LVIII, no.4, October-December, pp.89-112.

Gaan N. 1999. Environmental Degradation and Conflict: The Case of Bangladesh - India (New Delhi: South Asian Publisher, 1998).

__________, 1997. Environmental Scarcity of Fish and Conflict: The Case of India and Sri Lanka over Kachchativu Waters", International Studies Notes, Vol-22, No.3, Fall, pp.17-23.

Gaulin Ted. 2000. "To Cultivate a New Model: Where do Soyasa and Gleditsch Fall Short", Environmental Change and Security Project Report 6, pp. 104-107.

For GECHS see *http://www.gechs.org/* ; Janos Bogardi and Hans Guenter Brauch (2005) "Global Environ-mental Change: A Challenge for Human Security – Defining and conceptualizing the environmental dimension of human security", In: Andreas Rechkemmer, ed. *UNEO – Towards an International* Environ-ment, pp. 85-109. Nomos: Baden-Baden. GECHS will also be holding a conference on the mainstreaming of human security, "The International Conference on Human Security in Asia: Theory, Practice and Impacts will be held in Bangkok, October 4-5 2007 *http://www.ids.polsci.chula.ac.th/humansecurity.htm*

Gleick Peter H.1998. World's Water: The Biennial Report on Fresh Water Resources. Washington D.C.: Covels, California, Island Press.

Gorbachev M. 1987. "Reality and guarantees for a secure

world", Moscow News, No.39, p. 3287.

Gorz Andre Ecology and Freedom.1993. quoted in Ole Waever, "Securitization and Desecuritization", Working paper, vol.5, Centre for Peace and Conflict Research, Copenhagen, p.14.

Graham Kennedy. 2002. "Leadership ethics for the future: Tread Lightly on the planet', UNU Nexions, April. p.4.

Gurr Ted. 1993. Minorities at Risk: A Global view of Ethnopolitical Conflicts. Washington DC: US Institute of Peace Press.

Haftendorn Helga.2000. "Water and International Conflict", Third World Quarterly vol.21, no.1, pp.51-68.

Hatami Haleh and Peter H.Gleick.1992. "Chronology of Conflict over Water in the Legends, Myths and History of the Ancient Middle East", Report of the Pacific Institutes of the Studies in Development, Environment, and Security," Oakland, California, October.

Haque M.Shamsul. 2002. "Non-Traditional Security and the Environment in North east Asia", Work in Progress, Vol.16, No.3, Summer. P.24.

________________, 1999. "The Fate of Sustainable Development Under the Neoliberal Regimes in Developing Countries", International Political Science Review 20/2, pp.199-222.

Holsti O.R.1991. "International Systems, Systems Change and Foreign Policy," Diplomatic History 15: 94.

Ibrahim Mamman Aminu.1992. "The Information Drain: Obstacles to Research in Africa", Gatekeeper Series no.32. London: International Institute for Environment and Development.

Quotations from the IPCC rely on "Working Group II Contribution to the Intergovernmental Panel on

Climate Change, Fourth Assessment Report Climate Change 2007: Climate Change Impacts, Adaptation and Vulnerability, Summary for Policymakers, 6 April 2007 *http://www.ipcc.ch/SPM6avr07.pdf*.

Joffe J. 1992. "Entangled for ever", in C. W. Kegley Jr. and E.R. Wittkoff, eds., The Future of American Foreign Policy. New York: St. Martin's Press, P.35.

Kaldor M and R.Falk, eds, 1987. Dealignment: A New Foreign policy Perspective. Oxford: Basil Blackwell, 1987.

Kapitza Sergei. August 1999. "Anti Science Trends in the USSR", Scientific American, vol.265.no.2.

Kates Robert W. and B.L. Turner II and William Clark. 1990. "The Great Transformation", in B.L. Turner II, and William C. Clark, Robert W. Kates, John F. Richards, Jessica T. Matthews, William B. Mayer, eds., The Earth as Transformed by Human Action : Global and Regional Changes in the Biosphere over the Past 300 years. Cambridge: Cambridge University Press with Clark University, p.1.

Kessler Richard.1989. Rebellion and Repression in the Philippines. New Haven, Conn: Yale University Press.

Klare M and D.Thomas, eds. 1991. World Security: Trends and Challenges at Century's End. New York; St. Martin's Press.

Levy Marc A. Robert O.Keohane, and Peter M. Haas. 1993. "Improving the Effectiveness of International Environmental Institutions", in Peter M. Hass, Robert O. Keohane and Mark A. Levy eds., Institutions for Earth: Sources of Effective International Environmental Protection. Cambridge, MA: MIT Press.

Levy David L. and Daniel Egan. 1998. "Capital Contests:

National and Transnational Channels of Corporate Influence on the Climate Change Negotiations", Politics and Society, vol.26, no.3, September, pp.337-361.

Libiszewski Stephan. 1992. What is an Environmental Conflict? ENCOP, Occasional paper no. I, July, p.6.

Lipschutz R.D. and J.P Holdren, 1990. "Crossing Borders: Resource Flows, the Global Environment and International Security ", Bulletin of Peace Proposals, vol.21, pp.121-33.

Quoted by Littlecott Chris (2007) "Climate Change: The Global Security Impact"

February*http://www.e3g.org/index.php/programmes/climate-articles/climate- change-the-global-security-impact /*

Lodgaard, Sverre "Environmental Conflict Resolution," paper presented at the UNEP meeting on Environmental Conflict Resolution, Nairobi, 30 March 1990, p.18.

Lonergan S.C. 1999. ed., Environmental Change, Adaptation and Security, (Boston: Klewer, 1999).

Mack Andrew, "Human Security in the New Millennium," Work in progress, Vol.16, No.3, Summer 2002, p.5

Manning Michael and David Rejeski. 7-11 June 1993. "Sustainable Development and Risk: A Fit?" Paper presented at the Conference on Comparative Risk and priority Setting of Air Pollution Issues, Keystone, Colo.

Matthew Richard A, Ted Gaulin, and Bryan McDonald. 2001."The Elusive Quest: Linking Environmental Change and Conflict "submitted to Canadian Journal of Political Science, Revised Manuscript submitted; Dec 21, 2001, File Number: 01-12, p.7.

Moss Richard H., "Environmental Security? The Illogic of Centralized State Responses to Environmental Threats', in Paul Painchaud, ed., Geopolitical Perspectives on Environmental Security, Cahier du GERPE, no.92-05, Universite Laval, Quebec, 1990.

Myers Norman, 1986. "The Environmental Dimension to Security Issues", The Environmentalist, vol.6, Winter, p.251.

Myers Norman. 2001. "Sustainable Development : Tackling Problems – or Sources of problems ?" Paper presented at United Notions University Centre, 34 September.

Olson Mancur. 1982. The Rise and Decline of Nations: Economic Growth, Stagflation, and Social Rigidities. New Haven, Conn: Yale University Press.

Ostrom Elinor, Schroeder Larry and Wynne Susan. 1989. "Institutional Incentives and Sustainable Development" World Development, vol.17, no.9, pp.1375-87.

Peterson V. S. ed. 1992. Gendered States: Feminist (re)visions of International Relations Theory. Boulder, CO: Lynne Rienner.

Painchaud. 1993. Geopolitical Perspectives, quoted in Ole Waever, "Securitization and Desecuritization", Working paper, vol.5, Centre for Peace and Conflict Research, Copenhagen, p.14.

Pearce David and Kerry Turner.1990. Economics of natural Resources and the Environment. Baltimore; John Hopkins University Press.

Peluso Nancy and Michael Watts, ed. 2001. Violent Environments. Ithaca: Cornell University Press, pp.15-24.

Pirages Denis. 2004. Review Article of Paul Ehrlich and Anne Ehrlich's book One with Nineveh in

Environmental change of Security Project Report, Woodroid Wilson International Center for Scholars. Issue 10.

Porter Gareth. 1995. "Environmental Security as National Security Issue", Current History, May, p.218.

See: "Press Conference by Security Council President, 4 April 2007" *http://www.un.org/News/briefings/docs//2007/070404_Parry.doc.htm* .

Repetto Robert. 1987. "Population, Resources, Environment: An Uncertain Future", Population Bulletin, vol.42, no.2, pp.6-7.

Rifkin J. 1991. Biospheric Politics: A New Consciousness for a New Century. New York: Crown. p.2.

Rogers Katrina. 1995. "Rivers of Discontent – Rivers of Peace: Environmental Cooperation and Integration Theory", International Studies Notes, Vol.20, no.2, Spring , pp.17-18. See: Rohr Ulrike (2006) "Gender and climate change," *Tiempo* 59 (April): 3-7 *http://www.tiempocyberclimate.org/portal/archive/pdf/tiempo59high.pdf* .

Romer Paul.1994. "The Origins of Endogenous Growth", Journal of Economic Perspective, vol.8, no.1, pp.3-22.

Ben Russell and Nigel Morris (2006) "Armed forces are put on standby to tackle threat of wars over water", *Independent*, 28 February *http://news.independent.co.uk/environment/article348196. ece*

Ruttan Vernon and Hayami Yujiro.1984. "Towards a Theory of Induced Institutional Innovation", The Journal of Development Studies, vol.20, no.4.

Simon Julian. 1996. The Ultimate Resources (Princeton, N.J.: Princeton University Press, 1981), p.345; and Julian Simon, The Ultimate Resource 2. Princeton, N.J.: Princeton University Press, 1996.

Smith S. 1991. "Mature Anarchy, Strong States and Security," Arms Control, Vol.12, pp.325-29.

Smith D and E. P. Thompson, eds.1987. Prospects for a Habitable Planet. Harmondsworth: Penguin

Spring Ursula Oswald: "Climate Change: A Gender Perspective on Human and State Security Approaches to Global Security"; a summary is at: *http://womenand globalsecurity.org/index.php?option=com content &task=view&id=22&Itemid=33*;

Tickell Crispin Sir (2003) "Risks of conflict: Population and Resource Pressure", In: Hans Günter Brauch, P.H Liotta, Antonio Marquina, Rogers, Paul; Selim, Mohammed El-Sayed, eds. *Security and Environment in the Mediter-ranean. Concep-tua-lising Security and Envi-ronmental Conflict*, pp. 13-18. Hexagon Series on Human and Envi--ron-mental Security and Peace, vol. Springer: Berlin-Hei-delberg.

Tickner Ann. 1992. Gender in International Relations: Feminist Perspectives on Achieving Global Security. New York: Columbia University Press, P.6

Traub Joseph and Henryk Wozniakowski. January 1994. "Breaking Intractability", Scientific American, vol.270.no.1.

Ullman Richard H. 1983. "Redefining Security," International Security, vol.8, pp.129-53.

United Nations Development Program.1992. Human Development Report 1992. New York: Oxford University Press.

UNDP (1994) Human *Development Report: New Dimensions of Human Security*. UNDP: New York.

UNDP (2004) Reducing *Disaster Risk: A Challenge for Development*. Geneva: UNDP, Bureau for Crisis Prevention and Recovery *http://www.un.org/special-*

rep/ohrlls/ldc/Global-Reports/UNDP%20Reducing%20Disaster%20Risk.pdf .

UNDP (2007) *Human Development Reports http://hdr.undp.org/* ; see also UNDP, UNEP, World Bank,

ADB, AfDB, GTZ, DFID, OECD, and EC (2003) *Poverty and Climate Change: Reducing the Vulnerability of the Poor through Adaptation*. World Bank: Washington *http://www.undp.org/climatechange/adap01.htm* .

UNDP (2007) "Poverty Eradication, MDGs and Climate Change" *http://www.undp.org/climatechange/adap01.htm* .

U.S. Department of State. 1997. "Environmental Diplomacy: The Environment and U.S. Foreign Policy", U.S. Department of State, Washington, D.C.

Villiers Marq De. 1999. Water Wars, London: Weidenfeld and Nicolson, 1999); World in Transition: Ways towards Sustainable Management of Fresh Water Resources, German Advisory Council on Global Change, Annual Report 1997. Heidelberg: Springer – Verlag Berlin, 1999.

Quoted in Vogel Ben (2007) "Climate change creates security challenge 'more complex than Cold War'," *Janes.com http://www.janes.com/security/international_security/news/misc/janes070130_1_n.shtml*

WBGU website at:<http://www.wbgu.de/wbgu_ig2007_engl.html.

Wisner Ben and others, "Climate Change and Human Security" Simultaneously uploaded to Radix - Radical Interpretations of Disaster: *http://www.radixonline.org/cchs.html* & *http://www.radixonline.org/cchs.doc* ;

Disaster Diplomacy: *http://www.disasterdiplomacy.org*; Peace Research and European Security Studies

(AFES-PRESS): *http://www.afes-press.de/html/topical.html* .

World Commission on Environment and Development, Our Common Future (Brundtland Report (New York / London: Oxford University Press, 1987)) p.290.

Walzer Michael. 1992. Just and Unjust Wars: A Moral Argument with Historical Illustrations (New York: Basic Books.

______________, 1993. Spheres of Justice: A Defence of Pluralism and Equality. (Oxford: M. Robertson.

________________, 1994.Thick and Thin: A Moral Argument at Home and Abroad. Notre Dame: University of Notre Dami Press, 1994.

________________-, 1995. "The politics of Rescues ", Social Research 62, pp.53-67.

Wilson E.O. 30 May 1993. "Is Humanity Suicidal", New York Times Magazine.

World Bank. 1992. World Development Report 1992. New York: Oxford University Press.

Wright Robert. October 1991. "The Experiment That Failed: Why Soviet Science Collapsed", The New Republic, vo.205, no.18.

CHAPTER 5 : WOMEN DEFICIT AND VIOLENT CONFLICT

Boone, James L. (1983), " Noble family structure and expansionist warfare in the Late Middle Ages", In Rada Dyson-Hudson & Michael A. Little (Eds.), Rethinking human adaptation : Biological and cultural models, Boulder, CO : Westview, 79-86.

Boone, James L.(1986), " Parental investment and elite family structure in preindustrial states : A case study of late medieval-early modern Portuguese genealogies" American Anthropologist 88(4),859-878.

China State Statistical Bureau (2001). Major figures of the 2000 population census. Beijing : China Statistics Press.

Cincotta Richard P. and Elizabeth Leahy, 2006-2007, "Population Age Structure and Its Relation to Civil Conflict : A Graphic Metric", ECSP Report, 55.

Dalby S. 19990. "American Security Discourse : The Persistence of Geopolitics," Political Geography Quarterly, 9, pp.171-88.

Dreze, Jean, & Reetika Khera.(2000). " Crime, gender, and society in India : Insights from homicide data." Population and Development Review26(2),335-352.

Easterlin, Richard A. (1978). " What will 1984 be like ? Socioeconomic implications of recent twists in age structure", Demography 15(4), 397-432.

Easterlin, Richard A. (1987). Birth and fortune : The impact of numbers on personal welfare (second edition). Chicago : University Of Chicago Press.

Gourevitch, Philip. (1998). We wish to inform you that tomorrow we will be killed with our families : stories from Rwanda. New York : Farrar, Strauss and Giroux.

Holsti, O.R. 1991. "International Systems, Systems Change and Foreign Policy," Diplomatic History, 15.

Homer-Dixon, Thomas F.(1999). Environment, Scarcity, and Violence. Princeton, NJ & Oxford : Princeton University Press.

Homer Dixon, Thomas F.& Jessica Blitt (Eds). (1998). Ecoviolence : Links among Environment, Population and Security. Lanham, MD : Rowman&Littlefield.

Hudson, Valerie M.,& Andrea M. den Boer.(2004). Bare Branches : The Security Implications of Asia's Surplus Male Population. Cambridge,MA : MIT Press.

India Registrar General. (2001). Census of India,2001, Series 1 : India, Paper of 2001 : Provisional population totals. New Delhi, India : Office of the Registrar General.

Johnson, Norris R., James G. Stemler, & Deborah Hunter. (1977). "Crowd behaviour as 'risky shift' : A laboratory experiment." Sociometry 40(2),183-187.

Kahl, Colin H. (2002). "Demographic change, natural resources and violence", Journal of International Affairs 56(1), 257-282.

Kennedy, Paul (1993). Preparing for the twenty-first century, New York : Random House

Lancaster Carol, "Poverty, Terrorism and National Security", Environmental Change and Security Project Report, Woodrow Wilson International Center for Scholars, Washington, D.C : 2003, Issue 9, p.19

Mastany, Lisa. (2004, September/ October). " The hazards of youth". World watch magazine, 18-21.

Matthew, Richard A. (2002). "Environment, population and conflict". Journal of International Affairs 56(1),235-254.

Mazur, Allan,& Joel Michalek. (1998). " Marriage, divorce, and male testosterone", Social Forces,77(1), 315-330.

Miller, Barbara D. (2001). " Female-selective abortion in Asia : Patterns, policies, and debates." American Anthropologist 103(4),1083-1095.

Moller, Herbert.(1968). " Youth as a force in modern world)", Comparative Studies in Society and History 10(3), 237-60

National Intelligence Council. (2004). Mapping the global future : report of the national Intelligence Council's 2020 Project. Washington, D.C : Government Printing Office. Available online at http : /www.foia.cia.gov/ 2020.pdf

Oldenburg, Philip. (1992). " Sex ratio, son preference, and violence in India : A research note." Economic and Political Weekly 27(49-50), 2657-2662.

Oster, Emily. (2005, December). " Hepatitis B and the case of the missing women." Journal of Political Economy 113(6), 1163-1216.

Pape, Robert. (2005). Dying to win : The strategic logic of suicide terrorism. New York : Random House, Inc

Richard P. Cincotta and Elizabeth Leahy, 2006-2007, Population Age Structure and Its Relation to Civil Conflict : A Graphic Metric, ECSP Report, 2006-2007, p.55.

Sciolino, Elaine. (2001, December 9). " Radicalism : Is the devil in the demographics?" The New York Times, section 4, p.1

Sprinzak, Ehud. (2000, September/ October)." Rational fanatics", Foreign Policy120, 66-73

Urdal, Henrik. 2005 "Defusing the Population Bomb : Is Security a rational for Reducing Global Population Growth?", Environmental Change and Security Program Report, issue 11, 5-11.

United Nations Population Division. (1998). Too young to die : Genes or gender. New York : United nations.

Valerie M. Hudson and Andrea M. den Boer. Bare Branches : The Security Implications of Asia's Surplus Male Population (MIT Press, 2004)

CHAPTER 6 : DIGITAL AGE SECURITY THREATS

Adler, E (1992). "The Emergence of Cooperation : National Epistemic Communities and the International Evolution of the Idea of Nuclear Arms Control," International Organization 46(1) : 101-45.

Adler, E. (1997). "Seizing the Middle Ground : Constructivism in World Politics, : " European Journal of International Relations 3(3) : 319-63.

Adler, E. (2002). "Constructivism and International Relations," in W.Carlsnaes, T.Risse and B.A. Simmons (eds), Handbook of International Relations. London : Sage.

Agnew, J. And Corbrige, S. (1995). Mastering Space : Hegemony, Territory and International Political Economy. London : Routledge.

Alberts, D. (1996a). The Unintended Consequences of Information Age Technologies. Washington, DC : National Defense University

Alberts, D. (1996b). Defensive Information Warfare. Washington, DC : National Defense University.

Alberts, D. and Papp,D., eds (1997). The Information Age : An Anthology on Its Impacts and Consequences. Washington, DC : National Defense University.

Allan, P. and Goldmann, K.eds (1995). The End of the Cold War : Evaluating Theories of International Relations. The Hague : Kluwer Law International.

Allison, G.T. and Zelikow, P. (1999). Essence of Decision : Explaining the Cuban Missile Crisis, 2nd edn. New York : Longman.

Anderson, C. (1995). "The Accidental Superhighway. A Survey of the Internet," The Economist, July 1.

Applegate, M (2001), Preparing for Asymmetry : As Seen Through The Lens of Joint Vision 2020. Carlisle : Strategic Studies Institute.

Arquilla, J. and Ronfeldt, D. (1999). The Emergence of Noopolitik : Toward an American Information Strategy. Santa Monica, CA : RAND.

Arquilla, J. and Ronfeldt, D., eds (2001). Networks and

Netwars : The Future of Terror, Crime, and Militancy, Santa Monica, CA : RAND.

Ayoob, M. (1997) "Defining Security : A Subaltern Realist Perspective, "in K. Krause and M.C. Williams (eds), Critical Security Studies : Concepts and Cases. London : UCL Press.

Bauer, H. and Brighi, E. (2002). "Editorial Note," Millennium : Journal of International Studies 31(3) : iii-iv

Beck, U. (1992). Risk Society : Towards a New Modernity. London : Sage.

Beck, U. (1999). World Risk Society. London : Polity.

Bendrath, R. (2001). The Cyberwar Debate : Perception and Politics in US Critical Infrastructure Protection," Information and Security 7 : 80-103.

Bendrath, R (2003). "The American Cyber-Angst and the Real World – Any Link?" in R.Latham (ed.), Bombs and Bandwidth : The Emerging Relationship Between IT and Security. New York : New Press

Biddle, S.(2004). Military Power : Explaining Victory and Defeat in Modern Battle, Princeton, NJ : Princeton University Press.

Buzan, B. (1991). Peoples, States and Fear : An Agenda for International Security Studies in the Post Cold War Era, 2nd edn. Boulder, CO : Lynne Rienner.

Buzan, B., Waever, O. and De Wilde, J. (1998). Security : A New Framework for Analysis. Boulder, CO : Lynne Rienner.

Camilleri, J.A and Falk, J. (1992). The End of Sovereignty. The Politics of a Shrinking and Fragmenting World. Aldershot : Edward Elgar.

Campen, A., Dearth, D.and Goodden, T. (1996). Cyberwar : Security, Strategy and Conflict in the Information Age. Fairfax,VA : AFCEA International Press.

Castells, M. (1989). The International City : Information Technology, Economic Restructuring, and the Urban-Regional Process. Oxford : Blackwell.

Castells, M. (1996).The Information Age : Economy, Society and Culture, Vol. 1 : The Rise of the Network Society. Malden, MA : Blackwell.

Castells, M. (1997). *The Information Age Economy, Society and Culture, Vol. 2 : The Power of Identity,* Malden, MA : Blackwell.

Castells, M. (1998).). The Information Age Economy, Society and Culture, Vol. 3 : End of Millennium. Malden, MA : Blackwell.

Castells, M. (2000). Information Age : Rise of the Network Society, Vol. 1, 2nd edn. Malden, MA : Blackwell.

Checkel, J. (1997). Ideas and International Political Change : Soviet / Russian Behavior and the End of the Cold War. New Haven, CT : Yale University Press.

Choucri, N. (2000). "Introduction : CyberPolitics in International Relations," International Political Science Review 21(3) : 243-63.

CNN (1997), "Experts Prepare for an 'Electronic Harbor,'" November 7 URL (consulted February 27,2003) : *http : //www.cnn.com/US/9711/07/terrorism*, infrastructure.

Cordesman, A. (2002). Cyber-Threats, Information Warfare, and Critical Infrastructure Protection Defending the US Homeland. Westport, CT : Praeger.

De Borchgrave, A Cillufo, E.J., Cardash, S.L. and Ledgerwood, M.M. (2000). Cyber Threats and Information Security – Meeting the 21st Century Challenge. Washington, DC : Center for Strategic and International Studies.

Deibert, R. and Stein, J.G. (2003), " Social and Electronic

Networks in the War on Terror" in R. Latham (ed.), Bombs and Bandwidth, The Emerging Relationship Between IT and Security, New York : New Press.

Denning, D.E. (1999), Information Warfare and Security. Boston. M.A. Addison Wesley.

Denning DE. (2001a), "Activism, Hacktivism, and Cyberterrorism, The internet as a Tool for Influencing Foreign Policy," in J.Arquilla and J.Ronfeldt (eds), Networks and Netwars : The Future of Terror, Crime and Militancy. Santa Monica, CA : RAND.

Denning DE. (2001b), "Is Syber Terror Next?" Essays on September 11, Social Science Research Council, URL (consulted July 11, 2001) : *http : //www.ssrc.org/sept11/essays.denning.htm*.

Department of Defense (1998). Joint Doctrine for Information Operations, October 9, *URL : http : /www.dtic.mil/doctrine/jel/new_pubs/jp3_13.pdf.*

Der Derian, J. (2000). "Virtuous War/Virtual Theory," International Affairs 76(4) : 771-88.

Dewey, J. (1948) Reconstruction of Philosophy. Boston, MA : Beacon Press.

DSBTF (2001). 'Protecting the Homeland : Report of the Defense Science Board Task Force on Defensive Information Operations," Study Vol. II URL (consulted June 21, 2002) : http : //www.iwar.org.uk/iwar/index/htm.. Washington, DC : Department of Defense.

Duncan, R.W., Jancar-Webster, B. and Switky, B. (2003). World Politics in the 21st Century. New York : Longman.

Economist, The (2002). "A Survey of Digital Security," October 26 : 19.

Edelman, M. (1964). The Symbolic Uses of Politics, 2nd edn.. Urbana : University of Illinois Press.

Edelman, M (1977). Political Language : Words that Succeed and Policies that Fail. New York : Academic Press.

Edelman, M. (1985). The Symbolic Uses of Politics : With a New Afterword. Urbana : University of Illinois Press.

Edelman, M. (1988). Constructing the Political Spectacle. Chicago, II : Chicago University Press.

Edwards, J. (2002). Press release for the Cybersecurity Preparedness Act, January, URL : *http : // edwards.senate.gov/press/2002/jan28-pr.html.*

Erbschloe, M. (2001). Information Warfare : How to Survive Cyber Attacks. Berkeley, CA : Osborne and McGraw Hill.

Eriksson, J. (2001a). "Securitizing IT," in J. Eriksson (ed.), Threat Politics : New Perspectives on Security, Risk and Crisis Management. Aldershot : Ashgate.

Eriksson, J. (2001b). "Cyberplagues, IT and Security" Threat Politics in the Information Age," Journal of Contingencies and Crisis Management 9(4) : 211-22.

Eriksson Johan and Giampiero Giacomello, "The information Revolution, Security, and International Relations : (IR) relevant theory", International Political Science Review, Vol.27, No.3, July 2006, pp.221-244.

Everard, J. (2000). Virtual States : The Internet and the Boundaries of the Nation-State. London : Routledge.

Fearon, J. and Wendt, A. (2002)."Rationalism and Constructivism : A Skeptical View," in W. Carlsnaes, T.Risse and B.A. Simmons (eds), Handbook of International Relations. London : Sage.

Forno, R. (2002)/ Quotes on "Electronic Pearl Harbor," July 25, URL : *http : //www.soci.niu.edu/~crypt/other/ harbor.htm.*

Fountain, J.E. (2001). Building the Virtual State : Information

Technology and Institutional Change. Washington, DC : Brookings Institution.

Franda, M.F. (2001). Governing the Internet : The Emergence of an International Regime. Boulder, CO : Lynne Rienner.

Freedman, D.H. (2000)."How to Hack a Bank," URL (consulted July 25,2002) : *http : //www.forbes.com/asap/2000/0403/056.html*.

F-secure (2003). "Iraq War and Information Security," URL (consulted March 27, 2003) : *http : //www.f-secure.com{virus-info/iraq.shtml*.

Furnell, S, (2002). Cybercrime : Vandalizing the Information Society. Edinburgh : Pearson Education..

George, A and Bennet, A (2005). Case Studies and Theory Development in the Social Sciences Cambridge, MA and London : MIT Press.

Giacomello, G. (2005). National Governments and Control of the Internet : A Digital Challenge. London : Routledge.

Giacomello, G. and Mendez, f. (2001). "Cuius Regio, Eius Religio, Omnium Spatio? State Sovereignty in the Age of the Internet," Information and Security 7 : 15-27.

Gibson, W. (1984). Neuromancer. New York : Ace.

Gilpin, R. (1986). "The Richness of the Tradition of Political Realism," in R. Keohane (ed.), Neorealism and Its Critics. New York : Columbia University Press.

Goldman. E (2005), Information and Revolution in Military Affairs, London, Routledge.

Goldman, E. and Mahnken, T.G. eds (2004) The Information Revolution in Military Affairs in Asia, London and Basingstoke, Palgrave Macmillan.

Goldmann, K (1999), "Issues, Not labels, Please! Response

to Eriksson", Cooperation and Conflict 34(3) : 331-3.

Gongora, T and Von Riekhoff, H., eds (2000), Towards a Revolution in Military Affairs : Defense and Security at the Dawn of the Twenty-First Century, London : Greenwood Press.

Gourevitch, P, (1978), "The Second Image Reversed : The International Sources of Domestic Politics," International Organization 32(4) : 881-912

Haas. E, B (1990) : When knowledge is power, Three Models of Change in International Organizations, Berkeley : University of California Press.

Hammond, A.L (2001), "Digitally Empowered Development," Foreign Affairs, March-April, 80 : 96-106.

Harshberger E and Ochamanek, D (1999). " Information and Warfare, New Opportunities for US Military" in Z.M. Khalizad and J.P. White (eds) Strategic Appraisal, The Changing Role of Information in Warfare, Santa Monica, CA.RAND

Henry, R and Peartree C.E. eds (1998), The Information Revolution and International Security, Washington DC. Center for Strategic and International Studies.

Herd, G.P. (2000)"The Counter-Terrorist Operation in Chechnya : Information Warfare Aspect, "Journal of Slavic Military Studies, 13(4), 57-84.

Kaldor. M (1999), New and Old Wars, Organized Violence in a Global Era. London, Blackwell,

Katzenstein, P. (1996), The Culture of National Security, Norms and Identity in World Politics. New York, Columbia University Press.

Katzenstein, P. Keohane, R.O. and Krasner, S, (1998), "International Organization and the Study of World Politics," International Organization 52 (4) : 645-85

Keck, M and Sikkink, K.A. (1998), Activists Beyond Borders, Advocacy Networks in International Politics, Ithaca, NY : Cornell University Press.

Keegan, J (1993), A History of Warfare, London, Hutchinson.

Keohone, R and Nye, J.S. (1977) Power and Interdependence, World Politics in Transition, Boston, MA : Little Brown

Keohane, R and Nye, J.S. (1989), Power and Interdependence, New York, Harper Collins.

Keohane, R and Nye, J.S. (1998), "Power and Interdependence in the Information Age," Foreign Affairs, 77(5) : 81-94

Khalizad, Z White, J. and Marshall, A.W. (1999), Strategic Appraisal, The Changing Role of Information in Warfare, Santa Monica, C.A. : RAND

Klinenberg, E.and Perrin, A (2000) "Symbolic Politics in the Information Age : The 1996 Presidential Campaign on the Web," Information, Communication and Society 3(1) : 17-38.

Knox. M and Murray, W. eds (2001), The Dynamic of Military Revolution, 1300-2005. Cambridge, Cambridge University Press.

Krasner, S (1995), "Power Politics, Institution and Transnational Relations" in T. Risse Kappen (ed.) Bringing Transnational Relations Back In. Cambridge : Cambridge University Press.

Laird, R.F. (1999), Revolution in Military Affairs, Allied Perspectives, Washington, DC. Institute for National Strategic Studies, National Defense University.

Latham, R., ed (2003) Bombs and Bandwidth, The Emerging Relationship Between IT and Security, New York, New Press.

Lebow, R.N. and Raise. Kappen, T (1995), International

Relations and the End of the Cold War, New York : Columbia University Press.

Lewontin, R.C. (1992), Biology as Ideology, The Doctrine of DNA, New York, Harper Perennial.,

Libicki, M (1997), Defending Cyberspace Washington, DC : National Defense University.

Lonsdale, D.J. (1999) "Information Power : Strategy, Geopolitics, and Fifth Dimension" Journal of Strategic Studies, 22 (2-3) : 137-57.

Matthews, R and Tredderick, J. eds (2001), Mangaing the Revolution in Military Affairs, London and Basingstoke, Palgrave Macmillan,

Mearsheimer, J J (2001), The Tragedy of Great Power Politics, New York, Norton,

Merelman, R.M. ed (1993), Language, Symbolism, and Politics, Boulder, CO : Westview Press.

Moravcsik, A ed. (1998), Centralization or Fragmentation ? Europe Facing the Challenges of Deepening, Diversity and Democracy, New York, Council on Foreign Relations,

Moravcsik. A.Ed. (1999), The Choice for Europe : Social Purpose and State Power from Messina to Maastricht, London, UCL Press.

Morgenthau. H.J. (1993) Politics Among Nations, The Struggle for Power and Peace, brief edn, revised by K.W. Thompson, New York, McGraw Hill.

Mowlane, H (1997), Global Information and World Communication, New Frontiers in International Relations, London, Sage.

Muller, H (2002), "Security Cooperation" in W. Carlsnaes, T. Risse and B.A. Simmons (eds) Handbook of International Relations. London : Sage.

Norris, P. (2001), Digital Divide : Civic Engagement,

Information Poverty, and the Internet Worldwide, Cambridge, Cambridge University Press.

Nye. J.S.Jr (2002), The Paradox of American Power, Why the World's Only Superpower Can't Go It Alone Oxford, Oxford University Press.

Nye, J.S.Jr (2003), Understanding International Conflicts, An Introduction to Theory and History, 4th edn. New York, Pearson and Addison Wesley,

Nye, J.S.Jr (2004a), Soft Power, The Means to Success in World Politics, New York, Public Affairs,

Nye J.S. Jr (2004b), Power in the Global Information Age, From Realism to Globalization, London, Routledge.

O'Day A : ed. (2004), Cyberterrorism, Aldershot, Ashgate,

Onuf, NG. (1989), World of Our Making : Rules and Rule in Social Theory and International Relations, Columbia, University of South Carolina Press.

PBS Online (2002), "Frontline Hackers" URL (consulted July 25, 2002), *http : //www.pbs.org/wgbh/pages/frontline/shows/hackers/whoare/notable.html.*

PCCIP (2000), "Fact Sheet, President's Commission on Critical Infrastructure Protection, URL (consulted June 20, 2002), http//www.info-sec.com/pccip/web/backgrd.html.

Peirce. C.S. (1963), Collected Papers of Charles Sanders Peirce, Vol. 5, Pragmatism and Pragmaticism and Vol. 6 Scientific Metaphysics, C. Hartshorne and P. Weiss (eds.) Cambridge, MA and London, Belknap Press.

Pfaltzgraff, R.L. Jr and Shultz, R.H. Jr (1997), "Future Actors in a Changing Security Environment" in R.L. Pfaltzgraff Jr and R.H. Shultz Jr (eds), War in the Information Age : New Challenges for US Security Policy, Washington, DC and London, Brassey's

Philpott, D (2001), "Usurping the Sovereignty of

Sovereignty" World Politics, January, 53 : 297 – 324.

Polikanov, D., ed. (2001) Information Challenges to National and International Security. Moscow : PIR Center.

Ridge, T. (2002). Remarks by Homeland Security Director Tom Ridge to the Electronics Industry Alliance, Grand Hyatt Hotel, April 23, 2002. Washington, DC : White House, Office of the Press Secretary.

Risse – Kappen, T., ed. (1995). Bringing Transnational Relations Back In : Non – State Actors, Domestic Structures, and International Institutions. Cambridge : Cambridge University Press.

Rosecrance, R.N. (1999). The Rise of the Virtual State : Wealth and Power in the Coming Century. New York : Basic Books.

Rosenau, J.N. (1990). Turbulence in World Politics : A Theory of Change and Continuity. Princeton, NJ : Princeton University Press.

Rosenau, J.N. and Singh, J.P., eds (2002). Information Technology and Global Politics : The Changing Scope of Power and Governance. Albany : State University of New York Press.

Ruggie, J.G (1998). Constructing the World Polity : Essays on International Institutionalism. London : Routledge.

Russett, B and Antholis, W (1993), Grasping the Democratic Peace : Principles for a Post-Cold War World, Princeton, NJ : Princeton University Press.

Saco D (1999) : "Colonizing Cyberspace : National Security and the Internet", in J. Weldes, M.Laffey, H. Gusterson and R.Duvall (eds) Cultures of Insecurity : States, Communities and the Production of Danger, Minneapolis, University of Minnesota Press.

Schmidt : B.C. (2002), "On the History and Historiography in International Relations" in W.Carlsnaes, T. Risse and B.A. Simmons (eds.) Handbook of International Relations. London : Sage

Schwartau, W (1996).Information Warfare, Emeryville, Publisher Group West.

Schwartau, W (1997) "An Introduction to Information Warfare," in R.L.Pfaltzgraff Jr and R.H, Shultz Jr (eds) War in the Information Age : New Challenges for US Security Policy. Washington, D.C and London : Brassey's.

Sears D.O. (1993). "Symbolic Politics : A Socio – Psychological Theory," in S. Iyengar and W.J. McGuire (eds), Explorations in Political Psychology. Durham, NC : Duke University Press.

Sloan, E.C. (2002). Revolution in Military Affairs. Montreal : McGill-Queen's University Press.

Smith, G. (1998). "An Electronic Pearl Harbor? Not likely," Issues in Science and Technology, URL (consulted June 20, 1998) : *http : //205.130.85.236/issues/15.1/ smith.htm*.

Snyder, J (991). Myths of Empire. Ithaca, NY : Cornell University Press.

Sofear, A.D. and Goodman, S.E. (2001). The Transnational Dimension of Cyber Crime and Terrorism. Stanford, CA : Hoover Institution Press.

Stern, E. (1999). "The Case for Comprehensive Security," in D.Deudney and R.Matthew (eds), Contested Grounds : Security and Conflict in the New Environmental Politics. Albany : State University of New York Press.

Sundelius, B. (1983). "Coping with Structural Security Threats," in O. Holl (ed.), Small States in Europe and Dependence. Wien : Braumuller.

Sun Tzu (1963).. The Art of War, trans. S.B. Griffith. Oxford

: Oxford University Press.

Tengelin, V (1981). "The Vulnerability of the Computerised Society," in H. Gassmann (ed.), Information, Computer and Communication Policies for the '80s. Amsterdam : North Holland Publishing Company.

T Hart, P. (1993). "Symbols, Rituals and Power : The Lost Dimensions of Crisis Management, "Journal of Contingencies and Crisis Management (1) : 36-50.

Valeri, L. (2000), "Securing Internet Society : Toward an International Regime for Information Assurance," Studies in Conflict and Terrorism 23(2) : 129-46.

Van Creveld, M. (1991). The Transformation of War. New York : Free Press; Oxford : Maxwell Macmillan International.

Volti, R. (1995), Society and Technological Change, 3rd edn. London : St. Martin's Press.

Walker, R.B.J. (1993). Inside / Outside : International Relations as Political Theory. Cambridge : Cambridge University Press.

Walt, S. (1994). "The Renaissance of Security Studies," International Studies Quarterly 35(2) : 211-39.

Waltz, K.N. (1979). Theory of International Politics. New York : McGraw Hill.

Waever, O. (1995). "Securitization and Desecuritization," in R.D.Lipshutz (ed.) On Security. New York : Columbia University Press.

Waever, O. et al. (1993). Identity, Migration and the New Security Agenda in Europe. New York : St. Martin's Press.

Wendt, A. (1992). "Anarchy Is What States Make of It : The Social Construction of Power Politics," International Organization 46 : 391-425.

Wendt, A. (1999). Social Theory of International Politics.

Cambridge : Cambridge University Press.

Wight, C. (2002). "Philosophy of Social Science and International Relations", in W.Carlsnaes, T. Risse and B.A. Simmons (eds), Handbook of International Relations. London : Sage.

Williams, M.C. (2003). "Words, Images, Enemies : Securitization and International Politics," International Studies Quarterly 47(4) : 511-31.

Wolfers, A. (1962), Discord and Collaboration : Essays on International Politics. Baltimore, MD : Johns Hopkins University Press.

Yourdon, E. (2002). Byte Wars – The Impact of September 11 on Information Technology. Upper Saddle River, NJ : Prentice Hall PTR.

CHAPTER 7 : FEMINIST PERCEPTIVES ON SECURITY

Addams, Jane, Emily G. Balch, and Alice Hamilton. Women at The Hague : The International Congress of Women and Its Results. New York : Macmillan, 1916.

Agarwal, Bina, ed. Structures of Patriarchy : The State, the Community, and the Household. London : Zed Books, 1990.

Ardener, Shirley, ed. Perceiving Women. New York : Wiley, 1975.

Arendt, Hannah. On Violence. New York : Harcourt, Brace and World, 1969.

Aron, Raymond. Peace and War : A Theory of International Relations. Garden City, N.Y. : Doubleday, 1966.

Arvedson, Ingemund Hägg, Månans Lönnroth, and Bengt Rydén, eds. Economics and Values. Stockholm : Almqvist and Wiksell International, 1986.

Ashley, Richard K. "Untying the Sovereign State : A Double Reading of the Anarchy Problematique." Millennium : Journal of International Studies 17(2) (1988) : 227-

262.

Avery, William and David Rapkin, eds. America in a Changing World Political Economy. New York : Longman, 1982.

Axelrod, Robert. The Evolution of Cooperation. New York : Basic Books,1984.

Azar, Edward and Chung-in Moon. "Third World National Security : Toward a New Conceptual Framework." International Interactions 11(2) (1984) : 103-135.

Bandarage, Asoka. "Women in Development : Liberalism, Marxism, and Marxist-Feminism." Development and Change 15 (1984) : 495-515.

Barber, James David and Barbara Kellerman, eds. Women Leaders in American Politics. Eaglewood Cliffs, N.J : Prentice Hall, 1986.

Beauvoir, Simone de. The Second Sex. New York : Knopf, 1952.

Beitz, Charles. Political Theory and International Relations. Princeton : Princeton University Press, 1979.

Benn, S. I. and G. F. Gaus. Public and Private in Social Life. London : Croom Helm, 1983.

Bookchin, Murray. The Ecology of Freedom. Palo Alto, Calif. : Cheshire Books, 1982.

Bookchin, Murray. Toward an Ecological Society. Montreal : Black Rose Books, 1980.

Boserup, Esther. Women's Role in Economic Development. Aldershot, England : Gower, 1986.

Botkin, Daniel B. Discordant Harmonies : A New Ecology for the Twenty First Century. New York : Oxford University Press, 1990.

Boulding, Elise. Women in the Twentieth Century World. New York : Wiley, 1977.

Breines, Wini and Linda Gordon. "The New Scholarship on Family Violence." Signs : Journal of Women in Culture and Society 8(3) (Spring 1983) : 490-531.

Brock-Utne, Birgit. Educating for Peace : A Feminist Perspective. New York : Pergamon Press, 1985.

Brock-Utne, Birgit. Feminist Perspectives on Peace and Peace Education. New York : Pergamon Press, 1989.

Brock-Utne, Birgit. "Gender and Cooperation in the Laboratory." Journal of Peace Research 26(1) (1989) : 47-56.

Brown, Sarah. "Feminism, International Theory, and International Relations of Gender Inequality." Millennium : Journal of International Studies 17(3) (1988) : 461-475.

Brown, Wendy. Manhood and Politics : A Feminist Reading in Political Theory. Totowa, N.J. : Rowman and Littlefield, 1988.

Broverman, Inge K., Susan R. Vogel, Donald M. Broverman, Frank E. Clarkson, and Paul S. Rosenkranz. "Sex-Role Stereotypes : A Current Appraisal." Journal of Social Issues 28(2) (1972) : 59-78.

Buzan, Barry. People, States, and Fear, 2d ed. Boulder : Lynne Rienner, 1991.

Cardoso, Fernando and Enzo Faletto. Dependency and Development in Latin America. Berkeley : University of California Press, 1979.

Carr, E. H. The Twenty Years' Crisis, 1919-1939 : An Introduction to the Study of International Relations. New York : Harper & Row, 1964.

Carson, Rachel. Silent Spring. London : Hamish Hamilton, 1964.

Charlton, Sue Ellen M. Women in Third World Development. Boulder : Westview, 1984.

Choucri, Nazli and Robert C. North. Nations in Conflict : National Growth and International Violence. San Francisco : W. H. Freeman, 1975.

Cohn, Carol. "Sex and Death in the Rational World of Defense Intellectuals." Signs : Journal of Women in Culture and Society 12(4) (1987) : 687-718.

Common Security : A Blueprint for Survival. New York : Simon and Schuster, 1982.

Connell, R. W. Gender and Power : Society, the Person and Sexual Politics. Stanford : Stanford University Press, 1987.

Corr, Helen and Lynn Jamieson, eds. Politics of Everyday Life : Continuity and Change in Work and the Family. New York : St. Martin's Press, 1990.

Crapol, Edward P., ed. Women and American Foreign Policy : Lobbyists, Critics, and Insiders. New York : Greenwood Press, 1987.

Cynthia Enloe, Does khaki become you? The militarization of women's lives (London : Pandora, 1988).

——————, Bananas, beaches and bases : making feminist sense of international politics (London : Pandora,1989).

Dalby, Simon. "American Security Discourse : The Persistence of Geopolitics." Political Geography Quarterly 9(2) (April 1990) : 171-188.

Dankelman, Irene and Joan Davidson. Women and Environment in the Third World : Alliance for the Future. London : Earthscan Publications, 1988.

Deutsch, Karl W. Nationalism and Social Communication. Cambridge, Mass. : M.I.T. Press, 1954.

Deutsch, Karl W., Bruno Fritsch, Helio Jaguaribe, and Andrei S. Markovits, eds. Problems of World Modeling : Political and Social Implications. Cambridge, Mass. :

Ballinger, 1977.

Diamond, Irene and Gloria Feman Orenstein, eds. Reweaving the World : The Emergence of Ecofeminism. San Francisco : Sierra Club Books, 1990.

Dietz, Mary G. "Context Is All : Feminism and Theories of Citizenship." Daedelus 116(4) (Fall 1987) : 1-24.

Di Stephano, Christine. "Masculinity as Ideology in Political Theory : Hobbesian Man Considered." Women's Studies International Forum 6(6) (1983) : 633-644.

Eisler, Riane. The Chalice and the Blade : Our History, Our Future. San Francisco : Harper & Row, 1988.

Elshtain, Jean Bethke. Public Man, Private Woman : Women in Social and Political Thought. Oxford : Martin Robertson, 1981.

Elshtain, Jean Bethke. "Reflections on War and Political Discourse : Realism, Just War, and Feminism in the Nuclear Age." Political Theory 13(1) (February 1985) : 39-57.

Elshtain, Jean Bethke. Women and War. New York : Basic Books, 1987.

Elshtain, Jean Bethke and Sheila Tobias, eds. Women, Militarism, and War. Savage, Md. : Rowman and Littlefield, 1990.

Enloe, Cynthia. Bananas, Beaches, and Bases : Making Feminist Sense of International Politics. Berkeley : University of California Press, 1990.

Enloe, Cynthia. Does Khaki Become You? Boston : South End Press, 1983.

Falk, Richard A. "Contending Approaches to World Order." Journal of International Affairs 31(2) (Fall/Winter 1977) : 171-198.

Falk, Richard A., Samuel S. Kim, and Saul H. Mendolvitz,

eds. Toward a Just World Order. Boulder : Westview, 1980.

Finn, Geraldine. "Women and the Ideology of Science." Our Generation 15(1) (Winter 1982) : 40-50.

Flax, Jane. "Postmodernism and Gender Relations in Feminist Theory." Signs : Journal of Women and Culture in Society 12(4) (1987) : 621-643.

Galtung, Johan. "A Structural Theory of Imperialism." Journal of Peace Research 8(2) (1971) : 81-117.

Gee, Pauline W. "Ensuring Police Protection for Battered Women : The Scott v. Hart Suit." Signs : Journal of Women in Culture and Society 8(3) (Spring 1983) : 554-567.

Gerzon, Mark. A Choice of Heroes : The Changing Face of American Manhood. Boston : Houghton Mifflin, 1984.

Gill, Stephen and David Law. The Global Political Economy : Perspectives, Problems, and Policies. Baltimore : Johns Hopkins Press, 1988.

Gilman, Charlotte Perkins. Herland. New York : Pantheon, 1979.

Gilpin, Robert. The Political Economy of International Relations. Princeton : Princeton University Press, 1987.

Goetz, Anne Marie. "Feminism and the Limits of the Claim to Know : Contradictions in the Feminist Approach to Women in Development." Millennium : Journal of International Studies 17(3) (1988) : 477-496.

Grant, Rebecca and Kathleen Newland, eds. Gender and International Relations. Bloomington : Indiana University Press, 1991.

Griffin, Susan. Woman and Nature : The Roaring Inside Her. New York : Harper & Row, 1978.

Griscom, Joan L. "On Healing the Nature/History Split in Feminist Thought." Heresies 4(1) (1981) : 4-9.

Haas, Peter M. Saving the Mediterranean : The Politics of International Environmental Cooperation. New York : Columbia University Press, 1990.

Hanmer, Jalna and Mary Maynard, eds. Women, Violence, and Social Control. Atlantic Highlands, N.J. : Humanities Press International, 1987.

Hansson, Carola and Karin Liden. Moscow Women. New York : Pantheon Books, 1983.

Haraway, Donna. Primate Visions : Gender, Race, and Nature in the World of Modern Science. New York : Routledge, 1989.

Harding, Sandra. The Science Question in Feminism. Ithaca, N.Y. : Cornell University Press, 1986.

Harding, Sandra and Merrill B. Hintikka, eds. Discovering Reality. Dordrecht, Holland : D. Reidel, 1983.

Harris, Adrienne and Ynestra King, eds. Rocking the Ship of State : Toward a Feminist Peace Politics. Boulder : Westview, 1989.

Hartsock, Nancy C. M. Money, Sex, and Power : Toward a Feminist Historical Materialism. Boston : Northeastern University Press, 1983.

Higonnet, Margaret Randolph, Jane Jenson, Sonya Michel, and Margaret Collins Weitz, eds. Behind the Lines : Gender and the Two World Wars. New Haven : Yale University Press, 1987.

Hoffman John, Gender and sovereignty : feminism, the state and International Relations (London : Palgrave, 2001).

Holsti, K. J. The Dividing Discipline : Hegemony and Diversity in International Theory. Boston : Allen & Unwin, 1985.

Hooper Charlotte, Manly states : masculinities,

international relations and gender politics (New York : Columbia University Press, 2001).

Hunt, Michael H. Ideology and U.S. Foreign Policy. New Haven : Yale University Press, 1987.

Independent Commission on Disarmament and Security Issues, Common Security : A Blueprint for Survival. New York : Simon and Schuster, 1982.

International Studies Quarterly, Special Issue : Speaking the Language of Exile and Dissidence in International Studies, 34(3) (September 1990).

Isaksson, Eva, ed. Women and the Military System. New York : Harvester, Wheatsheaf, 1988.

Jackson, Robert H. and Carl G. Rosberg. "Why Africa`s Weak States Persist : The Empirical and the Juridical in Statehood." World Politics 35(1) (October 1982) : 1-24.

Jaggar, Alison. Feminist Politics and Human Nature. Totowa, N.J. : Rowman and Allanheld, 1983.

Jaquette, Jane S. "Women and Modernization Theory : A Decade of Feminist Criticism." World Politics 34(2) (January 1982) : 267-284.

Kaldor, Mary. "The Global Political Economy." Alternatives 11(4) (October 1986) : 431-460.

Keller, Evelyn Fox. A Feeling for the Organism : The Life and Work of Barbara McClintock. New York : W. H. Freeman, 1983.

Keller, Evelyn Fox. Reflections on Gender and Science. New Haven : Yale University Press, 1985.

Keohane, Robert O. After Hegemony : Cooperation and Discord in the World Political Economy. Princeton : Princeton University Press, 1984.

Keohane, Robert O., ed., Neorealism and Its Critics. New York : Columbia University Press, 1986.

Keohane, Robert O. and Joseph S. Nye. Power and Interdependence, 2d ed. Glenview, Ill. : Scott, Foresman, 1989.

King, Ynestra. "Feminism and the Revolt of Nature." Heresies 4(1) (1981) : 12-16.

Klassen, W., ed. Dialogue Toward Inter-Faith Understanding. Tantur/Jerusalem : Ecumenical Institute for Theological Research, 1986.

Kramarae, Cheris and Dale Spender, eds. The Knowledge Explosion. Elmsford, N.Y. : Pergamon Press, 1991.

Laclau, Ernesto and Chantal Mouffe. Hegemony and Socialist Strategy : Towards a Radical Democratic Politics. London : Vergo, 1985.

Lapid, Yosef. "The Third Debate : On the Prospects of International Theory in a Post-Positivist Era." International Studies Quarterly 33(3) (September 1989) : 235-254.

Leiss, William. The Domination of Nature. New York : George Braziller, 1972.

MacCormack, Carol P. and Marilyn Strathern, eds. Nature, Culture, and Gender. Cambridge, England : Cambridge University Press, 1980.

Macdonald, Sharon, Pat Holden, and Shirley Ardener, eds. Images of Women in Peace and War : Cross-Cultural and Historical Perspectives. London : Macmillan, 1987.

Machiavelli, Niccolò. The Prince and the Discourses. New York : Random House, 1940.

Mathews, Jessica Tuchman. "Redefining Security." Foreign Affairs 68(2) (Spring 1989) : 162-177.

McClelland, David. Power : The Inner Experience. New York : Wiley, 1975.

McGlen, Nancy E. and Meredith Reid Sarkees. "Leadership

Styles of Women in Foreign Policy." Unpublished paper, 1990.

McIntosh, Peggy. "Interactive Phases of Curricular Re-Vision : A Feminist Perspective." Wellesley, Mass. : Wellesley College Center for Research on Women, 1983.

Meadows, Donella H., Dennis L. Meadows, Jørgen Randers, and William Behrens III, The Limits to Growth. New York : Universe Books, 1972.

Merchant, Carolyn. Ecological Revolutions : Nature, Gender, and Science in New England. Chapel Hill : University of North Carolina Press, 1989.

Merchant, Carolyn. The Death of Nature : Women, Ecology, and the Scientific Revolution. San Francisco : Harper & Row, 1980.

Mies, Maria. Patriarchy and Accumulation on a World Scale : Women in the International Division of Labour. London : Zed Books, 1986.

Millennium : Journal of International Studies, Special Issue : Women and International Relations, 17(3) (Winter 1988).

Mische, Patricia M. "Ecological Security and the Need to Reconceptualize Sovereignty." Alternatives 14(4) (October 1989) : 389-427.

Molyneux, Maxine. "Mobilization Without Emancipation? Women's Interests, State, and Revolution in Nicaragua." Feminist Studies 11(2) (Summer 1985) : 227-254.

Moore, Henrietta L. Feminism and Anthropology. Minneapolis : University of Minnesota Press, 1988.

Morgenthau, Hans J. Politics Among Nations : The Struggle for Power and Peace, 5th ed. New York : Knopf, 1973.

Murphy, Craig and Roger Tooze, eds. The New International

Political Economy. Boulder : Lynne Rienner, 1991.

Myers, Norman. "Environment and Security." Foreign Policy 74 (Spring 1989) : 23-41.

Myers, Norman. Gaia : An Atlas of Planet Management. New York : Doubleday, 1984.

Nathanson, Stephen. "In Defense of Moderate Patriotism." Ethics 99 (April 1989) : 535-552.

North, Robert C. War, Peace, Survival : Global Politics and Conceptual Synthesis. Boulder : Westview, 1990.

Okin, Susan Moller. Justice, Gender, and the Family. New York : Basic Books, 1989.

Orr, David W. and Marvin S. Soroos, eds. The Global Predicament : Ecological Perspectives on World Order. Chapel Hill : University of North Carolina Press, 1979.

Parker, Geoffrey. Western Geopolitical Thought in the Twentieth Century. New York : St. Martin's Press, 1985.

Pateman, Carole. "God Hath Ordained to Man a Helper : Hobbes, Patriarchy, and Conjugal Right." British Journal of Political Science 19(4) (October 1989) : 445-464.

Pateman, Carole. The Sexual Contract. Stanford : Stanford University Press, 1988.

Peterson, V. Spike. "Clarification and Contestation : A Conference Report on `Women, the State and War' : What Difference Does Gender Make?" Los Angeles : Center for International Studies, University of Southern California, 1989.

Peterson, V. Spike, ed. Gendered States : Feminist (Re)visions of International Relations Theory. Boulder : Lynne Rienner, 1992.

Pettman Jan Jindy, Worlding women : a feminist international politics (London : Routledge, 1996).

Phillips, Anne, ed. Feminism and Equality. Oxford : Basil Blackwell, 1987.

Pierce, Diana. "The Feminization of Poverty." Journal for Peace and Justice Studies 2(1) (1990) : 1-20.

Pierson, Ruth Roach, ed. Women and Peace : Theoretical, Historical, and Practical Perspectives. London : Croom Helm, 1987.

Pietilä, Hilkka and Jeanne Vickers. Making Women Matter : The Role of the United Nations. London : Zed Books, 1990.

Pirages, Dennis. Global Technopolitics : The International Politics of Technology and Resources. Belmont, Calif. : Wadsworth, 1989.

Pitkin, Hanna F. Fortune Is a Woman : Gender and Politics in the Thought of Niccolò Machiavelli. Berkeley : University of California Press, 1984.

Plant, Judith, ed. Healing the Wounds : The Promise of Ecofeminism. Philadelphia : New Society Publishers, 1989.

Pursell, Carroll, ed. From Conservation to Ecology : The Development of Environmental Concern. New York : Thomas Crowell, 1973.

Reardon, Betty A. Sexism and the War System. New York : Teachers College Press, 1985.

Renner, Michael. National Security : The Economic and Environmental Dimensions. Washington, D.C. : Worldwatch Institute, 1989.

Ritvo, Harriet. The Animal Estate : The English and Other Creatures in the Victorian Age. Cambridge, Mass. : Harvard University Press, 1987.

Rosaldo, Michelle Z. and Louise Lamphere, eds. Women, Culture, and Society. Stanford : Stanford University Press, 1974.

Rosenau, James N., ed. International Politics and Foreign Policy. New York : Free Press, 1969.

Rosenberg, Emily S. "Gender." The Journal of American History 77(1) (June 1990) : 116-124.

Rourke, J. T. International Politics on the World Stage, 3d ed. Guilford, Conn. : Dushkin, 1991.

Ruddick, Sara. Maternal Thinking : Toward a Politics of Peace. New York : Ballantine Books, 1989.

Runyan, Anne Sisson. "Feminism, Peace, and International Politics : An Examination of Women Organizing Internationally for Peace and Security." Ph.D. diss., American University, 1988.

Runyan, Anne Sisson and V. Spike Peterson. "The Radical Future of Realism : Feminist Subversions of IR Theory." Alternatives 16(1) (1991) : 67-106.

Schelling, Thomas C. The Strategy of Conflict. Cambridge, Mass. : Harvard University Press, 1960.

Scott, Joan W. Gender and the Politics of History. New York : Columbia University Press, 1988.

Seager, Joni, ed. The State of the Earth Atlas. New York : Simon and Schuster, 1990.

Seager, Joni and Ann Olson. Women in the World : An International Atlas. London : Pan Books, 1986.

Segal, Lynne. Is The Future Female? Troubled Thoughts on Contemporary Feminism. New York : Peter Bedrick, 1988.

Sen, Amartya. "More Than 100 Million Women Are Missing." New York Review of Books 37(20) (1991) : 61-66.

Sen, Gita and Caren Grown. Development, Crises, and Alternative Visions : Third World Women's Perspectives. New York : Monthly Review Press, 1987.

Shiva, Vandana. "Ecology Movements in India." Alternatives 11(2) (April 1986) : 255-273.

Shiva, Vandana. Staying Alive : Women, Ecology, and Development. London : Zed Books, 1989.

Shiva, Vandana. "The Violence of Reductionist Science." Alternatives 12(2) (April 1987) : 243-261.

Small, Melvin and J. David Singer. Resort to Arms : International and Civil Wars, 1816-1980. Beverly Hills : Sage, 1982.

Snidal, Duncan. "Relative Gains and the Pattern of International Cooperation." American Political Science Review 85(3) (1991) : 701-726.

Spanier, John. Games Nations Play, 6th ed. Washington, D.C. : Congressional Quarterly Press, 1987.

Spender, Dale, ed. Men's Studies Modified : The Impact of Feminism on the Academic Disciplines. Oxford : Pergamon Press, 1981.

Sprout, Harold and Margaret Sprout. The Context of Environmental Politics : Unfinished Business for America's Third Century. Lexington : The University Press of Kentucky, 1978.

Sprout, Harold and Margaret Sprout. Toward a Politics of the Planet Earth. New York : Van Norstrand Reinhold, 1971.

Steuernagel, Gertrude A. and Laurel U. Quinn. "Is Anyone Listening? Political Science and the Response to the Feminist Challenge." Unpublished paper, 1986.

Stiehm, Judith Hicks. Arms and the Enlisted Woman. Philadelphia : Temple University Press, 1989.

Stiehm, Judith Hicks. Women and Men's Wars. Oxford : Pergamon Press, 1983.

Stiehm, Judith Hicks. Women's Views of the Political World

of Men. Dobbs Ferry, N.Y. : Transnational Publishers, 1984.

Stockholm International Peace Research Institute (SIPRI). Policies for Common Security. London and Philadelphia : Taylor and Francis, 1985.

Sylvester, Christine. "Some Dangers in Merging Feminist and Peace Projects." Alternatives 12(4) (October 1987) : 493-509.

Tannen, Deborah. You Just Don't Understand : Women and Men in Conversation. New York : Morrow, 1990.

Tickner J.Ann, Gendering world politics : issues and approaches in the post-Cold War era (New York : Columbia University Press, 2001).

Tickner J.Ann, Gender in International Relations : feminist perspectives on achieving global security (new York : Columbia University Press, 1992).

Tickner, J. Ann. "Hans Morgenthau's Principles of Political Realism : A Feminist Reformulation." Millennium 17(3) (Winter 1988) : 429-440.

Tickner, J. Ann. Self-Reliance Versus Power Politics : The American and Indian Experiences in Building Nation States. New York : Columbia University Press, 1987.

Tilly, Charles, ed. The Formation of National States in Western Europe. Princeton : Princeton University Press, 1975.

Tong, Rosemarie. Feminist Thought : A Comprehensive Introduction. Boulder : Westview, 1989.

Ullman, Richard H. "Redefining Security." International Security 8(1) (Summer 1983) : 129-153.

Vasquez, John, ed. Classics of International Relations, 2d ed. Englewood Cliffs, N.J. : Prentice Hall, 1990.

Vickers, Jeanne. Women and the World Economic Crisis. London : Zed Books, 1991.

Walker, R. B. J., ed. Culture, Ideology, and World Order. Boulder : Westview, 1988.

Wallensteen, Peter, ed. Peace Research : Achievements and Challenges. Boulder : Westview, 1988.

Wallerstein, Immanuel. The Modern World System. New York : Academic Press, 1974.

Waltz, Kenneth N. Man, the State, and War. New York : Columbia University Press, 1959.

Waltz, Kenneth N. Theory of International Politics. Boston : Addison-Wesley, 1979.

Waring, Marilyn. If Women Counted : A New Feminist Economics. San Francisco : Harper & Row, 1988.

White, Lynn. "The Historical Roots of Our Ecological Crisis." Science, March 10, 1987.

Williams, Michael C. "Rousseau, Realism, and Realpolitik." Millennium : Journal of International Studies 18(2) : 185-203.

Wilson, G. Kenneth and Peter Wallensteen. Major Armed Conflicts in 1987. Uppsala, Sweden : Department of Peace and Conflict Research, Uppsala University, 1988.

World Commission on Environment and Development. Our Common Future. Oxford : Oxford University Press, 1987.

Youngs Gillian, "Feminist International Relations : a contradiction in terms? Or : why women and gender are essential to understanding the world 'we' live in", International Affairs 80,1 (2004) : 75-87.

CHAPTER 8 : CONCEPTUALIZING HUMAN SECURITY

Alkire, S. 2003. "A conceptual framework for human security", CRISE Working Paper 2, Queen Elizabeth House, University of Oxford.

Amnesty International, 2003. "EU Summit on Iraq : Human Security Alongside Weapons Security : Amnesty International Calls on EU Leaders To Make the Fate of Civilians Their Top Priority", press release, EU Office, 13 February.

Ann. M.Florini and P.J.Simmons : - "The New Security Thanking A Review of the North American Literature : Project on World Security Rockefeller Brothers Fund, Washington Dc. And New York 1998, p- 32.

Axworthy Lloyd, 1997a. "Canada and Human Security : The Need for Leadership," International Journal Vol. LII (Spring), pp-183-96.

Axworthy, Lolyd, 1999. "NATO's New Security Vocation", NATO Review 47(4) : 8-11; available at *http : // www.nato.int/docu/review/1999/9904-02.htm*.

Axworthy, Lloyd, 2003. "Human security in the Era of Terrorism : The Responsibility to Protect", Working Paper no.14. Los Angeles, CA : School of Public Policy and Social Research, UCLA; available at http : // www.sppsr.ucla.edu/cgpr/docs/axworthy.doc.

Bajpai Kanti, 2003. "The Idea of Human Security", International Studies, vol.40, No.3, July-September.

Baldwin David, 1997. "The Concept of Security", Review of International studies. vol. 23. pp.12-18.

Bellamy, Alex J.and Matt McDonald, 2002. **"The** Utility of Human Security" : Which Humans? What Security? A Reply to Thomas and Tow, Security Dialogue 33(3) : 373-377.

Department of Foreign Affairs and International Trade (DFAIT), 1999. "Human Security : Safety for People in a Changing World", Ottawa : DFAIT; available at http : // summit-americas.org/Canada/ Human Security-english.htm.

Bernstein A. 2004. Respondent remarks, seminar at the National Council for Research on Women, Washington, DC, 11 March available at *http : // www.ncrw.org/interest/bernstein_remarks.htm.*

Burton, J.W.1990. Conflict : Basic Human Needs, New York : St Martin's Press.

Cincotta, Richard P., Robert Engelman, and Daniele Anastasion, 2003. The security demographic : Population and civil conflict after the Cold War. Washington, DC : Population Action International.

Commission on Human Security, 2003. Human Security Now, New York.

Donella H.Meadows, Dennis L.Meadows, Jorgen Randers and William W. BehrensIII, 1972. The Limits to Growth, New York : Universe Books.

Doyal, L. and Gough, I. 1991. A Theory of Human Need, Basingstoke : Macmillan.

Easterlin, Richard A. 1968. Population, labour force and long swings in economic growth : The American Experience, New York : national Bureau of Economic Research and Columbia University Press.

Easterlin, Richard A. 1978. "What will 1984 be like? Socioeconomic implications of recent twists in age structure", Demography 15(4), 397-432.

Easterlin, Richard A. 1987. Birth and fortune : The impact of numbers on personal welfare (second ed.), Chicago : University of Chicago Press.

Ehrlich Paul and Anne Ehrlich, 2004. One with Nineveh : Politics, Consumption, and the Human Future (Washington, D.C. : Island Press.

Elliot, Lorraine, 2001. " Regional environmental security : Pursuing a non-traditional approach", In Andrew T.H. Tan and J.D Kenneth Boutin, eds., Non-traditional security issues in Southeast Asia, Singapore : Select Publishing, Pp. 438-67.

Florini Ann M and P.J.Simmons,1998. "The New Security Thinking : A review of the North American Literature," Project on World Security, Rockefeller Brothers Fund, Washington, D.C, and New York.

Francois, Fouinat, 2004. "A comprehensive framework for human security", Conflict, Security and Development 4(3), December : 289-297.

Galtung, J. 1994. Human Rights in Another Key, Cambridge : Polity.

Galtung, Johan, 2004. " Human Needs, Humanitarian Intervention, Human Security and the War in Iraq", keynote speech, Sophia University/ICU, Tokyo, 14 December 2003 and Regional Studies Association, Tokyo, 10 January 2004; available at *http : // www.transnational*.org/SAJT/forum/meet/2004/ Galtung_Human Needs.html.

Gasper, Des, 2005. "Securing Humanity : Situating 'Human Security' as Concept and Discourse", Journal of Human Development 6(2) : 221-245.

Gasper, D. and T.D. Truong, 2005. "Deepening development ethics through the lenses of caring, gender and human security", paper for conference on Ethics and Development, Michigan State University.

Gewirth, A.1995. "Rights" in The Oxford Companion to Philosophy, Oxford : Oxford University Press.

Glasius, Marlies, 2008. "Human Security from Paradigm Shift to Operalization : Job Description for a Human Security Worker", Security Dialogue 39(1) : 31-54.

Goldewijk, B.K. and Fortman, B.de G. 1999. Where Needs Meet Rights, WCC Publications, Geneva.

Government of Canada, " Human Security : Safety for

people in A Changing World", paper prepared by the Department of Foreign Affairs and International Trade, Government of Canada (DFAIT), *http : // www.dfait.maeci.gc.ca/* foreign/Human Security/ secure.htm,p.1

Grayson, Kyle, 2004. "A Challenge to the Power over Knowledge of Traditional Security Studies", Security Dialogue 35(3) : 357.

Hampson, F.O; Daudelin, J; Hay, J.B; Martin T. and Reid, H. 2002. Madness in the Multitude : Human Security and World Disorder, Ottawa : Oxford University Press.

Haq Mahbub ul, 1994. "New Imperatives of Human Security", RGICS paper No.17, Rajiv Gandhi Institute for Contemporary Studies, Rajiv Gandhi Foundation, New Delhi, p.7.

Harvard Human Security Project, 2002. Definitions of Human Security, available at *http : // www.hsph.harvard.edu/hpcr/events/hsworkshop/ list_definitions.pdf.*

Hudson, Valerie M. and Andrea M. Den Boer, 2005. "Missing Women and Bare Branches : Gender Balance and Conflict", ECSP, Woodrow Wilson International Center for Scholars, Issue 11, 20-24.

Kaldor, Mary and Andrew Salmon, 2006." Military Force and European Strategy", Survival 48(1) : 19-34.

Kaldor, Mary; Mary martin and Sabine Selchow, 2007. "Human Security : A New Strategic Narrative for Europe", International Affairs 83(2) : 273-288.

Kerim, Srgian, 2008. Quoted in The Hindu, April 15 : 9.

Krause, Keith, 2004. "The Key to a Powerful Agenda, If properly Delineated", Security Dialogue 25(3) : 367-368.

Leaning Jennifer, 2004. "Psychosocial Well-Being over

Time", Security Dialogue 35(3) : 355-356.

Liotta, Peter, 2002. "Boomerang Effect : The Convergence of National and Human Security", Security Dialogue 33(4) : 473-488.

Mack, Andrew, 2004. "A Signifier of Shared values", Security Dialogue 35(3) : 366-367.

Mazur. Allan and Joel Michalek, 1998. "Marriage, divorce, and male testosterone", Social Forces, 77(1), 315-330.

Meadows Donella H., Dennis L. Meadows, Jorgen Randers and William W. Behrens- III, 1972. The limits to Growth. New York : University Books.

Mendowitz, Saul B. ed., 1975. On the Creation of a Just World Order, New York : The Free Press.

Najam, Adil. 2003. "The Human Dimensions of Environmental Insecurity : Some Insights from South Asia", Environmental Change and Security project Report, Woodrow Wilson International Center for Scholars. Issue no 9, p.61.)

Newman, Edward, 2004. "A Normatively Attractive but Analytically Weak Concept", Security Dialogue 35(3) : 358-359.

Pirages, Dennis, 2004. Review article on Paul Ehrlich and Anne Ehrlich' book One with Nineveh, in ECSP Report, Woodrow Wilson International Center for Scholars, Issue 10, p.84.

Ramphele, M.2004. "Reply", Seminar at the national Council for Research on Women, Washington, DC, 11 March, available at http : // www..nvrw.org/interest/ Bernstein_remarks.htm.

Robinson, M. 2003. Protection and Empowerment : Connecting Human Rights and Human Security, available at http : // www.oxan.com/about/news/ 2003-09-18.

Saul B. Mendowitz, ed., On the Creation of a Just World Order (New York : The Free Press, 1975)

Schulze, Kirsten, 2006. "Dealing with Destruction : Aceh a Year After the Tsunami", The World Today 62(1) : 11-12.

Sen, A.2003. "Human Security Now", Soka Gakkai International Quarterly, available at *http : // www.sgi.org/english/features/quarterly/0307/ feature1.htm*.

St. Clair, A.L. 2004a. "The Role of ideas in the United Nations Development Programme", in M. Boas and D. McNeill eds., Global Institutions and Development : Framing the World? London : Routledge.

St Clair, A.L. 2004b. Poverty Conceptions in the UNDP and the World Bank : Knowledge, Ethics and Politics, Department of Sociology, University of Bergen.

Star, S. and Griesemer, J. 1989. "Institutional ecology, 'translations' and boundary objects", Social Studies of Science, 19, pp. 387-420.

Staveteig, Sarah. 2005. "The Young and the Restless : Population Age Structure and Civil War", ECSP, Woodrow Wilson International Center for Scholars, Issue 11, pp. 12-19.

The Independent Commission on International Development Issues, North-South : A Programme for Survival, 1980. Cambridge, MA : The MIT Press.

The Independent Commission on Disarmament and Security Issues, Common Security : A Blueprint for Survival, 1982. New York : Simon and Schuster, 1982, pp-XV and 172 respectively.

The Stockholm Initiative on Global Security and Governance, 1991. "Common Responsibility in the 1990s" paper published by the Prime Minister's office,

Government of Sweden, Stockholm, pp.17-18.

The Commission on Global Governance, 1995. Our Global Neighbourhood. New York : Oxford University Press. P. 338.

Thomas, Nicholas and William T. Tow, 2002a. "The Utility of Human Security : Sovereignty and Humanitarian Intervention", Security Dialogue 33(2) : 177-192.

United Nations Development Programme, 1995a. "Redefining Security : The Human Dimensions", Current History, vol.94, May, pp.229-236.

Urdal, Henrik, 2006. "A clash of generations? Youth bulges and political violence", International Studies Quarterly 50, pp. 607-629.

Uvin, P. 2004. "A field of overlaps and interactions", Security Dialogue, 35(3), pp. 352-353.

Weigert Kathleen Maas. 1999. "Structural Violence", in Encyclopedia of Violence, Peace, and Conflict, vol.3. New York : Academic Press.

Williams, Jody, 2004. "Globalization, Human Security and Iraq", keynote speech to the 6th International Security Forum, Montreux, Switzerland, 4 October; available at http : // *www.icbl.org/campaign/ambassador/jody_williams/globaliz_iraq*.

Winslow, Donna and Thomas Hylland Eriksen, 2004. "A Broad Concept That Encourages Interdisciplinary Thinking", Security Dialogue 35(3) : 361-362.

Woodward, Emma, 1999. "Should We Think Before We Leap? A Rejoinder", Security Dialogue 30(3) : 277-281.

CHAPTER 9 : CONCLUSION

Acharya, Amitav, 2001. 'Human Security : East Versus West', International Journal 56(3) : 442-460.

Alkire, Sabina, 2001. 'A Conceptual Framework for Human Security', CRISE Working Paper 2. Oxford : CRISE.

Alkire, Sabine, 2003. 'Concepts of Human Security', in Lincoln C. Chen, Sakiko FukudaParr & Ellen Seidensticker, eds, Human Security in a Global World. Cambridge, MA : Harvard University Press (15-40).

Allard Tom, Mark Forbes and agencies. April 2007. " US braces for global warming", Sydney Morning Herald : 1).

Ayoob, Mohammed. 1997. " Defining Security : A Subaltern Realist Perspective" in K. Krause and M.C. Williams (eds) Critical Security Studies, Minneapolis : University of Minnesota Press.

Agamben Giorgio. 1998. Homo saucer : Sovereign power and bare life. Stanford : Stanford University Press.

Arendt Hannah. 1998. 2nd edn. The human condition. Chicago : University of Chicago.

Barkdull John. November 2000. "Why Environmental Ethics Matters to International Relations",vol.99. no. 640 : 366.

Barkin, J. Samuel and Cronin, Bruce. 1994. " The State and the Nation : Changing Norms and Rules of Sovereignty in International Relations", International Organization 48(1) : 107-30.

Biehl Janet.1991. Finding Our Way : Rethinking of Ecofeminist Politics. Montreal and New York, NY : Black Rose Books : . 89-90.

Biersteker, Thomas and Weber, Cynthia (eds) 1996. The Social Construction of Sovereignty. Cambridge : Cambridge University Press.

Booth Ken.2005 (ed). Critical security studies and world politics. Boulder : Lynne Rienner.

Booth Ken.1991. " Security as emancipation", Review of International Studies, 17(4) : 319.

Burke Anthony. 2001. 'Epilogue' in his In Fear of Security :

Australia's Invasion Anxiety. Sydney : Pluto Press Australia.

————————. 2001. " Caught between national and human security : Knowledge and power in post-crisis Asia", Pacific Review : Peace, Security and Global Change, 13 (3) : 215-39.

————————. 2007. Beyond security, ethics and violence : War against the other. London and New York : Routledge.

————————.June 2007. " What security makes possible : Some thoughts on critical security studies", working paper 2007/1, Reseach School of Pacific and Asian Studies, The Australian National University, Caberra.

Buzan Barry and Richard Little.2001. "Why International Relations has Failed as an Intellectual Project and What to do about it", Millennium; vol.30, no.1 : . 25.

Buzan, Barry, 2002. 'Human Security in International Perspective', presentation at the 14th Asia-Pacific Roundtable, Kuala Lumpur.

CNA Corporation.2007. National security and the threat of climate change, VA : CNA Corporation.

Cox, Robert.1986. " Social Forces, States and World Orders : Beyond International Relations Theory" in R. Keohane (ed). Neorealism and its Critics. New York : Columbia University Press.

Der Derian, James.1992. Antidiplomacy. Oxford : Basil Blackwell.

Dixon Thomas F.Homer.1991. " Environmental Change and Human Security", Behind the Headlines 48..

Doty Roxanne Lynn. 1998-99. " Immigration and the politics of security", Security Studies,8(2/3).

Engel J.Ronald and Engel Joan Gibb.1990. ed., Ethics of

Environment and Development Origins : NC Documentary Service 17, 3 March 1988, p.645; Quoted in "Introduction : The ethics of sustainable development", London : Belhaven Press, 1990, p.4.

Fay, Brian.1975. Social Theory and Political Practice. London : George Allen andUnwin.

Fierke Karin.2007. Critical approaches to international security. Cambridge : Polity.

Foucault Michael.1970. The Order of Things : Archaeology of the Human Sciences. London : Tavistock.

Guha Ram Chandra. November 2000. Report of the Wuppertal Institute for Climate, Environment, and Energy, quoted in his "the Paradox of Global Environmentalism", Current History, vol.99, no.640, November-2000 : . 370.

Hegel G.W.F.1967. Philosophy of right, trans. T.M. Knox. Oxford, London and New York : Oxford University Press.

Hall, Rodney Bruce and Kratochwil, Friedrich.1993. " Medieval Tales : Neo-Realist " Science and the Abuse of History", International Organization 47(4) : 479-500.

Jepperson, Ronald, Wendt, Alexander and Katzenstein, Peter. 1996. " Norms, Identity, and Culture in National Security" in P.Katzenstein (ed) The Culture of National Security : Norms and Identity in Word Politics> New York : Columbia University Press.

Jones Richard Wyn(ed). 2001. Critical theory and world politics. Boulder : Lienner Rienner.

Karliner Joshua. 1997, The Corporate Planet : ecology and politics in the age of globalization. San Francisco : Sierra Club Books : Chapter-7.

Krause Keith. 1998. "Critical Theory and Security Studies"

Cooperation and Conflict, vol.33(3) : 298-333.

Laferriere Eric. 1996. "Emancipating International Relation Theory : An Ecological Perspective". Vol.25. no.1.

Leaning, Jennifer & Sam Arie, 2000. 'Human Security : A Framework for Assessment In Conflict and Transition', working paper. Cambridge, MA : Harvard Center for Population and Development Studies.

Leopard Aldo. 1966. A Sand Country Almanac. New York, NY : Ballantine Books.

Litfin Karen T. Summer 2000. "Environment, Wealth, and Authority : Global Climate Change and Emerging Modes of Legitimation", International Studies Review, Special issue, vol.2, Issue no.2.

Mack, Andrew, 2002, 'A report on the Feasibility of Creating an Annual Human Security Report', Program on Humanitarian Policy and Conflict Research, Harvard University.

McRae, Robert Grant & Don Hubert, 2001. Human Security and the New Diplomacy : Protecting People, Promoting Peace. Montreal : McGill-Queen's University Press.

McSweeney Bill.1999. Security, identity and interests : A sociology of international relations. Cambridge : Cambridge University Press.

Measheimer, John.1995. " A Realist Reply", International Security 20(1) : 82-91.

Merchant Carolyn.1980. The Death of Nature : Women Ecology and the Scientific Revolution. New York, NY and Toronto : Harper and Row.

Owen, Taylor, 2003. 'Measuring Human Security : Overcoming the Paradox', Human Security Bulletin 2(3); available at http : // *www.prio.no/publications/*

archive/2003/ to 002.pdf.

Owen, Taylor, 2004, 'Are we Really Secure? Challenges and Opportunities for Defining and Measuring Human Security', Disarmament Forum 2004(3).

Owen Taylor.2004. "Human Security- Conflict, Critique and Consensus : Colloquium Remarks and a Proposal for a Threshold- Based Definition", Security Dialogue, Vol.35 (3) : 373-383.

Parkin Sara.1999. " Environmental Security : Issues and Agenda", Disarmament Forum : 41-48.

Paris Roland, 2001. "Human Security : Paradigm Shift or Hot Air?" International Security 26(2) : 87-102.

Paterson Matthew. 1999. "Interpreting trends in global environmental governance", International Affairs, vol.75, no.4, p.795; Lamont Hempel, Environmental governance : the global challenge (Washington D.C. : Island Press, 1996).

Paterson Matthew. 2000. Understanding global environmental politics : domination, accumulation, resistance. London : Macmillan.

Rolston Holms, III. 1988. Environmental Ethics : Duties to and Values in the Natural World. Philadelphia : Temple University Press : 174.

Ruggie, John. 1993. " Territoriality and Beyond : Problematizing Modernity in International Relations", International Organization 47(1).

Schmitt Carl.1985. Political theology. Cambridge, MA : MIT Press.

Schmitt Carl. 1996. The concept of political, trans. George Schwab. Chicago : Chicago University Press.

Smith Heather A. Winter 2000/ Spring 2001. "Facing Environmental Security", Journal of Military and

Strategic Studies. Available at *http : // www.jmss.org/2001/article3.html.*

Thakur, Ramesh Chandra; Edward Newman & United Nations University, 2000. New Millennium, New Perspectives : The United Nations, Security, and Governance. Tokyo & New York : United Nations University Press.

The Observer,22 February 2004.

Tickner J.Ann.1992. Gender in international relations : Feminist perspective on achieving global security. New York : Columbia University Press.

Tuchman-Mathews Jessica. Spring1989. "Redefining Security", Foreign Affairs.

Toulmin Stephen.1982. The Return to Cosmology : Postmodern Science and the Theology of Nature. Berkeley : University of California Press : 255-56.

Walt Stephen.1991. "The renaissance of security studies", International Studies Quarterly, 35(2) : 211-39.

Waever Ole.1995. " Securitization and desecuritization", in Ronnie D. Lipschutz (ed). On security, New York : Columbia University Press : 46-86.

Waever Ole, Jaap de Wilde and Barry Buzan.1998. Security : A new framework for analysis. Boulder : Lynne Rienner.

Walker, R.B.J.1990. "Security, Sovereignty and the Challenge of World Politics", Alternatives 15(1) : 3-27.

Wendt, Alexander. 1994. " Collective Identity Formation and the International State", American Political Science Review 88 : 384-96.

Wendt, Alexander 1995. " Constructing International Politics", International Security 20(10 : 71-81.

Williams Michael C.2003. "Words, images, enemies : Securitization and international politics", International Studies Quarterly, 47(4) : 511-31.